Unsolved Civil Rights
Murder Cases, 1934–1970

ALSO BY MICHAEL NEWTON
AND FROM McFARLAND

*Hate Crime in America, 1968–2013: A Chronology
of Offenses, Legislation and Related Events* (2014)

*White Robes and Burning Crosses: A History
of the Ku Klux Klan from 1866* (2014)

*The Texarkana Moonlight Murders: The Unsolved
Case of the 1946 Phantom Killer* (2013)

The Mafia at Apalachin, 1957 (2012)

*Chronology of Organized Crime
Worldwide, 6000 B.C.E. to 2010* (2011)

The Ku Klux Klan in Mississippi: A History (2010)

Mr. Mob: The Life and Crimes of Moe Dalitz (2009)

*The Ku Klux Klan: History, Organization, Language,
Influence and Activities of America's Most Notorious
Secret Society* (2007; paperback 2014)

*Encyclopedia of Cryptozoology: A Global Guide to Hidden
Animals and Their Pursuers* (2005; paperback 2014)

The FBI and the KKK: A Critical History (2005; paperback 2009)

The FBI Encyclopedia (2003; paperback 2012)

Unsolved Civil Rights Murder Cases, 1934–1970

Michael Newton

McFarland & Company, Inc., Publishers
Jefferson, North Carolina

LIBRARY OF CONGRESS CATALOGUING-IN-PUBLICATION DATA

Names: Newton, Michael, 1951– author.
Title: Unsolved civil rights : murder cases, 1934/1970 /
Michael Newton.
Description: Jefferson, N.C. : McFarland & Company, Inc.,
Publishers, 2016. | Includes bibliographical references and index.
Identifiers: LCCN 2015051033 | ISBN 9780786498956
(softcover : acid free paper) ∞
Subjects: LCSH: African Americans—Crimes against—History—
20th century. | Murder—United States—History—20th century. |
Hate crimes—United States—History—20th century. |
Racism—United States—History—20th century. |
Civil rights movements—United States—History—20th century.
Classification: LCC HV6250.4.E75 N497 2016 | DDC 364.152/308996073—dc23
LC record available at http://lccn.loc.gov/2015051033

BRITISH LIBRARY CATALOGUING DATA ARE AVAILABLE

ISBN (print) 978-0-7864-9895-6
ISBN (ebook) 978-1-4766-2362-7

© 2016 Michael Newton. All rights reserved

*No part of this book may be reproduced or transmitted in any form
or by any means, electronic or mechanical, including photocopying
or recording, or by any information storage and retrieval system,
without permission in writing from the publisher.*

Front cover images top and left to right: Birmingham's Sixteenth Street
Baptist Church, September 15, 1963 (Library of Congress);
George Washington Lee (National Archives); Rubén Salazar
(Library of Congress); Leon Jordan (Library of Congress);
Lamar Smith (Library of Congress); A. D. King (Library of Congress);
Willie Earle (National Archives)

Printed in the United States of America

*McFarland & Company, Inc., Publishers
Box 611, Jefferson, North Carolina 28640
www.mcfarlandpub.com*

For Heather,
for her constant love and support.

Contents

Acknowledgments ix
Preface 1
Introduction 3

Part 1: Official Civil Rights "Cold Cases" 7

Part 2: "The Forgotten" 97

Notes 261
Bibliography 275
Index 289

Justice delayed is justice denied.
—William Ewart Gladstone (1809–1898)

Acknowledgments

Librarians and journalists throughout the country were extremely generous in aiding my research for this book. I owe thanks to Greg Adams, editor-publisher of the *Wilk-Amite Record*; Johnny Adams, *Union Springs Herald*; Clellie Allen, editor and associate publisher of the *Wake Forest Weekly*; Mark Andrews, formerly with the *Orlando Sentinel*; Susan Blakeney, genealogist with the Laurel-Jones County Library System; Janet Boudet, associate director of the Roddenberry Memorial Library; Lucy Boyd, *Charleston Sun*; William Browning, *Columbus Dispatch*; Patti Burns, head of adult services at the Georgetown County Library; Germaine Butler, genealogy/reference librarian at the St. Tammany Parish Library; Holley Cochran, editor and general manager of the *Prentiss Headlight*; the Danville Public Library's Reference and Archives Department; Tim Davis, editor of the *Chatham Star-Tribune*; the Dayton Metro Library; Elizabeth DeGrie, managing editor of the *Ruston Leader*; Pam Edmondson, Edgecombe County Memorial Library; John Ellzey, Ricks Memorial Library; Jonathon Finley, editor of the *Montgomery Monitor*; Mercedes Franks, director of the Judy B. McDonald Public Library; Michelle Goad, head librarian for the *Arkansas Democrat-Gazette*; Irene Godwin, Ellen Payne Odom Genealogy Library; Polly Greene, *St. Tammany Farmer*; Rod Guajardo, news director for the *Natchez Democrat*; Susan Hedrick, *Chatham Star Tribune*; Carolyn Hemstreet, Hale County Library; Marianne Hill, Powhatan County Public Library; Thomas Hutchens, Huntsville-Madison County Public Library; Yvonne Keller, Courier Communications; Sheila Lence, Ripley Public Library; Andy Lewis, *Woodville Republican*; the Luverne Public Library reference staff; Alanna Maddox, reference librarian at the Decatur Public Library; Susan Martin, Live Oak Public Library; Professor Gary May, University of Delaware; Katrena McCall, *Walterboro Press and Standard*; Clay McFerrin, editor and publisher of the *Sun-Sentinel*; William McMullin, Mississippi's Northeast Regional Library; Jerry Mitchell, *Clarion-Ledger*; Stanley Nelson, *Concordia Sentinel*; Jason Niblett, *The Chronicle* in Laurel, Mississippi; the Olivia Raney Library's staff; Teresa Pennington, Paris Carnegie Public Library; Brenda Poke, Washington County Library System; Martha Powers-Jones, Ohoopee Regional Library System; Valerie Reddell, editor and publisher of the *Gonzales Inquirer*; the reference staff of the Waterloo Public Library; Linda Reynolds, director of the East Texas Research Center at Stephen F. Austin State University; Debbie Ryan, managing editor of the Nacogdoches *Daily Sentinel*; Evelyn Screws, adult services librarian at the Eufaula Carnegie Library; Carolyn Vance Smith, founder and co-chairman of the Natchez Literary and Cinema Celebration; Jan Smith, news research director for the *Commercial Appeal*; Jennifer Stapleton, San Pedro Regional Branch of the Los Angeles Public Library; Regina Strickland, Horseshoe Bend Regional Library; Maryann Struman, *Detroit Free Press*; Scott

Taves, Chicago's Howard Washington Library Center; Tanna Taylor, Tombigbee Regional Library; Claudine Tomlinson-Burney, director of marketing and public relations for the Orange County Regional History Center; Troy Valos, Slover Memorial Library's Sargeant Memorial Collection; Sheila Vance, Ripley Public Library; Anne Vanderleest, genealogy librarian at the Brandon Public Library; Lisa Wehrmann, the Library of Virginia; and Tiffany Woo, *Eufala Tribune*. Thanks also to my wife Heather for her loving forbearance as I navigated murky rivers of the human heart.

Preface

I grew up, in a sense, with the civil rights movement. Thirty-two months after my birth the U.S. Supreme Court issued its momentous ruling against public school segregation, and the rest is literally history: boycotts, sit-ins and freedom rides, black voter registration drives and white resistance to the point of death. On the eve of my 12th birthday Ku Klux Klansmen bombed an Alabama church, killing four girls ages 11 to 14. I was 16 before the movement touched me personally, with minority complaints against my alma mater—South High School in Bakersfield, California—for choosing a Confederate battle flag and a gray-clad "Johnny Rebel" mascot to represent a student body that was roughly one-third African American. It made no difference that Johnny Rebel, in my senior year, was a black student who sought the job and won election overwhelmingly. The heat was on in those years, and it left the ashes of tradition in its wake.

Down South—that land we read about and saw on television newscasts that appeared as foreign to our own experience as Vietnam or the embattled Belgian Congo—the ashes came from burned-out churches, homes, and meeting halls where people of color met to plead for simple justice. I was aware of certain murders, following the cases from a distance, but had no idea *how many* victims fell before one pundit or another finally decided that the movement was defunct. Most of its goals had been achieved, at least on paper, signed by presidents. What more was there to do, except forget about the years of pain and loss, focus on keeping Asian communism from our shores at any cost, and plowing on ahead toward Watergate?

Outside the towns where they were raised and killed, most of the victims were forgotten. My goal, in *Unsolved Civil Rights Murder Cases, 1934–1970*, is to light a candle to their memories, bringing them all together for the first time in one volume. Not everyone included here was active in the civil rights movement per se, but all were slain because their race or attitudes on race displeased their killers. This is their tribute, a monument of sorts, augmenting the Southern Poverty Law Center's Civil Rights Memorial in Montgomery, Alabama. That black granite fountain bears the names of 40 martyrs to the movement. But as we shall see, the final roll of sacrifice bears many, many more.

Lest we forget.

Introduction

The history of American race relations is written in blood. From 1492, when Christopher Columbus "discovered" a New World already populated by at least 30 million aboriginals—some estimates top 50 million—the annals of the Americas are an endless litany of enslavement, genocide, race riots and lynchings, codified and *de facto* racial discrimination. The first arrival of African slaves at Jamestown, Virginia, in 1619, paved the way for countless atrocities, pogroms, our nation's bloodiest war of all time, white terrorism in the postwar era, and the rise of "Jim Crow" legislation segregating every aspect of public life in 33 states on both sides of the Mason-Dixon Line, enforced by all-white courts, police, and vigilantes.

Eventually, inevitably, segregation spawned resistance movements, usually law-abiding, working through the court system at glacial speed, collecting victories that made small changes in the North and West, while they were stubbornly ignored in Dixie. After 1954, when the U.S. Supreme Court banned segregation of public schools, agitation for full racial equality increased, opposed by Southern politicians pledged to "massive resistance," white police departments, "respectable" Citizens' Councils practicing socio-economic intimidation, and violent "redneck" elements acting as Ku Klux Klans and similar groups.[1]

The result, once again, was bloodshed. In every Jim Crow state, where demonstrators marched, some died. Beyond the South, in wretched ghettos, no protests were necessary to produce an ever-rising body count. The final toll remains unknown, thanks in equal part to white public indifference, police cover-ups, and the refusal of some white-owned newspapers to cover crimes against minorities. In cases where the killers were identified, many were "cleared" on pleas of self-defense in preliminary hearings; others saw murder charges reduced to lesser felonies or misdemeanors prior to trial; and most, before December 1965, were swiftly acquitted by all-white juries, often including outspoken members of known racist hate groups.

So justice faltered and stalled. Minority anger festered as killers walked free, some boasting of their crimes behind the shield of double jeopardy. In 1965 the U.S. Department of Justice (DOJ) dusted off a statute from the Reconstruction Era, filing federal civil rights charges against murderers whom friendly juries had acquitted or racist prosecutors had refused to indict. By October 1967, jurors had convicted 12 killer Klansmen in three states, dispatching them to far-flung prisons with sentences capped at 10 years for conspiracy resulting in death. All were released before serving their full terms, returning to their hometowns and familiar lives.

More time passed, with more resentment mounting. African Americans in Dixie, finally enfranchised by the Voting Rights Act of 1965, elected members of their own race to political office and called white officials to account for failures of the past. In 1977, Alabama attorney general Bill Baxley convicted aging Klansman Robert Chambliss for a fatal 1963 church bombing, sending him to state prison for life. Encouraged by that victory, the 1990s brought a groundswell of demands for belated justice in Mississippi, witness to some of the civil rights era's most infamous slayings. Grudgingly at first, beset by white complaints that too much time had passed, too many witnesses had died, too many bits of crucial evidence had vanished, prosecutors built cases against the Magnolia State's most notorious racial terrorists. In 1994 an integrated jury convicted Klansman Byron De La Beckwith for the 1963 sniper slaying of civil rights leader Medgar Evers. Four years later, another Mississippi jury convicted former Klan leader Samuel Bowers of a murder he ordered in 1966. A new millennium dawned with the 2001 convictions of two more Alabama church bombers, Thomas Blanton, Jr., and Bobby Cherry, each sentenced to life on four counts of murder.

And there again, the drive for justice stalled, but not for long.

On May 10, 2004, the DOJ announced its reopening of an even older case, one of Dixie's most notorious. Black Chicago teenager Emmett Till had been visiting family in Mississippi during August 1955, when he allegedly whistled at or made provocative remarks to a white female storekeeper. Kidnapped from his relatives' home by the woman's husband and his half-brother, Till was tortured and shot, his body weighted down and dumped in a nearby river. The killers were acquitted by an all-white jury, then sold their confession to *Look* magazine for $10,000, scandalizing Mississippi and the nation at large, an open wound for many African Americans that never healed.

No federal charges were filed in Till's case, but grassroots rumblings across America eventually echoed in the halls of Congress. On February 8, 2007, Rep. John Lewis of Georgia, himself a renowned 1960s civil rights leader, introduced bill H.R. 293, subsequently known as the Emmett Till Unsolved Civil Rights Crime Act. One day later, Connecticut's Christopher Dodd introduced a corresponding bill in the Senate, S. 535. By mid–June another 83 representatives had signed on as co-sponsors of the House bill, while 19 other senators joined in sponsoring Dodd's bill by late July.[2]

The bill, as finally enacted by Congress and signed into law by President George W. Bush on October 7, 2008, directed the U.S. Attorney General to name a deputy chief in the Criminal Section of the DOJ's Civil Rights Division, responsible for investigating and prosecuting fatal violations of criminal civil rights statutes which occurred prior to January 1, 1970. The law, set to expire in December 2017 unless renewed by Congress, appropriated funds including $10 million per year for the DOJ and the Federal Bureau of Investigation (FBI), $2 million in grants to state or local law enforcement agencies aiding federal investigators, and another $1.5 million earmarked for the DOJ's Community Relations Service to bring together law enforcement agencies and communities to further the investigation of those homicides.[3]

The new law faced prodigious obstacles from its beginning. The most obvious was passing time, as DOJ investigators cast their net across eight decades, searching for crimes that fit the law's parameters. Local resistance to resurrecting the past, picking scabs from old wounds, was another stumbling block, exacerbated by the fact that many racial crimes spanning the era in question were poorly (if ever) reported. Finally, Congress itself seemed to abandon the law as soon as it took effect. Only two of 424 voting representatives had opposed the act when it passed in June 2007 (Lynn Westmoreland of Georgia and Ron Paul of Texas); the Senate vote had been unanimous. And yet, Congress appropriated no funds to the DOJ for its enforcement during 2008 or 2009, finally granting a mere $1.6 million of the authorized $13.5 million in 2010.[4]

Despite those handicaps, the DOJ and FBI persevered. Attorney General Alberto Gonzales issued the DOJ's first progress report in April 2007, recapping the department's history of civil rights investigations spanning half a century and noting that 40 federal prosecutors had been assigned to the new initiative.[5] A second report, issued by Attorney General Eric Holder in May 2010, provided more specifics, including a list of 122 victims slain between 1951 and 1968.[6] Holder's next report to Congress, filed in August 2011, added two more victims to the list, pushing the startup date backward to 1934. By that time, all but 38 of the selected cases had been closed once more, with no indictments filed.[7] Holder's third report, in August 2011, listed 125 victims, with 27 cases remaining open.[8] The last report as this book went to press, issued in January 2014, listed 126 victims killed in 113 separate incidents, 100 of those cases closed with only a single conviction in court.[9]

"Closing" a case officially brought no closure to families of murdered victims, who remain frustrated by what some regard as one more snub from federal authorities. As each case was dismissed in turn, pairs of FBI agents hand-delivered letters to surviving relatives of the victims, each leading with the bad news.

> We are writing to inform you that the Department of Justice and the Federal Bureau of Investigation recently conducted a review of the circumstances surrounding the death of your [relationship inserted], [name inserted], on [date inserted]. We regret to inform you that we are unable to proceed further with a federal criminal investigation of the matter because the man responsible for the death of your [relationship inserted] is deceased. Please accept our sincere condolences on the loss of your [relationship inserted].[10]

For most, it was too little, far too late. Of the remaining open cases, DOJ spokesmen admitted that "few, if any" would be prosecuted. Alvin Sykes, head of the Emmett Till Justice Campaign, spoke for many when he said, "The American people won't believe you made a full-faith effort if there wasn't a manhunt." Mark Potok, speaking for the Southern Poverty Law Center (SPLC), disagreed in principle, saying, "I think there is some utility in closing cases, if for no better reason than to assure the families that what can be done at this late date has been done. These are people who have been completely left out of the justice process for many decades. So the government does owe them a debt of attention. So I wouldn't say that it was a total waste of taxpayer money."[11]

Nonetheless, critical voices were the loudest, some coming from within the DOJ itself. FBI agent Cynthia Deitle, one-time leader of the cold case effort, posed a rhetorical question: "How does the Department of Justice write a letter that says that? The person that killed your father is very much alive, still lives in the hometown where you live, and admitted doing it ... and there's nothing that we can do or the state can do." John Gibson, executive director of the Arkansas Delta Truth and Justice Center, added his voice to the chorus, saying, "I hope we're not done." Alvin Sykes, noting Republican congressional refusal to fund the cold case program under President Barack Obama, added that the effort "hasn't lived up to its potential. I'm disappointed."[12] Charles Steele, Jr., president of the Southern Christian Leadership Conference (SCLC) founded by civil rights martyr Dr. Martin Luther King, called for public demonstrations if the law was allowed to expire in 2017. "We can never let people think they can get away with these types of horrific crimes," he declared.[13]

Part 1 of this book collects and examines cases reviewed under the Emmett Till Act for the first time in book form, recounting details of the crimes, where known, naming identified suspects, and relating why those cases barred from prosecution were officially closed. Part 2 details other cases, aptly described by SPLC spokesmen and some journalists as "The Forgotten," arbitrarily omitted from the DOJ's review of unsolved crimes. Readers having any further information on the cases found within, or any overlooked, are welcome contact the author though his website at www.michaelnewton.homestead.com.

Part 1: Official Civil Rights "Cold Cases"

Cases reviewed by the DOJ and FBI under the Emmett Till Unsolved Civil Rights Crimes Act of 2007 were selected arbitrarily, beginning curiously with a lynching case from 1934—one of thousands that mar U.S. history, occurring long before the recognized genesis of America's civil rights movement. That said, we must acknowledge that the crusade for racial equality did not begin in 1954, with a specific Supreme Court decision, nor did it end on New Year's Eve in 1969, as presumed by Congress. Some date the movement's origin from 1909, with the foundation of the National Association for the Advancement of Colored People (NAACP). Others note that early "freedom rides" occurred in 1947, when members of the Congress of Racial Equality (CORE) tried in vain to desegregate Southern bus terminals. In fact, Congress passed the first Civil Rights Act in 1866, with three more following by 1875, all universally ignored in Dixie, with the last ruled unconstitutional by an all-white U.S. Supreme Court in 1883. We may presume that DOJ and FBI officials did their best in selecting murders for review under the cold case initiative, although their effort—and the final disposition of those cases—satisfied virtually no one outside of Washington, D.C. Why were three lynchings chosen from the years 1934 to 1959, while 75 others from the same decades were ignored? How were certain killings by police distinguished from so many others equally suspicious? The following cases are listed chronologically, by the date of the specific crime where known, or by the date of its discovery. Some, regrettably, yield little detail after so much time has passed, while others are extensively detailed. All but one, including those "closed" by DOJ decree, remain officially unsolved.

Claude Neal
October 26, 1934; Jackson County, FL

Bride-to-be Lola Cannady, 19 or 20 years old (reports vary), set off from her family's rural home on October 18, to water the hogs they kept penned several hundred yards away. When she failed to return by nightfall, relatives and neighbors launched a search. Sheriff W. F. "Flake" Chambliss joined the search next morning, discovering signs of a struggle near the hog pen and its water pump. Soon afterward, searchers found Cannady's bludgeoned corpse in a grove of trees. Two doctors who examined Cannady found evidence of sexual intercourse, one calling it rape. Nearby, a bloody scrap of cloth lay with the stem and chain of a pocket watch. A man's footprints led Chambliss to the home of Sallie Smith, who shared her house with 23-year-old grand-nephew Claude Neal. When officers arrived, Smith was washing blood from Neal's clothing. Officers matched the bloody crime scene cloth to Neal's torn shirtsleeve, while the watch stem and chain fit his watch perfectly.[1]

Deputies found Neal sleeping in a white employer's corncrib and charged him with murder. Sheriff Chambliss, fearing vigilante action, shuttled Neal around various jails in Chipley, Panama City, and Camp Walton. A mob of would-be lynchers narrowly missed Neal in Panama City, then surrounded Chambliss's home on October 20, demanding surrender of the prisoner. By then, Neal was stashed across the state line, in Brewton, Alabama, while Florida newspapers predicted a Ku Klux Klan revival "to protect white womanhood." In custody, Neal used an "X" to sign a confession he could not read, and cousin Herbert Smith described the attack on Cannady, saying he and Neal met Lola while chasing a sow in a field near her family's hog pen. Neal asked Cannady for sex, whereupon she said, "You must be a fool." The two men then overpowered and raped her, Smith said, but left Cannady alive, covered with pine boughs.[2]

That discrepancy was problematic, coupled with Neal's insistence that Smith instigated the attack. On October 24, Smith confronted Neal in jail, and Neal confessed to sole guilt in the crime, saying his cousin "had nothing to do with it." Incredibly, despite Smith's prior confession to rape, officers freed Smith without filing charges and he remained unmolested in the ensuing ferocious mayhem.[3]

Shortly after midnight on October 26, a mob removed Neal from jail in Brewton, driving him back to Florida. Stopping at a point four miles from the Cannady crime scene, Neal's abductors issued a public invitation to his lynching, telling "all white folks" when and where he would be burned alive. From New York, NAACP spokesman Walter White wired Governor David Sholtz, requesting intervention "to avoid this disgrace upon the state of Florida." Sholtz demurred, saying he could not send troops without a request from Sheriff Chambliss, who had not asked for help.[4]

By 7:30 p.m., more than 2,000 people from 11 states had gathered at the Cannady home, swilling liquor, one telling reporters, "The womenfolk will do what they want to the nigger, then the men will get him." Neal, meanwhile, was held nearby, by a self-styled "Committee of Six," who sent word for the drunken mob to disperse. Instead of burning Neal alive, his captors shot him, then drove his corpse to the Cannady farm, where the body was beaten, shot more then 50 times, mutilated with knives, and run over by cars. Finally, as one "committee" member told author Dale Cox, "Somebody then said that if old Flake wanted him so bad, we should take him on up there and give him to him. So we took him up to the courthouse and hung him in a tree right outside Flake's office." Sheriff Chambliss cut down Neal's corpse at 6:32 a.m. on October 27. Later that day, photos of Neal's body sold on the streets for 50 cents each.

Sheriff Chambliss claimed that he could not identify Neal's killers, and NAACP investigator Howard "Buck" Kester had no better luck. By the time Sheriff John P. McDaniel reopened Neal's case in the 1980s, most of his suspects were dead or senile. Dale Cox found one witness who named an alleged triggerman, still living, but no solid evidence existed to support indictment.[5] The DOJ chose Neal's case as its oldest crime for review, under the Till Act, then closed the file without legal action on October 1, 2013.[6]

Maceo Snipes
July 18, 1946; Taylor County, GA

Born in 1909, Snipes worked his father's farm until the army drafted him in February 1943. He served for 30 months in World War II, including six in the Pacific Theater, then returned to Georgia with the novel notion that he was a full-fledged citizen. The U.S. Supreme Court agreed, having ruled in *King v. Chapman et al.*, on April 1, 1946, that Georgia's "white primary" elections illegally disfranchised African Americans. Snipes duly registered and was the only Taylor County African American to cast a ballot in the next primary, held on July 17, 1946.[7]

That was a volatile year in Georgia politics, with bitter white supremacist Eugene Talmadge seeking a fourth term as governor, backed by a newly resurgent Ku Klux Klan. As in the past, Talmadge condoned violence to suppress black suffrage. When Samuel Roper, an Atlanta policeman and KKK leader, sought Talmadge's advice on keeping blacks from the polls in July, Talmadge scrawled his answer on a notepad: "Pistols."[8] Intimidation kept most African Americans at home on election day, while those who dared to vote were marked for retaliation.

On July 18, one day after white votes swept Talmadge to victory, four white men drove to Snipes's rural home and called him out. One of the four—Edward Williamson, a fellow veteran who sometimes called himself "Ed Cooper"—shot Snipes three times on his porch, before the car departed. Stories differ as to whether Snipes collapsed immediately or walked three miles in search of help, aided by his mother. In any case, he died from blood loss on July 20, after a white physician said the hospital had no "black blood" available for transfusion. Relatives secretly buried Snipes that night, then fled the county in fear of their lives. When questioned by authorities, Williamson claimed self-defense, saying he tried to collect a $10 debt from Snipes, whereupon Snipes pulled a knife.[9]

Prosecutors filed no charges, and that stance persisted well into the 21st century. A Taylor County official, contacted by reporter Dan Barry in 2007, said of Snipes and Williamson, "Neither of them were exactly fine upstanding church-going citizens of the community."[10] Local obstinance led activists to contact the DOJ, which reviewed Snipes's case under the Till Act.

FBI agents retrieved their original file on the slaying, compiled in 1946, reporting that Snipes initially claimed "Mr. Williamson shot him because he had tried to get Mr. Snipes to work at a saw mill." Williamson and a companion, "Mr. Harvey," told agents Snipes owed Williamson $10 and that Williamson offered to let him work it off at the mill, but Snipes refused and threatened them with a knife. Williamson died in October 1983, followed by Harvey in March 2003, placing both beyond the law's reach.[11] Accordingly, the DOJ closed Snipes's case on April 12, 2010.[12]

Roger Malcom, Dorothy Malcom, George Dorsey and Mae Murray Dorsey
July 25, 1946; Moore's Ford, GA

One week after Maceo Snipes was shot in Taylor County (see July 18, 1946, above), another Georgia crime eclipsed his case in national headlines. The trouble began on

July 14, when 24-year-old Roger Malcom allegedly stabbed white Walton County farmer Barnette Hester. Witnesses to that event claimed Malcom suspected Hester of having sex with his—Malcom's—wife, who was seven months pregnant. Dorothy Malcom and her brother, 28-year-old war veteran George Dorsey, asked their white landlord, J. Loy Harrison, to bail Roger Malcom out of jail at Monroe, the county seat. Harrison, a reputed Ku Klux Klan member, initially refused, then changed his mind on July 25—Dorothy Malcom's 20th birthday—paying $600 for Malcom's release pending trial. At the time, Harrison told jailers he needed Malcom to work on his 1,000-acre farm, where the Malcoms and Dorseys resided as sharecroppers.[13]

At 5:30 p.m., as Harrison drove the Malcoms, George Dorsey, and George's wife Mae back toward Harrison's farm, a mob of armed white men blocked their way a Moore's Ford Bridge, on the border between Walton and Oconee counties. Various accounts estimate the mob's number between 12 and 30. The lynchers removed the Malcoms and Dorseys from Harrison's car, bound them to trees, and executed them with three volleys of gunfire. Afterward, one of the killers drew a knife and slashed open Dorothy Malcom's stomach, dashing her unborn fetus to the ground. Local rumors persist that the Dorseys were killed over George's alleged affair with a white woman.[14]

Harrison denied recognizing any of the lynchers, although none were masked. Speaking to authorities, he said, "A big man who was dressed mighty proud in a double-breasted brown suit was giving the orders. He pointed to Roger and said, 'We want that nigger.' Then he pointed to George Dorsey, my nigger, and said, 'We want you, too, Charlie.' I said, 'His name ain't Charlie, he's George.' Someone said 'Keep your damned big mouth shut. This ain't your party.'"[15]

President Harry Truman ordered an FBI investigation of the lynching, which compiled a list of 55 possible suspects, including George Hester, brother of Barnette. Agents interviewed 3,000 persons, telling FBI Director J. Edgar Hoover that gubernatorial candidate Eugene Talmadge met George Hester on July 15, two days before Georgia's primary election, and promised that if he won, he would guarantee immunity for anyone "taking care of" Roger Malcom. Ed Williamson, Monroe's assistant police chief, overheard that conversation on the county courthouse steps, later reporting it. Talmadge won the election, but died on December 21, before his inauguration.[16]

Governor Ellis Arnall offered $10,000 for information leading to conviction of the lynchers, and while the reward got no takers, he told reporters that "15 to 20 of the mob members are known by name." A federal grand jury convened on December 5, 1946, hearing 46 witnesses over the next three weeks. Those questioned included Loy Harrison, six members of the Hester family, three members of the Malcom family, Monroe police chief Ben Dickerson, and two FBI agents. On December 11, the panel indicted witness George Alvin Adcock on two counts of perjury, for denying he left home on July 25 or visited the crime scene on July 26. Aside from Adcock, however, the grand jury professed itself "unable to establish the identity of any persons guilty of violating the civil rights statute of the United States."[17]

Weeks later, white brothers James and Tom Verner entered Monroe's municipal ice house, spoke to manager Will Perry, then assaulted black employee Golden Howard, demanding to know what he had told the December grand jury. Perry suggested that they "take him out in back," where the beating continued for 15 minutes. U.S. Attorney John P. Cowart charged the Verners with "unlawfully injuring Golden Lamar Howard

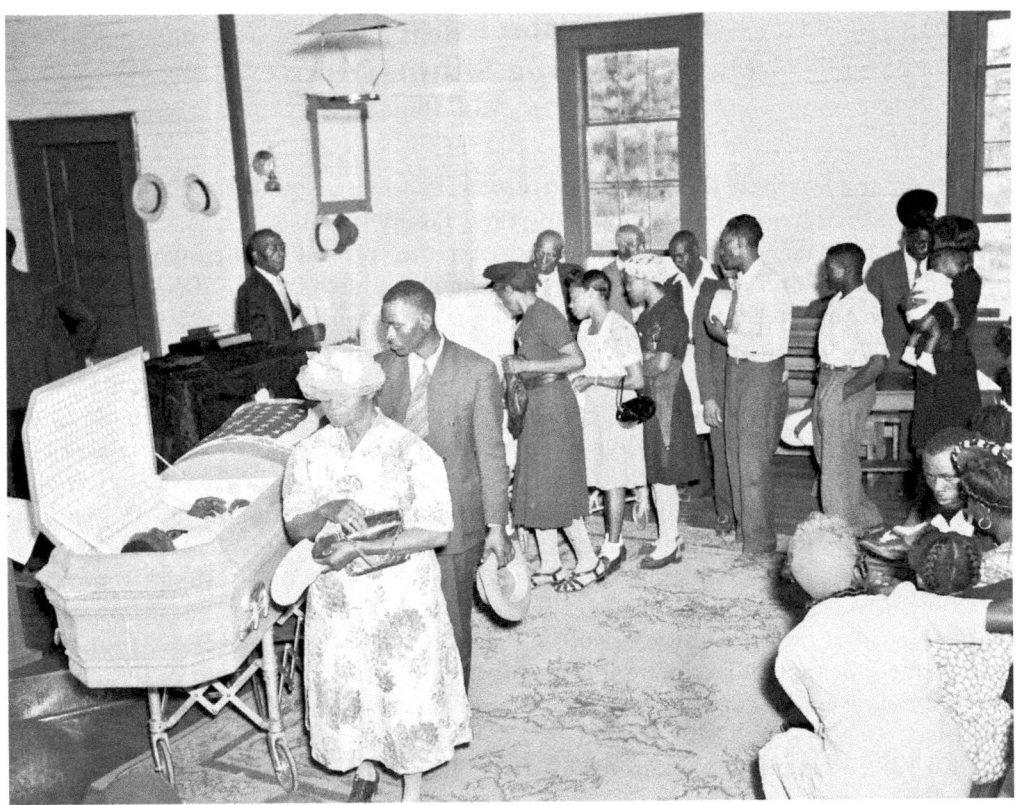

Funeral for Roger Malcom and his wife (Library of Congress).

because of his having testified before a federal grand jury" and "conspiring to injure" him. Walton County farmer H. L. Peters signed their $10,000 bonds, using his 316-acre farm as collateral. At trial, despite James Verner's admission that he beat Howard until his fists bled, white jurors acquitted both brothers.[18]

Local activist Robert Howard began researching the Moore's Ford case in 1968, aided by SPLC member Tyrone Brooks (now a Georgia state legislator). While reviving interest in the crime, they made no legal headway.[19] In 1991, white resident Clinton Adams admitting hiding in brush near Moore's Ford, watching the murders as a 10-year-old boy. Author Laura Wexler investigated that claim, concluding that Adams had "holes in his story."[20] Ten years later, when Governor Roy Barnes officially reopened the case, several of the FBI's original suspects were still alive, but none were charged.[21]

By 2006, FBI agents were back on the case. Passage of the Till Act accelerated their efforts, in concert with the Georgia Bureau of Investigation. In June 2008, FBI and GBI agents searched a Walton County farm near Gratis, collecting unspecified evidence they believed related to the lynching. GBI spokesman John Bankhead told reporters, "It was information that could not be ignored. We had to follow it."[22]

Whatever that evidence may be, it is still under wraps with the investigation ongoing. At last report from the DOJ, in January 2014, the Moore's Ford lynchings remain an open case.[23]

Harry Tyson Moore and
Harriette Vyda Simms Moore
December 25, 1951; Mims, FL

Harry and Harriette Moore had two reasons to celebrate on Christmas Day of 1951. Aside from the obvious holiday, bringing their family together, it was also their 25th wedding anniversary. After guests had departed, they retired for the night, happy and proud of their children, and of Harry's many accomplishments as Florida's leading advocate for African American equality. At 10:20 p.m., a powerful bomb exploded beneath heir bedroom, fatally wounding both victims. Harry died en route to a local hospital, while Harriette survived until January 3, 1952.[24]

Harry Moore was a natural target for Florida racists. Born in 1905, he founded Brevard County chapter of the NAACP in 1934, and three years later filed Dixie's first lawsuit to equalize pay for black and white public schools teachers. That effort prompted his dismissal as a school principal, while Harriette also lost her teaching job. Undaunted, Moore plunged full-time into civil rights work. Named as state president of the NAACP in 1941, he investigated lynchings and formed a Progressive Voters League to promote black suffrage statewide, registering 31 percent of Florida's eligible African Americans by 1950. His last great campaign involved defense of the "Groveland Boys," four young men framed for rape in Lake County (see July 26, 1949, and November 6, 1951, in Part 2).[25] Cumulative rage among white supremacists marked Moore for elimination racial terrorists.

Ku Klux Klansmen, blamed for 11 other Florida bombings in 1951 alone, were immediate suspects in Moore's slaying, though leader Bill Hendrix denied involvement, telling reporters, "If we caught one of our men doing it, we'd be the first to have him prosecuted." State investigation of the bombing was problematic under Governor Fuller Warren, himself a Klansman, who appointed fellow Kluxer J. Jefferson Elliott to lead the inquiry. FBI agents joined in the manhunt, focusing on three prime suspects: Joseph Neville Cox, "kligrapp" (secretary) of Orange County's Klan; Earl J. Brooklyn, who displayed a floor plan of Moore's home at Klan meetings; and Tillman H. Belvin, a friend of Brooklyn's known to join him in acts of Klan terrorism. Prior to settling in Florida, Belvin and Brooklyn were both expelled from Georgia's Klan for being too violent. All three suspects died over the next year, Cox by suicide after an FBI interrogation, Belvin and Brooklyn from apparent natural causes. Prosecutors filed no charges, but public interest in the case continued.[26]

In January 1978, dying from cancer, ex–Klansman Edward L. Spivey told Broward County officers he was present at the Moore bombing, planned by Joseph Cox to collect a $5,000 bounty placed on Harry Moore by persons unknown. Detectives were unable to identify the alleged contract's sponsor.[27]

Two months later, in March 1978, Raymond Henry, Jr., accosted local NAACP leader Charlie Matthews in Fort Pierce, raving drunk, telling him, "You raise a lot of hell around this town, but if I was active now, I'd do you like I did Harry T. Moore." Matthews took Henry home to sober up, inviting police to join them. Henry named three other members of a purported bombing team, including a lieutenant from the St. Lucie County Sheriff's Department, plus a policeman and a grocer from Fort Pierce, with a black man known only as "Cowboy." Strangely, Henry claimed the bombing had

The Moore home, shattered by a bomb on December 25, 1951 (Library of Congress).

occurred "just before Easter, 14 years ago"—i.e., in 1964. After missing a date with FBI agents and dropping from sight, Henry returned in November 1979 with a new conspiracy story, this one naming notorious Lake County sheriff Willis McCall as the crime's mastermind. Agents found no corroborating evidence, and in fact proved that the bombing's alleged "trigger man" was not in Florida in 1951. Sheriff McCall dismissed the tale as "some of the shit you reporters make up."[28]

State authorities launched a new investigation in 1991, after Dottie Harrington implicated ex-husband Frank in the bombing. Officers traced him to Hollywood, Florida, and cleared him after a polygraph test. Dottie then recanted her accusation, claiming Frank was "quite a talker with the boys," but admitting she would "never believe that he could be involved in any kind of violent crime."[29]

In December 2004, state attorney general Charlie Crist ordered yet another probe of the bombing, while Florida Crime Stoppers offered a $25,000 reward for information leading to identification of the killers. Archaeologists excavated debris from the blast site in December 2005, delivering that material to the FBI laboratory in Quantico, Virginia. The final report, published in 2006, named deceased Klansmen Belvin, Brooklyn, Cox, and Spivey as the only identified suspects.[30]

After passage of the Till Act, the DOJ added Harry and Harriette Moore to its list of cold case victims. Once again, the same quartet of dead Klansmen emerged as the only viable suspects.[31] Investigators closed the case without further action on July 15, 2011.[32]

Hilliard Brooks
August 12, 1952; Montgomery, AL

Segregated seating on city buses included all manner of racist abuse. Aside from seating blacks at the rear of a bus and whites to the front, many cities—including Montgomery—required blacks to surrender their seats if the "white" section filled and left riders standing. Black passengers had to board through the bus's front door, pay their fare, then exit and reenter through the rear, if the white driver did not drive away while they were on the sidewalk. Verbal disputes were frequent, one such leading to the death of Hilliard Brooks.

On August 12 the driver of Hilliard's bus called out to Patrolman Marvin E. Mills on the street, accusing Brooks of "creating a disturbance." An SPLC report says Brooks was ordered off the bus, accused of not paying his fare, but he refused to go, insisting that the money had been paid.[33] Whatever the issue, Officer Mills boarded the bus and soon thereafter shot Brooks, inflicting a wound that claimed his life on August 13. FBI agents reviewed the case under the Till Act and closed it without further action on April 9, 2010.[34] The FBI's letter of April 28 read, in part:

> Officer Mills stated that when he began to question Mr. Brooks, he came towards Officer Mills in an aggressive manner. Officer Mills pushed Mr. Brooks to the ground and warned him not to advance. Mr. Brooks got up, hit Officer Mills, and pulled the whistle and chain from Officer Mills's uniform shirt. Officer Mills fired a shot at Mr. Brooks, striking him in the abdomen. Mr. Brooks died from his injuries the following day.
>
> The MPD Board concluded that Officer Mills acted in self-defense, but recommended that the case be turned over to the Circuit Solicitor of Montgomery County to be presented before a grand jury. Montgomery Mayor John Goodwyn concurred with this recommendation. However, the Alabama State District Attorney's Office has no record of any grand jury proceedings or criminal trials pertaining to the death of Mr. Brooks.

Typical seating on a segregated bus in Montgomery, Alabama (Library of Congress).

In addition to the findings described above, the federal investigation determined that Mr. Mills died on May 30, 1993.[35]

Ladislado Ureste
April 27, 1953; San Antonio, TX

On April 22 a city police officer found Ureste, age 47, badly beaten with a chain in Concepcion Park, where Ureste worked as a watchman. The officer delivered him to a hospital, where Ureste died on April 27 without regaining consciousness. Investigators learned that Ureste was seen in a heated argument with white plumbers laying pipe through the park, after they complained of being forced to work behind a non-union African American ditch-digger. Police questioned the suspects but filed no charges.[36] The DOJ reviewed Ureste's case in 2009 and closed it without further action on April 20, 2010.[37]

Preston Bolden
May 8, 1953; San Antonio, TX

Passers-by found Bolden dead beside railroad tracks in the 600 block of North Walnut Street, with cause of death determined by an autopsy to be a broken neck. Although his death was an apparent homicide, no suspects were developed.[38] The DOJ reopened Bolden's case under the Till Act, asking relatives or others possessing knowledge to contact the San Antonio FBI office. Failing on that front, the department closed Ureste's case on May 26, 2011.[39]

Isadore Banks
June 4, 1954; Crittenden County, AR

Born in 1895, Banks served overseas in World War I, then returned to prosper, against all odds, in strictly segregated Arkansas. By 1954 he owned several business and 1,000 acres of land in Crittenden County, farming some and leasing more to others, helping black farmers buy seed and farm equipment, supporting a local black school with supplies.[40] In fact, he was too prominent and prosperous to live.

Banks left home for the last time on June 4, telling wife Alice he was off to pay their farmhands. Four days later, neighbor Carl Croom found Banks's truck abandoned in woodland outside Marion. Police soon found Banks, chained to a tree, mutilated, burned beyond recognition, with a can of gasoline nearby. Coroner T. H. McGough noted a wound in Banks's side, but could not say if it was caused by a blade or gunshot. With no signs of a struggle at the scene, McGough theorized that Banks was killed elsewhere, his 300-pound corpse transported by several assailants.[41]

Local police dragged their feet, identifying no suspects. Julian Fogleman, Marion's city attorney in 1954, could not recall in later years whether an inquest was even conducted.[42] The Grant Co-op Gin, run by Banks and other successful African Americans, offered a $1,000 reward for information in the case but got no takers. Arkansas civil rights activist L. C. Bates and the NAACP sought help outside the state, but all in vain.[43]

Several theories surround Banks's murder. One suggests that Banks was romantically linked to a white woman, another that he quarreled with a white man who made lewd advances to his daughter. The most likely suggestion involves Banks's property, coveted by less affluent white farmers. In the wake of Banks's slaying, whites did in fact acquire the property, although their names are lost to history. "What happened to his land?" son Jim Banks asked in 2011. "That's the $64,000 question, and all records have been destroyed. He owned a great deal of land and at that time, that wasn't common to have that kind of wealth for a black man. Offers had been made many times and he refused."[44]

Newspaper coverage of Isadore Banks's June 1954 torture slaying (author's collection).

While suspects remain elusive, the Civil Rights and Restorative Justice Project at Northeastern University's School of Law unearthed the missing land records in 2011, causing descendants of Banks to rejoice. "I just jumped for joy," granddaughter Marcelina Williams told television producer Chuck Hadad, "and I started calling people and saying, 'They found the land! They found the land!' All of the relatives were the same as I was—overwhelmed. We are going to have the biggest party on his land."[45]

Still, the murder remains unsolved today. The DOJ reviewed Banks's case under the Till Act, but made no headway, closing it without legal action on August 2, 2012.[46]

Isaiah Henry
July 28, 1954; Greensburg, LA

Isaiah Henry, called "Izell" in some reports, registered to vote in St. Helena Parish, when only a handful of the district's 52 percent black majority were allowed that privilege. He cast his first ballot on July 27, 1954, and paid the price one day later, when he was waylaid and savagely beaten by whites. Almost miraculously, he survived, but suffered major brain damage and was impaired until his death in 1959.[47] An alternate version of the event claims two unnamed individuals found Henry in a roadside ditch, a mile from his Greensburg home, and transported him to Lallie Kemp Hospital in Independence, where he died the same day.[48] The DOJ reopened Henry's case under the Till Act, then closed it again on May 21, 2012.[49]

George Washington Lee
May 7, 1955; Belzoni, MS

Lee was born in 1904, to an impoverished, illiterate sharecropping mother, mistreated by an abusive stepfather in Edwards, Mississippi. After his mother's death, an older sister took him in and supervised his high school education, rare in those days for black Mississippians. During years of labor in New Orleans, Lee took a correspondence course in typesetting, then found his calling as a minister in the 1930s, returning to Mississippi, where he led four churches around Belzoni. To support his family, Lee also ran a grocery store and operated a print shop from home.[50]

In 1953, a year before the Supreme Court's school desegregation ruling in *Brown v. Board of Education of Topeka*, Lee and fellow grocer Gus Courts founded an NAACP chapter in Belzoni, Lee doubling as the chapter's head and vice president of the Regional Council of Negro Leadership under Dr. T. R. M. Howard. In April 1955, an RCNL audience of 7,000 listened with rapt attention in all-black Mound Bayou, as Lee told them, "Pray not for your mom and pop. They've gone to heaven. Pray you can make it through this hell."[51]

The white-supremacist Citizens' Council, founded in July 1954, marked Lee and Courts as early targets for retaliation in Belzoni. The pair had registered 90 black voters in Humphreys County, and had led a boycott of local gas stations whose owners refused to install restrooms for African Americans. When threats failed to dissuade Lee and Courts from pursuing racial equality, violence was the next recourse. Near midnight on May 7, 1955, drive-by gunmen ambushed Lee on his way home from a shopping errand, blasting him with shotguns and propelling his car into a roadside shack. Lee died en route to a local hospital.[52]

Sheriff Isaac Shelton initially blamed Lee's death on reckless driving; when surgeons extracted shotgun pellets from his face, Shelton dismissed them as dental fillings, jarred loose by the crash. Informed that dentists do no use lead fillings, Shelton changed his tune, telling reporters, "This is one of the most puzzling cases I have ever had. If Lee was shot, it was probably by some jealous nigger. He was quite a ladies man." A local coroner's jury attributed Lee's death to "hemorrhage and probable asphyxiation from a wound, the cause of which is unknown." U.S. Attorney General Herbert Brownell, Jr., ordered an FBI investigation, but the agents accomplished nothing. No suspects were identified, no charges filed.[53]

George Washington Lee, murdered in Mississippi on May 7, 1955 (National Archives).

Threats continued against Gus Courts, prompting his resignation from the NAACP soon after Lee's murder. Still, he was not safe, as gunmen in a passing car shot up his store on November 25, 1955, leaving Courts badly wounded. He survived that attack, and witnesses described the shooters as white men, but Sheriff Shelton dismissed that testimony, launching a futile search for "light-skinned niggers." FBI agents returned, but showed no real interest in solving the case. When a physician offered them the buckshot pellets extracted from Courts, he was told to "keep them."[54]

The DOJ reviewed Lee's case under the Till Act, then closed it without further action on June 6, 2011.[55] Belzoni's crimes remain officially unsolved today.

Lamar Smith
August 13, 1955; Brookhaven, MS

Born in 1892, two years after Mississippi lawmakers rewrote the state's constitution to disfranchise African Americans, Lamar Smith was a veteran of World War I who returned from service overseas to join the Regional Counsel of Negro Leadership and work to register black voters in Lincoln County. He was one of the county's few black registered voters casting primary election ballots on August 2, 1955, and when that vote forced a runoff between leading candidates, scheduled for August 23, Smith worked overtime to sign up new voters. That task brought him to Brookhaven and the county courthouse on August 13, helping blacks fill out absentee ballots, thereby allowing them to vote without facing white mayhem at the polls.[56]

A 10 o'clock that morning, several white men approached Smith on the courthouse lawn, one drawing a pistol and shooting him at point-blank range. Sheriff Carnie E. Smith detained three men—Charles Falvey, Mack Smith, and Noah Smith—then released them after brief preliminary questioning. Lincoln County's district attorney told reporters Sheriff Smith refused to file charges "although he knew everything I know." According to the D.A., Sheriff Smith personally saw prime suspect Noah Smith "leave the scene with blood all over him. It was his duty to take that man into custody regardless of who he was, but he did not do it."[57]

On August 17, an article in the Communist Party's *Daily Worker* newspaper reported that a coroner's jury blamed Smith's death on "a gunshot wound in an altercation with Noah Smith, Mack Smith, Charles Falvey, and probably other parties unknown."[58] Despite that finding, an all-white grand jury, convened on September 13, indicted no one for the slaying and did not censure Sheriff Smith for his seeming negligence.[59]

Lamar Smith with his wife on their wedding day, date unknown (Library of Congress).

The DOJ reviewed Smith's case under the Till Act, closing it without legal action on April 12, 2010.⁶⁰ A letter from the FBI to Smith's survivors, bearing the same date, reported that Noah Smith died in June 1975, followed by Charles Falvey in December 1987, and Mack Smith in September 1992. With no known suspects surviving, agents could do nothing more.⁶¹

Emmett Louis Till
August 28, 1955; Money, MS

The son of Mississippi Delta natives, Till was born in Chicago on July 25, 1941. His parents separated the following year, but Emmett took life in stride, surviving a bout with polio that left him with a stutter at age six, known to family and friends as "a prankster, a risk-taker and a smart dresser who nevertheless did well in school." In August 1955, before he left to visit relatives in Mississippi, his mother warned him, "If you have to get on your knees and bow when a white person goes past, do it willingly." His personality was irrepressible, however—charming to his kinfolk, fatal for a black teenager in he South, three months after the U.S. Supreme Court ordered schools to integrate "with all deliberate speed."⁶²

Till arrived in tiny Money, Mississippi, on August 21. Three days later, he joined cousin Curtis Jones and other local boys to purchase candy at Bryant's Grocery and Meat Market. Outside, Till's companions later said, he showed them photos from his wallet of an integrated class, pointing out a white girl he claimed was his girlfriend. The boys dared Till to approach the store's white proprietor, 21-year-old Carolyn Bryant, and speak to her. All agree that Till took the dare, but what happened next remains in dispute.⁶³

Conflicting accounts claim that Till "wolf-whistled" at Bryant, took her hand and asked her for a date, or said, "Bye, baby" as he left the store. Another version says he told Bryant, "You needn't be afraid of me, baby, I've been with white women before." Bryant herself would testify that Till put his arm around her waist while mouthing "unprintable" words. In any case, she was alarmed enough to fetch a pis-

Emmett Till, shortly before his fatal trip to Mississippi in August 1955 (National Archives).

tol from her car, parked outside, whereupon the youths fled. Returning to the home of Till's great-uncle, Mose Wright, Till and Jones kept the matter secret for fear of being scolded.[64]

Roy Bryant, Carolyn's 23-year-old husband, was hauling shrimp to Texas when the incident occurred, returning to Money on August 27. Alerted by his wife, Bryant questioned several African American youths, obtaining Till's name and directions to his relatives' home. Several witnesses heard Roy discussing Till's abduction with 36-year-old half-brother John William Milam. In the predawn hours of August 28, Bryant and Milam—with a third unidentified man, described as black in some reports—abducted Till from Mose Wright's home at gunpoint, driving him to a shed owned by Milam. There, according to witnesses, a group of four to eight other men, white and black, observed Bryant and Milam beating Till, attempting to decide if they should kill him or simply leave him with a warning.[65]

Bryant's version of events, sold to author William Bradford Huie for $4,000 and later published in *Look* magazine, claimed that he merely hoped to frighten Till, extracting an apology, but Till allegedly cursed his abductors and refused to grovel, maintaining his claim that he'd "had" white women in Chicago. "Well, what else could we do?" Bryant said. "He was hopeless. I'm no bully; I never hurt a nigger in my life. I like niggers—in their place—I know how to work 'em. But I just decided it was time a few people got put on notice. As long as I live and can do anything about it, niggers are gonna stay in their place. Niggers ain't gonna vote where I live. If they did, they'd control the government. They ain't gonna go to school with my kids. And when a nigger gets close to mentioning sex with a white woman, he's tired o' livin.' I'm likely to kill him.... I stood there in that shed and listened to that nigger throw that poison at me, and I just made up my mind. 'Chicago boy,' I said, 'I'm tired of 'em sending your kind down here to stir up trouble. Goddam you, I'm going to make an example of you—just so everybody can know how me and my folks stand.'"[66]

Bryant shot Till, then joined Milam to weight Till's body with a 75-pound cotton gin fan, and dumped him in the Tallahatchie River, where he surfaced on August 31. Battered and swollen from immersion, the nude corpse was unrecognizable, but relatives identified Till by a ring he habitually wore, bearing his father's initials—"L. T." for "Louis Till"—and the date "May 25, 1943."[67]

Tallahatchie County Sheriff H. Clarence Strider hoped to bury Till quickly, but Till's mother demanded that the corpse be shipped home to Chicago for interment. Meanwhile, Strider encouraged rumors that Till was not dead, but was hiding with relatives in the North. A bitter racist, furious at the bad press Till's murder brought to his state, Strider told reporters, "We never have any trouble until some of our Southern niggers go up North and the NAACP talks to 'em and they come back home. If they would keep their nose and mouths out of our business we would be able to do more when enforcing the laws of Tallahatchie County and Mississippi." When Charles Diggs, an African American congressman from Michigan visited Tallahatchie County following Till's murder, Strider barred him from the sheriff's office on grounds that he—Strider—could not believe in the existence of "a nigger congressman."[68]

FBI agents investigated Till's murder, delivering an 8,000-page report to state authorities. Governor Hugh White condemned the slaying and called for "vigorous prosecution," sending a telegram to NAACP headquarters that said, "Mississippi does not condone such conduct." A grand jury indicted Roy Bryant and Milam for murder,

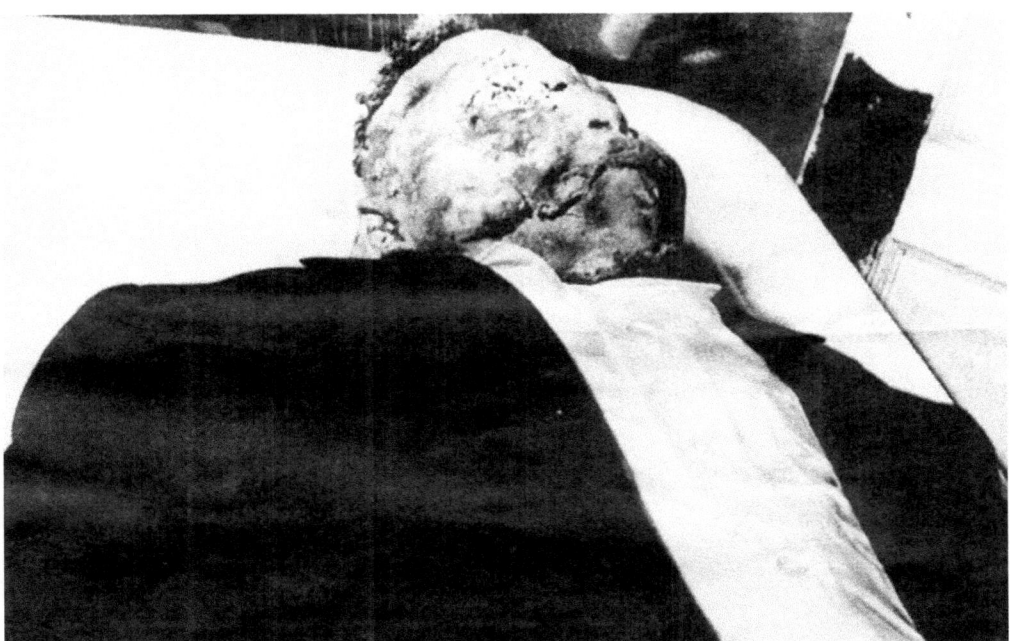

Emmett Till in his coffin, displaying damage that encouraged Mississippi authorities to dispute his identity (National Archives).

with Sheriff Strider granting that the evidence against them was "pretty good." But then, as northern criticism mounted, Mississippi's white press changed its tune, assailing "outside agitators" for the slaying and other similar crimes. Collection jars in public places raised $10,000 for Bryant's and Milam's defense. Sheriff Strider, on September 3, claimed that a wealthy black activist, Dr. T. R. M. Howard, had procured a cadaver to stand in for Till, placing Till's ring on the body.[69]

Prosecutor Gerald Chatham had misgivings when the trial began in September 1955. Till's relatives had witnessed his abduction, but Chatham was unaware of two witnesses to the crime itself: Levi Collins and Henry Lee Loggins, black employees of John Milam's brother. Upon learning what they had seen, Sheriff Strider jailed both men in Charleston, to prevent them from testifying. During the five-day trial, Bryant and Milam admitted kidnapping Till, but claimed they had released him alive and well. Sheriff Strider appeared as a defense witness, touting his fable of switched corpses, and harassed black spectators in court, addressing them with comments such as "Hello, niggers." A defense attorney, in summation, warned jurors that if they voted to convict, "your forefathers would turn over in their graves." The all-white panel acquitted Bryant and Milam after 67 minutes of deliberation, one juror telling reporters, "If we hadn't stopped to drink pop, it wouldn't have taken that long." After the verdict was announced, Sheriff Strider publicly congratulated the defendants.[70]

Despite that victory for racism, Mississippi's press continued harping on the case. In October 1955, the *Jackson Daily News* reported that Till's father had been hanged in 1945, while serving with the U.S. Army in Italy, for raping two women and killing a third. The defendants' published confessions offset that attitude somewhat in 1956, but Mississippi's Citizens' Council and State Sovereignty Commission still blamed the crime

Confessed slayers of Emmett Till, J. W. Milam (left) and Roy Bryant, at their murder trial (Library of Congress).

on northern agitators bankrolled by the NAACP. Folk singer Bob Dylan recorded a song titled "The Death of Emmett Till" in 1962. Bryant and Milam moved to Texas, but later returned to Mississippi. Both died from cancer—Milam in 1980, Bryant in 1994—but not before Bryant was twice convicted of food stamp fraud, in 1984 and 1988.[71]

Media interest in Till's case persisted. In 1996, documentary filmmaker Keith Beauchamp claimed that up to 14 people were involved in Till's slaying, including Carolyn Bryant. In 2003, PBS aired an installment of *American Experience* titled "The Murder of Emmett Till." A year later, the DOJ reopened Till's case, exhuming his corpse in 2005. The body was "in pretty poor shape," but still displayed extensive cranial damage, a broken left femur, two broken wrists, and metallic fragments in the skull consistent with a gunshot. DNA analysis conclusively identified the corpse as Till's.[72]

In March 2007, black District Attorney Joyce Chiles convened a grand jury to reexamine Till's case. The panel found no credible evidence supporting claims of 14 participants in the crime, and declined to indict 73-year-old Carolyn Bryant Donham, long divorced from Roy Bryant and remarried. The DOJ closed its case without further action on December 28, 2007.[73]

John Earl Reese

October 22, 1955; Mayflower, TX

The Supreme Court's *Brown* rulings of 1954–55, demanding integration of public schools with "all deliberate speed," generated as much racist passion in Texas as in any other Jim Crow state. Most counties would comply, dodging the hard-line response of Deep South white supremacists who answered "Never," but violence was not to be avoided, even so. Gregg County, in east Texas, witnessed some of the worst terrorism after a federal court ordered Kilgore Junior College to desegregate.[74]

On Saturday, October 26, 16-year-old John Reese went to the Hughes Café with younger cousins Johnnie and Joyce Nelson. Previously, nightriders had fired on local schools, and Johnnie Nelson later told an interviewer, "The word had come through that there was a possibility of a drive-by."[75] Undaunted, Reese and Joyce were dancing to music from the jukebox when bullets shattered the café's windows, killing Reese and wounding both of his cousins. Elsewhere in Mayflower that night, the shooters blasted mailboxes at black homes and shot up one house, cutting a resident with flying window glass in her bedroom, as she knelt to say her nightly prayers.[76]

Texas Rangers investigated the shootings, questioning some 300 potential witnesses. Research led them to 22-year-old Perry Dean Ross and 21-year-old Joe Simpson, who confessed their plan to "make a raid" against "uppity blacks." As Ross's lawyer, Gordon R. Wellborn, later told a jury, the men "wanted to scare somebody and keep the niggers and the whites from going to school together." In jail, Ross admitted driving the car and firing a .22-caliber weapon at various targets, while Simpson went along for the ride.[77]

A grand jury charged both men with murder on February 2, 1956, but a judge soon dismissed Simpson's charge, in exchange for testimony against Ross. At trial, attorney Wellborn argued that his client had been drunk, urging jurors to "call it a bad day and let the boy go on in life." District Attorney Ralph Prince, while arguing for jail time to "deter others from committing a similar crime," seemed to agree with Wellborn in principal, calling Reese's murder "a case of two irresponsible boys attempting to have some fun by scaring niggers." Jurors convicted Ross on April 23, 1956, but he need not have worried. After imposing a sentence of two to five years, the judge suspended it and sent Ross home.[78]

The DOJ reviewed Reese's case under the Till Act, closing it without further action on April 15, 2010.[79] As the FBI explained to his survivors, Perry Ross had died in January 1978, followed by Joe Simpson in June 1998, placing both beyond the reach of human justice.[80]

Clinton Melton
December 3, 1955; Glendora, MS

On Saturday, October 3, Elmer Otis Kimball, a white cotton gin operator, pulled into Lee McGarrh's gas station and, according to McGarrh, asked to have his tank filled. In fact, the car belonged to John Milam, Kimball's best friend and confessed slayer of recent murder victim Emmett Till (see August 28 above), with whom Kimball had spent the day hunting. McGarrh told 10-year employee Clinton Melton to fill the car's tank, but when he had done so, Kimball claimed he had only requested two dollars worth of fuel. An argument ensued, Kimball announcing his plan to fetch a gun from home and shoot Melton.[81]

True to his word, Kimball soon returned with a shotgun and his 13-year-old son, Sammy. While McGarrh watched from inside the station, Kimball approached, telling black bystander John Henry Wilson, "I'm going to kill that nigger." Wilson begged him to reconsider, whereupon Kimball said, "Get back or I'll kill you too." As Wilson retreated, Kimball shot Melton three times, killing him instantly. Melton left a widow, Beulah, and four young children.[82]

McGarrh, Wilson, and witness George Woodson described the slaying to Sheriff H. Clarence Strider as unprovoked murder. Kimball, when arrested, claimed self-defense and displayed a shoulder wound, claiming that Melton—though unarmed—had shot him first. Afterward, supposedly, he drove to Milam's home, passing a local doctor's residence, and Milam took him to a hospital in Charleston, 25 miles distant, passing by the doctor's house a second time.[83]

Elmer Otis Kimball, slayer of Clinton Melton in December 1955, acquitted on a plea of self-defense (National Archives).

A grand jury charged Kimball with murder. He faced trial in March 1956, in the same Sumner courthouse where friend Milam and half-brother Roy Bryant were earlier acquitted in the Till case. This time, cameras were barred from court, County Attorney Hamilton Caldwell and District Attorney Roy Johnson saying, "We don't want a press table here this time because the less seen of the press the better, because we'd like to see a conviction." In fact, only one reporter attended the trial, sent from Hodding Carter's *Delta Democrat-Times* in Greenville.[84]

Prosecution witnesses included Lee McGarrh, John Wilson, and George Woodson, all describing Melton as unarmed and innocent of any wrongdoing. Elmer Kimball, on the stand, claimed Melton cursed at him repeatedly, saying, "I wish you'd make up your damn mind" and "I'm not afraid of you or any other white son of a bitch." Kimball said he complained to McGarrh (who denied it), then announced he had to fetch more cash from home to pay his inflated bill. When he returned, Kimball told jurors, Melton shot him without warning, forcing Kimball to return fire. Sammy Kimball seconded his father's tale. Other defense witnesses—none of them present at the shooting—included Sheriff Strider (who also testified for the defense in Emmett Till's slaying), one of his deputies, and Glendora's police chief. County Attorney Caldwell final plea to the jury was plaintive: "Regardless of whether a man's white or black, you've got to be impartial. A nigger's a human being. He's got life. And you know that no nigger would call you those things, and you would just walk away."[85]

The all-white jury acquitted Kimball on March 13, as expected, but Beulah Melton did not live to hear that verdict. While working with NAACP field secretary Medgar Evers to investigate her husband's death, she mysteriously drove her car into a rural bayou and drowned on December 22, 1955. A relative driving past the crash site saved two of Melton's children from the car (see August 22, 1955, in Part 2).

The DOJ reopened Clinton Melton's case under the Till Act, then closed it on April 12, 2010.[86] A letter from the FBI to his surviving children, bearing that same date, reported Elmer Kimball's death in February 1985—and misspelled his name as "Kimbell"—thereby foreclosing any hope of further legal action.[87]

James E. Evanston
December 21, 1955; Long Lake, MS

An elderly schoolteacher, Evanston lived with his wife at Tutwiler, in Tallahatchie County, while teaching black elementary and high school students in Merigold (Bolivar County). He was not an NAACP member, but had attended the September murder trial of Emmett Till's killers and may have been marked for that reason. Three months later, on December 21, he left home to visit Tallahatchie County's Long Lake and never returned. Searchers pulled his body from the water on December 24, with cause of death unknown at last report.[88] The DOJ reviewed Evanston's case 55 years later—possibly hampered by spelling his surname "Evansington"—and closed it without result on April 12, 2010.[89]

Jesse James Shelby
January 21, 1956; Yazoo City, MS

On Friday night, January 20, Patrolman Marlon Manor and Jolly C. Thompson were dispatched to investigate a disturbance at the Silver Slipper, an all-black nightclub. Arriving on the scene, they reportedly found 23-year-old Jesse Shelby in a car outside the club, fighting with girlfriend Ruby Lee Little. On hearing Little's claim that Shelby had assaulted her, Thompson pulled Shelby from the vehicle to arrest him, shooting him in the stomach when Shelby allegedly grabbed Thompson's blackjack and struck him with it. Shelby died from his wound early on Saturday. A coroner's inquest, convened on January 24, heard "four or five witnesses," according to County Attorney Griffin Norquist, then ruled the shooting a justifiable act of self-defense.[90]

The DOJ reviewed Shelby's case under the Till Act, then closed it on May 24, 2010.[91] An FBI letter to Shelby's family reported that Officer Thompson died in February 1983, followed by Manor in October 1992.[92]

Jessie James Shelby, killed by police on January 21, 1956 (Civil Rights Archive).

Thomas Hency Brewer
February 18, 1956; Columbus, GA

Brewer, an African American physician born in 1894, joined Muscogee County's fledgling civil rights movement in the 1920s, founding the district's first NAACP chapter in 1939. Six years later, he raised funds to support a local civil rights case, *King v. Chapman et al.*, which invalidated Georgia's "white primary" elections. In 1951, his campaign to integrate the Columbus Police Department resulted in hiring of four black patrolmen. By 1955 he was embroiled in further controversy: an effort to integrate the golf course on Columbus's South Commons, and an allegation, staunchly denied, that as a prominent Republican with national party ties he had blocked a popular white Columbus citizen from serving as the city's postmaster.[93]

Dr. Thomas Brewer, killed by Lucio Flowers on February 18, 1956 (National Archives).

Those factors, and Brewer's professional success, made him a natural target for racists in Georgia, where the Ku Klux Klan enjoyed strong connections with the Democratic Party and in law enforcement. On February 18, 1956, Brewer died from seven point-blank gunshot wounds, in a clothing store downstairs from his First Avenue office. The triggerman, white store proprietor Lucio Flowers, claimed Brewer had entered his shop, started a quarrel over an incident of police brutality both men had witnessed 10 days earlier, then reached into his pocket, prompting Flowers to shoot in fear of his life. Investigators found a pistol in Brewer's pocket, carried due to frequent death threats, and while that gun was neither drawn nor fired, authorities ruled Brewer's shooting self-defense. One year later, in February 11, 1957, police found Flowers dead outside First Avenue's Old Dixie Theater, shot once in the head. His death was deemed a suicide, prompted by financial woes, but many African Americans believe Flowers was murdered to seal his lips, by someone involved in a plot to kill Dr. Brewer.[94]

Whatever the truth of that theory, Brewer's death prompted an exodus of black professionals from Columbus, including at least three physicians and one attorney. Brewer's surviving family also fled the area, stalling the local civil rights movement until Dr. Martin Luther King, Jr., launched a campaign in Georgia six years later.[95]

The DOJ reviewed Brewer's case under the Till Act, then closed it without further action on April 6, 2009.[96] The suspicious death of Lucio Flowers effectively precludes further investigation.

William Dallas Owens
March 5, 1956; New Bern, NC

City police arrested Owens, a disabled World War II veteran, for public drunkenness. He died in jail a short time later, from a skull fracture. The DOJ reopened his case in 2008 and closed it without result on April 3, 2009.[97] Curiously, a March 2007 report in the *Fayetteville Observer* says of Owens: "His published obituary suggests he was white: His Army unit had not been integrated during World War II and the church and funeral home that handled his burial is traditionally white."[98]

Bessie McDowell
June 14, 1956; Andalusia, AL

At age 58, Bessie McDowell was well known in her community, a member of the Veterans of Foreign Wars Auxiliary who frequently prepared meals for the local Junior Chamber of Commerce. Her death resulted from the actions of white loan collector Claude Ingle, who visited McDowell's home with son Bobby Ray on Thursday night, to collect money from her live-in nephew, Charlie C. Williams. Williams offered to pay on Friday, claiming he presently had no money, whereupon Bobby Ingle slapped him. As Williams ran back in the house, Claude Ingle fired a pistol through an open window, striking McDowell in the face as she slept. She died en route to a hospital.[99]

In custody, Claude Ingle claimed he fired because he thought Williams was running for a gun. A grand jury charged both Ingles with murder, but Bobby's charge was subsequently dismissed. White jurors convicted Claude on a reduced charge of manslaughter, whereupon the court imposed a one-year prison term and a $500 fine. The Alabama Court of Appeals affirmed that judgment on September 17, 1957.[100]

The DOJ reviewed McDowell's case under the Till Act, but could find no cause for further legal action, closing the matter on April 9, 2010.[101]

Maybelle Mahone
December 5, 1956; Zebulon, GA

In hard-core Jim Crow states, white supremacists demanded absolute subservience from African Americans. A case in point is that of Maybelle Mahone, a 30-year-old mother of six who allegedly "sassed" B. T. Dukes, a 71-year-old white farmer, at her home in Pike County, two miles from Molena. Dukes killed her with a shotgun on the spot, facing a murder charge that earned him a life prison term on August 1, 1957. He served only a fraction of his time, however, before an appellate court ruled him insane and released him.[102] The DOJ reviewed Mahone's case 52 years after the fact, then closed it without taking action on April 6, 2009.[103]

Willie Edwards, Jr.
January 23, 1957; Montgomery County, AL

In January 1957 members of the Ku Klux Klan heard rumors that Edward Wells, a black truck driver for the Winn-Dixie supermarket chain, was "making passes" at white women around Montgomery. Unknown to Klansmen, Wells called in sick on the night they planned to abduct him, and they snatched replacement driver Willie Edwards, Jr., instead. Calling him "Edward," refusing to believe they had the wrong man, the kidnappers drove Edwards to the Tyler Goodwin Bridge, forcing him to jump at gunpoint. Edwards plunged 50 feet into the Alabama River, his body retrieved from the water on April 23. Officials claimed decomposition barred them from determining a cause of death.[104]

The case languished until February 1976, when state attorney general Bill Baxley reopened the file. Ex-Klansman Raymond Britt, Jr., furnished an affidavit on February 20, in exchange for immunity, claiming he joined fellow "knights" Henry Alexander, Sonny Kyle Livingston, Jr., and James York in abducting Edwards and forcing him to leap from the bridge. (Britt and Livingston were previously charged with bombing black homes, but white jurors acquitted both Klansmen in 1957, despite their signed confessions.) Baxley charged the three suspects with murder, but Judge Frank Embry dismissed the case on grounds that no cause of death was determined for Edwards, saying, "Merely forcing a person to jump from a bridge does not naturally and probably lead to the death of such person."[105]

Sixteen more years slipped away before Alexander, on his deathbed from cancer, confessed his role in the murder to wife Diane. She penned a letter of apology to Edwards's survivors, after Henry died in December 1992, and met with the family in September 1993. On July 28, 1997, Malinda Edwards wrote to Montgomery County District Attorney Ellen Brooks, requesting reevaluation of her father's case. Later that year, State Medical Examiner Dr. James Lauridson exhumed the remains of Willie Edwards, pronouncing his death a homicide. Judge Charles Price ordered Alabama's Department of Vital Statistics to change Edwards's cause of death from "unknown," but that belated switch moved survivors no closer to justice. Ellen Brooks presented her case to a local grand jury in March 1999, but that panel returned no indictments, citing the death of key witnesses.[106]

The DOJ reviewed Edwards's case under the Till Act, then closed it without further action on July 2, 2013. No details of its findings have been published.[107]

Willie Joe Sanford
February 1957; Hawkinsville, GA

On March 1, 1957, a fisherman's hook snagged the nude corpse of Willie Joe Sanford, wired to the stalks of underwater plants in a Hawkinsville creek. A grand jury considered the case, and while no record of its findings survives today, prosecutors indicted no suspects.[108] An FBI press release announced that Sanford's case had been "fully assessed" by October 9, 2009, but the DOJ did not formally close the case until July 5, 2012.[109]

George Washington Singleton, Jr.
April 30, 1957; Shelby, NC

At age 34, Dr. Singleton was an army veteran described in press reports as a "prominent physician and husband of an Indianapolis socialite." The only African American surgeon licensed to practice at Shelby Hospital (now Cleveland Regional Medical Center), he "enjoyed a heavy practice" but was vacating his office and, in fact, leaving Shelby for Nashville, Tennessee, where wife Sarah was a university student. The couple's three children were scattered, two living with Sarah's mother in Indianapolis, one with George's mother in Newberry, South Carolina. Relatives said that Dr. Singleton planned to practice next in Indiana.[110]

At 2 a.m. on April 30, a fiery blast rocked Dr. Singleton's second-story office in Shelby. Police found his charred body in the ruins, near the doorway, and while police claimed no evidence of foul play, a theory circulated that Singleton had been clubbed with a blunt instrument, "probably wielded by an intruder seeking narcotics," who then set the place afire.[111]

The DOJ reviewed Singleton's death under the Till Act and closed the case on April 16, 2010.[112] A letter to his family read, in part:

> The local investigation revealed that, had Dr. Singleton not vacated the building by May 1, 1957, eviction proceedings would have commenced. Dr. Singleton's car was parked in front of the office, packed with clothing and belongings. Further, personal papers and records had been removed from the office and were located on the dining room table in Dr. Singleton's home, including insurance policies in the amount of $6,000 covering "office medical equipment, including books and supplies." An accelerate [sic], gasoline, was discovered at the scene of the fire, and latent fingerprints recovered from a can of gas recovered at the scene matched Dr. Singleton's. The medical examiner determined that Dr. Singleton died as a result of his third-degree burns and found no evidence of foul play.[113]

Charles Brown

June 18, 1957; Benton, MS

A white man named Walton shot Brown for "visiting" the gunman's sister at her home. FBI agents briefly investigated, then left prosecution to state authorities, who did nothing.[114] The DOJ reopened Brown's case under the Till Act, then closed it without taking action on April 16, 2010.[115] On that date FBI agents delivered a letter to Brown's survivors, relating details of the crime. Heavily censored prior to its release for public viewing, that letter read, in part:

> [DELETED] were interviewed by the FBI and stated that [DELETED] had heard from an unidentified source or sources that Mr. Walton had caught [DELETED] "in some action" and decided to lure Mr. Brown to the [DELETED] home to kill him. Mr. Brown was invited to dinner [DELETED] on the night of his death. Also present were [DELETED]. [DELETED] told [DELETED] that Mr. Walton had knocked on the door and when [DELETED] opened it, Mr. Walton entered and shot [DELETED] with a shotgun. [DELETED] also stated that the local prosecutor never consulted with [DELETED] concerning any effort to prosecute Mr. Walton….
>
> Mr. Walton, then a 50-year-old farmer, who had been previously incarcerated for the manslaughter of his son-in-law, admitted that he shot Mr. Brown in the heart with a shotgun as the victim sat in [DELETED] dining room. Mr. Walton claimed that he shot Mr. Brown because Mr. Brown had been "too friendly" with [DELETED] while her [DELETED] was out of town.
>
> Mr. Walton died on July 14, 1965.[116]

Rogers Hamilton
October 22, 1957; Lowndes County, AL

Hamilton was 18 years old on the night a pickup truck occupied by at least two white men appeared at his mother's home, on a farm owned by white landlord George McCurdy. One of the men called Rogers out by name and spoke briefly to him while Hamilton's mother watched from the house, then Rogers got into the truck and it rolled away. Beatrice Hamilton initially thought McCurdy was the driver, fetching her son for some late-night job, but instinct prompted her to follow the pickup on foot. Soon, she found the truck stopped, Rogers and one of the white men standing beside it. As she screamed, horrified, the white man drew a pistol, shot Rogers in the forehead, then got back in the truck and drove away.[117]

On October 23 Alabama Bureau of Investigation agent Oscar Coley visited Hamilton's home, escorted by Deputy Sheriff Joe Jackson—an officer whose alcoholic brother, Lux, was notorious for assaulting African Americans without provocation or subsequent punishment. Mrs. Hamilton described the murder vehicle and its occupants as best she could, but Coley refused to believe the killers were white. In his report, he wrote, "Since it was 1:30 in the morning, it is doubtful that Beatrice Hamilton could have determined the color of the truck or the color of the men who carried him away. It is the opinion of the writer that Beatrice Hamilton, although sincere in her belief that her statement is true, that due to emotional upset of her son being killed that in all probability she is mistaken in many respects to what she stated. At the present time, there is no clue as to what could have been the motive for this killing."[118]

A half-century later, investigative reporter John Fleming uncovered a possible reason for Hamilton's murder. Lucius Evans, a retired Lowndesboro mill worker, told Fleming that Hamilton and some friends often traveled to Hayneville, the county seat, to visit a woman they called "the white girl." In fact, Evans explained, "she wasn't white, she was real light-complected, and she had these three beautiful daughters." On other occasions, he said, "Rogers didn't always go to the 'white girl's' house, but kept going up the road, on up the way there, and back in a neighborhood on the far side of the road. I don't know who he was going to see. But he was going to visit someone else." Civil rights activist Bob Mants contends that Hamilton found himself smitten with "the wrong colored girl," specifically one desired by some unknown, jealous white man.[119]

The DOJ reviewed Hamilton's case under the Till Act, and it remained officially open at last report, in January 2014.[120]

Clarence Horatious Pickett
December 23, 1957; Columbus, GA

Police arrested Pickett, a part-time minister, for unknown reasons on December 21, severely beating him in his jail cell. He died from his injuries two days later, without regaining consciousness. Prosecutors filed no charges.[121] The DOJ reopened Pickett's case under the Till Act, mistakenly calling him "Charles," then closed it without taking any action on April 12, 2010.[122] Some websites today unaccountably confuse his case with that of Charles Brown in Mississippi (see June 18, 1957, above).[123]

George Love
January 8, 1958; Sunflower County, MS

A sheriff's posse killed Love near Ruleville or Indianola (reports differ), but serious questions remain as to why they were hunting him in the first place. Fifty years after the fact, FBI spokesmen said Love "allegedly shot and seriously wounded a Ruleville night marshal who sought to question Love about a robbery."[124] Conflicting sources, however, claim officers "believed he was responsible for a murder and arson." That source adds that Love "was later cleared of any connection to the murder."[125] The DOJ reviewed Love's case under the Till Act and closed it without taking any action on June 10, 2011.[126]

James Brazier
April 20, 1958; Dawson, GA

White racists in Terrell County despised Brazier as an "uppity nigger" whose prosperity—including purchase of new cars in 1956 and 1958—infuriated them. On Sunday, April 20, Brazier observed Sheriff Zachary T. Matthews and Dawson police chief Howard L. Lee arresting—some reports say beating—his father, Odell Brazier, for drunk driving on the road near Brazier's home. Chief Lee later claimed that Brazier interfered with the arrest, although they managed to secure his father and transport Odell to jail. Later that night, Assistant Police Chief Weyman Burchle Cherry and Officer Randolph McDonald visited Brazier's home, calling James out of the house, then pounding him with a blackjack and pistol while his wife and four children watched. (Some sources claim Sheriff Matthews and Chief Lee were also present, joining in the assault.) Tossing Brazier into the backseat of their patrol car, the officers kicked him twice in the groin, slammed the door on his dangling legs, and reportedly threw a hatful of sand into Brazier's bloody face before they drove away.[127]

At Dawson's jail, the officers dumped Brazier in a cell with his father, who used his own clothing as makeshift bandages for James's bleeding wounds. A physician, visiting the lockup to examine a white prisoner, saw Brazier bleeding from the ears and advised police to put him in a solitary cell, waking him every two hours. James was still unconscious on April 21, when Mayor V. L. Singletary fined Odell $115, then postponed James's trial for a week and released him. Relatives drove James to Terrell County's hospital, then on to Midtown Medical Center in Columbus, where he died after brain surgery on April 25. Odell, enraged and grieving, sped through Dawson in his car and was arrested once more, but Mayor Singletary waived his $25 fine.[128]

The public furor over Brazier's death prompted complaints from white merchants. Responding to that concern, authorities published Brazier's police record of traffic infractions and misdemeanors, then included an alleged quote from the victim following his beating: "When I first entered the door of the jail, 'X' hit me on the back of the head and knocked me down and said, 'You smart son-of-a-bitch, I been wanting to get my hands on you for a long time.' I said, 'Why you want me for?' 'X' said, 'You is a nigger who is buying new cars and we can't hardly live. I'll get you yet.'" Sheriff Matthews, speaking to a reporter from the *Washington Post*, made no secret of his racism, saying, "There's nothing like fear to keep niggers in line."[129]

Prosecutors filed no charges in Brazier's case. Exactly one month after Brazier's death, Weyman Cherry shot and killed another African American, Willie Countryman (see May 25, 1958, below), once more avoiding charges and advancing to serve as Dawson's chief of police for a decade. At his death in 1970, from a car crash, the *Dawson News* eulogized Cherry as being "instrumental in preserving law and order in the community." Pulitzer Prize-winning journalist Alan Bradley Schrade took a different view, writing: "W. B. Cherry had steely eyes, a menacing look, and virtually every black in Terrell County feared him because of his long list of atrocities against blacks."[130]

Widow Hattie Brazier filed a lawsuit against Matthews, Cherry, McDonald, and another policeman in 1962, but it was subsequently dismissed. The DOJ reviewed Brazier's case under the Till Act, then closed it without further action on April 6, 2009. A letter from the FBI to Brazier's family noted that Cherry had died in October 1970, followed by McDonald in June 1995.[131]

Edward Smith
April 27, 1958; State Line, MS

Smith, age 40, lived with wife Daisy on Route 1 in State Line, near the Alabama border in Greene County. On Sunday afternoon, L. D. Clark visited Smith's home, attempting to collect $2.50 that he claimed Smith owed to him. Smith denied owing the money and Clark left, but soon returned to resume the argument. After a few minutes of quarreling, Clark left again, then returned a third time, accompanied by another white man, John Colker. The argument picked up where it had ended earlier, Daisy Smith watching from the porch as Clark drew a pistol and shot Edward twice in the chest, killing him almost instantly. A justice of the peace placed Clark under $5,000 bond, pending action by the county's next grand jury. Daisy Smith and two other witnesses testified before that panel, which refused to charge Clark.[132] The DOJ reviewed Smith's case under the Till Act, closing it without legal action on November 5, 2009.[133]

John Larry Bolden
May 3, 1958; Chattanooga, TN

Chattanooga police received a white resident's complaint that he was "annoyed" by the noise of black youths idling near his home. White officers Lester Lee Shell and W. H. Taylor responded, confronting 15-year-old John Larry Bolden, his brother, and friend Henry Spencer. Bolden's brother and Spencer later said Officer Taylor slapped John, before both patrolmen struck him with their nightsticks. Taylor claimed he only used the club in self-defense, after Bolden "jumped" him. He then fired three shots into Bolden's chest after Bolden grabbed a trashcan, apparently planning to hit Taylor with it. Struck in the heart by one bullet, Bolden died at a local hospital on May 4.[134]

A grand jury charged Officer Taylor with manslaughter and he proceeded to trial, where an all-white jury acquitted him. Taylor died on January 16, 1975, followed by Shell on May 9, 1997.[135] The DOJ reviewed Bolden's case under the Till Act, then closed it without taking action on April 15, 2010.[136]

Willie Countryman
May 25, 1958; Dawson, GA

African Americans in Dawson, Georgia, feared white lawman Weyman Burchle Cherry. In April 1958, as assistant police chief, he was one of three officers named in the fatal beating of civil rights leader James Brazier (see April 20, 1958, above). On May 25 he shot Tobe Lattimer in the buttocks, allegedly for fleeing arrest with "a jar of shine" (bootleg whiskey). One day later, Cherry and partner Robert Hancock went to investigate "a commotion" at Willie Countryman's home. They found Countryman in the backyard, where he purportedly slashed Cherry's cap with a knife, prompting Cherry to kill him on the spot.[137]

An inquest on the latter incident proclaimed that Cherry shot Countryman "in self defense in the line of duty." He still faced a grand jury in Brazier's case, with Officers Edwin Harold Jones and Randolph Ennis McDonald, but the panel found them blameless in that slaying, as well. In early June, the *Washington Post* published a story claiming African Americans in Dawson and environs lived in constant fear of law enforcement officers. Police Chief Howard Lee rejected that assertion, insisting that "97 per cent of our Negroes are satisfied." FBI agents visited Dawson, then left with no recommendation for action.[138]

A year after Countryman's slaying, Dawson's city council promoted Cherry to chief of police, a post he held until his death, in a car crash, on October 25, 1970. In his obituary, the *Dawson News* claimed that, aside from coaching "midget football," Cherry "was instrumental in preserving law and order in the community."[139]

The DOJ reviewed Countryman's case under the Till Act, then closed it again on April 6, 2009.[140] A letter hand-delivered to surviving family members, reprising the Bureau's prior investigation, read in part:

[NAME DELETED] was interviewed by the FBI in 1958. [DELETED] stated that on the night of the shooting [DELETED] was standing with Mr. Countryman outside his house. At some point they heard what sounded like someone urinating in the back yard. Mr. Countryman went to investigate the sound. [DELETED] stated that [DELETED] heard Mr. Countryman say something to the effect of, "I'm sorry. I didn't know it was you all." [DELETED] then heard something fall followed by the sound of a gunshot....

Officer Cherry claimed that after Mr. Countryman was placed in an ambulance, DPD [DELETED] picked up Mr. Countryman's knife. [DELETED] told the FBI that he took the knife from the scene, but he claimed that he could not locate it at the station and that Officer Cherry might have had it. When questioned by the FBI, Officer Cherry said that he was in possession of the knife but, after checking two desks at the station, he also failed to locate it and claimed that it must have been at his home.

Officer Hancock stated that he was about 15 to 20 feet ahead of Officer Cherry as they moved through Mr. Countryman's property. Officer Hancock heard a commotion, turned, and saw someone lunging at Officer Cherry, whereupon Officer Cherry fired and the person fell to the ground. Officer Hancock stated that he did not see the knife.[141]

Hancock, deceased since 1991, could not be interviewed again, and so the case was closed.

Woodrow Wilson Daniels
July 1, 1958; Water Valley, MS

Yalobusha County Sheriff James G. "Buster" Treloar arrested Daniels, a 37-year-old deliveryman, at his home on June 21, charging him with reckless driving, drunkenness, and possession of untaxed whiskey. Five witnesses, both white and black, later described Treloar repeatedly and viciously assaulting Daniels at the county jail, beating him with a 10-inch blackjack. Dr. M. S. McMillan examined Daniels that night, in custody, reporting that he saw Treloar kick Daniels in the leg while telling him, "You son of a bitch, there's nothing wrong with you." When Daniels was released on June 22, his wife drove him to a Memphis hospital, where he suffered a fatal stroke on July 1. An autopsy confirmed severe head injuries from blunt force trauma.[142]

Local whites, vowing that justice would be served, prevailed on widow Annie Margaret Daniels not to contact the DOJ in Washington.[143] A grand jury indicted Treloar for manslaughter, and he faced trial in July 1958, before Judge Curtis Swango, who presided three years earlier at the trial of Emmett Till's slayers (see August 28, 1955, above). Prosecution witnesses included Dr. McMillan, two white acquaintances of Daniels, and a black couple who saw Treloar beating Daniels in jail. White witnesses Lucille Chapman and Lillian Gore testified that they had known Daniels for years, never seeing him drunk or in possession of liquor. Both agreed that Daniels was "normal before going to the jail, but was sick and injured after being released." L. O. Turner, another African American arrested on June 21, described Treloar stopping en route to the courthouse, to arrest Daniels at home, Daniels with a blackjack in his car. (Judge Swango ruled the liquor bottles, seized without a warrant, inadmissible and irrelevant to the pending manslaughter charge.) A black couple, Mr. and Mrs. H. S. Vaughn, witnessed one assault by Treloar on Daniels in jail, but five whites testified to their alleged "bad character" and drug addiction. Under cross-examination they admitted receiving "hypodermic shots" from a physician in the county jail, while detained on forgery charges later dismissed without trial.[144]

Buck Treloar—described by the white supremacist *Clarion-Ledger* as "the tall, handsome sheriff"—was his own star witness, denying or explaining every accusation lodged against him by the state. He "might have cursed" Daniels, Treloar admitted, but denied kicking the prisoner as Dr. McMillan described. Rather, "I nudged him back in the chair, so the doctor could continue his examination." McMillan had found "nothing wrong" with Daniels, Treloar said, but "gave him an injection" of some unknown drug.[145]

The trouble, said Treloar, began as soon as he arrested Daniels. En route to jail, Daniels repeatedly leaned over from the patrol car's backseat, arguing about the confiscated whiskey bottles, until "I finally reached back, slapped him with my open palm, and told him to sit back in the seat." On the county jail's second floor, Daniels allegedly refused to enter the cells reserved for African Americans, barging into a "white" cell instead. When Treloar followed him, Daniels reportedly grabbed his arm. "I jerked to free myself," Treloar testified, "then hit him across the shoulder with my slapstick. He fell to his knees. I hit him four or five more times on the seat of the pants and told him to go in the [black] cell." Daniels finally complied, and in Treloar's version, he suffered no more blows.[146]

Jurors had heard enough, deliberating less than half an hour before they acquitted

Treloar. Leaving the courtroom, Treloar told reporters, "By God, now I can get back to rounding up bootleggers and damn niggers."[147] One of his attorneys entertained spectators, telling them, "That jury knew that you can't kill a nigger by hitting him on the head. You gotta hit him on the heel."[148]

Annie Daniels, left destitute, fled Mississippi, saying, "I'm hurt and I'm scared. I don't know how I'm ever going to pay Wilson's medical and funeral expenses and take care of our five children."[149] In 1992, Treloar, pushing age 70, announced his candidacy for the Mississippi legislature, but voters rejected him. He died in 2006.[150] The DOJ reviewed Daniels's case under the Till Act, then closed it without further action on April 12, 2010.[151]

Richard Lillard
July 20, 1958; Nashville, TN

Lillard, a 38-year-old inmate of the Nashville City Workhouse, died from injuries suffered when he was beaten by three correctional officers: Superintendent John William Burnett, Officer Luolen Harris Debow, and Officer Clark Patterson. An autopsy revealed eight lacerations and three fractures, attributing Lillard's death to shock, hemorrhage, and cerebral concussion.[152]

Prosecutors charged Burnett and his subordinates with murder. At trial, they testified that Lillard had to be subdued after he armed himself with a blackjack and a broom handle, "acting oddly" and threatening others. An inmate witness testified that Burnett entered Lillard's cell with "a long dog stick," striking him repeatedly, and that the beating continued after Lillard was disarmed. An all-white jury acquitted the defendants on January 16, 1959.[153] All three officers were long dead by the time the DOJ reopened Lillard's case under the Till Act, prompting investigators to close it without further action on April 15, 2010.[154]

Ernest Hunter
September 13, 1958; Savannah, GA

Police arrested Hunter after he allegedly interfered with an officer's attempt to give Hunter's wife a traffic citation. Later that day, Hunter suffered fatal gunshots in a holding cell, reportedly while grappling with another officer.[155] The DOJ reviewed his case under the Till Act, closing it without further action on April 6, 2009.[156]

Joseph Franklin Jeter, Sr.
September 13, 1958; Atlanta, GA

Officers of the Atlanta Police Department shot Jeter in the midst of what they described as a melee occurring in and around a drugstore. An FBI report on the incident, heavily censored, reads, in part:

Shortly before the shooting, Officer Dempsey, Lt. Barrett, Officer Oliver, Officer Jones, and Officer Turner responded to a report of a man, later identified as [DELETED] pointing a gun inside a drugstore. The drugstore was located near the Perry Homes housing project. Shortly after arrival, the officers arrested [DELETED]. At that point, a neighborhood crowd began to form around the officers and [DELETED].

Numerous witnesses gave statements to the APD concerning the events that followed [DELETED] arrest. The majority of the witnesses stated that the officers beat [DELETED] after arresting him and when a woman from the crowd, [DELETED], protested, they began to beat her too. The [DELETED] approached the officers in an attempt to intervene and stop them from beating [DELETED]. An officer grabbed [DELETED] around the neck and lifted him off the ground, while another officer struck him. Mr. Jeter started to cross the street toward the officers to explain that [DELETED] was the housing [DELETED]. At that point, an officer, likely Officer Oliver, crossed the street and pushed Mr. Jeter backwards, and Officer Dempsey then shot Mr. Jeter.

The officers reported that when they arrested [DELETED] and placed him in a patrol car, a very large crowd approached and began yelling at them. Among them was [DELETED], Mr. Jeters' [DELETED]. The officers claimed that when Officer Oliver attempted to arrest his [DELETED], Mr. Jeter struck Officer Oliver from behind, knocking him to the ground. According to the officers, Mr. Jeter, [DELETED] jumped on top of Officer Oliver. Believing that Mr. Jeter was trying to take Officer Oliver's service weapon, Officer Dempsey shot and fatally wounded him.[157]

Prosecutors referred the shooting to Fulton County's grand jury, which questioned 30 witnesses. On September 30, 1958, the panel declined to indict Officer Dempsey, finding that he "acted in defense of himself and of his fellow officers." Officer Turner died in February 1978, followed by Dempsey in September 1993, Jones in November 1994, Oliver in July 1996, and Barrett in November 2003.[158] The DOJ reviewed Jeter's case under the Till Act, closing it without further action on May 2, 2010.[159]

Mack Charles Parker
April 25, 1959; Poplarville, MS

On the night of February 23, 1959, an old car driven by Jimmy Walter broke down on Black Creek Ford Road, in Pearl River County, Mississippi. Walter went to find help, leaving pregnant wife June and their four-year old daughter behind. In his absence, June later said, a black man arrived, forcing June and her daughter into his car after telling them, "I am an escaped convict and have killed five people. Two more won't make any difference." On a nearby logging road, the man raped June, then released his captives. They walked to the highway and June flagged down a passing trucker, telling him, "I've been raped by a nigger." The trucker drove them to Lumberton, where June found Jimmy using a public telephone.[160]

June Walters offered no description of her rapist beyond race, sex, and approximate age. On February 24, after conducting a suspect lineup, Sheriff W. Osborne Moody told reporters June had identified her attacker as Mack Parker, a 23-year-old truck driver. Moody arrested Parker and lodged him in the Hinds County jail to forestall lynching. Four friends of Parker—David Alfred, Tommy Grant, Norman Malachy, and Curt Underwood—seemed to support the prosecution's case, claiming they were out with Parker, after visiting an outlaw nightclub in Poplarville, when they passed the Walters' stranded car and Parker said, "Why don't we stop and get some o' that white stuff?"

An unidentified officer sprays Mack Parker's corpse with insecticide after its retrieval on May 4, 1959 (National Archives).

The companions all refused, and Parker dropped them at their homes before, presumably, returning to rape June.[161]

Parker, for his part, denied the crime. Police never found his alleged pistol, and tire tracks from the rapist's car, while "similar" to those of Parker's vehicle, were not a perfect match. A grand jury indicted Parker on April 13, and police returned him to Poplarville two days later, where he pled not guilty on April 17. Around 12:15 a.m. on April 25, a gang of eight to ten masked men removed him from jail, aided by Deputy Sheriff Jewel Alford, and drove Parker to a bridge spanning the Pearl River, on the Mississippi-Louisiana border. There, they shot him dead and dumped his body in the river, where it was recovered on May 4.[162]

While Governor James Coleman denied a lynching had occurred, calling the execution "straight-out murder," the DOJ sent 60 FBI agents to investigate Parker's death. Over the next two weeks, they identified eight suspects: jailer Jewel Alford, itinerant minister L. C. Davis, J. Floren Lee, his son J. F. "Jeff" Lee, Columbus "Crip" Reyer, Herman Schultz, Arthur Smith, and J. P. Walker, an ex-deputy sheriff. Reyer admitted that the lynchers used his car, but denied participation in the crime. Smith cracked on May 13, confessed, and named his coconspirators.[163]

Meanwhile, on May 11, the *Chicago Defender* published an anonymous interview with a white Poplarville resident, proclaiming Parker's innocence. The interviewee claimed June Walter was engaged in an adulterous affair with another white man, and had gone off with him while her husband sought aid for their broken-down car. Returning late and fearing exposure, June allegedly hatched a false tale of abduction and rape to conceal her infidelity. Such talk, and a recent Supreme Court ruling that challenged Dixie's all-white juries, allegedly motivated the lynchers to take Parker out before trial.[164]

One month after the lynching, FBI agents delivered their 370-page report to Governor Coleman, who passed it on to Pearl River County District Attorney Vernon Broome. Another all-white grand jury convened, under notoriously racist Judge Sebe Dale, Sr., who barred panel members from reading the FBI report, instead warning jurors to "preserve our way of life" and "keep your mouths shut." No indictments were returned, and lyncher J. P. Walker won election as Pearl River County's sheriff in 1963.[165]

The DOJ reopened Parker's case under the Till Act, in May 2009. As this book went to press, it remained under investigation, ostensibly seeking live suspects and charges on which to indict them.[166]

Samuel O'Quinn
August 14, 1959; Centreville, MS

Sam O'Quinn's life was an African American success story: born in 1901, a graduate of Tuskegee Institute and father of 11 children, he was a certified plumber, electrician and carpenter; a licensed mortician who ran his own funeral home; assistant town engineer for Centreville; operator of 33 jukeboxes across southwest Mississippi; owner of a 235-acre plantation; and proprietor of a Centreville café on Main Street. Inevitably, racist whites regarded him as "uppity" and envied his prosperity. Instead of being cowed by threats and opposition, O'Quinn joined the NAACP and spoke out publicly for black equality in Wilkinson County.[167]

Samuel O'Quinn, murdered in Mississippi on August 14, 1959 (Civil Rights Archive).

At 11 p.m. on August 14, 1959, O'Quinn retrieved his wife and seven-year-old son from the café, driving them home. On arrival, he left the car to open their gate, and was shot from the shadows while returning to his vehicle. Wife Ida and two of their adult children rushed O'Quinn to Centreville's Field Memorial Community Hospital, where doctors pronounced him dead on arrival.[168]

Police never solved O'Quinn's murder, but author Anne Moody offered a solution nine years after the fact, in her memoir *Coming of Age in Mississippi*. According to Moody, O'Quinn was slain after a visit to the North, purportedly consulting with NAACP leaders about a more aggressive civil rights movement in Centreville. She blames his murder on "The Guild," a local racist group resembling the Citizens' Council, acting in conjunction with black school principal C. H. Willis, whom Moody calls "one of the biggest Uncle Toms in the South." Moody wrote: "It was said that he [Willis] was the one who squealed on Samuel O'Quinn and also helped plot his death. Even later, a Negro on his deathbed confessed that he and another Negro, who is alive and healthy today, were paid five hundred dollars to murder Samuel O'Quinn and the money was delivered by Willis." As for motive, beyond pure racism, Moody says that O'Quinn "supposedly knew all the facts underlying the Taplin burning [see June 1956 in Part 2] and other mysterious killings in and around Centreville and Woodville. It never came out which whites were behind the killing, but everyone figured it was the same bunch that had pulled all the others."[169]

In December 1959, Mississippi State Sovereignty Commission investigator Zack J. Van Landingham visited Wilkinson County Sheriff, J. T. Falkenheimer in Woodville, afterward informing his employers, "The sheriff said that ever since the killing of the Negro Sam O'Quinn, there has been no activity on the part of the NAACP or the Negroes in that community."[170]

The DOJ reviewed O'Quinn's case under the Till Act, then closed it without legal action on May 4 2012.[171]

Booker T. Mixon
October 12, 1959; Marks, MS

A Mississippi native, born in 1934, Mixon served in the Korean War, then settled in Chicago with his wife and sired two children. In 1959 the family returned to Mississippi, living in Clarksdale while Mixon working as a gravel hauler for white employer J. A. Childs of Greenwood. Three days after he took that job, on October 12, Quitman County Sheriff's Deputy Ben Collins found Mixon naked and badly injured beside State Route 6 near Marks, with flesh torn from his back and torso. He lingered in a coma at Coahoma County Hospital until October 23, then died without regaining consciousness. Dr. Joseph Jones, Jr., a black Clarksdale physician, said that Mixon "had multiple abrasions and bruises on his face, head, abdomen, and legs.... Furthermore, there were brain injuries and head fractures. I would say he could have been dragged by a car, perhaps, over some grass."[172]

Authorities blamed Mixon's death on an unknown hit-and-run driver, while his relatives called it murder. They hired Memphis attorney J. F. Estes to investigate, but while Estes urged Governor James Coleman to launch a full investigation, he never obtained reports from the autopsy or coroner's inquest. Even the persons who drove Mixon from the scene remain unknown today, together with their reasons for choosing a hospital 100 miles distant. Likewise unexplained is the disappearance of his clothes. Suspicion is exacerbated by reports that lawman Ben Collins, later Clarksdale's police chief, spent much of his tenure harassing NAACP members and other civil rights activists during the 1960s.[173]

The DOJ reviewed Mixon's case under the Till Act, closing it without further action on August 13, 2012.[174]

Luther Jackson
October 30, 1959; Philadelphia, MS

Conflicting stories surround the death of Luther Jackson, a 27-year-old Korean War veteran who was visiting his native Mississippi to claim a deceased relative's body.

According to a sworn affidavit from Jackson's girlfriend, Hattie Thompson, they were parked in a borrowed car on Pine Street when a police car pulled up, occupied by Patrolmen Lawrence Rainey and Richard Willis. Both officers said they saw Jackson "slumped over" the car's steering wheel and presumed he was drunk. Approaching the vehicle, Rainey ordered both occupants out, pushing Jackson around the car toward the roadside. Thompson said Jackson asked, "What have I done wrong?" before Rainey shot him twice at close range, in the stomach and heart. Rainey and Willis said Jackson cursed at them and grabbed Rainey by the throat, forcing him to fire in self-defense.[175]

Thomas ran to Jackson's lifeless body, crying, "You have shot him for nothing." Rainey struck her and she hit back, whereupon he dragged her to the patrol car and shoved her into its backseat. He then radioed headquarters, saying, "Come on down here. I think I have killed a nigger." Two more patrolmen soon arrived, followed shortly by Chief Bill Richardson and Mayor Clayton Lewis. When Thomas again protested the shooting, Richardson struck her with his pistol, breaking her glasses. Again, she lashed back, and he clubbed her with a blackjack. When the chief poised to hit her again, a patrolman restrained him, saying, "We are in deep enough as it is."[176]

The officers jailed Thomas overnight, without medical treatment for her injuries, and she was swiftly convicted next morning, fined $25 for assault and $18 for public drunkenness. She subsequently told Jackson's sister that police had forbidden her from leaving Philadelphia or even going "across town."[177] Another witness to the shooting—Frances Culbertson, a cousin of Jackson's by marriage—had challenged Sheriff Ethel "Hop" Barnett after Jackson's slaying, then fled Philadelphia after she was assaulted and jailed by Rainey.[178] Thomas filed a complaint with U.S. Attorney General William Rogers and received an answer reading: "This matter will be given our careful consideration and should it develop that a violation of federal law is involved, appropriate action will be taken." The FBI announced an investigation, but Thomas received a second letter less than a month later, informing her that "the evidence does not indicate the violation of any federal statute. For that reason, there is no basis for any further action by this department."[179]

In 1967 Rainey, Willis, and Barnett were among Ku Klux Klan members indicted on federal charges of conspiring to murder victims James Chaney, Andrew Goodman, and Michael Schwerner. White jurors acquitted Rainey and Willis, while failing to reach a verdict on Barnett (see June 21, 1964, below).

The DOJ changed its mind about Jackson's case in 2009,

Lawrence Rainey, killer of Luther Jackson on October 30, 1959 (Library of Congress).

adding his name to the department's list of civil rights cold cases, but found that Philadelphia police possessed no record of the incident.[180] Lawrence Rainey, meanwhile, had died on November 8, 2002, unpunished for his crimes. The DOJ closed Jackson's case once again on April 16, 2010, sending his family a letter that misstated the date of his slaying as October 25, reported Rainey's death, and cast a shadow of possible guilt on suspect Earthy Culberson. That paragraph read:

> Mr. Culberson [sic] was reportedly involved in various illegal activities, including running gambling and prostitution rings and selling contraband alcohol. [Names deleted] believe that Officer Rainey took responsibility for the shooting because Mr. Culberson had connections in the PPD, and more specifically with Officer Rainey, providing Officer Rainey with prostitutes and alcohol in return for receiving early warnings of any impending police investigation of his activities. We did not find any corroboration for this theory. Mr. Culberson died in January 1994.[181]

William Roy Prather
October 31, 1959; Corinth, MS

Eight white youths "accidentally" killed 15-year-old William Prather in an attack that they afterward characterized as a "Halloween prank." Vague reports suggest one member of the gang was indicted for manslaughter, but no record of a trial exists today.[182] The DOJ announced a review of Prather's case under the Till Act, still open and ongoing as of January 2014.[183]

Mattie Green
May 16, 1960; Ringgold, GA

At 1:05 a.m. on May 16, a powerful bomb exploded beneath the home of Jethro Green, Sr., a 39-year-old mechanic employed at the Abney Motor Company in East Ridge, 11 miles northwest of Ringgold. The blast knocked Jethro unconscious, killed wife Mattie, age 32, and injured their infant son Larry, while sparing three other children. Initial newspaper reports claimed the bomb consisted of 25 to 30 pounds of dynamite, but further investigation identified the explosive as ammonium nitrate fertilizer mixed with diesel fuel and detonated by an electric blasting cap.[184]

Governor Ernest Vandiver, Jr., offered a $500 reward for information leading to arrest and conviction of the bombers, but found no takers. Catoosa Co. Sheriff J. D. Stewart investigated the crime, aided by agents from the Georgia Bureau of Investigation and the FBI, but no suspects were ever publicly identified. Attention focused on the fact that Green's house sat on the dividing line between black and white residential districts, with African American neighbors on one side and whites on the other. Even so, Jethro Green—a lifelong Ringgold resident—seemingly was well regarded by both races. A white neighbor called Green "one of the nicest colored men I've ever known—a real Christian who lives right and tries to bring his children up right." Green himself said, "I've never had any trouble. I thought everybody liked me."[185]

In the absence of hard evidence, three rumors grew around the Green bombing. The weakest suggests that Jethro may have bombed his own home, thereby risking his life, or that some black neighbor may have done it for personal reasons. During Dixie's violent years between 1954 and 1966, white law enforcement officers frequently blamed African Americans for bombing their own homes and churches, but Sheriff Stewart voiced no such suspicions and expressly absolved Jethro Green. As for other black suspects, FBI agents uncovered one's name in 2009, but the late subject's wife insisted he was home all night on May 16, 1960.[186]

A second theory calls the bombing a case of mistaken identity, with the terrorists planting their charge at the wrong residence. In that scenario, bombers targeted an African American known for fighting with whites but struck the Green home instead. Five decades after the fact, FBI agents found a onetime neighbor of the Greens who admitted teenage brawls with "white boys" in 1960, but he denied any knowledge of retaliation plots.[187]

The final, most persuasive theory pins the bombing on members of the Ku Klux Klan. In 2009 an unidentified informant recounted a long-ago conversation with Sheriff Stewart, in which he allegedly said "a white male named Lester Waters had confessed to the bombing and that the guilt had driven him crazy." Further investigation named Waters as a member of the violent Dixie Klans, based in Chattanooga, and a personal friend of Sheriff Stewart. The same informant claimed that Stewart personally delivered Waters to Georgia's Milledgeville State Hospital after his mental breakdown.[188]

Why would Klansmen target the Greens? One theory, unsupported by documentary evidence, claims Jethro Green had joined Ringgold's fledgling NAACP chapter, thus marking him as an "agitator."[189] Even without that tie to "radicals," however, Klansmen might have marked Green's home as a symbolic bridge between white and black neighborhoods, destroying it to emphasize the local color line.

When the DOJ revisited Green's case in 2007, misspelling the surname as "Greene," daughter Anna Ruth Montgomery told reporters, "I want this investigation to happen, but, at the same time, if they can't solve it, why go into it?" FBI agents closed the file without further action on May 4, 2012, citing lack of evidence.[190]

Marshall Johns, Ernest McPharland, Albert Pitts and David Pitts

July 23, 1960; Monroe, LA

A white man shot five of his black employees on July 23, 1960, killing four. Police detained the gunman, then released him without charges when he said the five had threatened him.[191] The DOJ reviewed this case under the Till Act, closing it without legal action on April 22, 2010.[192]

Fred Robinson

August 5, 1960; Edisto Island, SC

Robinson's corpse washed ashore on Edisto Island, one of South Carolina's Sea Islands, on August 5. Published accounts say that his skull was crushed, his eyes gouged out.[193] The DOJ reviewed this case under the Till Act, listing the date of Robinson's death as August 3, then closed the matter without legal action on February 2, 2012.[194] My inquiries to local libraries and newspapers elicited no further information.

Clarence P. Cloninger
October 10, 1960; Gaston, NC

Little is known of this case, beyond the fact that Cloninger (spelled "Cloniger" in some accounts) died while jailed in Northampton County. Afterward, his widow complained that he suffered a heart attack in custody and that jailers denied him life-saving medical treatment.[195] The DOJ briefly reviewed the case, then closed it without comment on April 3, 2009.[196]

Herbert Lee
September 25, 1961; Liberty, MS

Details of Lee's early life are vague, with conflicting reports dating his birth from 1909, 1911, and 1919. We know he was a dairy farmer, father of nine children, and a charter member of the NAACP's chapter in Amite County, led by E. W. Steptoe. Sheriff E. L. Caston raided the group's office in 1954, briefly seizing membership rolls until the FBI forced their return, but Lee persevered in civil rights activities, welcoming SNCC members when they entered Amite County to register black voters seven years later. In September 1961, DOJ officials interviewed various African Americans in Amite County, learning that state legislator Eugene H. Hurst and other local whites had threatened voting activists, including Lee.[197]

On Monday, September 25, Lee drove a load of cotton to a gin at Liberty, the county seat. Hurst was present at the same time, driving a truck owned by Billy Jack Caston—the sheriff's notoriously violent brother. As Lee parked his pickup, Hurst approached, shouting. An argument ensued, ending when Hurst drew a pistol

Herbert Lee with his wife, shortly before his slaying by Eugene Hurst on September 25, 1961 (Civil Rights Archive).

and shot Lee at close range, with a dozen witnesses watching. Sheriff Caston left Lee's body on the ground while he organized a hasty coroner's jury, coercing witnesses to testify that Lee attacked Hurst with a tire iron. Hurst claimed that he drew his gun in self-defense and struck Lee's hand with it to make him drop the tire iron, whereupon the pistol discharged accidentally. The jury swiftly voted Lee's death "justifiable homicide." A mortician from McComb came to collect Lee's corpse, when no one in Liberty would touch it.[198]

A footnote to that crime and cover-up involved witness Louis Allen, who soon recanted his false testimony and described Lee's murder to FBI agents. After twenty-eight months of harassment, Allen planned to leave Mississippi, but he was slain the night before his scheduled departure (see January 31, 1964, below).[199]

The DOJ reviewed Lee's case under the Till Act, closing it without legal action on April 16, 2010. A letter from the FBI to Lee's survivors summarized the false testimony of Hurst and other witnesses before the coroner's jury, then noted Hurst's death on April 20, 1990, which rendered any thoughts of prosecution moot.[200]

Eli Brumfield
October 13, 1961; McComb, MS

Patrolman B. F. Elmore shot Brumfield during a traffic stop, claiming Brumfield "jumped" from his car wielding a pocketknife.[201] The DOJ examined Brumfield's case under the Till Act, closing it without further action on September 24, 2013.[202]

Roman Ducksworth, Jr.
April 9, 1962; Taylorsville, MS

Corporal Ducksworth—a military police officer, nearing retirement after 10 years in the U.S. Army—was traveling from Fort Ritchie, Maryland, on emergency leave, to

The bus on which Roman Ducksworth, Jr., was slain, April 9, 1962 (Library of Congress).

visit wife Melva, and their newborn sixth child, when he died at the hands of Police Officer William Kelly. The official version of his death claims Kelly removed Ducksworth from the bus after the driver could not wake him, then shot Ducksworth in self-defense after the soldier attacked him. Relatives say Kelly found Ducksworth sleeping in a "white" seat on the bus, perhaps mistaking him for a "freedom rider," and woke him with a punch, then dragged him from the bus and continued to beat him before shooting Ducksworth in the heart. A town marshal alleged Ducksworth was drunk, and a local grand jury deemed his death a "justifiable homicide."[203]

The DOJ examined Ducksworth's case under the Till Act, closing it without legal action on April 12, 2010.[204] In a letter to Melva Ducksworth, FBI agents noted Officer Kelly's death in September 2004 and quoted a message Kelly sent to Ducksworth's parents, saying, "If I'd known it was your son I wouldn't have shot him."[205]

Joseph Hill Dumas
May 5, 1962; Perry, FL

Constable Henry Sauls "accidentally" shot 19-year-old Joseph Dumas during a routine traffic stop. Governor Farris Bryant suspended Sauls from office and a federal grand jury later indicted him for violating Dumas's civil rights, but no record of a trial survives today.[206] The DOJ reviewed this case under the Till Act, closing it without legal action on April 9, 2010.[207]

Paul Guihard
September 30, 1962; Oxford, MS

Guihard was a 30-year-old French journalist, covering the U.S. civil rights movement, when racists rioted against admission of African American James Meredith to the University of Mississippi, staging what historian William Doyle calls "the beginning of a Ku Klux Klan rebellion." Armed racists from across the South flocked to Mississippi for the "Battle of Oxford," wounding 166 U.S. marshals and 48 soldiers sent to protect Meredith on campus.[208]

While covering that outbreak, around 8:40 p.m., Guihard was shot in the back at close range with a .38-caliber pistol. Students found him dying in a clump of trees near Ward Hall, 165 yards from the Lyceum where U.S. marshals were besieged by snipers. Hundreds of interviews conducted by the FBI and Mississippi Highway Patrol failed to identify a suspect in Guihard's death, which remains unsolved today.[209]

The DOJ reopened Guihard's case under the Till Act, but had no better luck after the passage of a half-century. FBI agents closed the file again on July 19, 2011.[210]

A. C. Hall
October 13, 1962; Macon, GA

Around 9 p.m., a white married couple noticed a black male rummaging around inside their car, parked at their residence in Macon. Examining the vehicle after he fled, they found a pistol missing from its glove compartment and summoned police. Officer James L. Durden and his partner got the call, collecting the couple and cruising their neighborhood in search of the suspect. Moments later, they approached George Washington Carver Elementary School on Hazel Street, where 17-year-old A. C. Hall and a 16-year-old female companion had briefly stopped en route to a third party's house, for the girl to dump grit from her shoes.[211]

An undated FBI letter, sent to Hall's family 49 years later, describes what happened next, as follows:

> In 1962 the officers and the couple stated that Mr. Hall ran across the headlights of the patrol car, whereupon [DELETED] recognized him as the person [DELETED] had seen exiting their car and said, "that's him." The officers and the couple stated further that one or both the officers yelled at Mr. Hall to stop but he did not comply. According to the officers, when Mr. Hall ran over a dirt mound, [DELETED] stopped the car at the edge of the mound. At that point, Mr. Hall turned toward the car and pulled his right arm from behind his back. It was then that first Officer Durden, and then [DELETED] started firing at Mr. Hall. Officer Durden fired two shots and [DELETED] five. Mr. Hall continued running but eventually fell to the ground, having been fatally wounded. The couple confirmed that Mr. Hall turned and pulled an arm from behind his back. Neither the officers nor the couple stated that they saw something in Mr. Hall's hand, however.[212]

So, was Hall armed or not? That question should be easy to resolve, but the last page of the bureau's letter—unlike 45 others sent to grieving families and later published on the *New York Times*'s website—is curiously "missing" from FBI files.[213]

Fifteen hundred demonstrators marched on Macon's City Hall, protesting Hall's death, but prosecutors filed no charges.[214] Officer Durden died in September 2009. Agents interviewed his aging unnamed partner two years later, noting that he "could not remember many details of the shooting." Still, his memory was crystal-clear of "firing at Mr. Hall after Mr. Hall turned toward the officers and pulled a gun and Officer Durden warned him that Mr. Hall was about to shoot the officers."[215] How that gun was missed by all four witnesses in 1962, and what became of it—if it existed—still remains a mystery. The DOJ closed its review of Hall's case without taking further action, on July 27, 2011.[216]

Sylvester Maxwell
January 4, 1963; Camden, MS

Various newspaper accounts report the discovery of Maxwell's corpse, castrated and otherwise mutilated, near Highway 11 in Canton, Mississippi, on January 17, 1963, "less than 500 yards from the home of a white family." Both the date and place are incorrect, according to the FBI, which says Maxwell's brother-in-law found his body on January 9, near Old Highway 51 in Camden. Police soon arrested a black friend of Maxwell's, Thomas William Campbell, while Medgar Evers, Mississippi field secretary of the NAACP, called Maxwell's slaying a "probable lynching," saying that black killers "don't mutilate the body. That's done by bigots who normally take Negroes out and mob them."[217]

In fact, however, Campbell pled guilty to Maxwell's murder in September 1963 and received a life prison term. Before that plea, officers escorted Campbell to Maxwell's funeral, where he publicly apologized to the victim's family. Campbell served nine years and four months, was paroled in January 1973, and died in November 2001.[218]

In his confession to authorities, summarized in a DOJ letter to Maxwell's survivors, Campbell described the fatal incident as follows.

> On January 4, 1963, Mr. Campbell was driving your [DELETED] home after they had gone out drinking and they began to argue. Mr. Campbell stated that, during the argument, your [DELETED] "pulled a knife" on him. Mr. Campbell pulled out his own knife and cut your [DELETED] about five times across the chest with it. After killing your [DELETED] Mr. Campbell pushed his body out of the car and into a pasture. Mr. Campbell then drove to Memphis, Tennessee, where he stayed for four days and then returned to Mississippi and turned himself into [sic] the Madison County Sheriff's Office.[219]

Campbell's description of the stabbing does not explain Maxwell's emasculation or other injuries, generally described as gross and extensive mutilation. The FBI investigated Maxwell's case in 1964, and again in 2008, concurring with official findings on both occasions. The DOJ closed its review without further action on May 2, 2010.[220]

William Lewis Moore
April 23, 1963; Etowah County, AL

A white U.S. Postal Service employee and CORE member, born in 1927, Moore planned a one-man "freedom walk" from his home in Baltimore, Maryland, to Jackson, Mississippi, in early 1963. He planned to push a shopping cart festooned with signs supporting civil rights, and hoped to deliver a personal letter to white-supremacist Governor Ross Barnett on arrival Mississippi's capital. Along the way, Moore hoped to stay overnight with relatives in Birmingham—Charles and Helen Cagle, the former a Ku Klux Klansman later suspected in that city's fatal September church bombing—but they refused to have him in their home, Helen urging him to abandon his folly and leave them in peace.[221]

In fact, Moore never reached the "Magic City," even then embroiled in public demonstrations and police brutality. At 9 p.m. on Tuesday, April 23, a motorist found him lying beside the highway near Keener, shot twice with a .22-caliber weapon. The Cagles drove from Birmingham to identify their nephew's corpse.[222]

William Moore at the beginning of his one-man civil rights march through the South in April 1963 (Civil Rights Archive).

Investigation revealed that Klansmen Gaddis Killian and Floyd Simpson—a "klokan" (investigator) for the local Klan chapter—had stopped Moore on the highway near Colbran, where Simpson ran a grocery store, on the afternoon of April 23. They questioned him about his signs and politics, predicting Moore's imminent death, Simpson telling the postman, "Now I know who you are." The slugs from Moore's body matched Simpson's rifle, and Sheriff Dewey Colvard jailed both men on April 25, soon releasing Killian when he complained of claustrophobia. Simpson posted bond on April 28, and a grand jury convened on September 12 declined to indict him. Local KKK "exalted cyclops" George Killian—cousin of Gaddis—defended his klokan with the claim that some unknown "stranger" had used Simpson's gun to kill Moore.[223]

Two years later, FBI agents questioned Simpson about a recent spate of racist bombings in Birmingham. According to Bureau memos, "Simpson stated he had no information concerning the bombs ... and if he would have information, he is doubtful he would advise the FBI." Simpson apparently quit the Klan in 1968 and died in a nursing home 30 years later, at age 75.[224]

The DOJ reviewed Moore's case under the Till Act, but without a living suspect, agents closed the file on August 2, 2012.[225]

Andrew Lee Anderson
July 17, 1963; Crittenden County, AR

On Wednesday, July 17, a white resident of Crittenden County reported seeing Anderson, a 17-year-old African American, attempting to molest her eight-year-old daughter. A posse including six sheriff's deputies and an uncertain number of vigilantes chased Anderson into a soybean field near Marion, where he was shot in the leg with a high-powered rifle. Relatives say Anderson was questioned for two hours at the shooting scene, without receiving medical attention, dying from blood loss soon after he finally reached Crittenden County Memorial Hospital in West Memphis.[226]

Coroner T. H. McGough convened an inquest the same day, but by his own admission heard no testimony as to who had fired the fatal shot. McGough ruled Anderson's death "justifiable homicide," based on an Arkansas statute that permits any citizen to attempt apprehension of a fleeing felon.[227]

The DOJ reviewed Anderson's case under the Till Act, then closed it without legal action on April 9, 2010.[228]

Johnny Brown Robinson
September 15, 1963; Birmingham, AL

Riots erupted in Birmingham after Klansmen bombed the Sixteenth Street Baptist Church, killing four young African American girls. Soon after that blast, white racists began to cruise past the church and through Birmingham's black neighborhood, their cars festooned with Confederate flags and banners reading, "Nigger, Go Back to Africa," hurling soda bottles from their windows at black pedestrians. Those attacks, in turn prompted certain angry African American's to stone the passing cars.[229]

One of those enraged by the white joyriders was 16-year-old Johnny Robinson.

Ku Klux Klansmen bombed Birmingham's Sixteenth Street Baptist Church on September 15, 1963, killing four young girls and sparking riots that claimed the lives of Johnny Robinson and Virgil Ware (Library of Congress).

With other youths, he threw stones at a passing carload of racists draped in a large Rebel flag, but their stones missed and struck another passing car instead. At that point, a police car arrived on the scene, with several patrolmen inside. In the backseat, Officer Jack Parker had his shotgun pointed out the window. As the black youths ran into an alley, the patrol car stopped and cut off their retreat. According to FBI agent Dana Gillis, "The crowd was running away and Mr. Robinson had his back [turned] as he was running away. And the shot [from Parker's weapon] hit him in the back."[230]

The officers involved told conflicting stories. Parker claimed he fired his shotgun "towards the ground," surmising that buckshot pellets ricocheted from the pavement to strike Robinson.[231] Another patrolman said their driver slammed on the brakes, causing Parker to fire accidentally. Yet another thought the car "might have hit a bump in the road." Civilian witnesses disagreed, reporting that they heard two shots, fired into the alley without warning. A Jefferson County grand jury declined to indict Parker in 1963, and a federal grand jury likewise refused in 1964.[232] The DOJ reviewed Robinson's case under the Till Act, closing it without further action on April 9, 2010.[233]

Virgil Ware
September 15, 1963; Birmingham, AL

The sixth and final victim of Birmingham's bloody Sunday was 13-year-old Virgil Ware, an eighth-grade "A" student and football player who planned on attending law school. His dream was cut short when two white 16-year-olds, Michael Lee Farley and Larry Joe Sims went looking for trouble after the morning's tragic church bombing by Ku Klux Klansmen. Farley and Sims began their hunt with a stop at local headquarters of the neo-Nazi National States Rights Party, leaving there to cruise the streets on Farley's motorcycle. Driving aimlessly, they spotted Ware and his brother James, walking home from a shopping excursion. Farley urged Sims to "scare them," whereupon Sims fired two shots from a pistol borrowed from Farley, striking Virgil Ware in the cheek and chest. Prosecutors charged Sims with first-degree murder, but an all-white jury convicted him on a lesser charge of second-degree manslaughter. Farley pled guilty to the same offense, and while both boys were sentenced to seven months in jail, a friendly judge suspended that sentence, replacing it with two years on probation.[234]

The DOJ reviewed Ware's case under the Till Act, reporting that FBI agents were "unable to locate the court transcripts or any local investigative reports pertaining to the incident." A Jefferson County judge opined that Farley and Sims were likely tried as juveniles, with their records destroyed long ago.[235] Accordingly, the case was closed without further action on March 29, 2011.[236]

Ernest Jells
October 20, 1963; Clarksdale, MS

Members of CORE and the NAACP began organized civil rights activities in Clarksdale during August 1962, sparking waves of violence by city police and white vigilantes. On October 20, 1963, several patrolmen shot young Ernest Jells (spelled "Earnest" in some reports), after a white merchant accused him of stealing a banana. The officers claimed Jells threatened them with a rifle when they tried to arrest him. Prosecutors deemed the slaying "justifiable."[237] The DOJ reviewed this case under the Till Act, closing it without legal action on April 16, 2010.[238]

Gene Brown
1964; Canton, MS

The NAACP claimed that Brown—also known as "Pheld Evans"—was killed near Canton "under mysterious circumstances," on some unknown date in 1964.[239] The DOJ reviewed Brown's case under the Till Act and closed it without legal action on April 21, 2010.[240] Surprisingly, while attempting to debunk rumors of Ku Klux Klan involvement, FBI agents named a second, previously unreported victim in the case, casting blame for both deaths on a deceased relative of Brown. The FBI's explanation of the case reads, in part:

According to our review, sometime in 1964, Mr. Brown and his cousins, Eddie Brown, and Percy Mack, Jr., went to Kosciusko where Mr. Mack dropped the other two men off at a girlfriend's house. Later that night, Mr. Brown and Mr. Eddie Brown left the girlfriend's house and were walking on a dark road to meet Mr. Mack so he could drive them back home. According to [DELETED] the three cousins "were playing games" and Mr. Mack accidentally ran over and killed his cousins. Mr. Mack returned home and informed his parents, who then washed down the car. Eventually, a rumor started, likely by Mr. Mack's family, that Mr. Brown had been beaten to death by Ku Klux Klan members....

One of Mr. Brown's relatives, [DELETED], told the FBI that Mr. Brown had been murdered by Klan members. Another relative, [DELETED], similarly told the FBI that both Mr. Brown and Mr. Eddie Brown had been beaten and then run over, although [DELETED] did not identify the perpetrators. Neither [DELETED] nor [DELETED] identified the source of their information concerning Mr. Brown's death.

Three of Mr. Brown's other relatives, [DELETED] and [DELETED], told the FBI that they had heard the rumor of the Klan murder but they eventually also learned that Mr. Mack had, in fact, accidentally killed Mr. Brown and Mr. Eddie Brown.

Mr. Mack died on September 18, 1978.[241]

Louis Allen

January 31, 1964; Amite County, MS

Allen—born in 1919, a World War II veteran employed as a logger—was one of a dozen witnesses to the murder of civil rights activist Herbert Lee by white state legislator Eugene Hurst at Liberty, Mississippi (see September 25, 1961, above). Coerced by Sheriff E. L. Caston and Deputy Daniel Jones, Allen joined other witnesses at a coroner's inquest the same day, falsely testifying that Lee attacked Hurst with a tire iron before Hurst gunned him down "in self-defense." Allen's conscience soon got the better of him, however, and he told FBI agents the truth: that Hurst had approached Lee to provoke an argument, then shot the unarmed victim in cold blood. An FBI memo notes that Allen "expressed fear that he might be killed," but agents, as usual in those days, offered him no protection.[242]

Allen's second statement failed to produce an indictment of Hurst, but it unleashed a long, brutal campaign of harassment. On June 30, 1962, Deputy Jones arrested Allen for "interfering with the law," beating him with a flashlight and breaking Allen's jaw in two places. In July, Allen submitted an affidavit on that incident to the DOJ, which took no action against Jones. On August 21, 1962, Allen and two other African Americans tried to register as voters in Amite County, but Jones and other racists ejected them from the courthouse. In the summer of 1963, Jones assaulted Allen's cousin, John Wesley Horton, and jailed him on trumped-up charges. On September 11, 1963, Allen described his beating by Jones to a federal grand jury, but no indictment resulted. On November 6, 1963, Jones—newly elected as the county sheriff—arrested Allen for a "bounced check" and carrying a concealed weapon. NAACP members raised Allen's $800 bond three weeks later, while Amite County's prosecutor threatened him with three to five years in state prison.[243]

Meanwhile, incessant death threats continued. Near-miss gunshots followed Allen's August effort to register as a voter, and a white merchant told Allen, "Louis, the best thing you can do is leave. Your little family—they're innocent people—and your house could get burned down. All of you could get killed." On February 21, 1963, fire swept the home of Allen's ex-employee, Leo McKnight, killing McKnight, his wife, pregnant daughter and son-in-law. Locals said that warnings to break off all ties with Allen preceded the fire. When Allen reported those incidents to the FBI, agents passed his statements on to Sheriff Jones, despite a memo plainly stating that "Allen was to be killed and the local sheriff was involved in the plot to kill him." In fact, by that time, Sheriff Jones was a reputed member of Mississippi's recently revived Ku Klux Klan, while his uncle led the local KKK chapter as its "exalted cyclops."[244]

By January 1964, Allen was finally prepared to leave his lifelong home and move north for his family's safety. His time ran out on January 31—the night before his scheduled departure—when two shotgun blasts killed him in his rural driveway. Son Hank Allen drove to Sheriff Jones's home, to report the slaying. Jones, armed with a shotgun, followed Hank back to the crime scene and searched Allen's body, saying, "Let me see if I can find what caused the problem." Jones found Allen's wallet, containing his NAACP membership card, and held it overnight. When returned on February 1, the card was gone.[245]

There matters rested for over three decades, until Tulane University history professor Plater Robinson opened his own investigation of the murder. In 1998, Robinson interviewed elderly black preacher named Alfred Knox, who claimed that Sheriff Jones enlisted his son-in-law, Archie Weatherspoon, to "kill Louis Allen." At the last moment, Weatherspoon, refused "to pull the trigger," whereupon Jones allegedly shot Allen himself. Before the Till Act passed in 2007, both Knox and Weatherspoon were dead.[246]

Reporter Steve Kroft launched an 18-month investigation of Allen's murder for the television program *60 Minutes* in 2009, culminating in a broadcast aired on April 10, 2011. Ex-sheriff Jones, still living at that time, denied participation in Allen's murder, then invoked the Fifth Amendment when Kroft asked about his reputed Klan membership. A $20,000 reward, offered by Allen's survivors for information solving the crime, remains unclaimed.[247] The DOJ reviewed Allen's death under the Till Act, and at last report, in January 2014, the case remains open.[248]

Clifton Walker
February 28–29, 1964; Wilkinson County, MS

Natchez, Mississippi, was a hotbed of Ku Klux Klan activity in the 1960s. More than 40 Klansmen worked at the local International Paper Company's plant, where Clifton Walker—a 37-year-old African American father of five—also toiled from 3 to 11 p.m. Walker often rode to work in an integrated carpool, but he was alone when he left work on February 28, 1964, headed home to Woodville, 37 miles away. Friends had warned him to avoid a shortcut that would save a mile or so on driving, via Poor House Road, but on the last night of his life Walker ignored that sage advice. Three hundred yards from the turnoff, Walker drove into an ambush, multiple shotguns blasting his car and killing him instantly.[249]

A neighbor, Prentiss Mathis, spotted Walker's buckshot-riddled car at 1 p.m. on February 29 and called the Mississippi Highway Patrol—another refuge for KKK members, as noted in FBI documents from that era. One reputed Klansman on the force was Patrolman R. W. Palmertree, first to arrive at the crime scene and lead investigator on the case. Official reports say that Walker's windows were shot out, with part of the steering wheel blown away. Palmertree found Walker's keys dangling from the open glove compartment, where Walker carried a .38-caliber pistol for self-defense. Walker died before reaching the weapon—and relatives who later received the gun found it had been sabotaged, its firing pin filed down, incapable of detonating a cartridge primer. Officers who viewed Walker's body reported at least two close-range shotgun blasts to his face and neck.[250]

Highway Patrol reports on Walker's case ignored the atmosphere of racial violence in southwest Mississippi, including the tension between Klan members and black coworkers at International Paper in Natchez. Instead, the documents alleged adulterous affairs between Walker and at least nine local women, black and white, in a typical attempt to blame Walker for his own murder. FBI agents examined the case between March and December 1964, but filed no charges. A final Highway Patrol report, from November 1964, named two suspects to Natchez District Attorney Lenox Forman, recommending their arrest, but Forman demurred on grounds of "insufficient evidence," and the suspects' names have been redacted from copies released to the public.[251]

Clifton Walker, murdered in a Mississippi highway ambush on February 28–29, 1964 (Civil Rights Archive).

Nonetheless, investigative journalist Ben Greenberg has identified those suspects as Klansmen Ed Fuller and Gordon "Bud" Geter. In addition to nightriding with the Klan, state and federal documents uncovered by Greenburg name Fuller as a police informant associated with the Mafia in prostitution rackets and numerous acts of violence around Mississippi and neighboring Louisiana. He died in 1975. Klansman Geter, deceased since 1982, also served as a Wilkinson County constable and a deputy sheriff in the mid-1960s.[252]

Greenberg has also uncovered the names of three other potential suspects mentioned in Highway Patrol reports from 1964. One, white Woodville resident Carl Cavin, visited the home of his estranged wife at 1 a.m. on February 29, behaving in a manner that prompted her to say he "appeared to be extremely nervous and drinking heavily." Highway Patrol reports add that Cavin and another white man, Red Metcalf, were seen together on Poor House Road at 10:30 p.m. on February 28. FBI documents described Cavin and Metcalf meeting at Nettles Truck Stop on U.S. Highway 61, within a mile of Poor House Road, on February 28. Another Highway Patrol document named Walker's neighbor, Prentiss Mathis, as a suspect, but did not recommend his arrest.[253]

The DOJ reviewed Walker's case under the Till Act, and while at least three FBI agents were assigned to the investigation between 2007 and 2012, Greenberg reports that none ever spoke to members of Walker's family. Agent Bradley Hentschel, leading the investigation in 2012, refused to discuss particulars, but referred vaguely to "the reliance that we have on the public to provide us information because we have resource and personnel limitations." None of the Walkers had been interviewed when the DOJ closed the case, without further action, on October 1, 2013.[254]

Silas Ernest Caston
March 1, 1964; Hinds County, MS

Soon after midnight on Sunday, March 1, sheriff's deputies received a call of shots fired at the Sunshine Inn, a café catering to African Americans, near Jackson. Hinds County Sheriff Fred Pickett later said that, as his officers arrived, two suspects fled on foot, while one reentered the café, pursued by Deputy Herbert Hoover Sullivan. Inside the Sunshine Inn, 20-year-old Silas Caston allegedly turned, "as if to attack the deputy," and received a fatal gunshot to the stomach. A search confirmed he was unarmed, Pickett said, but Deputy Sullivan "had no way of knowing that."[255]

Caston's mother filed a $100,000 lawsuit against Sullivan and the sheriff's department, aided by attorneys from CORE and the NAACP. That action sent Mississippi's State Sovereignty Commission into full defensive mode, field agent Erle Johnston, Jr., reporting to headquarters that "John Reed, colored male, who was a good friend of Silas Caston," put the civil rights lawyers in touch with Caston's family. Johnston also quoted an unnamed black informer saying, "It is rumored that Caston had a pistol with him when deputies appeared at the scene, when he dropped it and ran into the Sunset Inn where he was shot as he turned on the Deputy in a dark hallway."[256]

The outcome of that lawsuit is unknown today, but Sullivan faced no criminal charges for killing Caston. The DOJ reviewed Caston's case under the Till Act, finding that Deputy Sullivan died in April 1986. An FBI report to Caston's family, hand-delivered on May 2, 2010, quotes a witness to the shooting—name deleted before public release of the report—as saying that when officers approached him, Caston "turned around and raised his hands in surrender, whereupon he was shot." The report found that Sullivan acted alone, and his death removed any potential legal remedies, therefore the case was closed.[257]

Johnnie Mae Chappell
March 23, 1964; Jacksonville, FL

Race riots rocked downtown Jacksonville on Monday, March 23. In the midst of that chaos, Chappell—a 35-year-old wife and mother of 10—left home with two neighbors to find a wallet she dropped near her home in Picketville, an all-black neighborhood. While they were so engaged, a car occupied by four white men passed by and a single shot was fired, striking Chappell in the stomach. She died en route to a local hospital.[258]

City detectives Lee Cody and Donald Coleman, assigned to the case, made no progress until August 1964, when Wayne Chessman approached them offering "help." He admitted being in the murder vehicle and implicated three friends—driver Elmer Kato, fellow backseat passenger James Alex Davis, and alleged triggerman J. W. Rich. Prosecutors charged all four with first-degree murder, but Cody and Coleman came under fire from the white community and were later dismissed from the police department, while the murder weapon "disappeared" from custody. Charges against Chessman, Davis and Kato were soon dismissed. Jurors convicted Rich of manslaughter and he received a 10-year sentence, but was favored with parole in 1968.[259]

Meanwhile, the slaying shattered Chappell's family. Authorities removed the five youngest children from father Willie Chappell's custody, and he sent the older five to live with relatives. Most of the children did not learn the story of their mother's death until a family reunion in March 1996.[260] Son Sheldon Chappell began a quest for justice, aided by ex-detective Cody. The Chappells filed a lawsuit alleging police misconduct in 2001, but a federal judge dismissed it on grounds that the statute of limitations had lapsed.[261] President George W. Bush, also requested a DOJ review of the case in 2002, without results.[262] J. W. Rich, in a 2003 interview, denied any part in the crime.[263] In April 2005, Governor Jeb Bush, the president's brother, ordered Florida's Department of Law Enforcement to reopen the case, but again the gesture accomplished nothing.[264]

The DOJ reviewed Chappell's case a second time, under the Till Act. As of last report, in January 2014, it was listed as an open case with investigation ongoing.[265]

Bruce W. Klunder
April 7, 1964; Cleveland, OH

Oregon native Bruce W. Klunder was a white Presbyterian minister who graduated from Yale University Divinity School, then moved to Cleveland in 1961, serving as assistant executive secretary of the Student Christian Union at Western Reserve University. Soon immersed in that city's civil rights struggle, he led a local CORE chapter. In 1962

Bruce Klunder, killed while protesting construction of a segregated school on April 7, 1964 (National Archive).

he led a restaurant sit-in in Sewanee, Tennessee, but generally focused his attention closer to home, picketing segregated public facilities and protesting discrimination in job hiring. In April 1964, when Cleveland's City School District announced plans for construction of new segregated schools, Klunder plunged headlong into active opposition.[266]

On April 6, some 50 protesters blocked construction equipment on Lakeview Road, at the proposed site for Stephen E. Howe Elementary School. Police intervened, arresting 23 and injuring two. The next day, Klunder led 1,000 marchers to the school, confronting dozens of police. Klunder and three companions dodged officers, lying down to block the progress of a bulldozer. Driver John White, seeking to avoid three demonstrators in front of him, backed over Klunder and crushed him to death.[267] Police ruled Klunder's death accidental, and while construction of Howe Elementary briefly stalled, the school was later completed and opened as a segregated facility.[268] Cleveland's schools remained segregated until 1978, when a federal court order mandated busing to desegregate all classrooms.[269]

The DOJ reviewed Klunder's case under the Till Act, but agents were unable to locate John White, reporting that he "is either deceased or could not be located using the variety of public and law enforcement databases available to FBI investigators." Based on media reporting of the incident, they did not deem Klunder's death a racially motivated homicide.[270] The case was closed without legal action on April 16, 2010.[271]

Henry Hezekiah Dee and Charles Eddie Moore
May 2, 1964; Homochitto National Forest, MS

On the eve of Mississippi's "Freedom Summer," Ku Klux Klansmen were inflamed by rumors of black militant activity throughout the state, including fanciful tales that Black Muslims were smuggling guns to African American activists. On Saturday, May 2, Klan members kidnapped 19-year-olds Dee and Moore from Meadville, driving them into the Homochitto National Forest for "interrogation." After being tortured, the still-living victims were chained to a Jeep motor and train rails, dropped in the Mississippi River to drown. Searchers recovered their mangled torsos on July 11–12, 1964, while searching for three civil rights workers killed in Neshoba County (see June 21, 1964, below).[272]

State police and FBI agents focused on Klansmen Charles Edwards and cousin James Ford Seale as suspects. Edwards confessed to abducting the victims with Seale and whipping them with beanpoles, but claimed they were released alive. He later recanted that statement, claiming it was coerced. Local prosecutors subsequently dropped the case.[273]

In 2000, *Clarion-Ledger* reporter Jerry Mitchell discovered that the murders had occurred on U.S. government property. The DOJ reopened its investigation, whereupon Seale's relatives spread false news of his death. That lie collapsed in July 2005, when documentary filmmaker David Ridgen and Charles Moore's brother, Thomas, found Seale still living in Roxie, Mississippi, at age 69.[274]

Another 15 months passed before federal prosecutors charged Seale, then 71, with two counts of kidnapping and one count of conspiracy to kidnap in January 2007. He pled not guilty, but jurors convicted him at trial in August 2007, resulting in imposition

FBI agent Jim Ingram examines chains removed from the corpses of Henry Dee and Charles Moore on July 12, 1964 (National Archives).

of three life prison terms.[275] That verdict was upheld on appeal in March 2010, and while a May 2010 report from the U.S. Attorney General's office rightly claims Seale's prosecution as a victory for the DOJ's Cold Case Initiative, he was actually convicted 14 months before formal enactment of the Till Act.[276]

James Earl Chaney, Andrew Goodman and Michael Schwerner

June 21, 1964; Neshoba County, MS

The Ku Klux Klan triple-murder of civil rights activists Chaney, Goodman and Schwerner, occurring immediately prior to the commencement of Mississippi's "Freedom Summer," ranks among the most notorious hate crimes of the turbulent 1960s. Multiple books and countless articles have reported the facts of that crime, in which racist police joined a lynch mob to snuff out three lives and Mississippi's legal establishment spent three years obstructing justice. None of the killers were charged with murder at trial in 1967, instead facing maximum 10-year sentences on charges of conspiring to violate the victims' civil rights.

In that case, jurors convicted seven of eighteen defendants: Jimmy Arledge, Horace Doyle Barnette, KKK leader Samuel Holloway Bowers, Jr., Deputy Sheriff Cecil Ray Price, Billy Wayne Posey, Alton Wayne Roberts, and Jimmie Snowden. The panel acquitted eight defendants: Bernard L. Akin, Travis M. Barnette (brother of Horace), Olen L. Burrage (owner of the farm where the victims were buried), James T. Harris, Frank J. Herndon, Sheriff Lawrence A. Rainey, Herman Tucker, and ex-policeman Richard A. Willis. No verdicts were returned for once-and-future Sheriff Ethel Glen Barnett, Edgar Ray "Preacher" Killen, and Jerry McGrew Sharpe. Charges against the latter three were dismissed after trial.[277]

In the 21st century, reporting by Jerry Mitchell at Jackson's *Clarion-Ledger* revived interest in the triple murder, prompting more than 1,500 Mississippi citizens to petition Governor Haley Barbour for justice in June 2004.[278] On January 6, 2005, Neshoba

Top: Remains of Klan victims James Chaney, Andrew Goodman and Michael Schwerner, exhumed by FBI agents on August 4, 1964. *Bottom:* Neshoba County defendants show amusement at their mass arraignment in 1965. Deputy Cecil Price (left) and Sheriff Lawrence Rainey occupy the front row (both photographs, National Archives).

County's grand jury indicted 80-year-old Edgar Killen on three counts of murder. Six months later, on the 41st anniversary of the slayings, jurors convicted Killen of manslaughter, resulting in three consecutive 20-year prison terms.[279]

The DOJ reviewed this triple-murder case under the Till Act, with two suspects still alive: Olen Burrage, acquitted of federal conspiracy charges in 1967, and Pete Harris, a former KKK "investigator" who reportedly made multiple telephone calls to gather Klansmen for their "job" on June 21, 1964.[280] At last report, in January 2014, the case remained open, with investigation ongoing.[281]

Jasper Greenwood
June 21, 1964; Vicksburg, MS

Relatives of tavern manager Jasper Greenwood feared foul play when he disappeared from Vicksburg on June 21, 1964. By the time two children found his body eight days later, it was badly decomposed, prompting a coroner's jury to list the cause of death as undetermined. Decades later, Greenwood's granddaughter, Linda Galvin, told reporters, "The black funeral home told me that he was castrated and he had what looked to be a stab wound in his throat area." The last person to see Greenwood alive said he was in the company of two white men. According to Galvin, "None of that showed up in the FBI report."[282]

The DOJ reviewed Greenwood's case under the Till Act and closed it without legal action on June 17, 2010.[283] An explanatory letter delivered to Greenwood's family read, in part:

> According to our review, on June 29, 1964, your [DELETED] body was found next to his car on a "lover's lane," about 100 yards off Main Street in Vicksburg.... According to a June 30, 1964 article in the *Vicksburg Evening Post,* no weapon was found near your [DELETED] body. Additionally, a purse containing $61 was found in his car, likely ruling out the possibility that he was killed during a robbery....
>
> Shortly after the discovery of your [DELETED] body, the VPD investigation determined that he had last been seen alive in the early hours of June 21, 1964, in the company of Flossie Lee Minor, a married African-American woman, whose husband had reportedly previously threatened your [DELETED] for dating his wife. Ms. Minor and her husband initially disappeared but, on July 3, 1964, the VPD arrested Ms. Minor. Ms. Minor reportedly admitted that she had gone with your [DELETED] to a "lover's lane," where, according to Ms. Minor, your [DELETED] suddenly died of an apparent heart attack and she fled the scene. She denied that there had been any foul play involved in your [DELETED] death....
>
> In 1964 the FBI investigated allegations ... that [DELETED] the funeral home owner who prepared your [DELETED] body for burial, told [DELETED] that he had noticed a hole at the base of your [DELETED] throat that could have been a stab or bullet wound. The FBI interviewed [DELETED] in 1964 and [DELETED] denied that he thought the hole had been caused by anything other than "nature" and stated that he specifically told [DELETED] that when [DELETED] asked about it.[284]

Joseph Edwards
July 12, 1964; Concordia Parish, LA

Edwards, a 21-year-old African American, worked as a porter at the Shamrock Motor Hotel in Vidalia, Louisiana, in 1964. On the morning of July 12, witnesses saw two white men in a new Oldsmobile sedan stop Edwards's blue-and-beige 1958 Buick on U.S. Highway 84 between Vidalia and Ferriday. Police found the Buick abandoned that Sunday; some accounts describe bloodstains inside it and a necktie knotted as a noose, found dangling from the steering wheel. FBI agents and Mississippi Highway Patrolmen searched for Edwards, but "Jo-Ed," as his friends knew him, was never seen again.[285]

Today, some researchers believe Edwards fell prey to an ultra-violent Ku Klux Klan faction known as the Silver Dollar Group, which met at the Shamrock and reportedly planned the murder of victim Frank Morris there a few months after Edwards disappeared (see December 10, 1964, below). As to motive, a cousin of Edwards, Carl Ray Thompson, told reporter Stanley Nelson in 2007: "Joe-Ed told me he had many close escapes. I begged him to quit that job. To be frank, Joe was fooling with them white women in Vidalia while he was working at that motel." Thompson was so worried that he "quit going anywhere with Joe-Ed," from fear of becoming a victim himself. Sometime later, Thompson and three friends were detained on suspicion of burglary and, Thompson says, beaten by Concordia Parish sheriff's deputies Frank DeLaughter and Bill Ogden, both now deceased. Before their release, DeLaughter allegedly asked the four if any of them were related to Edwards. When Thompson raised his hand, the deputy "indicated that Thompson and the others might face a similar fate as Joe-Ed." Thompson recalled rumors that Jo-Ed's corpse was buried "in that hole near the bowling alley," a pit dug to provide dirt fill for construction on U.S. 84 decades earlier.[286]

Joseph Edwards, circa 1963 (Civil Rights Archive).

In 2009, ex–FBI agent Billy Bob Williams, assigned to Natchez from July 1964 through August 1966, told the *Concordia Sentinel* that a Klan informant claimed Edwards had been kidnapped, driven into Mississippi, "skinned alive," then shot, wrapped in chains, and dumped into the Mississippi River. Rumors that FBI agents discovered a bloodstained shack, believed to be a Klan torture chamber, remain unconfirmed. Earcel Boyd, Jr., son of a

Vidalia's Shamrock Motel, once a gathering place for members of the KKK's Silver Dollar Group (author's collection).

notorious Klansman, told Stanley Nelson, "I think it was some of the Silver Dollar Group. Joe probably saw too much and heard too much. He had access all over the Shamrock and he could go anywhere he wanted to be there." Coupled with stories of his interracial dating, that suspicion was a recipe for sudden death.[287]

Despite being suspected in a rash of bombings and at least two other homicides, no members of the SDG were ever charged with any crimes. The DOJ reviewed Edwards's case under the till act, then closed the file without further action on February 20, 2013.[288]

James Powell
July 16, 1964; Harlem, NY

Off-duty police lieutenant Thomas Gilligan shot 15-year-old James Powell three times on
Thursday afternoon, after Powell allegedly rushed Gilligan with a knife. Neighbors acknowledged Powell had gone "a little wild" after his father's death, logging four arrests: one for attempted robbery (of which he was acquitted), one for breaking car windows, and two for boarding subways without paying the fare. Gilligan, for his part, had previously shot two other persons in violent encounters. Neighborhood witnesses insisted Powell held no knife and only raised his arm in a defensive attitude after Gilligan drew his pistol. Police reported finding a knife in the gutter, eight feet from Powell's body, and the shooting was deemed justified.[289]

After the shooting, some 4,000 residents of New York City's Harlem and Bedford-

James Powell's shooting on July 16, 1964, sparked rioting in Manhattan's Harlem ghetto (Library of Congress).

Stuyvesant ghettoes rioted against police from July 16 until the early hours of July 19, also looting and vandalizing stores. Before order was restored, one rioter was dead, 118 persons hospitalized, and 465 arrested on various charges.[290]

The DOJ reopened Powell's case under the Till Act and apparently accepted Gilligan's original account of the event, closing the file on February 9, 2012.[291]

Isaiah Taylor
June 26, 1964; Ruleville, MS

A policeman shot and killed Taylor during a traffic stop, afterward claiming that Taylor lunged at him with a knife. A coroner's jury deemed the slaying "justifiable homicide."[292] The DOJ reviewed Taylor's case under the Till Act, closing it without further action on April 12, 2010.[293]

Neimiah Montgomery
August 10, 1964; Merigold, MS

Montgomery stopped for gasoline at a service station on August 10, then allegedly refused to pay when the white attendant finished filling his tank. Official reports say Montgomery produced an axe handle, knocking the attendant down and threatening a female bystander before City Marshal L. L. Yarbrough arrived on the scene. According to Yarbrough, Montgomery then struck him with the axe handle, whereupon Yarbrough shot Montgomery in self-defense. Investigators deemed the shooting justified.[294] The DOJ reviewed Montgomery's slaying under the Till Act, closing the case on April 12, 2010.[295]

James Andrew Miller
August 30, 1964; Jackson, GA

The SPLC reports that Miller was beaten by white thugs several days prior to a second confrontation, occurring on August 30.[296] In the second incident, Miller and unnamed companions quarreled with a group of white men, one of whom—John Whittaker—shot Miller at close range. Staff at a nearby hospital pronounced Miller dead, while Whittaker drove to Covington, 19 miles north of Jackson, and there surrendered to police. A coroner's jury found that Whittaker fired in self-defense. He died in December 1987, 20 years before the DOJ launched its Cold Case Initiative.[297] The department reviewed Miller's case under the Till Act, closing it without further action on April 12, 2010.[298]

Herbert Orsby
September 7, 1964; Pickens, MS

In early September, 14-year-old Herbert Orsby—called "Hubert Orsby" and "Herbert Oarsby" in various published accounts—traveled from New Orleans to visit his grandparents in Pickens, Mississippi. They last saw him alive on September 7, walking in the general direction of the Big Black River. Two days later, strollers in Canton, 18 miles south of Pickens, saw Orsby's corpse floating in the river and summoned police. When pulled from the water, Orsby wore only shorts, but an FBI report says "the remainder of his clothing was found on a nearby riverbank." Holmes County's coroner, Dr.

Justin Kazar, denied finding any bruises or other evidence of violence on Orsby's body, and an inquest attributed his death to accidental drowning.[299]

Still, nagging questions remain. If, as implied by the coroner's verdict, Orsby left his clothes on the riverbank to go swimming, how and why did he travel from Pickens to Canton to do so? How did he plan to get back, after cooling himself in the treacherous river? A CORE press release claimed Orsby was last seen alive in a T-shirt bearing that organization's initials, which might have made him a target for local racists. Another report, never verified, described a young African American male abducted by whites at gunpoint, the day Orsby vanished. Also on that day, in Canton, presumed KKK members planted bombs at two grocery stores in Canton's black community, apparently retaliating for a black boycott of white merchants.[300]

FBI agents investigated Orsby's death in 1964, and again under the Till Act, 45 years later. Neither investigation revealed any evidence of a hate crime or identified any suspects. The DOJ closed Orsby's case without legal action on April 12, 2010.[301]

Frank Andrews
November 28, 1964; Lisman, AL

A white Choctaw County sheriff's deputy shot Andrews, allegedly while Andrews was attacking another officer. The county solicitor filed no charges.[302] FBI agents reviewed the case under the Till Act, and it remained open, with investigation ongoing, as this book went to press.[303]

Frank Morris
December 10, 1964; Ferriday, LA

In 1964, 54-year-old Frank Morris owned and lived in a shoe repair shop on U.S. Highway 84 in Ferriday, Louisiana, also hosting Sunday morning radio programs that featured religious music and sermons from various clergymen. Morris was affable, apparently well liked by blacks and whites alike. It shocked some local residents, therefore, when arsonists torched his shop and home on December 10, leaving Morris with burns that claimed his life four days later.

FBI agents interviewed Morris at Concordia Parish Hospital, transcribing his fragmented recollection of the attack. Morris woke to the sound of smashing glass and found two white men, one pouring gasoline around the shop, the other armed with a shotgun. When Morris tried to flee, the gunman snarled at him, "Get back in there, nigger." Seconds later, the shop was ablaze and the terrorists fled, leaving Morris to escape through a window with burns over most of his body. Drifting in and out of consciousness, he first claimed not to recognize his killers, then said, "I probably seen them before," adding, "I think they might work at Johns Manville [a building materials factory] or something like that over in Natchez." Speaking to other visitors, he called his assailants "two white friends," but refused to divulge their names.[304]

Two Ferriday policemen arrived with the fire still burning and drove Morris to the hospital. One officer who did not respond, though seen nearby, was Concordia Parish Deputy Sheriff Frank DeLaughter, a notorious racist who terrorized African Americans

Frank Morris's shoe repair shop after the December 10, 1964, arson attack (Civil Rights Archive).

throughout his tenure as a lawman and joined his sister in recruiting members for the Ku Klux Klan from her drive-in restaurant. On the night of December 10, gas station attendant Delbert Matthews saw DeLaughter talking to a white man in a green car bearing Mississippi license plates, while firemen fought the Morris fire two blocks away. Earlier, the green car's unknown driver had paid Matthews ten dollars to watch his car while it sat in the station's unused wash bay.[305]

Multiple motives surfaced in the Morris case. One involved an argument with Deputy DeLaughter, over boots Morris repaired, for which DeLaughter would not pay. After that quarrel, DeLaughter reportedly told fellow Klansman O. C. "Coonie" Poissot that Morris was not "acting right" and should be dealt with by the KKK. Another tale, discounted by the FBI, alleged that Morris was involved in civil rights activity. A third story noted Klan anger over Morris serving blacks and whites alike, further complaining that white mothers "depended on Morris to keep their families in shoes." A more serious charge claimed Morris had propositioned a white lawman's wife—or, perhaps, enraged her by rejecting her advances.[306]

Two stories apparently having some merit involved Morris peddling bootleg liquor and allowing interracial couples to have sex at his shop. After the fire, investigators found a suitcase in the rubble, filled with 14 half pints of bourbon, each individually wrapped in newspaper, plus "two or three empty half pint whiskey bottles on the floor of Morris's living quarters." Fireman and jailer Junior Harp told FBI agents that Morris had been suspected of bootlegging since 1961, but that police never "developed any positive information in this respect." As to the sexual liaisons, a friend of Morris, Robert "Buck" Lewis, told the *Concordia Sentinel* in 2008, "That's a fact. I knew it. I saw it. Frank only participated, as far as I ever knew, as a go-between. Why he allowed it to happen in his shop, I don't know." According to Lewis, some of the after-hours visitors were police officers and Klansmen.[307]

Suspects publicly identified suspects in the Morris arson-murder, besides Frank DeLaughter, include: Klansman Arthur Leonard Spencer of Rayville, who died in May 2013, accused by his son, ex-wife, and ex-brother-in-law in 2011; and O. C. Poissot, deceased since 1992, who allegedly confessed the crime to Spencer's then-wife in the early 1970s. Around the same time, Frank DeLaughter—dead since 1996—was convicted on federal charges of beating a white prisoner in 1965, and, with Concordia Parish Sheriff Noah Cross, for racketeering related to the Morville Lounge, a Concordia Parish gambling den and brothel. Meanwhile, Edward McDaniel, a Natchez Klan leader and FBI informer, told agents in 1966 that he suspected Klansmen Tommy Lee Jones, E. D. Morace, James Scarborough, and Thore L. Torgersen as the killers. All belonged to the Silver Dollar Group, a brutal faction formed by members of various Klans who resented their organizations restraining terrorism. Like other suspects in the case, all four are now deceased.[308]

The DOJ reviewed Morris's case under the Till Act, but with no identified suspects still living, agents closed the file for the last time on December 30, 2013.[309]

Jose Weisheimer Cano
January 1, 1965; Brookville, FL

A Texas native, called "Jesse" or "Jessie" in most published accounts, Cano vanished from his Brookville, Florida, home on New Year's Day. Officers of the Hillsborough County Sheriff's Office (HCSO) and the Florida Department of Law Enforcement (FDLE) investigated the case, without result.[310] The DOJ reviewed Cano's case under the Till Act and closed it without legal action on June 3, 2011.[311] A letter to Cano's survivors, dated the following day, read in part:

> According to our review, [DELETED] contacted the HCSO in 1999 and alleged that you had told your [DELETED] that [DELETED] told you during a fishing trip that the Ku Klux Klan (KKK) had killed Mr. Cano, then placed his body on the railroad tracks to cover up any evidence of homicide. The HCSO, then the FDLE, conducted investigations into these allegations, but did not find any evidence that Mr. Cano was the victim of a racially-motivated homicide. On November 2, 2008, you were interviewed by the FBI and denied that the conversation your [DELETED] had described between you and [DELETED] had ever taken place. You stated further that to your knowledge, [DELETED] had never been involved with the KKK. Based on your statements and the lack of evidence to substantiate the allegation that Mr. Cano was the victim of a racially-motivated homicide, the FBI closed its investigation into this matter.[312]

Marshall Scott
January 1965; New Orleans, LA

Scott, an African American inmate at the Orleans Parish Prison on South Broad Street, died from uncertain causes while held in solitary confinement. Relatives complained that he was denied proper medical care, but no charges were filed in the case.[313] The DOJ reviewed Scott's case under the Till Act, closing it without further action on May 25, 2012.[314] My inquiries to local libraries and newspapers revealed no further details, including the date of his death.

Selma Kelly Trigg
January 21, 1965; Hattiesburg, MS

In its annual report for 1965, the NAACP claimed that a "Mrs. Saleam K. Triggs" was "mysteriously burned to death" in her Hattiesburg home on January 23, 1965. Four decades later, FBI agents, investigating that report under the Till Act determined that the victim, 76-year-old Selma Kelly Trigg, had been trapped in her bedroom by a fire of undetermined origin, on January 21. Firefighters removed her through a bedroom window, and doctors pronounced her dead on arrival at a local hospital.[315] The DOJ closed Trigg's case on May 2, 2010, citing insufficient evidence to prove a crime had occurred.[316] Nonetheless, an anonymous website still lists "Saleam Triggs" as a civil rights martyr, repeating the NAACP's initial inaccurate data.[317]

Ollie Shelby
January 22, 1965; Jackson, MS

Shelby suffered fatal gunshot wounds while incarcerated at the Hinds County Jail.[318] The DOJ reviewed his case under the Till Act, closing it on April 16, 2010, without further action.[319] My inquiries to local libraries and media outlets elicited no further information on the case.

Jessie Brown
January 23, 1965; Winona, MS

White farmer Reese Marlon Gipson killed black farmhand Jessie Brown with a shotgun blast inside Gipson's home. Police arrested Gipson the following day, and District Attorney Chatwick Jackson briefly investigated the slaying, accepting Gipson's story that Brown was drunk and armed with an ice pick, attacking both Gipson and Gipson's wife. Brown's family believed "there was more to the shooting than was revealed at the time," but a grand jury filed no charges. Gipson died in June 1977, three decades years before the DOJ launched its Cold Case Initiative.[320] FBI agents reviewed Brown's case under the Till Act, closing it without further action on April 19, 2010.[321]

Jimmie Lee Jackson
February 18, 1965; Marion, AL

On Thursday night, February 18, 26-year-old woodcutter Jimmie Jackson joined his mother, Viola, and 82-year-old maternal grandfather Cager Lee, and other African Americans in a march from Marion's Zion United Methodist Church to the city jail a half-block distant, planning to sing freedom songs for incarcerated civil rights worker James Orange. En route, they were attacked by a group of city police, sheriff's deputies, and Alabama State Troopers who chased some marchers into nearby Mack's Café. There, officers clubbed Cager Lee and Viola Jackson to the floor. When Jimmie Lee came to his mother's defense, Trooper James Bonard Fowler shot him in the stomach. Colonel Albert Lingo, commander of the state police and an ally of the Ku Klux Klan, served Jackson with an arrest warrant in his bed at Selma's Good Samaritan Hospital, but Jackson would never stand trial. Infection of the bullet wound claimed his life on February 26.[322]

Contemporary activists and civil rights historians credit Jackson's slaying as a major motivating factor for Dr. Martin Luther King, Jr.'s later march from Selma to Montgomery, which in turn prompted Congress to pass the Voting Rights Act of 1965. Colonel Lingo concealed Fowler's identity, and a grand jury ruled Jackson's slaying "justified" in September 1965. Journalist John Fleming reports that no FBI agents bothered to question Fowler until Fowler himself admitted the shooting, in a March 2005 interview with Fleming for the *Anniston Star*. In that conversation, he claimed Viola Jackson attacked another trooper with "an old timey Coke bottle," whereupon other blacks swarmed the officer. Fowler intervened, he said, and shot a man who tried to grab his pistol. Two other troopers filed conflicting affidavits, saying *Fowler* was struck with the bottle, before firing in self-defense. Exuding confidence, Fowler told Fleming, "I don't think legally I could get convicted for murder now no matter how much politics they got 'cause after 40 years they ain't no telling how many people is dead." That parting comment may have been a reference to Nathan Johnson, Jr., another African American whom Fowler shot and killed 15 months after slaying Jackson (see May 8, 1966, below).[323]

Jimmie Lee Jackson, fatally wounded by Alabama state trooper James Bonard Fowler on February 18, 1965 (Civil Rights Archive).

In fact, a Perry County grand jury indicted Fowler on May 10, 2007, charging him with both first- and second-degree murder for Jackson's killing. Legal maneuvers delayed his trial until late 2010, when Fowler dodged a jury verdict by pleading guilty to a reduced charge of second-degree manslaughter on November 15. In what District Attorney Michael Jackson called "a fair resolution," Circuit Judge Tommy Jones sentenced Fowler to six months in prison and six months of unsupervised probation.[324]

Having apparently delayed investigation of Jackson's death by four decades, the DOJ was equally slow to abandon the case after Fowler's guilty plea. Jackson's file, reopened under the Till Act, was finally closed on May 3, 2011.[325] FBI agents investigated Nathan Johnson's slaying a bit longer, but ultimately filed no charges.[326]

William Henry Lee
February 25, 1965; Rankin County, MS

Mystery surrounds the death of William Lee, in part because he sometimes used the name "John Patrick Lee" in daily life. That alias has led some researchers to claim two separate murders from Rankin County in February 1965, when in fact only one has been documented.[327]

Racist violence was commonplace in Mississippi during 1964 and 1965, centered on areas where African Americans staged protests against segregation or asserted their right to vote. Lee reportedly attended various civil rights meetings around Rankin County, which boasted four active Ku Klux Klan chapters. On February 16, 1965, the U.S. Civil Rights Commission launched five days of public hearings in Jackson, focused on black disfranchisement. As those hearings closed, on February 22, ex-governor Ross Barnett addressed a racist audience Selma, Alabama, warning his listeners that they faced "absolute extinction of all we hold dear unless we are victorious" in defense of white supremacy. According to Northeastern University's Civil Rights and Restorative Justice Project, four African Americans were slain in Mississippi over six days after Barnett's speech—including William Lee.[328]

Various accounts of Lee's death report that his battered body was found beside a country road or railroad tracks near Goshen Springs, Mississippi. In fact, the two may not be contradictory, since train tracks often cross or run parallel to roads traveled by automobiles. Although his corpse bore wounds suggesting Lee was beaten, the Southern Poverty Law Center reports that postmortem tests blamed his death on strangulation. More specifically, the Arkansas Delta Truth and Justice Center names the specific cause as "strangulation from gas." Local police surmised Lee's car had broken down, and that he died while seeking help, but no records survive to indicate active investigation.[329]

The DOJ reopened Lee's case under the Till Act, but apparently found no new evidence. The case was closed without legal action on May 5, 2011.[330]

Donald Rasberry

February 27, 1965; Okolona, MS

Information remains sketchy on the death of 19-year-old Donald Rasberry, reportedly shot by his white plantation boss five days after ex-governor Ross Barnett regaled a racist audience with threats of "absolute extinction" should white supremacy cease to prevail in the South. Local authorities filed no charges against the unnamed slayer.[331] The DOJ reopened Rasberry's case under the Till Act—misspelling his surname "Raspberry"—then closed it without legal action on May 17, 2010.[332]

James Reeb

March 9, 1965; Selma, AL

A Kansas native, born in 1927, Reeb served in World War II, then attended St. Olaf College in Northfield, Minnesota, where he met his future wife. After graduation, he attended Princeton Theological Seminary, graduating in 1953, and was granted fellowship as a Unitarian Universalist minister six years later. Settled in Boston with his growing family, Reeb devoted himself to social work and causes related to civil rights, joining Dr. Martin Luther King, Jr.'s SCLC. On March 7, 1965, after viewing television footage of police beating black marchers on Selma's Edmund Pettus Bridge, he booked a flight to Alabama with fellow Unitarian ministers Orloff Miller and Clark Olsen.[333]

By noon on March 9, the three friends joined 450 other out-of-town clergymen in Selma, causing local racists to rant against northern "outside agitators." That evening, after prayer services, Reeb, Miller, and Olsen dined at a local restaurant, then inadvertently took a wrong turn past the Silver Moon Café, an all-white establishment known as a Ku Klux Klan hangout. As they passed, four men emerged from the café, shouting, "Hey, niggers!" The men attacked, one fracturing Reeb's skull with a baseball bat, afterward saying, "Now you know what it is like to be a real nigger down here."[334]

James Reeb, fatally beaten by Klansmen in Selma, Alabama, on March 9, 1965 (Library of Congress).

Knowing that Selma's white hospital was likely to reject them, Miller and Olsen took Reeb to the all-black Burwell Infirmary, where chief D. W. Dinkins deemed Reeb's injuries too severe for local treatment. A black funeral home's ambulance transported Reeb to the University of Alabama at Birmingham's hospital, 100 miles away. Delayed further by a flat tire en route, Reeb finally arrived, survived emergency surgery, but died on March 11 without regaining consciousness.[335]

On March 11, Selma police arrested four suspects—41-year-old Elmer L. Cook, 36-year-old William Stanley Hoggle, his 30-year-old brother Namon O'Neal "Duck" Hoggle, and 30-year-old R. B. Kelly—then quickly released them on bail. Two days later, an airplane dropped fliers over Selma, urging "white citizens" to bankroll the quartet's defense. Klan leaders spread false rumors that Reeb was "already dying from cancer," as if that excused his murder. On April 13, after Circuit Judge James Hare delivered a 50-minute rant blaming civil rights workers and the FBI for racial violence in Selma, Dallas County's grand jury indicted Cook and the Hoggles for murder, while voting "no bill" against Kelly.[336]

Prior to trial, prosecutor Blanchard McLeod warned reporters, "I don't have a very strong case." FBI memos called McLeod an "adamant segregationist," declaring, "It cannot be anticipated from the attitude which he has displayed that he has any intention of forcefully and aggressively prosecuting the case." During jury selection, when McLeod asked the panel en masse whether racism would prevent them from rendering a fair verdict, all but three stood mute. Judge L. S. Moore ruled, and McLeod accepted, that silence equaled a negative answer. The case lurched on from there, with one prosecution witness missing and another deemed mentally incompetent by Judge Moore. Ministers Clark and Olson positively identified Elmer Cook as one of their assailants, but were less sure of the Hoggles. While jurors considered their verdict, racist Sheriff Jim Clark—who deputized Klansmen for his "special posse"—visited the jury room for reasons unknown. The result: acquittal of all three defendants.[337]

Years later, FBI informer Gary Rowe revealed that at least one of Reeb's attackers was a fellow Klan member. On March 25, 1965, shortly before Rowe's wrecking crew murdered white activist Viola Liuzzo, they stopped at the Silver Moon Café. There, Kluxer Eugene Thomas recognized one of the Reeb defendants dining alone and spoke to him briefly. I parting, the man said, "God bless you boys. We have done our job. Now it's up to you." Rowe, now deceased, never named the man in his FBI reports or later Senate testimony, but described him as six feet tall, 220 pounds, "hard talking," and proud of personally clubbing Reeb to death.[338]

The DOJ reviewed Reeb's case under the Till Act, closing it without legal action on May 18, 2011.[339] Two weeks later, Reeb's family received a letter from the FBI, explaining that three of the suspects were dead: Cook in February 1975, Kelly in March 1994, and William Hoggle in June 1996. Namon Hoggle lived on, but the statute of limitations on civil rights prosecutions from the 1960s had expired, prohibiting indictment.[340] Namon survived at least until May 2013, listed online as organizer of Bama Motors of Selma.[341]

Hosie Miller
March 15, 1965; Newton, GA

On Monday, March 15, several cows owned by white farmer Cal Hall, Jr., roamed onto the property of African American neighbor Hosie Miller. When Hall came to collect them, he also tried to claim one of Miller's cattle. Miller, a 40-year-old Baptist deacon, refused to give up his animal, whereupon Hall drew a pistol and shot him. Relatives drove Hall 10 miles to a hospital in Camilla, where he died on March 25.[342]

Police initially arrested Hall for assault with intent to kill, then issued a warrant for murder on March 24, the day before Hall's death. A grand jury convened on October 27, 1965, declined to indict him on any charges. Miller's family filed a wrongful death lawsuit, but white jurors found Hall blameless on September 12, 1966. He died 10 years later, in June 1976.[343]

Miller's case was forgotten by most Americans until July 2010, when his daughter, Shirley Sherrod, was dismissed from her job as Georgia State Director of Rural Development for the U.S. Department of Agriculture. The basis for her firing was supposed "racist" remarks Sherrod made before an NAACP audience four months earlier, including a reference to her father's murder. Far-right blogger Andrew Breitbart posted truncated clips from that speech on his website, distorting Sherrod's remarks and prompting her dismissal. Later, when the full transcript was published, the White House apologized for its hasty reaction and Secretary of Agriculture Tom Vilsack offered Sherrod a new position.[344]

The DOJ reviewed Miller's case under the Till Act, closing it without further action on June 21, 2011.[345] One week later, Miller's family received a letter stating that no charges could be filed because the sole killer involved had died 35 years earlier.[346]

Oneal Moore
June 2, 1965; Varnado, LA

On June 1, 1964, Washington Parish hired Creed Rogers and Oneal Moore, a 33-year-old army veteran and father of four, as its first black deputy sheriffs in an effort to relieve racial tensions caused by white violence and black protests. One year later, while the partners were riding together, gunmen in a pickup truck ambushed their patrol car, killing Moore with a rifle shot to the head, blinding Rogers in his right eye with a shotgun blast. Rogers remained conscious long enough to broadcast a description of the dark-colored murder vehicle, including its Confederate flag bumper sticker.[347]

One hour later, police arrested 41-year-old Ernest Raphael "Ray" McElveen in Tylertown, Mississippi, 28 miles northwest of Varnado. He drove a black 1954 pickup with a Rebel flag sticker and carried a pistol, but officers found no other weapons. Cards in McElveen's wallet identified him as a member of the KKK, Citizen's Council, and the neo-Nazi National States Rights Party; he was also an "honorary special agent" for the Louisiana State Police. Jailers held McElveen overnight, then shipped him back to Louisiana, where Sheriff Dorman Crowe predicted more arrests. As Crowe told reporters, "You can't shoot a high-powered rifle and a shotgun and drive a pickup truck at the same time."[348]

Oneal Moore in military service, prior to his assassination by Louisiana Klansmen on June 2, 1965 (Civil Rights Archive).

In fact, no other suspects were identified. McElveen told detectives he was camped alone near the state border when he suffered a back injury and sought treatment in Tylertown.

Widow Maevella Moore with other mourners at her husband's funeral (Civil Rights Archive).

Though charged with murder, he was soon released on bond, Bogalusa's white judge and prosecutor deeming it unfair to keep him jailed until Creed Rogers was able to testify. Two days after the ambush, drive-by gunmen shot up the home of Washington Parish's chief deputy, a white officer assigned to investigate Moore's murder. Governor John McKeithen offered a $25,000 reward for the arrest of Moore's killers, telling journalists, "We're going to catch them all," but he got no takers. Prosecutors soon dismissed McElveen's murder charge for lack of evidence.[349]

FBI agents reopened Moore's case in 1990, and again in 2001, offering a still-unclaimed $40,000 reward for information. One tip prompted them to excavate a concrete patio, seeking the murder weapons, but they found nothing. A woman dying from cancer claimed her boyfriend had confessed to killing Moore, but no proof emerged. Later, a second, unnamed suspect in the case was questioned, but claimed amnesia dating from a 12-year-old car accident. McElveen died in 2003, taking his secrets with him. Creed Rogers followed McElveen to the grave five years later.[350] The DOJ reviewed Moore's case again, under the Till Act, and at last report, in January 2014, it was still considered "open," with investigation ongoing.[351]

James Waymers
July 10, 1965; Allendale, SC

A white man shot Waymers during an argument sparked by Waymers's attempt to furnish a black neighbor's home with electrical power.[352] An all-white jury accepted the gunman's plea of self-defense, acquitting him at trial.[353] The DOJ reviewed his case under the Till Act, closing it without further action on April 15, 2010.[354]

John Wesley Wilder
July 17, 1965; Ruston, LA

Around 1 a.m., a white policeman patrolling Ruston's mostly black Washington Heights district observed a large group of African Americans on the street, engaging in what he described as boisterous behavior. Stopping his car, the officer—unnamed in presently available reports—attempted to arrest one man for disturbing the peace, whereupon other members of the group reportedly attacked him. Struck by some object thrown from the crowd, the officer retrieved his shotgun from the patrol car, but it was snatched from his hands. Wilder then allegedly rushed the officer, grabbing him by the throat, whereupon the patrolman shot him five times. A local newspaper article from July 19 states that a coroner's inquest deemed the shooting justifiable.[355]

The DOJ reviewed Wilder's case under the Till Act, closing it without further action on May 25, 2011.[356] A letter to Wilder's survivors, dated June 1, reveals discrepancies in police testimony—one alleged responding officer denied being on duty the night of the slaying—while other patrolmen described Wilder's killer as "bothered by the shooting," claiming he "had not wanted to shoot Mr. Wilder." Although the officer was still alive in 2011, a five-year statute of limitations barred filing of civil rights charges.[357]

William Piercefield
July 24, 1965; Concordia Parish, LA

Piercefield, age 42, died in what newspaper accounts called a gun battle with sheriff's deputies and police from Ferriday, a town whose population was three-fourths African American in 2010. According to reports in the *Concordia Sentinel*, officers responded to a domestic disturbance involving a hostage. Piercefield then fired at officers, whereupon they pumped tear gas into the house and kicked in a door to kill him.[358] The DOJ reviewed Piercefield's case under the Till Act, and it remained open as this book went to press.[359]

John Queen
August 8, 1965; Fayette, MS

Journalist Joseph Shapiro writes, "In the segregated South in 1965, John Queen was about as insignificant as a man could be." A 65-year-old African American, paralyzed below the waist by a childhood accident, he crawled along Fayette's Main Street, where whites called him "Crippled Johnny" or "Shoe-Shine Johnny." Acquaintances enjoyed "riling him up," to hear Queen rattle off profanity, but that habit was perilous in racially mixed company.[360]

On Sunday, August 8, 36-year-old Jasper Burchfield—a white part-time constable from a neighboring county—stopped at Fayette's icehouse with his mother and 12-year-

Demonstrators protest the August 8, 1965, slaying of John Queen in Fayette, Mississippi (Civil Rights Archive).

old sister. Queen, as usual, was parked on the sidewalk outside, with his shoeshine boxes. Teenage witness Martha Wallace later said, "All I remember: I heard the word 'shit' or 'damn,' or something like that. And I know the man said, 'Don't talk like that in front of my wife and daughter.' And John, you know, John had kind of a big mouth. John said, 'I can say shit whenever I get ready.' And that was it. And the next thing I heard was a shot."[361]

Burchfield claimed that he fired in self-defense, after Queen drew a pistol and shot first at him. Martha Wallace and another "ear-witness" heard only one shot, but Charles Dawkins arrived moments after the shooting, saying he saw Queen dead, with a gun in his hand. Other witnesses referred vaguely to a bullet hole in a house across the street. The Rev. Percy Turner, a friend of Queen's, recalled Queen showing him a pistol Queen carried in one of his shoeshine boxes. Wallace says that when Jefferson County Deputy Sheriff Robert Pritchard arrived on the scene, he shook Burchfield's hand "in a friendly manner." Within the hour, Coroner R. A. "Sonny Boy" Cupit convened an inquest. Its one-line verdict reads: "Johnny Queen, came to his death by reason to-wit: Four gunshot wounds (.38 S & W special pistol) fired by J. W. Burchfield, in our opinions, in self-defense."[362]

Information from declassified FBI files brands Burchfield a bitter racist and Ku Klux Klan member, based on statements from undercover informants. Six months before Queen's death, agents had questioned Burchfield about his Klan membership, noting that "Burchfield spoke in a very derogatory manner of what he referred to as the 'Nigger situation,' and talked at length about the manner in which the quote 'Jews' were handling the United States, and the effect they have had on the American dollar and the American economy." Burchfield's name was also on a list of Mississippi Klansmen published by the House Committee on Un-American Activities in 1966. Employed by day with other Klansmen at the International Paper Company's plant in Natchez, while serving as night constable in nearby Fenwick, Burchfield was named by Adams County investigators as a suspect in the kidnapping and flogging of several black men.[363]

FBI agents reopened Queen's case in 2009, under the Till Act, and interrogated Burchfield, who denied Klan membership while telling them, "I get along with blacks myself. I never had no trouble with no blacks. Not a one." Burchfield's sister, a witness to Queen's slaying, confirmed that Queen was first to draw a gun, but contradicted her brother and mother, saying Queen never fired because his pistol jammed.[364] Hampered by conflicting testimony and the statute of limitations on 1960s civil rights violations, agent's closed Queen's case on July 26, 2013.[365]

Freddie Lee Thomas, Jr.
August 19, 1965; Sidon, MS

Sparse, contradictory sources confound investigation of 16-year-old Freddie Thomas's death. No cause of death is listed on the two websites that briefly mention the event. One site claims Thomas died in Sidon, on August 20; the other places his death in Greenwood, 10 miles farther north, either on August 20 or September 3. The FBI, presumably a more authoritative source, lists his death as occurring Sidon, on August 19. Thomas's brother believes he was slain as a warning to would-be black voters, but no suspects have been publicly identified.³⁶⁶ The DOJ reopened Thomas's case under the Till Act, then closed it without further action on June 9, 2011.³⁶⁷

Arthur James Hill
August 20, 1965; Villa Rica, GA

On the last day of his life, Hill and three friends argued with several white men at a gas station, after which a station employee killed him, also wounding one of Hill's companions. Held on a voluntary manslaughter charge, the killer claimed Hill was armed with a shotgun when slain.³⁶⁸ Jurors acquitted Hill of all counts in October 1965. The DOJ reviewed Hill's case under the Till Act, closing it without legal action on May 18, 2011.³⁶⁹ A letter from the FBI to his survivors, censored before public release, explains more details of the crime:

> According to our review, Mr. Green shot and killed Mr. Hill and shot and wounded [DELETED] on August 20, 1965. As you told the FBI, shortly before the shooting [DELETED], Mr. Hill, [DELETED], and [DELETED] stopped at a gas station in Villa Rica. After [DELETED] pumped gas, he and an unidentified white man began to argue and fight. When a second unidentified white man approached [DELETED], Mr. Hill intervened. It was then that Mr. Green, an employee of the gas station, approached [DELETED] lifting his pistol. As Mr. Hill was getting back into the car, Mr. Green shot and fatally wounded him, and then shot [DELETED]. [DELETED] then drove a short distance to a hospital, but Mr. Green was deceased by the time he arrived there.
>
> Mr. Green was indicted on a charge of manslaughter for killing Mr. Hill and on a charge of assault with intent to murder for shooting [DELETED]. According to an October 14, 1965 article in the *Carroll County Georgian*, Mr. Green was acquitted of all charges. According to the article, two white men, [DELETED], testified that they were stopped at a red light when a car occupied by five African-American men and women stopped in front of them and someone in the car "called [DELETED] names." [DELETED] then followed the other car to a gas station where the two groups began to argue. Mr. Green then told everyone to leave, [DELETED] left, but [DELETED] group did not. According to the article, Mr. Green gave an unsworn statement in which he claimed that Mr. Hill refused to leave, and "called him all sorts of names in the presence of women." Mr. Green stated further that Mr. Hill then reached to the floorboard of his car and Mr. Green saw the butt of a weapon. At that point, Mr. Green yelled at Mr. Hill, "don't do that." Mr. Green claimed that Mr. Hill replied, "I'm going to blow your guts out, you SOB," whereupon Mr. Green fired his pistol nine times, killing Mr. Hill and wounding [DELETED].
>
> Mr. Green died on January 3, 1973.³⁷⁰

Jonathan Myrick Daniels
August 20, 1965; Hayneville, AL

Daniels, a 26-year-old Episcopal seminarian from Keene, New Hampshire, flew to Selma, Alabama, on the same plane that carried James Reeb to his death (see March 9, 1965, above). Daniels lasted longer than Reeb, joining civil rights protests in "Bloody Lowndes" County, where he was jailed with Father Richard Morrisroe and 30 African Americans on August 14, for picketing a segregated store in Fort Deposit. Released into sweltering heat on August 20, Daniels, Morrisroe, and two black teenagers—Joyce Bailey and Ruby Sales—approached a nearby store, hoping to buy soft drinks. At the store, a white man with a shotgun ordered them to leave the premises. When they did not move fast enough to suit him, the man took aim at Sales. Daniels pushed her aside, and died from a blast to the chest. Morrisroe, fleeing, received the second charge of buckshot in his back.[371]

Triggerman Thomas L. Coleman was an engineer for the state highway department and a member of one of the county's oldest families. His sister, like their father before her, was superintendent of Lowndes County's schools. Tom Coleman was a "special" sheriff's deputy, present at the county courthouse when Daniels, Morrisroe, and the rest were freed on August 20. After shooting Daniels and Morrisroe, he returned to the sheriff's office, fielded a call reporting the murder, then phoned Albert Lingo, chief of Alabama's state police, saying, "I just shot two preachers. You'd better get down here." Lingo arrived with a bail bondsman known as a KKK member, chauffeured by Coleman's son, a highway patrol officer.[372]

For the remainder of his life, Coleman—a proud Citizens' Council member—denied Klan membership, but substantial evidence contradicts him. In February 1965 he joined known Klansmen to threaten members of the all-black Mt. Carmel Church over their civil rights work. A short time later, he warned state attorney general Richmond Flowers, "If you don't get off this Klan investigation, we'll get you off." Nor did targets of his threats regard them as idle. Six years before killing Daniels, in August 1959, Coleman shot and killed a black inmate at Greenville's prison camp, when guards professed themselves unable to control the prisoner.[373]

Prosecutors charged Coleman with first-degree murder for slaying Daniels, and assault with intent to commit murder for wounding Morrisroe. The trial, staged in September, was a farce with a foregone conclusion. Richmond Flowers opened for the state, then was banished by Judge T. Werth Thagard for "trifling with the court" when Flowers sought a postponement, to permit testimony from hospitalized witness Richard Morrisroe. Jury selection sparked laughter when Coleman's name appeared on the venire list, and another prospective juror, asked if he had any preconceived opinion on the case, replied, "I do. Not guilty!" While Klansmen including Viola Liuzzo's murderers thronged the courtroom, the prosecutor raised no objection to defense claims that Daniels and Morrisroe were armed with a knife and pistol, respectively (neither found at the scene). Leaving court to deliberate, one juror winked at Coleman in passing, and the panel's "not guilty" verdict surprised no one.[374]

Richmond Flowers described that verdict as the "democratic process going down the drain of irrationality, bigotry and improper law enforcement."[375] Coleman died in June 1997, untroubled by any further charges. Six years before Coleman's death, the Episcopal Church named Daniels as one of 15 modern-day martyrs, commemorating his sacrifice with an annual pilgrimage to Hayneville on August 14.[376]

The DOJ reviewed Daniels's case under the Till Act, closing it without further action on April 26, 2011.[377] An FBI letter to Richard Morrisroe, bearing the same date, reminded Morrisroe of Coleman's acquittal and subsequent death, closing with "sincere condolences on the loss of your friend."[378]

Thad Christian
August 28, 1965; Calhoun County, AL

On Saturday, August 28, father of seven Thad Christian left his home in Central City, west of Anniston, to catch fish for dinner with friend Shelley Kirby. He never returned, killed by a shotgun blast to the stomach, fired by white assailant Robert E. Haynes on a rural road south of Jacksonville. After charging Haynes with murder, Calhoun County Sheriff Roy Snead told reporters, "Apparently Christian and a companion were fishing in a creek, and this fellow went down to run them off." Kirby described Haynes driving by and shouting, "You niggers get out from down here," then returning to shoot Christian without provocation. Two other passersby, Lucille Edmondson White and her husband, saw Kirby sitting on the bumper of a car parked in the middle of the road, already shot, while Kirby stood nearby, shouting for help. As they slowed down, "This white man came from around the car with a shotgun under his arm. We were scared to death. He looked at us, and we backed up and got out of there. We didn't know what he might do, so we had to leave."[379]

Haynes's family told a different story, though none of them were present, claiming that Christian was armed and behaved in a threatening manner. Aubrey Haynes stands by his brother's unsupported claim that Christian carried a rifle and was accompanied by "many men," rather than Kirby alone. "They were yelling and fighting and cussing, and Robert went down there to break all that up, to run them away from there," Aubrey told reporter John Fleming. "He was up there on his porch in the cool of the day, trying to relax after working in that cussed pipe foundry all day long. He was up there drinking a six-pack of beer, and these fellows were making that racket down there by the road. Now, if that's a lie, then that's what Robert told me."[380]

Be that as it may, Robert Haynes pled guilty to manslaughter and served prison time, then died in a 1968 auto accident. In 2010, son Jerry Haynes told Fleming, "They auctioned off our farm for $10,000 on the steps of the Calhoun County Courthouse. We lost everything. My dad had too much to drink that night, but he didn't go down there with the intention of hurting anyone."[381]

The DOJ reviewed Christian's case under the Till Act, closing it without further action on April 6, 2011.[382] Two days later, FBI agents delivered a letter to Christian's family, citing Haynes's death and the 1960s statute of limitations on civil rights charges as factors precluding further investigation.[383]

Jimmie Lee Griffin
September 24, 1965; Oktibbeha County, MS

Police found Griffin's body on a highway near Sturgis, Mississippi, blaming his death on a hit-and-run driver.[384] According to the Arkansas Delta Truth and Justice Center, a coroner's report said Griffin "was run over at least twice," strongly suggesting murder.[385] The DOJ reviewed Griffin's case—misspelling his surname as "Griffith"—then closed it without further action on August 14, 2012.[386]

Jimmie Lee Griffin (left) with unidentified friend, circa 1964 (Civil Rights Archive).

Robert McNair
November 6, 1965; Pelahatchie, MS

Constable Luther Stevenson shot McNair, a 26-year-old father of six, while reportedly trying to serve McNair with a warrant for child neglect, issued by a local justice of the peace. Stevenson told investigators that he found McNair in a "juke joint," then chased him into a nearby field of waist-high grass, when McNair fled that establishment. In the field, McNair allegedly drew a pocketknife and lunged at Stevenson, whereupon Stevenson fired once in self-defense. A civilian witness, Fred White, told friends that he heard McNair beg Stevenson not to shoot him. Another witness, unnamed in FBI reports, reported hearing two gunshots, rather than one.[387]

Unknown to most acquaintances of Stevenson's in 1965, he led a double life, drawing his normal paycheck as a constable while serving as a covert informant for the Mississippi State Sovereignty Commission, a shady government agency active from 1956 to 1977, created to "protect the sovereignty of the state of Mississippi, and her sister states" from "federal encroachment"—i.e., racial integration. During its existence, the commission used informants such as Stevenson, along with members of white racist groups, to compile dossiers on more than 87,000 persons active in the civil rights movement nationwide.[388]

What role, if any, did Stevenson's secret work for the commission play in his shooting of Robert McNair? At the time, the Mississippi Freedom Democratic Party (MFDP) was active in Rankin County, seeking election of black representatives to the Agricultural

Stabilization and Conservation Service. MFDP chairman Lawrence Guyot asked the DOJ to investigate McNair's death, and while FBI agents apparently launched an inquiry, to results were ever published. Observers in Rankin County reported that "many [black] community residents appeared to take the McNair killing as a warning against participation in the ASCS process."[389]

Luther Stevenson was still alive when the DOJ reviewed McNair's case in 2010, under the Till Act, but his interview with FBI agents raised more questions than it answered. As detailed in an undated bureau letter to McNair's family, with the former constable's name omitted:

> [DELETED] told the FBI that he was charged, tried, and acquitted of murder charges. Moreover, [DELETED] stated that the FBI investigated the shooting in 1965 and that he was interviewed by the FBI at that time. However, the FBI was not able to locate any records or articles referencing the trial. Further, although the FBI retrieved 1964 records referencing [DELETED] those records did not pertain to an investigation of your [DELETED] shooting. The records stated that a confidential informant had reported that [DELETED] may have been a member of the Ku Klux Klan.[390]

That said, the DOJ could not file charges against Stevenson, since the five-year statute of limitations on civil rights violations—amended in 1994 to exempt crimes resulting in death—had long since expired. The department closed its review without further action on May 26. 2011.[391]

Samuel Leamon Younge, Jr.
January 3, 1966; Tuskegee, AL

A biography of Samuel Younge, penned by black activist James Forman in 1968, describes Younge as "the first black college student to die in the black liberation movement."[392] In fact, that dubious honor apparently belongs to Charles Eddie Moore (see May 2, 1964, above), an observation that takes nothing from Younge's sacrifice 20 months later.

An Alabama native, born to middle-class parents in 1944, Younge joined the U.S. Navy in 1962, participated in a tense blockade during the Cuban Missile Crisis, then received a medical discharge in July 1964, after surgical removal of a failing kidney. Returning to his hometown of Tuskegee, he enrolled at all-black Tuskegee Institute in January 1965 and joined a campus civil rights group—the Tuskegee Institute Advancement League—allied with SNCC. He marched with protesters in Selma, in March 1965, and traveled to Mississippi a month later, helping SNCC and the Mississippi Freedom Democratic Party register black voters. On July 18, 1965, a white mob attacked Younge and 30 other demonstrators when they tried to integrate a white Tuskegee church. Three months later, Opelika police arrested Younge and six other activists for transporting Lee County residents to register as voters.[393]

Near midnight on January 3, 1966, while engaged in yet another voter registration drive, Younge stopped at a Tuskegee gas station and tried to use its whites-only restroom. A dispute ensued, with 67-year-old white attendant Marvin L. Segrest, who shot and killed Younge on the spot. Macon County's grand jury stalled until November 1966 before indicting Segrest on a second-degree murder charge, and his December trial followed a pattern painfully familiar from preceding cases.[394] White bus driver W. B. Patterson testified that he "heard a shot, I didn't see what at," then entered the gas station to buy a soft drink. Emerging, he saw Segrest fire another shot, allegedly trying to miss Younge. According to Patterson, "I was looking over his shoulder, down the barrel" of Segrest's pistol, and clearly saw Segrest wait until Younge was "completely out of his line of fire." In fact, Patterson said, it seemed that Segrest was aiming "at a post."[395]

Segrest, meanwhile, claimed that he shot Younge in self-defense. According to Segrest, Younge arrived at his station "cursing and ranting and raving," demanding directions to the restroom. Segrest claimed that he politely answered, telling jurors that the only segregation of his station's toilets "is between ladies and men." Upon receiving directions to the men's room, Younge allegedly told Segrest, "I don't go to the goddamn back for nobody. The sooner you goddamn white folks know I don't do to the back, the better it will be for you." Segrest said he then told Younge to leave the station, whereupon Younge drove next-door to the Greyhound bus depot, then returned on foot "beyond himself," brandishing "this lead pipe or whatever it was." Segrest testified that he fired one shot into asphalt near Younge's feet, causing Younge to retreat behind a parked bus. Moments later, Younge returned, and Segrest fired the fatal shot, "aiming high" over Younge's head but striking him in the face.[396]

Three black witnesses disputed Patterson's and Segrest's testimony, saying that when Younge asked to use the restroom, Segrest "immediately pulled a gun" and ordered Younge to leave, then shot Younge when he verbally protested. Police sergeant George Prince arrived moments after the shooting, recalling in court that Segrest "complained about Younge's behavior" but mentioned no weapon. Still, officers claimed they found a golf club—not a lead pipe—lying underneath Younge's body. That was enough to satisfy the all-white jury, which acquitted Segrest.[397]

The DOJ reviewed Younge's case under the Till Act, closing it without legal action on March 28, 2011.[398] An FBI letter to Younge's survivors cited Segrest's acquittal and his death in 1986 as bars to any further investigation.[399]

Adlena Hamlett and Birdia Beatrice Clark Keglar
January 11, 1966; Leflore County, MS

On the same day NAACP member Vernon Dahmer died from burns inflicted by Ku Klux Klansmen in Hattiesburg, death claimed two more civil rights activists near Sidon, 152 miles farther north. Mystery surrounds that incident today, 50 years after the fact.

Adlena Hamlett, born in 1887, was a retired schoolteacher and one of the first African Americans to vote in Tallahatchie County. Birdia Keglar, 21 years Hamlett's junior, filed a federal lawsuit against Sheriff Ellett R. Dogan, Circuit Clerk Tom Harris, and Judge George Payne Cossar in November 1961, after they refused to accept her state-mandated poll tax. At a hearing in December, county officials suddenly announced that Keglar was "already listed" on Tallahatchie voting rolls, though Sheriff Dogan denied she had ever applied. Two years later, Keglar organized the county's first NAACP chapter, collecting dues through a Masonic lodge to keep membership secret.[400]

That effort was in vain. Mississippi's State Sovereignty Commission, founded in 1955 to preserve white supremacy, opened a file on the "problems" Keglar caused with fellow activists S. N. Drake and Grafton Gray. Keglar and Gray reported strange cars trailing them on travels through the county and around the state, sometimes pursuing them at high speeds. In 1965 Keglar warned young civil rights workers of a murder plot by the Ku Klux Klan, permitting them to escape the grim fate shared by so many others. Klansmen retaliated by hanging Keglar and Adlena Hamlett in effigy.[401]

On January 11, Hamlett and Keglar traveled to Jackson with Gray, Jesse J. Brewer, and Richard L. Simpson, a white volunteer from Massachusetts, for a "secret" meeting with Senator Robert F. Kennedy, who planned hearings in Mississippi to address disfranchisement of African Americans. On their return trip, midway between Sidon and Cruger, the party suffered a head-on collision with another car, driven by a local white man, Brown Lee Bruce, Jr. Hamlett and Keglar, seated in front with driver Grafton Gray, were killed instantly; Gray, Brewer and Simpson—both in the backseat—survived with serious injuries, Simpson admitted to a separate white hospital. Bruce, for his part, was reportedly unharmed.[402]

Local authorities dismissed the pile-up as an ordinary highway accident, but their response was hardly typical. Police kept survivors of the two slain women away from the crash site at first, then apparently disposed of Keglar's car, a 1965 Plymouth Fury II, without allowing relatives to see it. White hospital staff barred African Americans from visiting Richard Simpson, and he, too, seemed to vanish without a trace. Keglar's granddaughter, Alma Chism, suggested to author Susan Klopfer that Simpson, "if he survived, was probably taken out of Mississippi and sent home as soon as possible. That would have been the only way to keep him safe." Gray and Brewer recovered slowly, Gray's great-niece Gwen Dailey later telling Klopfer that he "was never the same" and refused to discuss the crash, after receiving several threats. Members of Hamlett's family spoke to Brown Bruce, a granddaughter informing Klopfer, "He was rude and unwilling to help. But he knew exactly what we were talking about."[403]

Adlena Hamlett, killed in a January 11, 1966, car crash with fellow activist Birdia Keglar (Civil Rights Archive).

Questions persist about the injuries suffered by Hamlett and Keglar. Relatives report that Keglar was decapitated, while Hamlett had both arms "cleanly severed," prompting rumors that they were dragged from the car and murdered, then replaced in the vehicle. Hamlett's granddaughter, Nina Zachary-Black, regards those mutilations as a sign of Klan involvement. Hamlett's great-granddaughter states categorically (without citing evidence) that both women "were marched to the edge of the woods where they were tortured, killed and mutilated in the style of the White Knights of the Klu Klux Klan [sic] of Mississippi." Adding insult to injury, Keglar's life insurance company refused to pay off on her policy after the crash.[404]

Following passage of the Till Act, Adlena Hamlett's relatives complained that FBI agents resisted adding Hamlett's and Keglar's names to the list of cases slated for review.

Dedication of Mississippi's Birdia Keglar Memorial Highway (Library of Congress).

Nonetheless, both appeared on the first list of cold-case victims published by the DOJ, in May 2010.[405] According to nearly-identical letters from FBI headquarters, Keglar's party was southbound on Highway 49B when they were "struck by a drunk driver (Mr. Bruce). The impact caused the hood of car [sic] to break loose and move through the windshield, fatally injuring" Hamlett and Keglar. Jesse Brewer and Richard Simpson, agents wrote, were "sleeping in the back seat" when the crash occurred. A paragraph presumably describing injuries suffered by Hamlett and Keglar, gleaned from interviews with an unnamed mortuary employee, who collected their bodies from the crash site, was deleted by FBI censors before the letters were released to journalists.[406]

Agents uncovered an accident report from the Mississippi Highway Patrol—long withheld from survivors, by officers who claimed no such paperwork existed—and asserted that Brown Bruce was charged with driving on the wrong side of the road. Despite the FBI's reference to his intoxication, Bruce was not charged with drunk driving, and the letters cite no disposition of his case. Bruce was unavailable for questioning, deceased in August 1996, while Grafton Gray died in December 1990 and Jesse Brewer in July 1998.[407]

That left only Richard Simpson, traced by agents who reported that his memory "confirmed the basic details" of the MHP report from 1966. Incredulous, Nina Zachary-Black asked reporters, "How can you be asleep and be an eyewitness at the same time?"[408] Ignoring that discrepancy, the DOJ closed Keglar's case for the last time on May 18, 2011, followed by Hamlett's eight days later.[409]

Nathan Johnson, Jr.
May 8, 1966; Alabaster, AL

Alabama state trooper James Bonard Fowler and a local patrolman arrested Johnson, age 34, on suspicion of drunken driving. At Alabaster's jail, while being booked, Johnson allegedly grabbed the city officer's baton and began to strike him with it, whereupon Fowler shot and killed him. Johnson was the second African American slain by Fowler, preceded by Jimmie Lee Jackson (see February 18, 1965, above), whose death inspired the historic civil rights march from Selma to Montgomery in March 1965. Forty-five years after the fact, Fowler pled guilty to manslaughter in Jackson's case, receiving a six-month sentence.[410] The DOJ reviewed Johnson's shooting under the Till Act, closing the case without further action on April 21, 2011.[411]

Vincent Dahmon
June 1966; Natchez, MS

Dahmon's case remains one of the most mysterious reviewed under the Till Act. I initially suspected that his listing as a victim might be a garbled reference to NAACP activist Vernon Dahmer, slain by Ku Klux Klansmen at Hattiesburg in January 1966, but

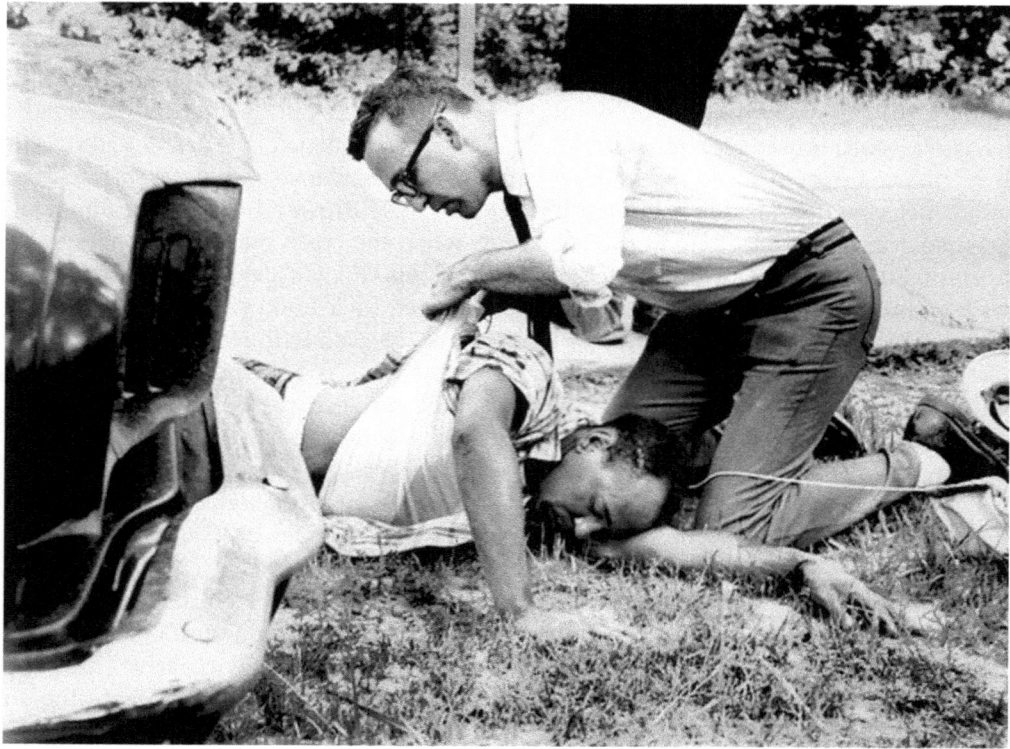

Unidentified physician examines James Meredith after he was shot on June 7, 1966. Klansmen murdered Ben White as a lure for Dr. Martin Luther King, Jr., when King took over Meredith's "March Against Fear" in Mississippi (Civil Rights Archive).

vague reports of the case insist that Dahmon—65 years old, compared to Dahmer's 57—was shot in the head at Natchez, "around the time of a march in support of James Meredith."[412]

Meredith began a one-man "March Against Fear" on June 5, 1966, bound from Memphis, Tennessee, to Jackson, Mississippi. A reputed Klansman wounded him with shotgun blasts on June 6, near Hernando, Mississippi, forcing Meredith to abandon the march. Other African American leaders, including Dr. Martin Luther King, Jr., and SNCC's Stokeley Carmichael, continued the pilgrimage, reaching Jackson on June 26.[413] During that time, on June 10, Klansmen kidnapped elderly farmer Ben Chester White (see June 10, 1966, below) and murdered him, in hopes Dr. King would visit the crime scene and thus make himself a target, but nothing more is known of Vincent Dahmon's death.

The DOJ reviewed this case under the Till Act, listing the date and place of his death as unknown, then closed the matter without further action on April 12, 2010.[414] My inquiries to Natchez libraries and newspapers elicited no further information on the case.

Ben Chester White
June 10, 1966; Homochitto National Forest, MS

Black activist James Meredith launched his one-man "March Against Fear" on June 6, 1966, planning to walk alone from Memphis, Tennessee, to Jackson, Mississippi, in defiance of white terrorists. One day later, reputed Ku Klux Klan member Aubrey Norvell wounded Meredith with shotgun fire, but Dr. Martin Luther King, Jr., and others vowed to continue the pilgrimage.[415] For Klansmen, after years of failed murder attempts, the time seemed ripe to assassinate King.

Specifically, the plotters this time were Ernest H. Avants, Claude Fuller, and James Lloyd Jones, members of a Klan faction known as the Cottonmouth Moccasin Gang. As bait for Dr. King, they planned to abduct and murder a black victim chosen at random, then kill King when he came to view the crime scene or attend the victim's funeral. On June 10 the trio offered 67-year-old handyman Ben White two dollars and a soft drink to help them find a lost dog, then drove him to Pretty Creek in the Homochitto National Forest near Natchez. There, Fuller shot White 15 times with a .30-caliber carbine, while Avants fired a shotgun blast into White's head. In the process, the clumsy killers shot up Jones's car, prompting them to set it on fire as a means of destroying evidence.[416]

That ploy failed to deceive Mississippi Highway Patrol investigators, who traced the car to Jones and obtained his confession to kidnapping, naming Fuller and Avants as White's slayers. Avants also confessed in custody, claiming that White was dead from Fuller's carbine fire before Avants administered the 12-gauge *coup de grâce*. Prosecutors charged all three Klansmen with murder, but Mississippi justice went awry once more. Jones recanted his confession, confusing white jurors enough that they deadlocked at trial, in December 1966, whereupon authorities dismissed his murder charge. Alleged arthritis and ulcers spared Fuller from trial, and his charges were also dismissed. Avants faced trial in 1967, acquitted when an all-white jury accepted his claim of "only" shooting a corpse.[417]

Thirty-six years passed, with Jones and Fuller dying, before FBI agents realized that White was killed on U.S. government land. That fact trumped claims of double jeopardy in June 2000, when a federal grand jury indicted Avants for aiding and abetting White's murder. Various legal delays, mostly pertaining to the defendant's poor health and alleged memory deficits resulting from a series of small strokes, stalled trial until February 2003, but Avants would not escape justice this time. Jurors convicted him, resulting in a life prison sentence, and his appeals were denied. Avants died in prison at age 72, in June 2004.[418]

White's case is an anomaly, solved more than four years before the Till Act was signed into law. Even so, the DOJ listed White among the victims whose deaths were reviewed under the new law, citing the file's closure date as October 16, 2003.[419]

Eddie James Stewart
July 9, 1966; Jackson, MS

Published reports disagree on the location where 24-year-old Eddie Stewart was slain by police, some accounts placing the event in Jackson, others in Crystal Springs—also considered part of the larger Jackson Metropolitan Statistical Area, although it lies in Copiah County, while Jackson is in Hines County. All reports agree that a group of state, county, and local officers beat and shot Stewart at his home, claiming lethal force was necessary because he "tried to escape" during an attempted arrest.[420]

When prosecutors took no action, Stewart's widow filed a $20 million federal lawsuit in August 1966, alleging that her husband was secure in custody when he was shot. Defendants in that case included Colonel T. B. Birdsong, state commissioner of public safety; A. D. Morgan, chief of the Mississippi Highway Patrol; Copiah County Sheriff Herbert Deaton; Hinds County Sheriff Fred N. Pickett; Crystal Springs police chief Boyce Ferguson; Highway Patrolman T. L. Oglesby; and a Copiah County sheriff's deputy identified only as "Walker."[421] My inquiries in preparation for volume found no disposition for that case, suggesting that it may have been dismissed. The DOJ reviewed Stewart's death under the Till Act, and closed the case without further action on May 26, 2011.[422]

Collie Hampton
August 14, 1966; Winchester, KY

White police officers answered a disturbance call to Hampton's home around 2 a.m., first confronting him outside, then following him into the house with drawn guns, reportedly intending to arrest him for "breach of the peace." At that time, officers said, Hampton kept one hand in his pants pocket, threatening to shoot them if they entered his home. A civilian witness also said that Hampton tried to shut the door, but officers forced it open, one of them slapping Hampton's face while another circled behind him.[423]

Chaos ensued from there. Police said Hampton grabbed the gun hand of the officer who slapped him, whereupon that officer shouted, "He has my gun!" A civilian witness, fleeing the scene, heard one shot followed closely by two more. An autopsy performed the same day, at Lexington's University of Kentucky Medical Center, found four gunshot wounds in Hampton's chest, two entrance and two exit wounds, with at least one shot piercing his heart. Kentucky State Police investigated the slaying, arresting four Winchester patrolmen on August 15. Each of the four posted $5,000 bond and left jail on August 16. Their trial began on December 13, 1966, and jurors acquitted the defendants three days later, after failing to determine whose gun fired the fatal shots.[424]

All four officers were still alive in 2011, when FBI agents reviewed Hampton's case under the Till Act. A letter to Hampton's family, dated May 27, explained that no new charges could be filed, since all four had been acquitted in state court and the five-year statute of limitations on federal civil rights offenses had expired.[425] Oddly, the DOJ did not officially close Hampton's case until June 1, five days after telling his survivors that no further action could be taken.[426]

Hulet M. Varner, Jr.
September 10, 1966; Atlanta, GA

On Saturday night, September 10, a drive-by shooting claimed the life of 15-year-old Hulet Varner and wounded 16-year-old companion Roy Wright. Also wounded was a white policeman rushing toward the shooting scene. Witnesses Eddie Foote and Ronald Warbington observed the shooting from a laundromat, telling police the car was driven by a white woman, while her white male companion shot the victims after asking, "What did you say, boy?"[427]

The incident touched off three nights of ghetto rioting, which left 20 persons injured, 90 jailed, and two stores burned. Fulton County's grand jury first indicted militant activist Stokeley Carmichael on riot charges, and then, on September 14, charged 42-year-old William Haygood James with murder. The panel also bound over James's wife, 31-year-old Edna Ruth James, as a material witness, releasing her on $2,000 bond while her husband remained in jail. On February 8, 1967, jurors convicted William James and recommended a life prison term, which Judge Stonewall Dyer imposed.[428] Georgia's Supreme Court reversed James's conviction on October 9, 1967, citing 12 procedural errors by the judge and prosecution.[429] James was not retried for Varner's slaying, but he was arrested once again in July 1973, for robbing a liquor store. Conviction on that charge brought another life sentence, that on affirmed on appeal.[430]

The DOJ reviewed Varner's case under the Till Act, closing it without further action on April 6, 2009.[431]

James Earl Motley
November 20, 1966; Wetumpka, AL

Around 1:40 a.m., Elmore County sheriff's deputy Harvey Conner stopped a car driven by Reuben Clark, with U.S. Air Force airman James Motley riding in the backseat. Motley allegedly objected to the stop, and to Conner demanding Clark's driver's license, whereupon Connor beat him over the head with a blackjack. Accompanied by two state troopers, Connor drove Motley to the county jail, where he died two hours later.[432]

Elmore County's coroner called Motley's death accidental, blaming a fall against his jailhouse bunk, and a January 1967 grand jury refused to charge Conner with homicide, but a federal grand jury indicted him for violating Motley's civil rights. At trial in April 1967, defense attorneys offered the jury of 11 whites and one African American three contradictory theories of Conner's innocence. First, they said Conner struck Motley, drawing blood, only when Motley resisted arrest. Second, they claimed no bloodshed occurred until Motley reached jail, where he "fell" and suffered fatal injuries. Finally, they alleged that Motley's skull "was unusually thin, so that a light blow might have crushed it."[433]

Reuben Clark destroyed the second argument, describing Conner's beating of Motley that left "blood all over" Conner's patrol car, later cleaned up at the jail. Conner himself admitted that, during the roadside arrest, "I hit him twice, or three times—I think it was twice—and some blood came." Debate over the relative thickness of Caucasian and Negroid skulls proved fruitless, but state toxicologist Guy Purnell testified that Motley's cranium was "thinner than adults I've seen before," and in fact the thinnest he had ever seen. No federal investigators testified for the prosecution, convincing local blacks that Washington had no real interest in the case, and jurors acquitted Conner on April 12.[434]

The DOJ reopened Motley's case under the Till Act, then closed it without further action on April 12, 2010.[435] Sixteen days later, FBI agents delivered a letter to Motley's family in Wetumpka, relating the published facts and noting Conner's death in November 1980. Their conclusion: "After careful review of this incident, we have concluded that the now deceased Harvey Conner acted alone when he assaulted the victim and therefore, we have no choice but to close our investigation."[436]

Alphonso Harris
December 1, 1966; Albany, GA

Albany was the scene of civil rights protests led by Dr. Martin Luther King, Jr., in 1962, which in turn prompted church burnings and other acts of violence by the Ku Klux Klan. It is unclear what role Alphonso Harris played in King's protests, but SPLC spokesmen assert that his slaying, four years later, occurred "in response to previous civil rights activity there."[437] An SPLC staff bulletin from 1966 describes Harris as a movement activist who spent time in "many jails" and had recently secured a recording contract for his music trio, the Freedom Singers.[438] Most recently, on August 10, 1966, Harris had been assaulted by whites while leading a protest march through troubled Grenada, Mississippi.[439]

An FBI report to Harris's family described his final hours as follows:

> According to our review, on December 1, 1966, [DELETED] shot and killed Alphonso Harris, while the two men were grappling over a pistol owned by [DELETED]. The shooting occurred outside the Los Antes Club in Albany. The incident reportedly began when a man named [DELETED] bumped into [DELETED] girlfriend inside the club and they began to argue. Sometime during the argument [DELETED] exited the club, and retrieved a pistol from his car. [DELETED] then approached the table where Mr. Harris was sitting with three other men and told them that he thought he was about to be shot. Mr. Harris and the three other men exited the club with Mr. Toomer and ran into [DELETED] who was returning to the club, armed with a pistol. [DELETED] fired one shot into the ground. He and Mr. Harris then began struggling over the pistol. During the struggle, the pistol discharged twice and Mr. Harris

sustained a fatal gunshot wound to the stomach and [DELETED] sustained a gunshot wound to a thigh. According to local court records, [DELETED] was charged in March 1967 with carrying a weapon without a permit. He pled guilty in May 1967, and paid a $200 fine and $45 in court costs.[440]

After reviewing Harris's death as a possible hate crime under the Till Act, the DOJ closed its case without further action on April 12, 2010.[441]

Wharlest Jackson, Sr.
February 27, 1967; Natchez, MS

In 1960s Mississippi, the price of a proud black man's life was 17 cents. Wharlest Jackson, born in 1930, was a 12-year employee of the Armstrong Tire & Rubber plant in Natchez when he received a promotion to chemical mixer in January 1967, with a raise of 17 cents per hour—enough in those days for wife Exerlena to quit her job as a cook and spend more time with the couple's five children.[442] Tragically, the promotion was also a sentence of death.

Many of Jackson's white coworkers at Armstrong were members of the Ku Klux Klan, with ample cause in their minds to despise him. Aside from his promotion to a formerly "white" job, edging out two Caucasian competitors, Jackson was also treasurer of the local NAACP chapter, recruited by best friend George Metcalfe, another Armstrong worker who served as the group's president. Jackson sometimes carpooled to

Police examine Wharlest Jackson Sr.'s pickup truck, bombed by Klansmen on February 27, 1967 (National Archives).

work with Metcalfe until August 25, 1965, when members of the Klan's Silver Dollar Group wired a bomb to the ignition of Metcalfe's 1955 Chevrolet sedan, nearly killing him. Afterward, Jackson took extra care driving to and from work—at least, until Monday, February 27.[443]

Leaving work shortly after 8 p.m. that night, Jackson began driving home through a rainstorm. As he neared his house, a bomb wired to his pickup truck's turn indicator detonated, shattering the vehicle and killing him instantly. Exerlena heard the blast at home and cried, "Oh, Lord, that's Jackson! They got Jackson!"[444]

Ex-FBI agent Billy Bob Williams, assigned to Natchez at the time, later told the *Concordia Sentinel* that Police Chief J. T. Robinson "was very upset that the Jackson case was never solved and he very much wanted the case to be reopened by the FBI."[445] The prime suspect in Jackson's murder, although never charged, was Raleigh Jackson "Red" Glover, a white Armstrong employee, Klansman, and reputed leader of the Silver Dollar Group. An FBI informant in the Klan, O. C. Poissot, named Glover as the bomber, noting Glover's history of demolitions training in the U.S. Navy. According to FBI files, Glover's stepson and fellow Klansman, James Edward Watts, stored stolen dynamite at his home and was proficient in wiring automobile electrical systems.[446]

Natchez police apparently reopened Jackson's case in the 1990s, claiming all identified suspects were dead. The department then delivered its files to the FBI, where they remain classified today.[447] The DOJ reviewed Jackson's death under the Till Act and, according to the last report in January 2014, the file remains open with investigation continuing.[448]

Benjamin Brown
May 11, 1967; Jackson, MS

Born in 1945, Brown joined the Mississippi civil rights movement as a teenager, participating in freedom rides, voter registration campaigns, and working with the

White students from Jackson's Millsaps College protest the May 11, 1967, police slaying of Benjamin Brown. They were photographed and marked for investigation by Mississippi's State Sovereignty Commission (Civil Rights Archive).

Delta Ministry "Freedom Corps" until the latter months of 1966, when he married a fellow activist and found work as a trucker in Jackson. Police in Mississippi's capital already knew him well, from seven prior arrests in local demonstrations.[449]

During those years, all-black Jackson State College was a center of student unrest, due in equal parts to racial discrimination and the escalating war in Vietnam, viewed by many African American's as a white man's war against people of color. On May 10, 1967, city police chased a speeding student onto the Jackson State campus and tried to arrest him, sparking a two-day protest that brought state police and National Guardsmen to quell the disorder. On May 11, during a demonstration on Lynch Street, city and state officers fired on the crowd with live ammunition. Benjamin Brown, reportedly a spectator that day, suffered two shotgun wounds—both fired from behind him. He died on May 12, his 22nd birthday.[450]

As usual in such cases, Brown's death received minimal investigation. On May 10, 1968, Brown's widow and mother sued city and state authorities in federal court, charging wrongful death and seeking release of all files on Brown's death. A district judge denied that motion, then was reversed by the Fifth Circuit Court of Appeals. Another judge dismissed the lawsuit without prejudice in August 1970, permitting the plaintiffs to refile if new evidence emerged.[451]

In May 1998, Jackson Deputy Police Chief Eddie Wilson reopened Brown's case. Three years later, on May 29, 2001, Hinds County's grand jury named ex-Mississippi Highway Patrol Officer Lloyd Jones (later Simpson County's sheriff for 19 years) and ex-Jackson police captain Buddy Kane as Brown's slayers, reporting that "there is evidence to support a conclusion that Brown was struck by at least two separate shots from shotguns fired by the Jackson police officer and the Mississippi Highway Patrol officer." The panel issued no indictments, but its report allowed Brown's family to renew litigation against the City of Jackson and the Mississippi Department of Public Safety. Those defendants settled out of court in 2002, for an undisclosed sum.[452]

The DOJ reviewed Brown's case under the Till Act, closing it without further action on March 19, 2013.[453]

Rodell Williamson
May 20, 1967; Wilcox County, AL

Rodell Williamson was a member of the Wilcox County NAACP, active in urging other African Americans to register as voters. On May 22, 1967, David Morgan and another fisherman, trolling the Alabama River near Camden, snagged his floating corpse and called the sheriff's office.[454] From that point onward, mystery surrounds the 31-year-old man's death.

Sheriff Percy "Lummie" Jenkins denied any signs of foul play on Williamson's body, and the county coroner told journalists an autopsy would be performed, but researchers from Northeastern University's School of Law report that no record of that postmortem existed in 2007, either at the state Department of Forensic Sciences or at the Brownlee Funeral Home that received Williamson's body. Nor, they said, was there any record of a police investigation in the case.[455]

Fred D. Campbell told a different story, after identifying his cousin's corpse. "It was hard to tell who he was," Campbell said, "but I went back four or five times to make sure. It really seemed to me that his neck was natural-born broken, and his head all covered up, smashed. I asked Mr. [Charles] Brownlee to pull back the rag over the head but he wouldn't do it. He sure looked to me like something was done to him. There was a gash around the back of his neck and bruises on his chest." Brownlee, owner of the mortuary, also urged Williamson's mother not to view her son, but she persevered to identify Rodell from his "rough" heels. Meanwhile, a sheriff's deputy told reporters that any talk of foul play in the case was "a damn lie." Mortician Brownlee added, "I don't think it was racial. You know what I mean."[456]

A relative of Williamson, David McCaskey, said that Williamson roused him from sleep, calling at his door on the night of May 20, but McCaskey did not answer, despite recognizing his voice. Sometime later, a nurse en route to visit a patient reportedly saw a man crawling along the roadside. "He was beaten and on his knees," Fred Campbell said. "He looked real bad, but she didn't stop because she was afraid. We asked the sheriff about it, but he didn't say anything."[457]

FBI agents announced an investigation of Williamson's death in June 1967, and uncovered two more witnesses, whose names are excised from reports released four decades later.[458] Both were residents of Lower Peachtree, 10 miles southwest of Camden. One saw Williamson walk past her home, while a neighbor saw a state police vehicle pass seconds later and heard a car door slam. Both witnesses recanted their statements when interviewed by FBI agents in 2010, prompting the DOJ to close Williamson's case once more on May 2.[459]

The department's official letter quoted David Morgan, his fellow fisherman, and an unnamed "special deputy" who recovered Williamson's corpse as saying "there were no marks on it or injuries to it. The autopsy report also indicates that there was no evidence of physical trauma to Mr. Williamson's head, body or brain. Muddy water and debris from the river was found in Mr. Williamson's lungs, which shows that he was still breathing when he entered the river, and the cause of death was likely drowning. The manner of death was classified as accidental. A toxicological analysis of Mr. Williamson's blood revealed an extremely high alcohol level (0.32 gram percent)."[460] African Americans familiar with the Wilcox County Sheriff's Office under Lummie Jenkins reject that finding categorically.

Carrie Brumfield
September 12, 1967; Franklinton, LA

Police found Brumfield, an African American, dead in his car, shot once in the chest with a .22-caliber weapon, on a rural road outside Franklinton, where he resided. They developed no suspects and the homicide remains officially unsolved.[461] The DOJ examined Brumfield's death under the Till Act, closing it without further action on September 24, 2013.[462]

Archie Wooden
December 25, 1967; Camden, AL

Wooden, age 16, allegedly "jumped or fell onto a sapling in a ditch," severing his femoral artery and bleeding to death within minutes. FBI agents reportedly made a civil rights inquiry at the time, results of which are unknown.[463] The DOJ revisited Wooden's case under the Till Act, then closed it without legal action on April 20, 2010.[464]

Samuel Ephesians Hammond, Jr., Delano Herman Middleton and Henry Ezekiel Smith
February 8, 1968; Orangeburg, SC

Disheartened by the war in Vietnam, President Lyndon Johnson declined to seek reelection in November 1968, creating a leadership vacuum within the Democratic Party at a critical moment in U.S. history. Before year's end, the nation was rocked by assassinations and riots, climaxed by the election of Richard Nixon, beginning the grim

Police examine slain victims of the February 8, 1968, "Orangeburg Massacre" (National Archives).

march toward Watergate. Before any of those historic events, however, came the Orangeburg Massacre.

Founded in 1896 as the Colored Normal Industrial Agricultural and Mechanical College of South Carolina, South Carolina State College (now South Carolina State University) was created as the state's sole college for African Americans.[465] In February 1968, near the close of a tumultuous era, its students engaged in protests against the Vietnam War and against exclusion of blacks from the All Star Bowling Lane, on U.S. Highway 301. Demonstrations at All Star began on February 5. The following night, police beatings sent nine students to the hospital. On February 8 protesters built a bonfire on campus, drawing firefighters and Highway Patrol officers. More than 100 were retreating from the bonfire when someone threw a banister railing, striking Patrolman David Shealy in the face. Moments later, at 10:33 p.m., other officers opened fire with shotguns, carbines and pistols, wounding 31 students, most of them shot in the back while fleeing, or in the soles of their feet while lying prone. Three of those shot—Samuel Hammond, Jr., Delano Herman Middleton, and Henry Smith—died from their wounds. A fourth death, the miscarried infant of Louise Kelly Cawley, a pregnant woman beaten by police while taking gunshot victims to the hospital, is largely forgotten today.[466]

Media outlets initially reported the shooting as a pitched battle between police, black snipers, and protesters hurling Molotov cocktails. The Associated Press called it "a heavy exchange of gunfire." A local newspaper told its readers that "about 200 Negros [sic] gathered and began sniping with what sounded like 'at least one automatic, a shotgun and other small caliber weapons' and throwing bricks and bottles at the patrolmen." Governor Robert McNair blamed the violence on outside "Black Power" agitators, falsely claiming that the shooting occurred off-campus.[467]

Of the 66 South Carolina Highway Patrol officers present, nine—Lieutenant Jesse Alfred Spell, Sergeant Henry Morrell Addy, Sergeant Sidney C. Taylor, Corporal Norwood F. Bellamy, Corporal Joseph Howard Lanier, Patrolman First Class John William Brown, Patrolman First Class Colie Merle Metts, Patrolman Edward H. Moore, and Patrolman Allen Jerome Russell—admitted firing into the crowd of protesters. One Orangeburg city patrolman—later promoted to chief of police—also confessed to firing at the demonstrators with a shotgun. A federal grand jury indicted the nine highway patrolmen on misdemeanor charges of "imposing summary punishment without due process of law." All pled self-defense, despite a dearth of evidence that demonstrators carried any weapons, or that gunfire was directed toward police. Jurors deliberated less than two hours before acquitting all accused.[468]

The only defendant convicted of any offense at Orangeburg as Cleveland Sellers, Jr., a 23-year-old African American serving as national program director of the Student Nonviolent Coordinating Committee. State authorities charged him with "inciting to riot" for events occurring at the All Star Bowling Lane on February 6, when police sent nine students to the hospital. White jurors convicted Sellers at trial in autumn 1970. He served seven months in prison, and while he received a full pardon from Governor James Hunt, Jr., in 1995, Sellers chose not to have his record expunged, retaining the conviction as "a badge of honor."[469]

Today, South Carolina University's gymnasium is named for the three students killed in 1968. On February 8, 2001, Governor Jim Hodges addressed an overflow crowd at the school's Martin Luther King, Jr., Auditorium, expressing "deep regret" for the massacre and calling it "a great tragedy for our state."[470]

FBI spokesmen initially denied plans to reopen the massacre case in December 2007, but it was later added to the DOJ's list of cold cases picked for review under the Till Act.[471] Unlike most such cases, the deaths of Hammond, Middleton and Smith remained open pending further investigation, as of January 2014.[472]

Larry Payne
March 28, 1968; Memphis, TN

On February 11, 1968, some 1,300 black sanitation workers walked off their jobs in Memphis, protesting years of discrimination and dangerous working conditions, climaxed by the death of workers Echol Cole and Robert Walker, crushed in the compactor of their garbage truck while trying to escape torrential rain. On March 28, Dr. Martin Luther King, Jr., led a protest march that degenerated into window-smashing violence, initiated by a group of militants called The Invaders, thought to be infiltrated by police *agents provocateurs*. During that riot, Patrolman L. D. Jones killed 16-year-old Larry Payne with a close-range shotgun blast as Payne emerged from a boiler room of the Fowler Homes housing development.[473]

Jones claimed that he and partner Charles F. Williams followed a group of looters

Larry Payne (in white shirt) observes Memphis police clashing with protesters shortly before his slaying by officers on March 28, 1968 (Library of Congress).

carrying television sets from a department store on Third Street to the Fowler Homes, where the young men ducked into the basement. Jones "hollered" for the suspects to emerge, but only Payne appeared, wielding a knife and forcing Jones to fire in self-defense. Oddly, police found no more suspects—and no TV sets—inside the boiler room, nor do crime scene reports reflect discovery of any knives. Against the story told by Jones, 25 civilian witnesses maintained that Payne was empty-handed when he left the boiler room.[474]

FBI agents began investigating Payne's death on March 30. Their final report, issued in 1971, mentioned no knife, additional looters, or stolen property found at the Fowler Homes, but concluded that available evidence "cannot disprove subject's claim of self-defense." A spokesman for the U.S. attorney's office in Memphis went further, saying that the shooting was "obviously executed in self-defense on the part of the police officer." Shelby County's grand jury concurred, deeming Payne's death a case of justifiable homicide.[475]

Payne's mother left Memphis for Michigan in 1969, saying that Larry's death "has got the best of my life. It's taken everything out of me. I was in my living room watching *As the World Turns*. A lady ran in and told me Larry had been shot by the police. I ran out. I ran to touch him. The police would not let me touch him. He said, 'Get back, nigger.' He put the barrel of the gun right into my stomach. I could feel it." A lawsuit, filed on her behalf against police by attorney Irvin Salky, was eventually defeated. During those proceedings, Salky noted that officers could not produce the knife in question, claiming it was "mistakenly collected with older evidence from the police property room" and dumped into the Mississippi River. As Salky told reporter Michael Lollar, "We had a lot of skepticism over that."[476]

The DOJ reviewed Payne's case under the Till Act but found no new evidence, closing the file once more on July 5, 2011.[477]

Ann Thomas
April 8, 1969; San Antonio, TX

Police found Thomas's partly clothed body near the intersection of Hamel Avenue and Rotary Street, north of Onslow Park. An autopsy determined that she had been raped and shot four times in the head.[478] The DOJ examined Thomas's still-unsolved murder under the Till Act, and closed the case on April 15, 2010, without developing any suspects.[479]

Part 2: "The Forgotten"

This part of collects "forgotten" victims of the civil rights struggle, omitted for reasons unknown from the DOJ's master list of cases compiled between 2007 and 2014. The list is not definitive, as noted earlier, because hate crimes were appallingly routine during the period examined and, in many cases, were ignored entirely by local and national news media, rendering comprehensive tabulation impossible. Even so, the roster includes 295 cases with 335 victims slain. Of those, 114 cases involved law enforcement officers; 75 involved lynch mobs or vigilante "posses"; 11 were the work of organized hate groups; and civilian individuals committed 85 of the crimes. Seven cases represent false or mistaken reports, including four persons wounded or narrowly missed by assassins but later reported as murdered, and three alleged victims for whom no information was available at press time. Two cases—those of Horace Bell and Clyde Kennard, involve deaths by natural causes, though Bell remains on several lists of murder victims, while Kennard's cancer—diagnosed in a Mississippi prison and left untreated by the state until it was incurable—may be viewed as a weapon in the fight for white supremacy. Likewise, the suicide of civil rights activist Juliette Hampton Morgan resulted directly from longstanding racist harassment. Whenever possible throughout this work, I strive to set the record straight.

Rexwell Scott
January 24, 1934; Hazard, KY

Scott reportedly engaged in a fistfight with white coal miner Alexander Johnson on East Main Street, around 6 p.m. on January 22. Johnson was hospitalized in critical condition, while officers arrested Scott and lodged him in the Perry County jail. Two days later, at 7:45 p.m. on January 24, a "well organized, well disciplined and fast moving" mob of 30 men, masked and heavily armed, invaded the jail, removing Scott from the custody of jailer Troy P. Combs and Deputy W. C. Knuckles. Pausing at the intersection of Main and High Streets, the lynchers fired 100 random shots, then roared out of town. Patrolman Tolbert Holliday heard the gunfire and pursued the mob in a taxi, but he arrived too late to save Scott, found hanging near Sassafras with 22 bullet wounds. Back in Hazard, Johnson died from his injuries roughly an hour after Scott was lynched.[1]

Unlike some of their Southern counterparts, Perry County officials launched an immediate investigation. Judge A. M. Gross issued arrest warrants for three men by midnight, detained with a fourth for questioning overnight.[2] On February 7 a special grand jury indicted white miners Ed Bentley, Petie Carroll, Ordley Fugate, Lee Gibson, Bill "Wooden" Kinser, George Watkins, and John Watts on murder charges.[3] Judge Sam M. Ward granted bond to the defendants on February 14, after a two-day hearing.[4] Governor Ruby Laffoon removed Troy Combs from office, declaring the jailer's post vacant, while Kentucky's state legislature adopted a resolution condemning Scott's murder without a single dissenting vote.[5]

Convicting the lynchers, however, was something else entirely. Despite jurors imported from Owsley County by Judge Ward, the first defendant placed on trial, Lee Gibson, basked in the sympathy of "mountain kinship."[6] Even with his boast on record of being first to shoot Rex Scott, even with a witness who had seen him riding on the running board of one lynch vehicle, the panel managed to acquit him on May 23 without much deliberation. The *Hazard Herald* declared the prosecution's case "purely circumstantial," opining that none of it linked Gibson to the crime.[7] With one acquittal on the books, charges against the other six defendants were dismissed.

Robert Johnson
January 30, 1934; Tampa, FL

On January 24 police arrested 40-year-old Robert Johnson on suspicion of raping a white woman but found no evidence linking him to the crime. Rather than release him, they charged him with stealing chickens, and Johnson reportedly confessed to that offense. Since Tampa led the state in lynchings, local officers planned to lodge him in the Hillsborough County jail, but their scheme played into the hands of white vigilantes. At 2:30 a.m. on January 30 detectives handed Johnson to Deputy Constable Thomas Graves. Graves later explained the unusual hour by saying, "I went to the police station to transfer him to the county jail, thinking with that out of the way, I would not have to get up so early the next morning." In fact, three carloads of lynchers were waiting, disarming Graves, driving him and Johnson to their selected murder site on the Hillsborough River where others waited. There, Graves said, one member of the unmasked mob told Johnson, "You son of a bitch, you know you did it." Johnson allegedly replied, "Yes, white folks, but I am sorry," before one of the lynchers shot him four times with the constable's revolver.[8]

On January 31, under pressure from Governor David Sholtz, State's Attorney Rex Farrior announced a grand jury investigation of Johnson's lynching, telling reporters, "We must not tolerate such a happening that spreads a blot on Tampa's history." The panel questioned 12 witnesses but returned no indictments. Afterward, Farrior told Governor Sholtz, "I did everything in my power to get an indictment," reporting that a majority of the grand jurors were in "sympathy with the lynching" and voted against removing Thomas Graves from office. The crime remains officially unsolved.[9]

Joe Love and Isaac Thomas
June 8, 1934; Alligator, MS

Accused of attempting to rape a white plantation manager's wife in Sledge, farmhands Love and Thomas were arrested in Greenwood, then seized by lynchers from

Sheriff W. T. Haynes and Deputy J. R. Spidle as they transported their prisoners to Clarksdale in Coahoma County. The mob hanged Love and Thomas from a railroad trestle near the tiny town of Alligator, in Bolivar County. Afterward, Deputy Spidle said both suspects had confessed to the attempted rape. Authorities made no arrests.[10]

Son Griggs
June 21, 1934; Kirbyville, TX

Jasper County's sheriff arrested 80-year-old Son Griggs for "consorting with" a wealthy white planter's 17-year-old daughter, whom the sheriff found in Griggs's cabin. Fearing a lynch mob, the sheriff sought to lodge Griggs in a stronger jail, at Orange, but some 200 whites intercepted his vehicle, seizing Griggs and hanging him from a roadside telephone pole, then riddling his corpse with bullets. Afterward, the lynchers cut him down and dragged him through the countryside behind a car. Authorities made no arrests.[11]

Richard Louis Wilkerson
June 24, 1934; Manchester, TN

On the evening of June 24 eight white men, including some from neighboring Franklin County, invaded an ice cream social held at Patton's Chapel Negro Church in Manchester. Their advances toward a black girl led to fighting and expulsion of the trespassers. Several of the men next visited Justice of the Peace Lee Cash at home, swearing out a warrant for "Dick Lou" Wilkerson's arrest on assault charges. Unsatisfied with that step, the eight next drove to Wilkerson's house, ransacking the place when they found he was not present. They finally overtook Wilkerson, walking home from the church, and shot him, afterward stripping his body and smashing his skull with an axe.[12] In a departure from Southern custom, the eight killers were indicted and convicted of manslaughter, but no record exists of any serving his prescribed prison time.[13]

Andrew McLeod
July 9, 1934; Bastrop, LA

Accused of attempting to rape a white woman, young farmer Andrew McLeod allegedly confessed his crime before a mob of 300 whites stormed the Morehouse Parish jail in broad daylight, battered down the doors, and hanged him from a tree in the courthouse square after slashing his throat. Police made no arrests.[14]

James Sanders
July 16, 1934; Bolton, MS

Residents of Bolton accused 25-year-old James Sanders of writing an "indecent letter" to a white girl. Lynchers seized him on July 16, then surrendered Sanders to three relatives of the girl who received the letter. Cast in newspaper accounts as "rescuers," the trio drove Sanders out of town, then stopped their car on a country lane, where Sanders allegedly grabbed a pistol from C. D. Lancaster's pocket and opened fire, forcing his son and brother to kill Sanders in self-defense. Hinds County's district attorney attended their preliminary hearing and recommended dismissal of all charges. A white businessman told reporters, "It was something that just had to be done."[15]

Henry Bedford
July 24, 1934; Pelahatchee, MS

Bedford committed the capital crime of "speaking disrespectfully" to a white man. On July 24 a mob dragged him from his home and whipped him to death. Authorities made no arrests.[16]

Grafton Page
August 3, 1934; Bethany, LA

White vigilantes whipped Page to death after accusing him of public drunkenness. Caddo Parish authorities filed no charges.[17]

Smith Houey and Robert Jones
August 13, 1934; Michigan City, MS

On July 2, 1933, an unknown bandit robbed and murdered white merchant Connis Gillespie in Michigan City, afterward setting fire to his store. While investigating that crime, Benton County deputy sheriff Mark Mason and another officer arrested two young sons of African American Frank Jones, then reportedly heard a pistol shot near Frank's home. Approaching the house without a search warrant, Mason kicked in the door and was killed by a shotgun blast from within. Robert Jones, a third son of Frank, admitted the shooting, saying he was in bed when Mason kicked the door, the officers had not announced themselves, and he believed the house was being robbed. At trial, an all-white jury convicted Jones of Mason's murder and sentenced him to die.[18]

Mississippi's Supreme Court startled the world on June 22, 1934, reversing Jones's conviction and ordering a new trial. The court proclaimed: "It is clear from the evidence that the constable had no right to enter the dwelling house at the time he was killed. The appellant was in his home and no person or officer had a right to enter except in strict accordance with the law. No matter how humble, a man's home is his castle and no one can enter without his consent."[19] That ruling led the *Kentucky New Era* to chastise "certain of our radical friends," declaring that Southern justice "is not always the ghastly travesty some of our critics like to make it," but the editors spoke too soon.[20]

The Jones verdict struck Benton County like a bombshell. In the period since Robert Jones had been imprisoned, officers had nabbed another black suspect, Smith Houey, in the Gillespie case, charging him with murder and confining him at Holly

Springs. Both prisoners were on their way to Ashland, Benton County's seat, for trial on August 13, Jones coming from Tupelo, with both under guard by sheriff's deputies. Those officers proved helpless when two mobs of white men seized their prisoners, then brought the pair together near Michigan City, hanging Jones and Houey from a tree 150 yards distant from the site of Deputy Mason's death. Sheriff R. H. Hudspeth and District Attorney Fred Belk promised a "thorough investigation," but no arrests resulted.[21]

Unidentified Man
August 23, 1934; Birmingham, AL

On this Thursday evening a black man armed with a pistol accosted three white girls passing through a city park on their way to a religious tent meeting, demanding any valuables they carried. While two girls grappled with him for the gun, the third ran a block to the tent gathering and summoned help. Armed men pursued the would-be bandit through darkness to an alley, where he was cornered and shot. The man, still unidentified today, died at a local hospital on August 24, without regaining consciousness. According to a newspaper report, "Police have not decided who fired the fatal shot that killed the Negro."[22]

Jerome Wilson
January 11, 1935; Franklinton, LA

On July 21, 1934, white "range rider" Joe McGee visited the Wilson farm in Franklin Parish, to inspect their livestock for mandatory "dipping" to kill parasites. He claimed that one mule was untreated, while the Wilsons denied it. McGee summoned help in the form of sheriff's deputies Delos C. Wood and McCauley McCain, accompanied by white civilian Brad Spears. Wood attempted to arrest Jerome Wilson and violence ensued, leaving Wood and Moise Wilson fatally wounded by gunfire, while Jerome Wilson and brother Luther suffered less serious wounds. Jurors convicted Jerome of murder on July 31 and sentenced him to die, but the state's supreme court overturned that verdict on January 8, 1935, finding that Wilson was denied a "fair and impartial trial." Three days later, before dawn on January 11, several white men entered the parish jail and shot Wilson dead in his cell. Sheriff J. C. Brock, still mourning the loss of his deputy, told reporters, "There wasn't any lynching. There wasn't any mob. There were just about six or eight men who were going about their business." No charges were filed in Wilson's murder.[23]

Anderson Ward
March 3, 1935; Maringuoin, LA

Local authorities arrested Ward for beating a white man who threatened him with a pistol. A white mob removed him from jail, hanged him from an oak tree, and shot his dangling body dozens of times. Police made no arrests.[24]

Ab Young
March 12, 1935; Slayden, MS

In March of 1935, African American suspect Ab Young was accused of killing a white highway worker in Marshall County. He fled to Rossville, Tennessee, where a mob of some fifty men captured him on March 12 and returned him to Mississippi. En route, the vigilantes debated whether they should burn Young alive or deliver him to the county sheriff at Holly Springs. Vengeance won out, although the murdered victim's brother pleaded with the lynchers not to mutilate Young. The mob allowed Young to sing a hymn before he was hanged at a schoolyard, his corpse used for target practice afterwards.[25] One witness to the crime, a Marshall County justice of the peace, told reporters, "I'm an officer, but my friends mean more to me than being an officer."[26] Authorities made no arrests.

T. A. Allen
March 21, 1935; Hernando, MS

The Rev. T. A. Allen was active in the Southern Tenant Farmers Union, organized in 1934 to challenge the power of white plantation owners. Worse than that, the union welcomed black and white sharecroppers on an equal basis. Violence plagued union organizers throughout the South, and Allen was one of the fatalities, kidnapped from Hernando and found in the Coldwater River, his corpse weighted with chains.[27] One report says authorities listed Allen's death as a "suicide."[28]

Daughter of A. B. Brookins
March 21, 1935; Poinsett County, AR

Sexagenarian minister A. B. Brookins was an organizer for the Southern Tenant Farmers' Union, seeking to improve the lot of impoverished serfs in Dixie, without regard to race. Whites reacted violently, beating Brookins at a black local meeting in Cross County, on November 20, 1934. Four months later, an armed mob attacked his home in Poinsett County, riddling the house with gunfire. Today, certain anonymous websites claim that Brookins lost an unnamed daughter to that murderous barrage, when in fact no one was killed.[29] According to contemporary reports, while the mob blazed away, "Brookins fled in his night clothes and his wife and child escaped the rain of bullets by hiding under the bed."[30]

Mary Green
March 22, 1935; Mississippi County, AR

Green, the wife of an African American minister, reportedly died from fright when a mob of white vigilantes invaded her home, seeking to lynch her husband.[31] Local inquiries revealed no further details on this case.

R. J. Tyrone
March 25, 1935; Lawrence County, MS

White neighbors fatally shot farmer R. J. Tyrone for being "too prosperous" during the Great Depression. Authorities made no arrests and the case remains officially unsolved.[32]

Unidentified Man
March 28, 1935; Hernando, MS

Local residents found the corpse of an African American man, still unidentified, shot several times and hanging with a rope around his neck in a gully outside town. In his pockets the victim carried several copies of Louisiana senator Huey Long's pamphlet "Every Man a King." A coroner's jury returned a verdict of suicide, although no firearm was found with the body.[33]

R. D. McGee
June 22, 1935; Wiggins, MS

Accused of raping an 11-year-old white girl, R. D. McGee was seized by a mob of some 300 lynchers. They hanged him from an oak tree near a local cemetery, riddled his dangling body with bullets, then cut McGee down and hanged him a second time, from a tree closer to the town's main highway. Authorities made no arrests.[34]

Bert Moore and Dooley Morton
July 15, 1935; Columbus, MS

White residents of Columbus blamed black farmers Moore and Morton for raping a white girl and attempting to rape a white married woman on July 10. Deputy Sheriff Parker Harris arrested the men on July 15 and was driving them to jail in Aberdeen, when six carloads of lynchers blocked his way. "Unable to resist," Harris surrendered his pris-

Bert Moore and Dooley Morton, lynched in Mississippi on July 15, 1935 (National Archives).

oners to the mob, which drove them eight miles south of Columbus to the Zion Church, there hanging both from a tree in the churchyard. A third suspect, named in press reports as Rayfield Sutton, evaded lynchers and bloodhounds, escaping into Alabama.[35]

Reuben Stacey
July 19, 1935; Fort Lauderdale, FL

Broward County sheriff's deputies arrested Stacey, a homeless tenant farmer, for allegedly staging "a murderous assault" on white victim Marion Jones. Subsequent accounts claimed Stacey had stabbed Jones, or at least threatened her with a knife, but a *New York Times* report said Stacey "had gone to the house to ask for food; the woman became frightened and screamed when she saw Stacy's face."[36] As threats of lynching spread, authorities decided to lodge Stacey in Dade County's jail for safekeeping, but a mob of 100 masked men lay in wait for the transfer. Seizing Stacey from Deputy Sheriff Virgil Wright, the lynchers took Stacey back to the Jones farm, hanged him near the house, and shot his dangling body 17 times. Police made no arrests.[37]

Spectators view Reuben Stacey, lynched in Florida on July 19, 1935 (National Archives).

Govan Ward
August 3, 1935; Louisburg, NC

Franklin County Sheriff J. T. Moore arrested Ward, a mentally retarded African American, for allegedly beheading a white farmer with an axe. A mob removed Ward from Moore's custody and hanged him, afterward firing dozens of bullets into his body. Authorities made no arrests.[38]

Bodie Bates
August 5, 1935; Pittsboro, MS

Calhoun County Sheriff Jack W. Powell jailed Bates for attempting to rape a white girl. Lynchers removed him from the lockup and hanged him from a bridge over the

Yalobusha River. Sheriff Powell made no arrests, claiming he possessed only "meager information" about the lynching.[39]

Elwood Higgenbotham
September 17, 1935; Oxford, MS

Lafayette County prosecutors charged Higgenbotham with killing a white planter. His trial concluded on September 17, with the jury retiring to consider its verdict at 6 p.m. Fifty impatient lynchers refused to wait, removing Higgenbotham from the Lafayette County jail at 9:30 p.m. and hanging him from a nearby tree. Police made no arrests.[40]

Lewis Harris
September 28, 1935; Vienna, GA

On September 22 Sheriff Bos Vinson received a report of a "disturbance" at "a Negro meeting" near Vienna, the seat of Dooly County. Arriving on the scene, Vinson found Harris with a jar of liquor, banned under Georgia's prohibition statute, and attempted to arrest him. Harris allegedly threatened Vinson with a pistol, then fled, but was hunted with bloodhounds and captured. Threats of lynching spread, and Vinson decided to move Harris on September 29, for safekeeping. While en route to Fitzgerald, in Ben Hill County, Vinson's vehicle was stopped by four carloads of white men who seized Harris, hanged him, and shot him multiple times. Authorities made no arrests.[41]

Bo Bronson
October 17, 1935; Moultrie, GA

While searching for another African American, suspected of killing a white man, a posse met Bronson in rural Colquitt County, beating and shooting him. He died soon after entering a local hospital. Although no evidence linked him to the recent murder, his slaying went unpunished.[42]

Two Unidentified Men
November 1, 1935; Gretna, LA

Jefferson Parish sheriff's deputies arrested two African American men on a charge of attempting to rape a white woman and transported them to a "mob-proof" jail in New Orleans, across the Mississippi River, for safekeeping. That night, three white men entered the jail and shot both prisoners dead in their cell. Authorities made no arrests.[43] No records survive to identify the victims.

Baxter Bell
November 4, 1935; White Bluff, TN

A constable arrested Bell for assault and battery after Bell allegedly struck a white woman in a rural tavern catering to African Americans. While en route to the Cheatham County jail in Ashland, the officer's car was stopped by five white men, including the woman's husband and four relatives, who overpowered the constable and kidnapped Bell. Searchers found him 30 minutes later, shot through the lungs at roadside. Authorities made no arrests.[44]

Ernest Collins and Bennie Mitchell, Jr.
November 11, 1935; Columbus, TX

Police arrested teenagers Collins and Mitchell for the rape and murder of white victim Geraldine Kollmann on October 17, 1935. The suspects reportedly confessed in custody, while a third, older man was briefly detained, then released with no charges filed. Colorado County Sheriff Frank Hoegemeyer transported Collins and Mitchell to jail in Houston for safekeeping, then returned with Deputy Berry Townsend to collect them for trial on November 11. White lynchers blocked the sheriff's car on a river bridge between Altair and Eagle Lake, seizing the prisoners and delivering them to the original crime scene, where a mob of 700 waited to hang them. Before his death, Mitchell implicated the older man released by Sheriff Hoegemeyer, who had since disappeared and was never apprehended.[45] After the lynching, county prosecutor O. P. Moore said, "I do not call the citizens who executed the Negroes a mob. I consider their action an expression of the will of the people."[46] None of the lynchers were arrested or publicly identified.

Mace Gray
January 16, 1936; Carthage, TX

A vigilante posse hunted Gray, after he struck two white girls with his car. Gray barricaded himself inside a barn, but was dragged out and riddled with bullets. Prosecutors filed no charges against the lynchers.[47]

Willie Jones
February 14, 1936; Mangum, OK

A mob of some 300 men hunted Jones for an alleged attack upon a white woman and her daughter, riddling him with bullets when they captured him. Greer County's sheriff called the original attack a bungled robbery.[48]

Philip Baker
March 14, 1936; Cusseta, GA

Sheriff's deputies arrested Baker on December 31, 1935, charging him with violent assaults on three women, two of them white. He was jailed in Macon for safekeeping, but a mob of 30 to 40 men was waiting when Chattahoochee County's sheriff brought him back for trial on March 14. The lynchers hanged Baker and riddled him with bullets. Although they were unmasked, the sheriff made no arrests.[49]

Lint Shaw
April 28, 1936; Danielsville, GA

Lynchers tried to seize Lint Shaw when he was charged with attempting to rape a white woman, but Judge Berry T. Moseley rose from his sickbed to stall the mob while Shaw was spirited away to Macon for safekeeping. Deputies later returned him to Danielsville, but another mob formed, prompting Shaw's relocation to a small jail in Royston, 10 miles distant. Vigilantes followed him and seized Shaw from the lone night watchman, returning him once more to Danielsville, where they riddled him with bullets. Police made no arrests.[50]

Willis Kees
April 29, 1936; Lepanto, AR

On April 18, white residents of Lepanto accused 19-year-old Willis Kees of attempting to rape a white woman. The mob showed rare leniency, whipping Kees and ordering him to leave town, but he returned on April 29 and was arrested by the town marshal. Before the officer could reach the local lockup with his prisoner, a masked mob seized Kees and shot him dead. Authorities made no arrests.[51]

John Rushin
May 3, 1936; Pavo, Georgia

Thomas County authorities blamed Rushin, a 55-year-old African American, for the death of a white man. Deputy Sheriff Herbert Kennedy arrested Rushin, but claimed a mob of some 200 men "snatched" the prisoner when he—Kennedy—turned his head to answer a question, while walking Rushin to his patrol car. The lynchers carried Rushin off and riddled him with bullets. Police made no arrests.[52]

A. L. McCamy
September 6, 1936; Dalton, GA

Whitfield County Sheriff J. T. Bryan suspected 21-year-old A. L. McCamy of attempting to rape a white woman. Despite the "victim's" denial of any criminal assault, and her insistence that she could not identify the man who invaded her residence, Bryan jailed McCamy at the county seat in Dalton. A mob of some 150 men arrived on September 6, and the lone jailer gave them his keys. Sheriff Bryan found McCamy's corpse four hours later, beneath a roadside tree where he had been hanged. No arrests resulted from the lynching.[53]

Buckie Young
September 11, 1936; Greenville, FL

A white lynch mob shot Young to death after he was accused of attempting to rape a white woman. Madison County's coroner refused to hold an inquest and authorities made no arrests.[54]

Tom Finch
September 12, 1936; Atlanta, GA

Tom Finch had worked for 10 years as an orderly at Grady Hospital, with an exemplary record, when he was accused of raping a mentally retarded white patient. The rape allegedly occurred in a small closet just off the crowded reception room of Grady's white clinic, adjacent to a busy doctor's office. Physicians, nurses, and other staff members agreed unanimously that the crime had not occurred. Police arrested Finch at home, at 9 p.m., and delivered him to the hospital seven hours later, near death from gunshot wounds. Officers claimed they shot Finch when he resisted arrest and attacked a policeman, then tried to flee on foot. Hospital records state that he was "shot five times in the breast" at close range. The slaying was deemed "justifiable homicide."[55]

J. B. Grant
December 4, 1936; Laurel, MS

According to the *Memphis Press-Scimitar*, a white mob lynched 17-year-old J. B. Grant (called "J. D." in one account), shooting him more than 100 times, then dragging his corpse through town behind a car before hanging it from a railroad trestle.[56] Oddly, neither report available today lists Grant's supposed offense, and his name does not appear on any other lists of U.S. lynching victims. My inquiries to local libraries and newspapers revealed nothing more on this case.

Mack Henry Brown
December 23, 1936; Roswell, GA

Brown, an apartment house janitor in Atlanta, allegedly "insulted" a white female tenant by kissing her hand. He disappeared soon afterward and was found weeks later, on December 23, floating in the Chattahoochee River at Roswell, handcuffed, with his feet bound, shot twice in the chest. On December 29, Fulton County Coroner Paul T. Donehoo blamed Brown's death on "a party or parties unknown." The crime remains unsolved.[57]

Wes Johnson
February 2, 1937; Headland, AL

Henry County Sheriff J. L. Corbitt charged Johnson with raping a white woman. Twenty-five carloads of white men seized Johnson from the county jail in Abbeville on February 2, hanged him near Headland, and shot his body to pieces. State attorney general A. A. Carmichael charged that "the wrong Negro was lynched" and filed impeachment proceedings against Sheriff Corbitt, charging him with willful neglect of duty. Alabama's supreme court exonerated Corbitt by a vote of four to two. No lynchers were indicted.[58]

Robert McDaniels and Roosevelt Townes
April 13, 1937; Duck Hill, MS

On December 30, 1936, an unknown gunman robbed and murdered white merchant George Windham at his store outside Duck Hill, in Montgomery County. Investigators learned that Roosevelt Townes had been seen in Duck Hill before the killing and left afterward, prompting a multi-state alert for his capture. Memphis police arrested Townes in April 1937, reporting that he had confessed and implicated acquaintance Robert "Bootjack" McDaniels. Delivered to Sheriff E. E. Wright on April 13, the prisoners were jailed at Winona and pled not guilty to the charges. Soon afterward, a mob formed at the courthouse and 12 men invaded the jail, seizing both inmates without resistance from Wright. A witness later said, "It was all very carefully planned and executed. Apparently each man had a job to do and did it with dispatch."[59]

Carried to some nearby woods, McDaniels and Townes were chained to trees before a mob of 300, including women and children. Torture began with blowtorches applied to each victim in turn, burning off fingers and ears, searing their torsos, before wood was piled around their feet, doused in gasoline and set ablaze, burning both men to death. A physician described the men as "burned to a crisp." Their death certificates cited "homicide by a mob ... burned with a blowtorch & dead wood."[60]

The torture slayings shocked America, at least above the Mason-Dixon Line. NAACP investigator Howard Kester reported his conclusion "that mob action was anticipated; that the sheriff of Montgomery County took no real precaution whatever to insure the accused a fair trial; that he made no effort to defend his prisoners against the mob; that he did not try to rescue the prisoners from the mob. Your investigator is reasonably convinced that the sheriff was in sympathy with the mob leaders and did not intend to permit the accused men to stand trial; and further that no effort will be made to identify the lynchers or to prosecute the murderers of Townes and McDaniels; and finally that local officials are incompetent to cope with such occurrences and that only the Federal government can safely intervene in such matters on behalf of justice and fair play."[61]

He was correct. Despite a former mayor of Duck Hill's statement that "there are a thousand people in Montgomery County who can name the lynchers," authorities filed no charges.[62]

Willie Reed
May 24, 1937; Bainbridge, GA

Accused of murdering two white women, one of whom was also raped, black suspect Willie Reed fled to Dothan, Alabama, and was captured there. Decatur County sheriff's deputies H. G. Pollock and R. A. Stephens retrieved him, fatally shooting Reed while en route to Bainbridge, when he allegedly tried to escape. A mob of 100 frustrated lynchers stormed the funeral home that had accepted Reed's body, burned the corpse, then dragged it through Bainbridge behind a car. Authorities declared Reed's shooting a case of justifiable homicide. No charges were filed against the rioters.[63]

Richard Hawkins and Ernest Powders
August 2, 1937; Tallahassee, FL

Police jailed Hawkins and Powders on charges of stabbing a city patrolman. Four masked whites removed the prisoners from jail, two blocks from the Leon County courthouse, and shot both fatally. When no arrests were made, Governor Frederick Cone told reporters, "This is a murder, not a lynching."[64]

Albert Gooden
August 17, 1937; Covington, TN

Authorities charged Gooden with fatally shooting Deputy Sheriff Chester Doyle on July 18, 1937, jailing him in Memphis for safekeeping. Tipton County Sheriff W. J. Vaughn was transporting Gooden back to Covington for trial on August 17, when six men stopped his car, seized the prisoner, and hanged Gooden. Vaughn made no arrests.[65]

Kirby
September 3, 1937; Mount Vernon, GA

White vigilantes executed a man known only as Kirby during their hunt for an African American rape suspect. Mount Vernon's mayor and another white man suffered wounds while trying to save Kirby's life.[66]

J. C. Evans
October 4, 1937; Milton, FL

Santa Rosa County Sheriff Joe Allen arrested Evans for robbing a gas station and committing an "unnatural crime" against a white boy. Four white men took Evans from the sheriff at gunpoint and subsequently executed him. Sheriff Allen made no arrests, saying he did not recognize the killers and had no means of identifying them.[67]

Washington Adams
June 10, 1938; Columbus, MS

On this Sunday, a white physician, Dr. James Lipscomb, was called to the home of handyman Washington Adams, where he found his long-time employee and friend in "moribund condition." Barely able to speak, Adams gasped that he was "choking to death," then described being dragged behind a car, prior to a three-hour beating by one "Mr. Thomas," a white man who had employed Adams sporadically over the past decade. Dr. Lipscomb transcribed Adams's last words, and signed his death certificate when Adams expired the same day.[68]

One version of this story claims that Adams owed ten dollars on his late wife's funeral expenses but was unable to raise the money in the midst of the Great Depression. On June 10 three white men reportedly accosted him, demanding the money, then beat him when he could not produce it.[69] Why an occasional employer of Adams would concern himself with such a debt remains unclear.

Lowndes County prosecutors ignored the incident, but Dr. Lipscomb soon became embroiled in controversy with Dr. R. W. Whitfield, Mississippi's director of vital statistics. Although we do not have Whitfield's original remarks, it seems that he took issue with comments penned by Dr. Lipscomb on the Adams death certificate. Lipscomb responded on July 4 with the following letter, presented here as he typed it, without corrections.

> I regret that I must take issue with you in regard to leaving out the "emotion" in the case of the death of Washington Adams. I am of the opinion that it played a very important part in this mans death for the following reasons:
> I knew this negro intimately—he worked at my house for four or five years—paddled my boat while I was fishing once or twice weekly—he had an Exopthalmic Goitre, also an enlarged knee—was not robust.
> I was talking to Wash in front of Caines Drug Store in Columbus Miss. at 5 p.m. June 10, 1938—he was in his usual state of health—at 8:45 p.m. of the same day I was called to his house—found him in a moribund condition—cold clammy sweat—pulseless at both wrists—eyes set in his head—hollering and screaming "I am dying," "I am choking to death"—tossing from one side of bed to other, saying first an auto mobile dragged me—then asking the people to go out of the room and saying feebly—"Mr. Thomas beat me, he beat me three hours, I am dying." I gave him 1/4 gr Morphine hypodermically waited about twenty minutes—still no pulse—he quieted a little—I did not want to see him die so I left. Died 9:30 p.m.
> Now then:
> He showed evidence along left side with some stripes, extending all the way to neck and left ear swollen, with lump above it—thyroid glands much enlarged—left buttock badly contused—no autopsy performed.
> The injury to body as manifested by objective symptoms did not seem sufficient to justify death, but Appletons Medical Dictionary, page 751 under definition of SHOCK, has this to say:
> SHOCK
> "A sudden depression of the vital functions, especially of the circulation, due to the

nervous exhaustion following an injury <u>or</u> a sudden <u>Overwhelming emotion</u>, and resulting either in <u>IMMEDIATE DEATH</u> or in prolonged prostration."

I respectfully submit that this highly nervous individual, with a goitre, being beaten by a man who he has regarded as his friend, he having worked for the ten or more years, was so Overwhelmed by the fact that he died of—

Cause of Death: SHOCK
Contributory Causes: Injury and OVERWHELMING EMOTION.[70]

Willie McDonald
July 1938; Newton, MS

Described in one newspaper account as an "insurance man," 26-year-old Willie McDonald allegedly entered a white woman's home dressed only in underwear, sometime in late July. Newton County sheriff's deputies arrested him for disturbing the peace, but while in transit to the county jail, McDonald (called "McDonnell" on his death certificate) reportedly struck Deputy J. M. Wells and tried to escape, whereupon he was shot multiple times and died instantly. Reference to "a mob" involved in McDonald's death suggests a lynching, but details are vague and no charges were filed.[71]

Tom Green
July 6, 1938; Sharkey County, MS

On the day in question, 48-year-old blacksmith Tom Green quarreled with his employer, white planter R. Purdy Flanagan, over the size of Green's latest paycheck. Furious, Flanagan fired Green on the spot and began sorting through Green's belongings, prior to Green leaving the plantation. Flanagan found a rifle, claiming it was his, while Green insisted that he owned the gun. As Flanagan brandished the weapon, Green drew a pistol and shot him three times, killing him. Green then fled to his cabin, a quarter-mile distant, and barricaded himself inside. Sheriff M. C. Keating rallied a 300-man posse to storm Green's home, resulting in Green's death when one L. H. Harris burst into the cabin and "blew the negro's head off" with a shotgun. Not satisfied, the mob tied Green's corpse behind a car, dragged it back to the scene of Flanagan's death, and set fire to the body. Still not sated, the lynchers dragged Green to the county seat at Rolling Fork and burned him a second time. With the sheriff involved, no charges were filed.[72]

John Dukes
July 6, 1938; Arabi, GA

A policeman sent to arrest Dukes for drunk and disorderly conduct shot the unarmed African American, but Dukes was still alive when a white mob gathered, dragged him several hundred yards from the shooting scene, then doused him with gasoline and burned him to death. Authorities made no arrests.[73]

Claude Banks
July 21, 1938; Canton, MS

On Thursday, July 21, white mill worker O. B. McAdams borrowed $50 from his boss and traveled 24 miles north from Brandon to Canton, ostensibly to visit his ailing daughter and pay her hospital bill. That evening, McAdams told police he was attacked and robbed by a knife-wielding black man, while walking through Canton's white residential district. According to Jackson's *Daily Clarion-Ledger*, a staunchly white-supremacist newspaper in those days, the fiend stabbed McAdams "numerous times about the face and body. He threw the white man to the ground and stamped on him with his boots officers said," leaving McAdams hospitalized "in critical condition."[74]

There is another version of that story, told by an undercover civil rights investigator who claimed McAdams suffered only "a few minor abrasions and scratches." Furthermore, he was last seen in Canton's black district, where friends from Brandon speculated that he had been seeking entertainment, either in a gambling den or elsewhere, being "frisked out of" the borrowed money. His daughter's bill had not been paid, and McAdams lost his job soon afterward.[75]

In any case, police and vigilantes responded to the claim of black-on-white crime in typical style, forming posses to track down the culprit. One group brought bloodhounds, following them to the home of a black minister named Jackson, where they arrested 26-year-old Earl Pate (called "John" in some reports), conveying him to jail. Meanwhile, other whites patrolled downtown streets, still seeking the robber. While that was underway, 23-year-old Claude Banks left a party at his girlfriend's house with companion Willie Jones, driving toward home. They met a group of white men bearing guns and flashlights, unaware of what was happening, and passed the "blockade" before shots rang out. At least one bullet struck Banks, killing him at the wheel, whereupon his car swerved and rolled into a roadside ditch. Jones, knocked unconscious, was arrested and dragged off to jail as another suspect. Mayor Charles N. Harris permitted reporters to photograph the corpse, but forbade any shots of the "posse."[76]

The *Clarion-Ledger* admitted that Banks was "believed to have no connection with the stabbing, but refused to heed warnings of the posse to stop and be questioned and paid with his life for his heedlessness." The legible portion of his death certificate reads, "Shot—hit by stray bullets," as if the shooting were an accident. Jones was released two hours after his arrest, with a warning to keep quiet or risk lynching, but later told friends of a debate among the shooters, one saying, "We've killed one, we might as well kill the other." Earl Pate spent several weeks in jail, then was freed in turn, despite police claims that they found him with blood-soaked clothing. No charges were filed against him, and Canton's whites made no attempts at extralegal punishment.[77]

Willis Banks, Claude's father, contacted Mayor Harris, requesting compensation for his son's death and the damage to his car. Harris refused, claiming the killers were not deputized and therefore did not represent the city. Witnesses who claimed police were present at the shooting and arrest of Willie Jones suggested that might be the reason why Harris prohibited photos of the posse.[78] No one was ever charged for killing Banks or for robbing O. B. McAdams.

Otis Price
August 9, 1938; Perry, FL

Accused of attempting to rape a white woman, Price was taken by lynchers from the Taylor County sheriff's custody and killed in a hail of bullets. Authorities made no arrests.[79]

W. C. Williams
October 13, 1938; Ruston, LA

Authorities in Lincoln Parish suspected 19-year-old W. C. Williams (called "R. C." in one report) of killing white victim R. M. Blair and beating (some accounts say raping) Blair's female companion. While Sheriff A. J. Thigpen tried to locate Williams, three white teenagers met him on a rural road and kidnapped him at gunpoint, delivering him to a lynch mob of some 3,000 persons. Sheriff Thigpen reportedly tried to negotiate with the mob, but in vain. The lynchers tortured Williams before he was hanged, shot, and burned.[80] In a letter to Louisiana senator A. J. Ellender, NAACP executive secretary Walter White predicted that no one would be charged with the crime. A parish grand jury proved him right on October 28, refusing to vote indictments despite the fact that the lynchers were unmasked and some were photographed.[81]

Louisiana lynchers with victim W. C. Williams, October 13, 1938 (Library of Congress).

Wilder McGowan
November 21, 1938; Wiggins, MS

At 8 p.m. on Sunday night, November 20, a 74-year-old white woman from a prominent family, mother of the town's only doctor, reported being robbed and raped at her home by "a light-colored negro with slick hair." A mob of some 200 whites organized, with bloodhounds, trailing 24-year-old suspect Wilder McGowan to his grandmother's home. They found him preparing to leave for Gulfport, where he worked at a fertilizer plant and was engaged to a schoolteacher. Reports differ as to whether the mob hanged McGowan at once, or held him in the woods until his supposed victim identified him—unlikely, it seems, since McGowan was dark-skinned, with "natural" hair.[82] Stone County Sheriff S. C. Hinton called the murder an "orderly lynching," telling reporters there was "no shooting and no disorder in the mob," then he ducked further questions, telling reporters he was "out investigating the case."[83]

While that investigation led nowhere, the NAACP conducted its own, collecting the names of 17 suspects and transmitting them to U.S. Attorney General Frank Murphy. According to the NAACP's report to Murphy:

> It is generally known that McGowan was innocent of the crime for which he was put to death and that the alleged crime was merely used as an excuse to lynch McGowan because he was a Negro who "did not know his place."
>
> We are informed that he was manly and refused to be intimidated by the ruffianly whites of Wiggins and had on several occasions been engaged in altercations when they sought to abuse and mistreat him; that on one occasion when a mob of armed drunken whites in an automobile ordered all the Negroes to run McGowan refused to do so and was attacked by the mob.
>
> He fought back and took a revolver from one of the white men, whereupon the mob let him alone. However, they bitterly resented his refusal to let them treat him as they wished.
>
> Recently, he was suspected of having slashed with a knife one of a group of whites who visited a Negro dance hall "looking for some good-looking nigger women." It is known that he was one of two or three young Negro men who resented this slur on their women and had a fist fight with the whites. He called for the lights to be put out and in the dark the whites were badly beaten and one cut on the arm.[84]

Lee Snell
April 29, 1939; Daytona Beach, FL

African American cab driver Lee Snell struck and killed a 12-year-old white bicyclist with his taxi. A policeman arrested him, but two older brothers of the accident victim took Snell from the officer's custody and fatally shot him. NAACP spokesmen called the murder a lynching, but leaders of the Southern Women for the Prevention of Lynching disagreed, saying that two killers did not constitute a "mob." In either case, the result was the same. Prosecutors filed no charges against the killers.[85]

Joe Rogers
May 8, 1939; Canton, MS

A church deacon and choir member, Rogers (sometimes spelled "Rodgers") worked at the Dinkman Lumber Mill in Canton. In May 1939 his white foreman told Rogers to move his family from their present lodgings to a house owned by the company, but Rogers refused, since rent on the new place was higher. On May 6 Rogers found an unexpected sum deducted from his weekly pay to cover rent on the house he had rejected. When Rogers confronted his foreman on May 8, the supervisor struck him with a fist, then reached for a nearby shovel. Rogers grabbed the spade first and struck the foreman with it before bystanders separated the two men. Rogers left work and was never seen alive again. On May 11 a constable pulled his corpse from the Pearl River, bound hand and foot, badly beaten and shot several times, with wounds suggesting torture with hot irons. The local *Madison County Herald* ignored the murder, and police warned African Americans not to discuss it. The case remains officially unsolved.[86]

O'Dee Henderson
May 9, 1940; Fairfield, AL

Henderson was an African American employee of the Tennessee Coal and Iron Railroad Company, a major mining firm with extensive railroad operations. Around 7:30 a.m. on May 9, 1940, he bumped into white coworker M. M. Hagood outside the company's office in Fairfield, and an altercation ensued. Hagood summoned Patrolman W. T. Glenn, telling him that Henderson had knocked him—Hagood—to the ground. Glenn immediately handcuffed Henderson, permitting Hagood to beat the prisoner while Glenn dragged him toward Glenn's patrol car. At the police station, Glenn handcuffed Henderson to a chair and the beating continued, while Henderson pleaded, "Have mercy on me" and "Let me explain." According to witness D. M. Flourney, Hagood struck Henderson repeatedly with a blackjack, a leather strap, and a rubber hose. Officer Thomas Nelson also beat Henderson with a blackjack, while Officer Glenn and Sergeant W. G. Cook stood watching. Finally, when Henderson was barely recognizable, Nelson shot him three times in the chest, killing him instantly.[87]

Fairfield's coroner ruled Henderson's death an "unjustifiable homicide," while Methodist minister Ted Hightower called for a city council investigation. Mayor Claude N. Gilley convened the council, requesting that Officers Cook, Glenn and Nelson be dismissed. Nelson was suspended for 30 days pending further investigation, during which Sgt. Cook testified that 20 to 30 similar beatings had occurred at Fairfield police headquarters during his three years with the department. Nonetheless, a resolution to dismiss the trio lost by one vote from the council. Prosecutors charged Nelson with first-degree manslaughter, but white jurors accepted his self-defense plea at trial, voting for acquittal.[88]

Elbert Williams
June 20, 1940; Brownsville, TN

Few white residents of Brownsville noticed when African Americans organized a local chapter of the NAACP in early 1940, but that changed in May, when members tried to register as voters for the year's presidential election. Shortly after midnight on June 16, Night Marshal Tip Hunter led a mob of 60 men who snatched Elisha Davis from his home and carried him to the bank of the Forked Deer River, where they threatened to lynch him if he did not reveal the NAACP chapter's membership and future plans. Davis told them everything he knew, whereupon Hunter ordered him to leave Brownsville and never return under pain of death. Again, Davis complied, soon followed by his family, abandoning their home, farmland, livestock, and a prosperous filling station to settle in Michigan.[89]

Four days after kidnapping Davis, vigilantes abducted Elbert Williams, secretary off the Brownsville NAACP chapter. Marshal Hunter initially lodged him in jail with Thomas Davis, Elisha's brother, then released Davis while keeping Williams in custody. Three days later, Williams's body surfaced in the Hatchee River, bearing obvious signs of torture. Annie Williams identified her husband's corpse before leaving Brownsville forever. NAACP investigators Walter White and Thurgood Marshall identified members of the mob, passing their names to state authorities, but Haywood County's grand jury refused to indict the killers. The FBI conducted a pro forma investigation, working closely with Marshal Hunter throughout, and reported no grounds for federal prosecution.[90]

Jesse Thornton
June 21, 1940; Luverne, AL

Thornton was a chicken farmer and general handyman, living in Luverne, the seat of Crenshaw County, with wife Nellie Thomas, since 1935. On the last day of his life, Thornton was idling with friends outside the town's barbershop with Officer Doris Rhodes approached, prompting Thornton to say, "There comes Doris Rhodes, boys." Overhearing the "disrespectful" comment, Rhodes confronted Thornton, demanding, "What did you say?" Thornton amended his remark to say "Mr. Doris Rhodes," whereupon Rhodes snarled, "No you didn't nigger." After Thornton grudgingly confessed, "I did say Doris Rhodes," Rhodes struck him with a blackjack, knocking him down, then placed him under arrest.[91]

Walking Thornton to jail, Rhodes momentarily released his grip to unlock the cell door, and Thornton bolted, trying to escape. Outside, a crowd had gathered and began to pelt the fugitive with bricks and stones. Though injured, he outdistanced them, until a flurry of five gunshots struck him from behind. Even then, he ran on for three-quarters of a mile before collapsing in exhaustion, weak from loss of blood. The mob seized Thornton, placed him in a pickup truck and drove him to a dead-end street, then dragged him off into a nearby marsh and pumped more bullets into him. From there, the lynchers returned to the barbershop, learned Thornton's address, and descended on his home. Pretending innocence, they asked Thornton's wife where he was, then threatened to return later, at which time they said she had "better tell" his location.[92]

Apparently planning an alibi, the mob next visited Mayor Tima King at his downtown office. On King's orders, the lynchers kidnapped Thornton's wife that night and held her prisoner for hours, threatening her life if she told anyone about their visits to her home. A fisherman found Thornton's vulture-ravaged body near the Pataylagga River on June 28 and called authorities, who identified Thornton from a gold watch in his pocket. Learning of the murder, NAACP attorney Thurgood Marshall wrote to the

Death certificate of Jesse Thornton, shot for failing to call a policeman "sir" (Civil Rights Archive).

DOJ on August 13, requesting an investigation of official complicity in Thornton's lynching. U.S. Assistant Attorney General John Rogge ordered an investigation on August 26, but FBI agents took their cue from racist Director J. Edgar Hoover, already at war with the DOJ's recently formed Civil Liberties Unit. The investigation, if it ever occurred, achieved nothing.[93]

Austin Callaway

September 8, 1940; LaGrange, GA

Police charged Callaway with attempting to rape a white woman. Near midnight on the day of his arrest, six masked men removed him from the Troup County jail and shot him to death. Authorities made no arrests.[94]

Bruce Tisdale

February 25, 1941; Andrews, SC

Five white men—Earl Barnes, John Cribb, Carl Eagerton, Lonnie Fulton, and Luther Morris—attacked 37-year-old Bruce Tisdale without apparent motive on February 20,

1941, inflicting head wounds that claimed his life, at a local hospital, five days later. A coroner's inquest found that all five "are all responsible for the death of Bruce Tisdale and are to be held for higher courts."[95] Georgetown County's grand jury indicted all five for murder, but matters were never that simple in Jim Crow South Carolina. At trial, after presentation of the state's evidence, prosecutors *nol prossed* the charges against defendants Barnes, Eagerton and Fulton, leaving them unpunished for their roles in Tisdale's murder. White jurors convicted Cribb and Morris on a reduced charge of manslaughter, resulting in seven-year prison terms. Both appealed those verdicts, then dropped their appeals on April 13, 1942, and began serving their time.[96]

Felix Hall

April 1941; Fort Benning, GA

Private Felix Hall volunteered for service in the U.S. Army and was stationed at Fort Benning, Georgia, for training with an all-black military unit. On April 3 soldiers found his corpse hanging from a tree in a wooded area of the base, dressed in full uniform, hands tied or wired behind his back. Postmortem examination revealed that Hall had been dead "for some time" when found. Other African American recruits reported the incident in letters home to their families in Columbus, Ohio, and copies of those letters found their way to the local NAACP chapter, which reported the apparent lynching to that organization's Washington headquarters. NAACP leaders wrote to President Franklin Roosevelt and Secretary of War Henry Stimson, demanding a full and open investigation. Base commanders initially ignored the condition of Hall's body, calling his death a suicide, then relented and admitted they had no idea who might have been responsible. Eight months later, the Japanese raid on Pearl Harbor and America's entry into World War II eclipsed Hall's case, which remains officially unsolved today.[97]

Robert Sapp

May 6, 1941; Blakely, GA

Accused of stealing from his white employer, Sapp was beaten by three men armed with clubs and a piece of heavy machine belting. He suffered fatal injuries and died several days later. Police filed no charges.[98]

A. C. Williams

May 13, 1941; Quincy, FL

Police charged Williams, an African American, with attempting to rape a 12-year-old white girl. A gang of lynchers removed him from jail and beat Williams severely, leaving him for dead, but passers-by found him alive and called for help. An ambulance arrived and was conveying Williams to a hospital when the lynch mob learned of his survival and waylaid the emergency vehicle, this time shooting him fatally in a rare case of "double lynching."[99]

Bob White
June 11, 1941; Conroe, TX

A plantation laborer from Houston, White traveled to Livingston, Texas, in summer 1937 to help his mother pick cotton. One August night, white resident Ruby Cochran reported that a black stranger had raped her in her home. Her description of the rapist said only that he "was barefooted, that he had very offensive breath, and was undoubtedly a negro." The next day, acting without arrest warrants, Polk County's sheriff and Cochran's three brothers seized 16 black workers from a nearby cotton field, ordering them to parrot the threats Mrs. Cochran recalled from her ordeal. On that evidence alone, she declared herself certain that White was the rapist. Held incommunicado for a week, beaten daily by Texas Rangers, White finally signed a confession.[100]

At his first trial, with would-be lynchers loitering outside Polk County's courthouse, White was convicted and sentenced to die. In 1938 the Texas Court of Criminal Appeals reversed that verdict, ordering a new trial on grounds that the prosecutor's prejudicial closing argument effectively denied White due process.[101] Defense attorney J. P. Rogers secured a change of venue to Conroe, 50 miles from Livingston, but a second white jury once again voted to execute White. This time, White appealed to the U.S. Supreme Court, which ordered a retrial on grounds that his confession was coerced.[102]

White's third trial convened in Conroe on June 11, 1941. Before opening arguments began, W. S. "Dude" Cochran—Ruby Cochran's husband—rose in court and shot White in the back of the head, killing him instantly. Spectators shook Cochran's hand before deputies led him away, soon to be released on $500 bond. At his murder trial, a week later, the prosecutor asked jurors to acquit Cochran and they happily agreed, deliberating less than two minutes before finding him "not guilty."[103] Cochran's widow was too frightened to claim his body, which lay in the morgue until it was consigned to a pauper's grave.[104]

Cleo Wright
January 25, 1942; Sikeston, MO

In the predawn hours of Sunday, January 25, a black intruder entered the home of Grace Sturgeon, a white soldier's wife. The stranger attacked her, slashing Sturgeon's abdomen so deeply with a knife that her intestines spilled out. Almost incredibly, she managed to survive, while the invader fled on foot. Thirty minutes later, night marshal Hess Perrigan and civilian neighbor Jesse Whittley were driving toward Sunset Addition, Sikeston's black ghetto, when they spotted Wright, a 26-year-old oil mill worker. Noting blood on his clothes, they stopped him, removed a bloodstained knife from his pocket, and placed him under arrest. En route to jail, while Perrigan beat him and held a gun to his head, Wright drew a second knife and stabbed the constable in his face, whereupon Perrigan shot Wright at least four times (some versions say eight).[105]

The night's three victims all reached Sikeston's small General Hospital, where doctors saved their lives. From there, officers took Wright to jail, where he allegedly confessed, not once but twice, to stabbing Grace Sturgeon. At 11:35 a.m. a mob stormed the jail, brushing aside prosecutor David Blanton, and carried Wright from his unguarded cell, dragging him behind a car to Sunset Addition, there stopping outside a black Baptist church. Horrified worshipers watched while the mob doused Wright with gasoline and burned him to death in the street. FBI agents identified 20 members of the lynch mob, who acted unmasked in broad daylight, but when a grand jury convened six weeks later, none were indicted.[106]

Howard Wilpitz
February 21, 1942; Brookshire, TX

A recent army draftee, 32-year-old Howard Wilpitz was celebrating his last night at home in Brookshire, 35 miles west of Houston, when two armed white men crashed the party. Constable Fred "Fritz" Abel, accompanied by civilian night watchmen Hope Cooper, accused Wilpitz of disturbing the peace and ordered him to leave town at once. When Wilpitz protested, Abel pistol-whipped him, then shot Wilpitz in the leg as he fled. Drawing his own gun, Wilpitz shot the revolver from Abel's hand, then ran on to hide in an outhouse behind the Negro Odd Fellow's Hall, two blocks from his home. Abel and Cooper summoned reinforcements, leading a mob of 25 to 30 men who laid siege to the privy, riddling it with bullets, continuing the fusillade even after Wilpitz tumbled from the outhouse, lifeless.[107]

Two white women informed Olivia Jacobs that her common-law husband was dead, but white mortician A. H. Muske refused to let Jacobs or any other African Americans view the corpse, holding it for a week until members of the "posse" wrapped it in a sack containing lime and acid, burying Wilpitz outside Brookshire at an undisclosed location, without any funeral service. Next, the lynchers went door-to-door, warning black residents to keep silent under threat of death. A reporter from the Associated Negro Press broke the story in March, prompting an NAACP investigation, but attorney Thurgood Marshall described the incident as "an exchange of gunfire," whereupon headquarters lost interest. A Waller County grand jury returned no indictments.[108]

Thomas P. Foster
March 22, 1942; Little Rock, AR

Foster was drafted into the U.S. Army in June 1941, in Baltimore. Assigned to the 92nd Engineers, he had earned sergeant's stripes by the time his company moved to Camp Joseph T. Robinson, in North Little Rock, shortly after the Japanese raid on Pearl Harbor. At 5:45 p.m. on March 22, two white military policemen arrested Private Albert Glover, a member of Foster's African American company, for public intoxication at the corner of West Ninth and South Gaines Streets. Glover later admitted being drunk and denied clear memories of the event, but published reports say he resisted arrest, encouraged by a crowd of black onlookers. City patrolmen Abner J. Hay and George Henson soon arrived and joined the struggle, beating Glover with their nightsticks.[109]

Sergeant Foster, who outranked the two MPs, stepped forward, demanding to know why they let civilian police beat a soldier. According to the hundreds of eyewitnesses, Hay and Henson then dragged Foster to the steps of a nearby church, clubbing him to the pavement. As Foster lay dazed, Hay stood over him and shot him five times at close range, while the MPs held bystanders at bay with drawn pistols. After the shooting, Hay reloaded his revolver, then calmly stood smoking a pipe until his superiors arrived. Foster was transported to University Hospital, where he died several hours later. Subsequent reports claim Hay was "looking for a nigger" to kill, as revenge for the slaying of his father—a city detective—by a black felon some time earlier.[110]

NAACP leaders joined members of 92nd Engineers and the Citizens Committee of Greater Little Rock in petitioning U.S. Attorney General Francis Biddle for an investigation and prosecution of Officer Hay. Meanwhile, the army welcomed Hay into its ranks before a federal grand jury convened. That panel, by a vote of 19 to 4, declined to indict Hay for murder. A marginal notation, handwritten on the application for Foster's headstone, reads: "Death was not in line of duty and was result of own misconduct."[111]

Willie Vinson
July 13, 1942; Texarkana, TX

Vinson was hospitalized when a white woman accused him of rape. Unrestrained by authorities, a lynch mob snatched him from his bed, dragged him through town behind a speeding car, and hanged him from a cotton gin's winch. Governor Coke Stevenson dismissed the murder, telling reporters, "Even a white man would have been lynched for this crime."[112]

James Edward Persons
October 12, 1942; Vermilion County, IL

White residents of Vermilion County and neighboring Vigo County, Indiana, cowered in their homes during an autumn "reign of terror" by an unidentified black man, said to approach farmhouses after nightfall. The prowler injured no one, but roused public wrath by appearing at J. W. Strickland's farm and others, shouting, "Water, water, give me water!" Sheriff John Trierweiler organized a posse and scoured the countryside, spotting a suspect on October 12 and firing shots as he climbed over a fence, then lost him in dense timber.[113]

On November 26 two hikers found the fugitive dead on the Van Wright farm, a mile from the October shooting scene. Papers on the corpse identified him as 33-year-old James Edward Persons, from Somerville, Tennessee. According to a local newspaper, the documents suggested that Persons "may have been" a deserter from the U.S. Army's Fourth Battalion Quartermaster Corps, based in Louisiana.[114]

Questions surrounded the case, including the legality of gunning down a man who had committed no known crime. Two exhumations and belated autopsies prompted hearings by a special federal grand jury, convened in East St. Louis on July 12, 1943. One day later, the panel indicted 13 posse members, including John Trierweiler and three former deputies: Herbert Beasley, James Elliott, and Pearl Miller. The rest were farmers drafted for the manhunt: Errett Bozarth, brother Kenneth Bozarth, Edward Garwood, James Houston, Martin Kiado, Guy C. Morris, Ernest Poynter, Charles Price, and Hubert Tweedy. The indictment charged Kiado and Morris with shooting Persons; the others were charged with conspiracy to violate his civil rights.[115]

Eight of the farmers posted bond on July 14. Kenneth Bozarth, having joined the U.S. Navy since the shooting, would be served with his arrest warrant in boot camp. Ex-sheriff Trierweiler and his three former aides declined to grace the court with their presence, but turned up on July 16 to request a special hearing. Twelve of the defendants entered not-guilty pleas on November 12, 1943, while Kenneth Bozarth remained at his wartime duty station.[116]

Further disposition of the case awaited the demise of Adolf Hitler's Third Reich and the Empire of Japan. On December 9, 1946, the nine farmers—hailed by defense attorney W. M. Acton as "the cream of their community"—pled *nolo contendere* to their conspiracy charge and paid fines of $200 each. Assistant U.S. Attorney Ray Foreman then *nolle prossed* the indictments of Trierweiler and his three deputies, effectively absolving the former lawmen of any responsibility for their posse's actions.[117]

Ernest Green and Charles Lang
October 12, 1942; Clarke County, MS

Fourteen-year-olds Green and Lang were scavenging for scrap metal and rubber along Highway 45, south of Shubuta, when their path crossed that of a white girl, 13-year-old Dorothy Martin on October 10. She displayed no fear, remained to talk with them, and failed to note a passing motorist who saw the three and hurried into town. What happened next remains a matter of debate. The busybody either roused Clarke County Sheriff Lloyd McNeal, reporting an attempted rape in progress, or approached Martin's father directly, claiming he had seen two "niggers" chasing and harassing Dorothy. When Dorothy came home to angry parents, she had no choice but to rubber-stamp the lie.[118]

A few hours later, Deputy Sheriff Ed McClendon arrested Green and Lang at their respective homes, presenting them to Justice of the Peace W. E. Eddins. In what Sheriff McNeal later called "a fair-and-square hearing," both youths allegedly confessed to attempted rape. Dorothy, meanwhile, experienced a change of heart and urged her father to exonerate the boys, but he was in no mood for reason. Lodged at the Clarke County jail in Quitman, Green and Lang remained secure until October 12, when a group of white men "tricked" their way inside and "forced" town marshal G. F. Dabbs to surrender his keys. Later that day, authorities found Green and Lang dangling from Shubuta's infamous "hanging bridge," site of a previous quadruple lynching in 1918.[119]

Madison Jones, youth secretary of Mississippi's NAACP, described the victims' injuries. Aside from being hanged, he said, "Their reproductive organs were cut off. Pieces of flesh had been jerked away from their bodies with pliers and one boy had a screwdriver rammed down his throat so that it protruded from his neck." Once removed from the bridge and returned to their families, Green and Lang were buried outside Shubuta's "white" graveyard by a work gang from the county prison.[120]

The double lynching, perpetrated in the midst of America's second world war to "save democracy," sparked outrage in the North. FBI agents exhumed the victims in a futile search for evidence, discomfiting Governor Paul B. Johnson, Sr., who—despite expression of "regrets" and a promise to "investigate" the lynching—told reporters, "These prejudices are in-born in us. You know there's nobody down here would sit down with a Negro and eat with him at the same table. You know we'd rather die first.

Our feelings toward the Negro are our own business, and certain people in the North are trying to make it their business. The President's wife, for instance. And that's bad. We're a very proud people in the South, in Mississippi, and you just make us mad that way."[121]

Johnson need not have feared that justice would prevail. No charges were filed in the double lynching, although Deputy McLendon, years later on his deathbed, allegedly confessed remorse for his role in the murders.[122]

Howard Wash
October 17, 1942; Laurel, MS

Five days after the lynching of Ernest Green and Charles Lang, Mississippi racists claimed another victim, some 30 miles distant from the double-hanging scene. African American laborer Howard Wash stood convicted of killing his employer, a white dairy farmer. At trial, Wash pled self-defense, and several white jurors apparently believed him, since they recommended life imprisonment over execution. Furious, a white mob removed Wash from the Jones County jail and hanged him on October 17. Authorities made no arrests.[123]

Robert Hall
January 30, 1943; Newton, GA

In 1943 the federal government rated Baker County among the most backward regions of Georgia, lacking even a railroad depot. Its racial climate was equally archaic, with a black majority of 60 percent rigidly controlled by the county's white minority. In 1936, believing that Sheriff Jack Griffin, Jr., "coddled" African Americans, white voters chose Mack Claude Screws—a 39-year-old farmer-turned-grocer—to succeed him and "manage" the problem.[124] Seven years later, through a revolting act of brutality, Screws made legal history.

One method Screws employed to "handle" blacks was randomly disarming them, in defiance of Georgia state law and the U.S. Constitution's Second Amendment. Late in 1942, learning that 22-year-old mechanic Robert Hall had acquired a pearl-handled revolver, Deputy Frank Jones stole it from the glove compartment of Hall's pickup truck and gave it to Screws. Hall's father made the first attempt to retrieve it, but Screws dismissed him. Next, Hall tried the county grand jury, which summoned Screws and questioned the illegal confiscation. Screws replied, "If any of these damn Negroes think they can carry pistols, I am going to take them." He then cursed the panel and warned its members "if the grand jury thought they could do anything to stop him, to go ahead and do it."[125]

Frustrated but determined, Hall hired white attorney Robert Culpepper, Jr., to sue Screws for return of the pistol. Culpepper sent Screws a warning letter, received on January 29, 1943, which triggered a brutal chain of events. Raging at Hall as "biggety Negro" and "a leader among the colored," Screws forged an arrest warrant charging Hall with stealing a nonexistent truck tire. Late that night, accompanied by Deputy Jones and city policeman Jim Bob Kelley, Screws arrested Hall at home, handcuffing him in full view of his wife and father. The officers began beating Hall en route to jail in Newton, and continued on arrival, dragging Hall to a public pump in the center of town, where they beat Hall for 15 to 30 minutes with fists and a two-pound iron blackjack. The assault and Hall's outcries roused multiple white witnesses who watched the entire episode. Finally, the trio dragged Hall inside the jail by his feet and dumped him into a cell.[126]

In the early hours of January 30 black ambulance driver Manley Poteat received a summons to the jail. He described Hall's condition as follows: "He was bloody and full of dirt and he was unconscious but crawling around on his all fours. The back of his head was beaten to a pulp and he was in a pool of blood. His head was swollen so that his eyes were closed.... There was a hole in his left temple. There was a gash an inch and one-half in the top right side of his head." Poteat drove Hall to a black hospital in Albany, 22 miles away, where he died within an hour of arrival. Mortician Walter Poteat, Manley's father, received Hall's corpse and noted the evidence of a savage beating.[127]

FBI agents investigated Hall's death after a the local prosecutor declared himself "helpless in the matter."[128] Screws visited various witnesses, trying to intimidate them with expressions of a hope that they "can still be friends." Most persevered to testify before a federal grand jury, which indicted all three officers for violating Hall's civil rights. At trial, Screws tried to rewrite history, telling the jury Hall had not been handcuffed when arrested, and that he had pulled a hidden sawed-off shotgun on arrival at the jail, firing a blast that barely missed Screws, forcing the officers to beat him down. Jones struck Hall "a lick or two" with his blackjack, Screws said, while the sheriff "was beating him about the face and head with my fist." Once Hall was disarmed, Screws testified, "We didn't hit him on the ground."[129]

Every civilian witness to the beating contradicted Screws, flatly denying any gunshots or the presence of a shotgun, which was never entered into evidence by the defense. Attorneys *did* produce staged photographs, attempting to discredit prosecution witnesses, but FBI experts revealed that they were fraudulent.[130] More damning still was the testimony of James P. Willingham, relating a conversation with Deputy Jones.

> He told me that the Negro had a mighty good pistol and they had taken it away from him and the Negro acted so damn smart and went before the court in some way trying to make them give it back to him ... and they went out there that night with a warrant and arrested him and handcuffed him and brought him to town and the Negro put up some kind of talk about wanting to give bond or something to that effect and they beat hell out of him; then, that when they got him up to the well they whipped him some more and he died shortly afterwards. He said the Negro attempted to shoot them at the well; said the Negro attempted to shoot them at the well with a shotgun and said he hit him with a blackjack pretty hard and I asked him about how in the world did the Negro try to shoot you and you had him handcuffed and he said well we finished him off and that is all.[131]

Jurors convicted the three officers, followed by imposition of the maximum one-year prison term with a $1,000 fine. The Eleventh Circuit Court of Appeals upheld their conviction, but the U.S. Supreme Court accepted the case for review in April 1944, based on a defense complaint that "there is a special division of the Department of Justice of the United States commonly known as the Civil Rights Division whose personnel is militant in seeking to expand the law by the prosecution of state officers for assaulting prisoners." Both sides presented arguments on October 20, 1944, and the court overturned the convictions by a vote of five to four, on May 7, 1945. All nine justices deemed Hall's murder "a shocking and revolting episode in law enforcement," but five declared that Hall's slayers had not "willfully" set out to violate his civil rights by killing him.[132]

A public murder did not harm to Sheriff Screws, politically. Baker County whites overwhelmingly elected him to a third term in 1944, and to three more after that, retaining Screws as sheriff until 1957—when they elected him to Georgia's state senate. Screws served one two-year term, then retired from politics. He died in February 1965, 11 days short of his 68th birthday.[133]

William Walker
May 30, 1943; Centreville, MS

Walker joined the U.S. Army in Chicago, following the Pearl Harbor raid, and was assigned to the all-black 364th Infantry Regiment, initially posted to protective guard duty with the Western Defense Command's Southern Land Frontier Sector at Phoenix, Arizona. While there, the unit was involved in two serious disturbances: first when 500 soldiers refused their commander's order to disperse, and again on November 26, 1942—Thanksgiving night—when 100 soldiers engaged in a firefight with military police, leaving three persons dead and 12 seriously wounded. Sixteen participants in that affray received 50-year prison terms, while the regiment's commander and executive officer were replaced.[134]

In May 1953 the 364th was transferred to Camp Van Dorn, near Centreville, Mississippi, arriving in two groups on May 26th and 28th. Black soldiers resented the move to a rigid Jim Crow atmosphere, revealing their displeasure through slovenly dress, discourtesy to officers, and curfew violations. On May 28, when a post exchange closed early due to "threatening behavior" by members of the 364th, several hundred looted and vandalized the shop. The following day, 75 soldiers roamed through Centreville, allegedly cursing at whites, confronting police and deputized civilians, dispersing only when MPs arrived.[135]

In that atmosphere, on May 30, white MPs accompanied by Wilkinson County Sheriff Richard Whitaker stopped William Walker in Centreville, challenging him for being out of uniform (a button missing from his shirt) and leaving base without a pass. Some sources say a fight ensued; others claim the MPs clubbed Walker and he defended himself, prompting an MP sergeant to order his summary execution. Whichever version is correct, Walker was fleeing when Sheriff Whitaker shot him in the back, killing him instantly.[136]

When word of Walker's death reached Camp Van Dorn, several hundred soldiers stormed the armory, seizing rifles with intent of raiding Centreville. Colonel R. E. Guthrie, commanding the base, dispatched black MPs to disperse the mob, wounding one soldier before tenuous order was restored.[137] Governor Paul Johnson, Sr., dispatched National Guardsmen and highway patrolmen to Centreville, but military officers met them near Brookhaven, informing them that the situation was under control.[138]

Unconvinced, Johnson contacted Mississippi senators Theodore Bilbo and James Eastland, seeking a federal investigation and assurances that no more black soldiers would be garrisoned in the Magnolia State. Centreville mayor Omer Carroll sent the War Department a telegram reading: "Urgently request that steps be taken to have the

364th infantry recently ordered here removed by the war department to northern station. This regiment is fomenting race riots and openly boasts they have come to clean Mississippi out. Have had no trouble with other colored troops until arrival of this regiment from Arizona some days ago. Consider this request of utmost urgency as serious race riots are expected if this regiment is allowed to remain here."[139]

General Lesley James McNair, commander of Army Ground Forces, refused to transfer the 364th. Instead, he ordered the unit confined to base and stripped of privileges until it "demonstrated its worthiness," beginning with exposure of the regiment's "real troublemakers." Major General Virgil Peterson, the army's Inspector General, agreed, and relative peace was restored until July 3, when soldiers from the 364th disrupted a dance at the camp. Finally, Peterson declared that "due to the attitude of civilians in this locality relative to racial matters and to the presence of large numbers of northern Negroes, there exists considerable danger of racial disturbances in the general vicinity of this camp." He recommended transfer of the unit overseas.[140]

Army records indicate that the 364th was shipped to the Aleutian Islands in March 1944, replacing a white unit on garrison duty and remaining there until war's end in 1945.[141] A radically different story surfaced in 1998, when Mississippi banker-turned-author Carroll Case published *The Slaughter*, a "fact-based novel" describing the alleged mass murder of 364th Regiment soldiers—1,227 in all—by white MPs at Camp Van Dorn in autumn 1943. Case quoted one alleged participant in the massacre, the late William Martzell, as saying, "We had the whole area sealed off—it was like shooting fish in a barrel. We opened fire on everything that moved, shot into the barracks, shot them out of trees, where some of them were climbing, trying to hide." Afterward, the dead were allegedly buried in mass graves, subsequently covered by a 12-acre lake, while survivors of the 364th began their long journey to the Aleutians.[142]

Publication of *The Slaughter* prompted calls for an investigation from NAACP leaders, Mississippi congressmen, and black journalists. Army headquarters denied all charges, published aerial photos of Camp Van Dorn revealing no lakes nearby, and released personnel records from the 364th Infantry. Carroll Case himself, while citing two civilian witnesses to the alleged massacre, admits that during 15 years of research he failed to find another soldier who supported his account, except the William Martzell.[143] Still, doubts linger in some minds, encouraged by a letter penned to the *Philadelphia Tribune* by Corporal Anthony Smirely, Jr., of the 364th in 1943. It read, in part:

> I appeal to you for some kind of investigation of this matter and hope that the negro-hating man of the United States can be made to see the light. I have heard of what may happen if I write, but I am not afraid of the consequences if my story can bring to life the truth of the matter. If I fail in what I am undertaking now, I might as well reserve a berth in Hell, for that is what it will be here.... I beg of you to please, from my heart, please do something for the fellows and myself whom are among the unfortunate to be in this State of blood—Negro blood—that is constantly flowing in the streets.[144]

Cellos Harrison
June 16, 1943; Marianna, FL

On February 5, 1940, white storekeeper Johnnie Mayo was robbed and fatally beaten in his shop. Before dying, he blamed "a yellow negro" for the attack. Police detained 30-year-old Cellos Harrison and two other African American men, questioning them as suspects, but released all three based on lack of evidence. Newly elected Jackson County Sheriff Barkley Gauss reopened the case, arresting Harrison again on May 19, 1942. That time, Harrison allegedly confessed to striking Mayo with a hammer and stealing some $30 from the store's cash register. A grand jury indicted him on June 13, and his murder trial began on June 23, with the confession admitted over objections from Harrison's lawyer. White jurors convicted Harrison on June 24, and he received a death sentence.[145]

So far, the handling of Harrison's case was routine for Jim Crow Florida, but he appealed the verdict and the state's supreme court overturned his conviction January 20, 1942, based on faulty instructions to the original jury the rules pertaining to confessions. The court ordered a new trial, with Harrison's statement excluded, and he was freed until a new indictment sent him back to jail, awaiting trial in June 1943.[146]

Whites in Jackson County—one of Florida's most active regions for the Ku Klux Klan since 1867, scene of the Claude Neal lynching (see October 26, 1934, in Part 1) and many others—were not prepared to let Harrison slip through a legal loophole. Shortly after midnight on June 16, four men arrived at the county jail in Marianna, allegedly telling night jailer Tom Belser they had a drunken man to drop off. Belser later said the men were masked, yet he admitted them, sans prisoner, whereupon one drew a gun and the others seized Harrison, dragging him off into the night. A highway patrolman found his corpse near dawn, in a roadside ditch. A coroner's jury found that Harrison "came to his death from wounds inflicted by a blunt or sharp instrument in the hands of an unknown person or persons."[147]

Sheriff Gauss missed the lynching, absent at a sheriff's convention in Ocala. Governor Spessard Holland ordered an investigation, led by Lieutenant Red Clifton of the state highway patrol, but officers identified no suspects.[148] FBI agents took on the case, developing several persons of interest, but finally closed the file without recommending prosecution.

Willie Lee Davis
July 3, 1943; Summit, GA

Davis, a 25-year-old army private, was on furlough, staying his widowed mother, when he visited Sanford's, an African American roadhouse, on the eve of Independence Day.[149] According to witness Joe Stokes, a "little fight" broke out at 10 p.m., between patrons Enoch Brooks and Arthur Cross, ending when Brooks fled the tavern. Moments later, Chief of Police James Mitchell Bohannon "drove up in his car and sat there a few minutes and then drove off," only to return an hour later "with his son and some other white man." That time, Bohannon "walked in the juke joint, looked around and walked out on the porch," where Willie Davis sat talking to a young woman, Cleo Cotton.[150] According to Stokes,

> Bohannon went up behind W. L. Davis ... and patted him around the belt and I assumed he wanted to see if W. L. had any weapons. W. L. looked back and slapped Bohannon's hand away and then Bohannon slapped W. L. W. L. said, "You ain't got any right to hit me. I'm not your man. I'm Uncle Sam's man." W. L. either hit or tried to hit Bohannon and they "tied up." They fought a few minutes on the porch and then

stepped down on the ground in front of the porch and continued fighting. W. L. broke away from Bohannon and ran around the side of Sanford's house which is next door to the juke joint and seemed to be trying to get away. The chief, Bohannon, yelled at the other man to head W. L. off and the chief's boy turned a flashlight on W. L. down in the alley.... A few second after W. L. ran around the house I saw Bohannon then draw his gun and shoot in the direction where W. L. ran. Bohannon then drew a line on the ground and told everyone present not to go past it and he and his boy and the other white man left. When he had left we went back and saw W. L. lying face down on the ground.[151]

Davis's death certificate states that he died from a "gun shot wound in body, killed instantly," adding that he was "killed by officer who was attempting to quell disorder."[152] While Georgia authorities accepted the slaying as self-defense, an investigator from the War Department arrived in Summit on July 5, subsequently filing a report with the DOJ that concluded: "In light of the evidence presented and the apparent indifference of civil authorities, it is the opinion of the investigating Officer that T/5th Grade Davis was unjustifiably shot and killed." Even then, nearly a year elapsed before the FBI began its own investigation. Finally, on October 10, 1944, U.S. Attorney J. Saxton Daniel charged Bohannon with violating Davis's civil rights by shooting him "wilfully [sic], unlawfully and without provocation."[153]

Bohannon answered the charge by claiming he "felt a knife" in Davis's pocket, firing his pistol only after Davis struck him, tried to grab his gun, and was "advancing on him."[154] Trial was scheduled for January 15, 1945, then postponed while the U.S. Supreme Court considered the case of another Georgia lawman, Sheriff Mack Screws, convicted on similar charges for beating a suspect to death (see January 30, 1943, above). In that case, the court found that murder by police did not, in itself, prove specific intent to violate the victim's civil rights. Discouraged, Saxton Daniel *nolle prossed* Bohannon's case, leaving him unpunished.[155]

Holley Willis
November 7, 1943; Fulton County, IL

The U.S. Army Service Forces Unit Training Center at Camp Ellis, surrounded by the towns of Bernadotte, Ipava, and Table Grove, opened on April 16, 1943, training soldiers from various engineering and transportation companies, while doubling as a prison camp for captured German soldiers.[156] Private Holley Ellis was among its trainees when was accused of insulting white women over the telephone. A lynch mob pursued him to a farmhouse, gunning him down as he tried to escape. Prosecutors filed no charges against the lynchers.[157]

Willie James Howard
January 2, 1944; Live Oak, FL

Howard worked at a dime store in Live Oak, where he developed an adolescent crush on coworker Cynthia Goff. Both were 15 years old, but Goff was white, Howard an African American. At Christmas, Howard sent cards to several fellow employees, signing Goff's "with L," for "love." She must have voiced displeasure, since he handed her another note on New Year's Day, asking her not to be angry. Howard signed off: "I love your name, I love your voice, for a S. H. ["sweetheart"] you are my choice."[158]

Fatal last words.

At 11 a.m. on January 2, Cynthia's father, Phil Goff, appeared at Howard's home with companions S. B. McCullers and A. M. "Reg" Scott. They asked for Howard's father, learned he was at work, then dragged Willie from his mother's arms at gunpoint, forcing him into their car.[159] Goff described what followed in an awkward, rambling affidavit penned later that day. Uncorrected, it reads:

> We took Willie James in the car with us and went to Bond-Howell Lumber Co. in Live Oak, Fla and explained the circumstances to his father who agreed to go with us and chastise the boy himself for his misdeed. We immediately drove to a place near the Suwannee river, a place just east of Suwannee Springs. When we arrived at point I tied the boys feet and hands to keep him from running so that his father could whip him. James the boys father took the boy and carries him some ten or twelve feet from the car where he was to whip him. But the boy making the statement he would die before he would take punishment from his father or anyone else made his way to the river where he jumped in drowned himself. His father stood by and viewed the son without attempting to prevent this happening.
>
> Reg Scott walked back to the car. S. B. McCullers and I walked back to cut a switch for his father to whip him with and the boy hollered that he would jump in the river. We were about 25 feet from him when he said this and I told him not to do that as he would surely drown in that water as it was deep. He said again that he would die before he let any man dady or white man put a licking on him, as I look around he was crawling near the bank of the river. I made a dash to get ahold of him so did Mr. McCullers and Mr. Scott but we were too late. He rolled over the bank into the river before we could reach him.[160]

James Howard, clearly terrified, signed the affidavit saying, "This I acknowledge to be true," but later said the white kidnappers, after binding Willie, gave him a choice of being shot or jumping into the river. Five days later the Howards sold their house and moved to Orlando, where Lula Howard reported a threatening visit by a white man "who claimed to be a lawyer from Madison, Florida, and said he was sent by the Government."[161] Meanwhile, the ink was barely dry on Goff's affidavit when Suwannee County Sheriff Tom Henry ordered black mortician Ansel Brown to collect Howard's corpse and bury it immediately. No death certificate was filed, and Howard's grave was unmarked until 2005.[162]

Despite pressure from the NAACP, led by activist Harry T. Moore (see December 25, 1951, in Part 1), local authorities accepted Phil Goff's statement and filed no charges. Governor Spessard Holland condemned the murder and ordered an investigation, but told NAACP attorney Thurgood Marshall, "I am sure you realize the particular difficulties involved where there will be the testimony of three white men and probably the girl against the testimony of one Negro man."[163]

In 2006 historian Marvin Dunn produced a documentary film, titled *Murder on the Suwannee River*, and tried without success to have state attorney general (and governor-elect) Charlie Crist reopen the case.[164] The DOJ ignored Howard's death, like so many others passed over for review under the Till Act, between 2007 and 2014.

Isaac Simmons
March 26, 1944; Amite County, MS

Simmons, a minister and renowned "medicine man," was unusually prosperous for an African American in Mississippi's Amite County during World War II. His father had purchased 278 acres of land between 1887 and 1895, leaving the property and a bank account containing $412.64 to his heirs when he died in 1933. Soon, Isaac controlled the estate, with various relatives living in homes scattered around the property. White neighbors coveted the land, as well as Isaac's secret remedies for treating sick livestock.[165] In 1941 false rumors also spread about oil being found on the land.[166]

In February 1944, after Simmons cut some timber on his property, two white men—Vaughn Lee and Noble Rider—warned him to cut no more, also demanding his recipes for animal remedies. Simmons consulted a lawyer to stop the harassment, and abstained from cutting any further trees in the meantime.[167]

There matters stood at 11 a.m. on March 26, when six white men arrived at the home of Isaac's son, Eldridge Simmons. He later identified them as Noble Rider, two of Rider's brothers, Harper Dawson, Rabbit Stillman, and a sixth man Eldridge did not recognize. They asked Eldridge to show them the property line, then attacked him, beating him and ripping off his shirt, forcing him into their car at gunpoint. Driving off toward Isaac's house, they called Eldridge and his father "smart niggers" for hiring a lawyer.[168]

On arrival at Isaac's home, Noble Rider and two others approached the house, while their three companions held Eldridge in the car. They soon returned with Isaac, one man gripping each of his arms while the third shoved and punched him from behind. When they had Isaac in the front seat, Eldridge in the rear, the gang drove to a nearby side road and stopped, dragging Isaac from the car while Eldridge once again remained behind. Soon afterward, Eldridge heard gunshots and the whites returned alone, debating whether they should kill him. Eldridge begged for his life and Noble Rider finally relented, warning, "If this comes up again you had better not know anything about it."[169]

Weak and half blind from his beating, Eldridge reached a relative's home and gathered help to search for his father. The party found Isaac's corpse at 1 p.m., shot three times, one arm broken with a club lying nearby, most of his teeth knocked out, and his tongue cut from his mouth. Amite County Sheriff Wiley Mize and Constable George Hazelwood staged a hasty "inquest" at the crime scene, declaring that Simmons "met his death at the hands of unknown parties."[170]

On March 29, the day after Isaac's funeral, Deputy Sheriff Nick Travers drove Eldridge Sim-

Isaac Simmons, killed by Mississippi whites for being too prosperous (Civil Rights Archive).

mons to Magnolia, in neighboring Pike County, and jailed him "for his own protection." Finally released on April 8, Eldridge traveled to New Orleans and contacted the NAACP. FBI agents initially refused to investigate the case, stating on July 24, "since no police officers appeared to be involved," but headquarters reversed that decision on August 3, deeming that action "should be taken under the 13th Amendment to the Constitution and under Section 42, (252) Title 18, United States Code."[171] Curiously, that section seems unrelated to civil rights, reading: "The Surgeon General shall provide for making, at places within the United States or in other countries, such physical and mental examinations of aliens as are required by the immigration laws, subject to administrative regulations prescribed by the Attorney General and medical regulations prescribed by the Surgeon General with the approval of the Secretary."[172]

On September 5, 1944, FBI agents confronted one murder suspect at a sawmill in Liberty, arresting him for assault when he threatened them with an axe. On October 25, after reviewing evidence collected by the bureau, Amite County's grand jury voted murder indictments against Noble Rider and his brother Narville; Harper Dawson, with sons Mann and Roger; and John Brown. Despite eyewitness identifications from Eldridge Simmons, the panel filed no charges against Vaughn Lee or Rabbit Spillman. Noble Rider faced trial alone, winning acquittal "on insufficient evidence," and "since the case against him was said to be the strongest," charges against the other five defendants were dismissed. Survivors of the Simmons family abandoned their land, and the trail of title soon disappeared in Amite County's "partial, tattered tax records for the period."[173]

Henry Hauser
March 27, 1944; New Orleans, LA

On March 22, Officers Lester Bach and Lloyd O'Brien arrested Hauser, a 35-year-old laborer, and white neighbor Taylor J. Alford on charges of public intoxication and disturbing the peace. Alford's wife Bernice and daughter Maud later described the two policemen beating Hauser at the time of his arrest, while Taylor Alford testified that the beating continued en route to the 7th Precinct in the Carrollton district. Unconscious on arrival, Hauser was placed in a cell, then doused with a bucket of water before Bach, O'Brien, and two other officers resumed the beating, hammering his abdomen with fists, blackjacks, and a rubber mallet. Released on bond after a night court hearing on March 26, Hauser crawled away to catch a streetcar on Magazine Street, reached his home with aid from a friend, and was admitted to Charity Hospital.[174]

Staff physicians found him in shocking condition, including a ruptured ileum (lower section of the small intestine) and other injuries, while reports that one or both of Hauser's eyes were "knocked out" remain unconfirmed.[175] He died at 11 a.m. on March 27, his death certificate listing multiple causes: "Right bronchial pneumonia; plastic peritonitis with perforation of illeums [sic] sutured at Charity Hospital; septic hepatitis."[176] In layman's terms, that means he had inhaled stomach contents into his right lung, suffered inflammation of the stomach lining due to trauma and infection, and succumbed to septic shock.

After the Alfords told their story, NAACP President Daniel E. Byrd assigned Hauser's case to attorney Thurgood Marshall. On April 29, 1944, Marshall sent affidavits from Hauser's relatives and the Alfords to U.S. Attorney General Francis J. Biddle, who in turn passed the matter on to Herbert Christenberry, U.S. attorney for the Eastern District of Louisiana. Christenberry ordered an FBI investigation, but J. Edgar Hoover's agents advised against prosecution on civil rights charges. Christenberry agreed, in his report to Assistant Attorney General Tom C. Clark. Although the Alfords were prepared to testify, Clark closed the investigation on December 18, 1944, falsely stating that "there were no witnesses to support a prosecution."[177]

While some biographers paint Clark as a crusading pioneer for civil rights, we should note his frequent lapses in personal ethics. Allied with underworld elements since his early years in Dallas, Texas, Clark was promoted to Attorney General in June 1945 and cut a deal with imprisoned Chicago mobsters a few weeks later, first arranging transfers for the convicts to softer quarters, then pressing their case for early parole. One of the lucky gangsters, Murray "The Camel" Humphreys, testified before Congress in October 1964—five years after Clark's elevation to the U.S. Supreme Court—saying that Clark "always was 100 percent for doing favors," for which he was handsomely paid.[178]

Joshua C. Collins
July 25, 1944; Jackson, MS

Collins, age 32, worked with wife Thelma as sharecroppers on a plantation owned by W. F. Farmer, nine miles south of Jackson. On July 19, while Collins was plowing a cotton field, Farmer ordered him to stop and plow a nearby cornfield instead. Collins replied that he would start the new job when his present work was done, and Farmer left in a huff to plow the other field himself. Two days later, a pair of white men Collins did not recognize arrived at the plantation, warning him to leave immediately under pain of beating or worse. Collins fled the property, one of the strangers firing pistol shots over his head, and sent a friend to collect his family's belongings on July 22.[179]

Resettled with Thelma in Jackson, Collins was looking for work when Detective W. A. Bigner, Jr., stopped him on Congress Street, downtown. As Police Chief Joel D. Holden later told reporters, an unidentified black man had entered the home of J. L. Peters on North Congress Street, taping a girl's mouth shut as she lay in bed and attempting to loot the house. Bigner, according to Chief Holden, planned to question Collins as a suspect in that crime, but Collins ran, initiating what the *Clarion-Ledger* called an "exciting chase," joined by two soldiers and two white civilians. The mini-mob caught Collins on South Farish Street, where he allegedly grappled with Bigner, kicking the detective in his "lower stomach." Bigner then shot Collins twice in the chest, killing him instantly.[180]

Thelma Collins contacted NAACP representatives, who reported the slaying to FBI agents. A preliminary federal investigation "failed to reveal any connection between Farmer and Higner [sic] or that anyone was with Higner when shooting occurred, or that Higner was one of the two white men who ran Collins off his farm."[181] Aside from misspelling Bigner's name, that report also flatly contradicted the *Clarion-Ledger*'s coverage, stating that four other whites aided Bigner in capturing Collins. Jackson authorities deemed the slaying "justifiable homicide."

Jose Davila
October 6, 1944; Hart, MI

A Mexican-American farm worker from Brownsville, Texas, Davila was nearly 1,400 miles from home when Sheriff Marland "Mid" Littiebrant shot and killed him in Hart, the seat of Oceana County, Michigan. One quirky local newspaper, the *Mears Newz*, described Davila as 19 years old, while others pegged his age at 32—a difference that seemed to have some bearing on the circumstances of his death.[182]

All sides agree that on the day he died, Davila took a pair of eyeglasses from Maxine English, a young white girl, outside Hart's only drugstore. *Mears Newz* publisher George Swift Lathers described the incident as an innocent prank between friends; other reports claimed the adult Davila "accosted" English and "stole" her glasses maliciously during a struggle. Maxine's guardian, Harry Brokering, demanded return of the spectacles, and went with bystander Warren Holmes to fetch the sheriff when Davila refused. The trio overtook Davila at a drinking fountain, at the corner of State and Washington Streets, where witnesses say Littiebrant—a 1920s amateur boxing champion—arrested Davila, then began punching him. Davila hit back, whereupon Littiebrant switched to his blackjack, and the brawl continued until Littiebrant shot Davila in the abdomen, fatally wounding him.[183]

Mainstream reports of the killing cast Davila as a rootless drifter with a history of violence, one article claiming that police in Texas knew him as "man who shot and stabbed to kill," formerly convicted on a murder charge in 1939, for which he allegedly served two years of a paltry five-year sentence. Coroner M. G. Wood examined Davila, but as with the rest of the case, conflicting accounts dispute what he found. One report claims Davila carried "one small utility knife," while others describe two knives of illegal length, including "a stiletto with a razor-sharp edge." Davila pulled no knives on Littiebrant during their fight, although the sheriff claimed that he was "reaching for his pocket" when Littiebrant opened fire. An inquest convened by Coroner Wood on October 10 cleared Littiebrant of any wrongdoing.[184]

George Lathers took a very different view. Despite friendly relations with Littiebrant, whose boxing prowess he had praised two decades earlier, Lathers branded the Davila shooting "murder." Charged with criminal libel, Lathers faced trial before Justice R. W. Mason in late October.[185] Confronted with a stream of "almost countless" prosecution witnesses, defense counsel grilled each in turn and "apparently gave a number of them some uneasy moments as he questioned them closely on their direct testimony." According to the *Pentwater News*, "Calling of witnesses came to a dramatic close shortly after the prosecution rested. Objections to the presentation of certain matters by the defense brought the announcement by Attorney Andelman that he would not call any further witnesses."[186] In any case, the six-member jury had heard enough, acquitting Lathers on November 3.[187] Littiebrant died in November 1970, at age 66.[188]

James Thomas Scales
November 23, 1944; Pikeville, TN

Scales was a troubled youth, logging eight arrests between the ages of nine and 16, when a purse-snatching conviction sent him to the Tennessee State Training and Agricultural School for Colored Boys in October 1944. Before his last arrest, he joined the U.S. Navy at 15, with connivance from his father, who lied about his age. That, too, went badly, ending with a discharge "by reason of inaptitude" in May 1944, due to rebellious, violent behavior including a stabbing.[189]

Soon after Scales entered the reformatory, Superintendent, H. E. Scott made him a "trusty," assigned to work as a servant at the home Scott shared with his wife and their married daughter, Gwendolyn Scott McKinney. In Scott's absence, around 7:30 a.m. on November 23, Assistant Superintendent William S. Neil sent two inmates to Scott's home with some freshly butchered meat. No one answered their knock, and Neil soon noticed that Notie Scott was missing from her matron's post at the school. Around 9 a.m. he led guard and storekeeper George Virgil Davis to the house, where they forced entry and found both women dead, hacked and beaten to death with weapons including an axe, a hammer, two butcher knives, and a shotgun barrel detached from its stock.[190]

An inmate headcount soon revealed that Scales was missing. Around 8:30 a.m., farmer Walter Hale and his uncle saw Scales near Winesap, north of Pikeville, and drove him back to the reformatory, hoping to collect the standard $10 reward for runaways. On arrival, William Neil would later tell the FBI, he asked Scales, "Boy, why'd you do it?" Scales allegedly replied, "I just don't know," and then, Neil said, confessed to striking

Death certificate for James Scales, lynched in Tennessee on November 23, 1944 (Civil Rights Archive).

both victims with a hammer. Neil sent Davis and the Hales to deposit Scales at the Bledsoe County jail, in Pikeville. They left him there with the only person present: teenage cook Ruth Douglas, watching the jail with her infant child while Sheriff Henry Goforth worked his second job at a mill out of town.[191]

An hour later, Neil allegedly phoned the jail, asking that Scales be searched for a missing pistol. Ruth Douglas told him Scales was gone, collected by three "guards" from the reformatory. In fact, the men were imposters, part of a lynch mob waiting on Pikesville's outskirts. They drove Scales back to the school and were about to hang him from a tree near the Scott home when Neil reportedly attempted to dissuade them. They relented to the point of removing his noose, then one or more lynchers shot Scales repeatedly in the face and head. That done, other inmates were forced to parade past his corpse, being told, "This is for you. This is what will happen to the rest of you if you can't take orders." Stories differ as to who spoke those words, a member of the mob or William Neil himself. Neil told the FBI, "While I was in the office calling Nashville to report the incident to my superiors I understand that someone marched some of the inmates outside of the dormitory so they could view James Scales' body but I did not see this happen."[192]

While Superintendent Scott returned from a Nashville meeting with the Commissioner of Institutions, Governor Prentice Cooper sent Department of Safety Chief Lynn Bomar to investigate the lynching, promising a full report and offering a $500 reward for capture of the killers. Pledges from Nashville's Ministers' Alliance and the International Labor Defense pushed that total over $1,800, but no one came forward. Assistant U.S. Attorney General Tom Clark ordered a "full and immediate" FBI investigation on November 24, but agents focused chiefly on Scales's criminal record and the DOJ closed its case in the second week of January 1945. Chief Bomar filed his report, but it was not released as promised, either by Governor Cooper or his successor, Jim Nance McCord.[193]

Dissatisfied African Americans pursued their own inquiries. The *Nashville Globe* claimed Scales was innocent, based on the number of weapons employed in the double slaying, suggesting he was lynched "because he may have been able to tell who were the actual murderers of the two women." Robert Lucas, from the *Chicago Defender*, interviewed Ruth Douglas. When he asked if she could name the men who kidnapped Scales, Deputy A. F. Goforth—the sheriff's son—answered for her, "No, she couldn't." Sheriff Goforth then delivered a harangue on the difference between race relations in Tennessee and Chicago. More productive was the probe conducted by Z. Alexander Looby, a Nashville attorney and member of the NAACP's National Legal Committee. He obtained eyewitness affidavits naming the triggerman as reformatory guard Fee "Pop" Morris, aided by others including one "Davis, first name unknown." A grand jury reviewed those findings in January 1945 but returned no indictments.[194]

Debate continues over who shot Scales. In 2004 a researcher recorded the statement of an aged witness, saying "a Davis from Van Buren County went and shot him. Killed the shit out of him." Davis, he said, was a "little old short feller. He wore a mustache." The same witness said William Neil personally took Scales from jail to be lynched, and afterward ordered the parade of inmates viewing his corpse. By the time that witness shared his memory, both Neil and Davis were deceased.[195]

Madison Harris
April 10, 1945; Atlanta, GA

White motorman T. H. Purl shot Harris, a disabled army veteran, after Harris disembarked from Purl's streetcar on Mitchell Street. Multiple witnesses testified that as Harris reached the sidewalk, Purl called out, "Boy, give me that gun." Harris turned with both hands empty, raised above his head, whereupon Purl shot and killed him. Police detained Purl, then released him "on copy"—with no bond posted—when he claimed self-defense. Officers claimed that a pistol was found under Harris's corpse.[196]

At a hearing in Recorder's Court, on April 18, eight witnesses agreed that Harris had no gun in hand when he was shot and did not threaten Purl. Some said that when police arrived, they pulled a pistol from the right hip pocket of the dead man's pants. A ninth witness, Ed Atkins, claimed Harris died with the gun in his hand, thus contradicting every other witness in the case. Judge A. W. Callaway cleared Purl, saying, "To me, this is nothing but a case of justified homicide."[197] A grand jury considered Purl's case in May 1946 but declined to indict him, voting "no bill" on the same day it cleared Arthur Frieberg for Phinazee Summerour's murder (see November 28, 1945, below). Witnesses in each case agreed that "both slayings appear to be unwarranted."[198]

Denice Harris
June 6, 1945; Atlanta, GA

Harris, a 22-year-old war veteran, drove a white male acquaintance to his adulterous rendezvous with a married white woman, unaware that the woman's husband had overheard a phone call arranging the tryst and had notified police. An officer waiting at the site shot Harris, perhaps in the mistaken belief that he was the woman's lover. A Fulton County coroner's jury deemed the killing "justifiable homicide."[199]

Bedsole Lamar
June 30, 1945; Autauga County, AL

In April 1945 a federal jury convicted Lamar, age 70, of operating an illegal whiskey still. The court imposed five years' probation, but it seems he failed to learn from that experience. Lamar vanished from home on June 30 and was found by relatives the next day, near a still he had constructed on his farm, midway between Prattville and Selma. According to a newspaper report, Lamar was "scalded with hot mash which had apparently been poured over him, and with two fractures of the skull, either one of which could have caused death." Sheriff Allen Stewart declared the death a homicide, but made no arrests.[200]

Prentiss McCann
July 7, 1945; Mobile, AL

McCann, a 22-year-old civilian truck driver employed by day at Brookley Army Air Field, left his home in Mobile's black Mayfield section around 8:45 p.m., en route

Prentiss McCann, slain by Alabama police on July 7, 1945 (Civil Rights Archive).

to a nearby grocery store. Along the way, he stopped outside the Midway Club, a tavern on Dublin Street, to watch a dice game. The gamblers scattered at 9:15, when Officers Pat Gibney and Melvin Porter rolled up in their cruiser, but McCann remained, described by witnesses as standing with his arms crossed, talking to a friend.[201]

What happened next remains a matter of dispute. State Solicitor Carl M. Booth, urged to investigate by Police Chief Dudley F. McFayden, told the *Mobile Register* that "Prentise" McCann was shot in self-defense after he "advanced toward Officer Porter with a threatening attitude and the officer struck him with his fist. The negro then reached into his pocket as if to draw a weapon and Porter told the negro to stop twice. When the negro continued to advance the officer drew his service pistol and fired the bullet hitting McCann in the right temple."[202] A drunken dice player helped the officers place McCann in their cruiser for the trip to City Hospital, where he died soon after midnight. Police neglected to inform Rena McCann of her husband's death, leaving neighbors to break the news.[203]

If the placement of McCann's wound seemed peculiar for a face-on confrontation, the official version of his death also omitted two key facts: he was shot *twice*, and proved to be unarmed. Another witness to the shooting claimed that Porter fired from the passenger's window of the police car, before stepping out, and afterward said, "I'm sorry it happened. The gun got caught up in the door." State Solicitor Booth accepted the identical stories told by Porter and Gibney, ruling McCann's death a "justifiable homicide."[204] The *Chicago Defender* took a different view, calling Porter "trigger happy," editorializing that McCann's death "would ordinarily be classed as a case of cold-blooded murder."[205]

NAACP attorney Thurgood Marshall sent eyewitness affidavits to U.S. Attorney

General Tom C. Clark, prompting an FBI investigation. Under apparent coaching by agents, two witnesses revised their original statements to conform more closely to the police version of events. Agents also detailed the prior arrest records of several bystanders, presumably to discredit them, while Chief McFayden assured G-men that Porter "had previously encountered no difficulty in handling negroes." Agents in Mobile predicted a grand jury investigation of the shooting, but none occurred. Rena McCann, now destitute with three small children, left Mobile to live with her parents in Waynesboro, Mississippi.[206]

Porter Flornoy Turner
August 1945; DeKalb County, GA

Ku Klux Klansmen suspected Turner, an African American taxi driver, of accepting white women as fares. One August night, a Klansman's wife entered his cab outside Atlanta's bus station, then drew a pistol and directed Turner to a secluded stretch of Pryor Road, where members of the Klan's violent "Klavalier Klub" waited. The Klansmen beat and kicked Turner, firing shots at his feet, then ordered him to run while they followed in his cab and other cars, eventually running over him. Authorities dismissed his death as a hit-and-run accident until May 1, 1946, when Klavalier leader and "chief ass-tearer" Cliff Vittur addressed the crime at a Klan meeting, chastising the killers for driving Turner's cab and failing to wipe their fingerprints off the steering wheel. They were only saved from "hot water," said Vittur, when a "brother Klansman" on Atlanta's police force eradicated the evidence.[207]

Unknown to the Klavaliers, one member present was Stetson Kennedy, an infiltrator employed by the Nonsectarian Anti-Nazi League. He reported Vittur's comments to the FBI and the Georgia Bureau of Investigation, and while no prosecutions resulted, state authorities used the incident, with others, to revoke the Klan's corporate charter.[208] Subsequently, in his memoirs of infiltrating the Klan, Kennedy dramatized the murder, falsely claiming to have witnessed it and changing the victim's name to "James Martin," while setting the crime in nonexistent "Rockledge County."[209]

Lila Bella Carter
August 15, 1945; Pine Island, SC

A white insurance agent raped and murdered 16-year-old Lila Carter, breaking her neck and jaw, leaving her body facedown in a pool of water to simulate accidental drowning. Carter's father collected evidence against the killer, but was jailed himself when he approached police, demanding a full investigation. The crime remains officially unsolved.[210]

Ervin Jones
August 21, 1945; Portland, OR

Three plainclothes policemen invaded Jones's home without warrants and without identifying themselves as lawmen. When Jones attempted to defend his family from strangers he believed were criminals, one officer shot him in the back with a sawed-off shotgun, killing Jones instantly. Successive hearings by a coroner's jury and a grand jury absolved the officers of any wrongdoing.[211]

Tom Jones, Jr.
September 8, 1945; Woodville, MS

Jones, a 24-year-old longshoreman, planned to visit family when he rode a Teche Greyhound Lines bus from New Orleans to Wilkinson County, Mississippi, with girlfriend Ruby Mae Williams. That visit—and his life—was cut short at the Woodville bus depot, when Jones forgot a basic point of Jim Crow courtesy toward whites.

Four friends of Jones—Albert Bell, Willie Bell, William Lee Ferguson, and Prentiss Gaines—were waiting at the Woodville station. While they greeted Ruby Williams, Jones waited at the bus to claim his luggage. Driver Buddy Dawson asked Jones if he was sure he had bags aboard, and Jones replied, "Yes." As described in affidavits filed by Albert Bell and Ruby Williams, Dawson snapped at Jones, "You are in Mississippi now, not New Orleans. My name is Mr. Dawson." Dawson struck Jones on the head with a flashlight, trying a second swing that Jones blocked with his forearm, punching Dawson in the face. Dawson then shouted, "You black son of a bitch, I am going to kill you!" Ducking inside the bus, Dawson returned with a blackjack, missing several swings while Jones retreated, then ran off to summon help.[212]

Dawson returned moments later with Woodville night marshal David McDonald, his pistol already drawn. Grabbing Jones by his shirt collar, McDonald twice shouted, "Nigger, where is the knife?" When Jones denied being armed, McDonald then yelled, "Nigger, what do you mean hitting a white man?" and shot Jones in the chest three times at point-blank range. According to Bell's affidavit, Jones died with his hands raised, making no attempt at self-defense.[213] After shooting Jones, McDonald ordered Williams, the Bells and their friends away from the scene. They watched from a distance as Dawson and McDonald stood over Jones, laughing and making no attempt to seek help.[214]

Tom Jones, Jr., killed by Mississippi officer David McDonald on September 8, 1945 (Civil Rights Archive).

At length, a hearse arrived from Woodville's Standard Burial Association, transporting Jones to the National Funeral Home, where Coroner Matt Walker examined his corpse. Walker found one entry wound at the right side of Jones's chest and two on the left, all three bullets having passed through his torso. Millie Jones Arbuthnot pressed the NAACP to investigate her son's slaying, generating national publicity, sometimes inaccurate.[215] The *Chicago Defender*, for instance, described Jones as 17 years old and placed the shooting in Belmont, 292 miles northeast of Woodville.[216]

NAACP attorney Thurgood Marshall sent several affidavits to U.S. Attorney General Tom C. Clark, prompting Clark to request an FBI investigation on October 11, 1945. Four agents reviewed the case, including George A. Gunter of New Orleans, later accused by 1960s civil rights activists of threatening their lives, linked by documentary evidence to the racist Mississippi State Sovereignty Commission. Under Gunter's guidance, agents questioned Jones's former New Orleans employers, recording observations that he was a "smart aleck," a "troublemaker," and "a ringleader among the negroes working." Specifically, Jones had protested the disparity in Shipyard Union dues for black and white members, resigning from the union in protest. Throughout the brief investigation, agents questioned none of Jones's African American coworkers. Gunter also found two white bus passengers who claimed Jones had a knife (never found) and that he "lunged" at Marshal McDonald with the vanished weapon. On May 1, 1946, FBI headquarters sent the DOJ a memo recommending against further action.[217]

Moses Green

September 9, 1945; Ellenton, SC

Green, a veteran of World War I, returned home from a shopping excursion and was shot by two Aiken County sheriff's deputies driving past his house. Green was unarmed, had no criminal record, and was not wanted on any charges. Prosecutors declined to charge the officers.[218]

Sam McFadden

September 21, 1945; Suwannee County, FL

McFadden, a war veteran and farm laborer, left home to buy groceries on September 21 and never returned. Two fishermen found his corpse in the Suwannee River near Live Oak on October 21. Governor Millard Caldwell sent a state police investigator, and suspicion focused on county constable Tom Crews, a wealthy turpentine producer who used peon labor. Despite testimony from 20 witnesses that Crews had lashed McFadden with a bullwhip, forcing him to jump into the river where he drowned, a county grand jury refused to indict the lawman.[219]

In 1946 a federal grand jury charged Crews with violating McFadden's civil rights "under color of law." Jurors convicted him that December, and he received the maximum one-year prison term with a $1,000 fine. Crews appealed that verdict to the U.S. Fifth Circuit Court of Appeals, which overturned his conviction on March 16, 1947. At that hearing, defense attorney Charles Cook Howell argued that Crews had not killed McFadden while acting in his official capacity, and that he possessed no "specific intent" to violate McFadden's rights. District Attorney Herbert S. Phillips cited "ample proof" that Crews placed McFadden under "virtual arrest" and used his authority to conceal the crime, but the three-judge panel disagreed.[220]

Wilbert Cohen
November 1, 1945; Location unknown

The Civil Rights Congress, in its 1952 genocide petition to the United Nations, described this case as follows: "Fourteen-year-old Wilbert Cohen was killed when two bullets from a policeman's gun were fired at him as he was leaving a friend's house. No action was taken against the policeman, either by the grand jury or by the police department."[221] Online searches revealed no further information on Cohen's death, and omission of the incident's location rendered local inquiries impossible.

Nicey Brown
November 1945; Selma, AL

A drunken off-duty policeman beat Mrs. Brown, age 70, to death with a bottle. At his murder trial, the officer's defense attorney told the all-white jury, "If we convict this brave man who is upholding the banner of white supremacy, then we may as well give all our guns to the niggers and let them run the Black Belt." The panel deliberated briefly before voting to acquit.[222] Local inquiries, seeking the killer's name and other details, went unanswered.

St. Claire Pressly
November 17, 1945; Johnsonville, SC

Pressly, a recently discharged war veteran, was returning home to Hemingway, South Carolina, when his train stopped in Johnsonville, seven miles from his destination. Stepping off to refresh himself, Pressly met a police officer identified in press reports as "Parrot," who arrested him on suspicion of involvement in a minor disturbance occurring two days earlier. Holding Pressly's belt from behind, Parrot drew his pistol and jammed it against Pressly's side, despite Pressly's insistence that he was not resisting arrest and the gun was unnecessary. As they proceeded toward police headquarters, Pressly unwisely taunted Parrot, saying, "You don't have the nerve to shoot me." Parrot then shot Pressly in the stomach and summoned a Jim Crow ambulance. Pressly was dead on arrival at Johnson Hospital in Hemingway. No charges were filed against Officer Parrot.[223]

Phinazee Summerour
November 28, 1945; Atlanta, GA

While riding a city streetcar, Summerour became embroiled in an argument over smoking with a white passenger. Details of that squabble are obscure, but it was settled peaceably before Summerour prepared to disembark at the corner of Angler Avenue and Bedford Place. A second white passenger, postal worker Arthur Frieberg, then shot Summerour, killing him instantly, afterward telling police that Summerour had cursed him and threatened him with a knife. Officers briefly detained Frieberg for "disorderly conduct," then freed him without bond pending a November 30 hearing in Recorder's Court.[224]

At that hearing, District Attorney William Schley Howard called the shooting "simply a case of blooded murder," while defense attorney A. L. Henson described it as "justifiable homicide." No witnesses corroborated Frieberg's claim that Summerour was armed or cursed him, maintaining instead that "few words, if any, transpired between Frieberg and the deceased." Despite early claims of an "open knife" found in Summerour's pocket, no weapon was produced. Judge A. W. Callaway held Frieberg over for a grand jury, on a charge of manslaughter, fixing his bond at $1,000.[225]

When that panel convened, in May 1946, it declined to indict Frieberg. On the same day, May 6, grand jurors refused to charge motorman T. H. Purl in the earlier streetcar slaying of Madison Harris (see April 10, 1945, above). Witnesses to each shooting agreed that "both slayings appear to be unwarranted."[226]

Jesse Hightower and Edgar Thomas
December 1945; Union Springs, AL

The Civil Rights Congress, in its 1952 genocide petition to the United Nations, described this case as follows:

December—Two persons were killed when a reign of terror swept over the Negro community of Union Springs, Alabama. A third Negro was wounded and a fourth was hounded out of town. The white policeman who was the murderer was known. Edgar Thomas was murdered when the white policeman heard him discuss the Negro question with a friend in Thomas' own store. Jesse Hightower was also murdered. Ed Day Gary, a veteran, had one eye shot out. Rev. J. L. Pinckney was ordered to leave town because he had been a witness to Thomas' murder.[227]

Such a crime spree should have rated media attention, but online searches proved fruitless, and my inquiries to local sources went unanswered.

O'Day H. Short Family
December 16, 1945; Fontana, CA

A longtime resident of Los Angeles, O'Day Short moved his family 47 miles eastward to Fontana, in the San Fernando Valley, seeking a better atmosphere for children than the crowded city. What he found, instead, was bigotry and death.

Soon after the Shorts arrived, they received a visit from San Bernardino County sheriff's deputies "Tex" Cornelison and Joe Glines. The officers warned Short that he was "out of bounds," advising him to avoid "disagreeableness" by moving to Baseline, Fontana's black ghetto. Complaints had been received, Glines said, though later he admitted that he "didn't get the complaints from any particular person. He just heard them on he streets." Next came J. Sutherland, the white real state broker who sold Short the Fontana property. Arriving on December 3, he said, "Short, the vigilante committee had a meeting on your case last night. They are a tough bunch to deal with. If I were you, I'd get my family off this property at once." Instead, Short reported the threats to FBI agents, and to an African American newspaper, the *Los Angeles Sentinel*, which headlined the story on December 6.[228]

Ten days later, on Sunday night, December 16, an explosion rocked the Shorts' home, instantly engulfing it in flames. Neighbors heard screams and rushed to assist them, extricating all four Shorts from the inferno. Seven-year-old Carol Ann died first from her burns, followed by nine-year-old brother Barry the same night, and mother Helen the following morning. O'Day Short survived the longest, lingering in agony for five weeks before he finally succumbed to trauma and infection, on January 21, 1946. Meanwhile, the *Fontana Herald News* reported the blaze on December 18, in a brief story headlined "Three killed when home accidentally burns in Fontana."[229]

The sources for that "accident" report were Deputies Cornelison and Glines. The county coroner resisted holding an inquiry until pressure from the black press and the NAACP compelled it. Convened on December 22, the hearing opened with District Attorney Jerome B. Kavanaugh's apology to local vigilantes for calling them a "pressure group." Kavanaugh then read a transcript of his hospital interview with O'Day Short, during which, Kavanaugh claimed, Short repeatedly declined to make a statement, pleading that he was too ill to testify, then grudgingly admitted that the fire was accidental. The coroner's jury endorsed that finding and closed the case.[230]

On its face, the verdict sounded reasonable. Short's home had no electric power on the night it burned, leaving the family to cope with potentially dangerous kerosene lamps. The story did not end at that, however. NAACP officials hired Paul T. Wolff, former chief arson investigator for the Los Angeles Fire Department, to examine the case privately. After visiting the burned-out house, Wolff told the *Sentinel*, "Some highly inflammable or explosive substance other than kerosene was present. How a substance of that character got there is unknown. But it was definitely present."[231] Wolff sent copies of his final report to D.A. Kavanaugh and California Attorney General Robert Kenny, reading in part:

> The specimens indicated an extremely high degree of heat—in the neighborhood of some 1600 degrees fahrenheit [sic] to 1700, but I found no evidence of any oils.... My analysis shows kerosene in considerable quantities.... This kerosene was found in the southeast corner of the living room, and in the northeast corner of the same room in the earth underneath.[232]

Refuting observations from local fire officials, Wolff added, "Statements I have seen in which it was stated kerosene will explode at 40 degrees fahrenheit are positively erroneous, as kerosene does not become volatile or throw off inflammable gas until in the neighborhood of 177 degrees fahrenheit."[233]

The Civil Rights Congress included the Short case in its 1952 genocide petition to the United Nations, garbling O'Day Short's name, transforming son Barry into a daughter, and misplacing the fire on December 23. In closing, the brief item offered a theory to solve the mystery: "While the Shorts were away, people broke into their home, sprayed the interior with an inflammable chemical, and left. When the Shorts returned, the father struck a match, and the lamp fuel, believed to be kerosene, exploded."[234]

While that theory remains unproven scientifically, attempts to suppress the Short case are undeniable, extending even to the local Catholic Church. When Jesuit activist George H. Dunne reported on the fire for *Commonweal* magazine, then wrote a play about the incident titled *Trial by Fire*, performed nationally in 1946, his superiors transferred him to a remote parish in Arizona. Eight years later, September 1954, Fontana finally abolished segregated zoning.[235]

Walter Campbell
December 26, 1945; Little Rock, AR

Campbell, an organizer for the Congress of Industrial Organizations' Food, Tobacco, and Allied Workers of America, suffered fatal stab wounds while recruiting black workers to protest 12-hour workdays and a pay rate of 50¢ per hour. A white man reportedly confessed to the slaying, then was released.[236] My inquiries to local sources failed to discover the killer's name or any other pertinent details.

Frank Allen
February 1946; Memphis, TN

In its 1952 genocide petition to the United Nations, the Civil Rights Congress included the "suspicious" death of cab driver Frank Allen, shot by two white policemen. The anonymous officers claimed that Allen fired the first shot, but another version of events asserted that he was unarmed, dragged from his taxi and murdered in a nearby vacant lot.[237] My inquiries to local libraries and newspapers revealed no further information on this case.

Alfonzo Ferguson and Charles Ferguson
February 5, 1946; Freeport, Long Island, NY

The four Ferguson brothers from Roosevelt, Long Island—Alfonzo, Charles, Joseph, and Richard—hoped for a relaxing night on February 5, 1946. Alfonzo was the quartet's lone civilian: Charles and Richard were both in the army, while Joseph was U.S. Navy seaman. Their night began badly, when a white café proprietor refused to serve them, claiming his establishment was "out of coffee," though white patrons on all sides were drinking theirs. The brothers protested, then left, whereupon the proprietor phoned police to complain about the incident.[238]

It took some time for rookie officer Joseph Romeika to locate the "misbehaving Negroes." In fact, the Fergusons were walking back to their bus stop, prepared to leave Freeport, when Romeika overtook them, placing them under arrest for disorderly conduct and ordering all four—plus a curious black passerby—to line up against a wall. When Charles and Joseph questioned the validity of their arrest, Romeika kicked both men in the groin, then drew his pistol and opened fire, killing Charles and Alfonzo, wounding Joseph in the shoulder. Romeika later claimed that Charles threatened him with a pistol, but none of the brothers were armed. Police swarmed the bus depot, armed with Tommy guns and tear gas, in the words of their chief, to prevent "a possible uprising of local Negroes."[239]

Navy shore police took custody of Joseph Ferguson, lodging him in the brig, while Richard was convicted of disorderly conduct the following day, sentenced to 100 days in jail.[240] At his trial, Judge Hilbert Johnson proclaimed, "Four fellows going out looking for trouble, they are going to find just what they were looking for. And I commend any police officer who can keep trouble away from this village." Nassau County District Attorney James H. Gehrig called Officer Romeika's actions "unquestionably justified." On February 22 an all-white grand jury declined to indict Romeika, while denying an attorney for the Ferguson family any opportunity to question witnesses.[241]

Five months of intensive black protests in Freeport prompted Governor Thomas Dewey to order a special investigation, climaxed by endorsement of local officials that African Americans deemed a whitewash.[242] Subsequently, the navy cleared Joseph Ferguson of any misconduct and Richard's conviction was overturned on appeal. The army issued a "Scroll of Honor" to Charles Ferguson's widow, signed by President Harry Truman, memorializing "Private First Class Charles R. Ferguson who died in the service of his country in the American Area, February 5, 1946." Five-star general Henry H. Arnold, Commander of the Army, also issued a citation praising Ferguson as a martyr.[243]

Nathaniel Jackson
February 9, 1946; Granville, WI

Private Jackson was confined at the army's U.S. Disciplinary Barracks when African American inmates protested the lack of meat in their diet. A white guard shot Jackson with a submachine gun, killing him instantly. Press reports mention two other unnamed black inmates injured by guards as they quelled the "disturbance."[244]

Timothy Hood
February 17, 1946; Bessemer, AL

A white streetcar conductor shot Hood five times after Hood attempted to tear down a Jim Crow sign directing blacks to sit at the rear of the car. A city policeman arrived to find the war veteran dying and finished him off with another gunshot. Jefferson County's coroner deemed both shootings "justifiable."[245]

Kenny Long
February 25, 1946; El Campo, TX

Army veteran Kenny Long was drinking soda at a gas station, with cousin Meron Long and friend Cosby Clay, when a white idler made racist comments and began to order Clay about. Enraged by the young black man's "disrespectful" answer, the white man called the Wharton County sheriff's office. Three deputies soon arrived, once introducing himself with the comment, "Don't you know I hate a goddamn nigger?" While assaulting the three African Americans, one officer drew his pistol and killed

Kenny Long. Meron Long and Cosby Clay were handcuffed, beaten further, and charged with "resisting arrest."[246]

William Gordon and James Johnson
February 28, 1946; Columbia, TN

On February 25, U.S. Navy veteran James Stephenson joined his mother to retrieve a radio left for repair at a Columbia department store. Discovering that her radio had been sold to another customer, Gladys Stephenson quarreled with white clerk William Fleming. His threatening attitude moved James to step between them and a fight ensued, ending when James shoved Fleming through a plate glass window. Police arrested both Stephensons for disturbing the peace, then released them after payment of a $50 fine. The matter might have ended there, but Fleming's father swore out a warrant charging James Stephenson with assault with the intent to commit murder. Black mortician A. J. Morton joined entrepreneur brothers Julius and Sol Blair in posting bond to secure Stephenson's release.[247]

Agitated whites began to gather at Maury County's courthouse, while African Americans armed themselves for self-defense in the nearby "Mink Slide" ghetto, blacking out the district's stores and shooting out streetlights. Columbia's police chief led three officers into Mink Slide, in an unmarked car, ignoring shouted warnings to turn back. Someone fired on them from the shadows, wounding all four, and the siege of Mink Slide began. Lynn Bomar, Tennessee's Commissioner of Public Safety, soon arrived with 67 highway patrolmen, followed closely by General Jacob Dickinson with 59 troopers from the Tennessee State Guard. To avoid martial law, Sheriff J. J. Underwood and local magistrate C. Hayes Denton deputized Bomar, Dickinson, and their men as county officers.[248]

First, deputies and white vigilantes surrounded Mink Slide. Next, police planned to invade the ghetto at 7 a.m. on February 26, but Bomar jumped the gun, leading what amounted to a pogrom against the black community. Officers riddled black shops with gunfire, paying particular attention to property pledged as bail for James Stephenson. At Sol Blair's barbershop, patrolmen "returned fired" against nonexistent snipers, leaving the shop a shambles and arresting two unarmed men, Lloyd Kennedy and William Pillow, on attempted murder charges. Julius Blair's store was likewise trashed and looted. At Morton's Funeral Home, officers ran amok, causing $2,000 damage ($25,000 today), defacing one large casket with the letters "KKK." Throughout Mink Slide, police stole cash and merchandise from stores, searched homes without warrants, confiscated any firearms found, and arrested more than 100 African Americans on vague charges. None were granted bail or access to attorneys.[249]

Three of those caught in the dragnet were William Gordon, James Johnson, and Napoleon Stewart. During a closed-door interrogation, one of them allegedly grabbed a confiscated weapon—conveniently left loaded within the prisoners' reach—and fired a shot that grazed Deputy Tom Darnell. The ensuing fusillade left Gordon and Johnson mortally wounded, while Stewart somehow escaped serious injury. Instead of driving Gordon and Johnson to Columbia's hospital, Bomar sent them to Nashville's all-black Meharry Hospital, 38 miles distant. Both men died en route.[250]

As the smoke cleared over Mink Slide, 25 African Americans faced charges of attempted murder for wounding the officers shot on February 25. At trial, white jurors surprised their neighbors with a compromise verdict, dubbed "approximate justice," convicting two defendants and acquitting the rest. Lloyd Kennedy and William Pillow received a similar split decision at their separate trial: jurors acquitted Pillow and convicted Kennedy of second-degree attempted murder. He received a five-year maximum sentence and was paroled after a few months in prison. James Stephenson was never tried for his brawl with William Fleming.[251]

Before those trials, a federal grand jury convened on April 8, 1946, before Judge Elmer D. Davies, a 1920s Klansman. That panel found no violations of federal law by any officers during the "Mink Slide riot," although Lynn Bomar admitted searching many homes without warrants and proclaimed that he would do the same again, in similar circumstances. Columbia's coroner held no inquest in the deaths of William Gordon and James Johnson, ruling that officers shot them in self-defense. Throughout those proceedings and subsequent criminal trials, police constantly harassed NAACP lawyers Thurgood Marshall and Z. Alexander Looby with false arrests for drunkenness and fabricated traffic violations.[252]

George Collins
April 1946; McAlester, OK

Collins was a U.S. Navy shore patrolman assigned to McAlester's naval ammunition depot and marine barracks (now McAlester Army Ammunition Plant) when a white city policeman killed him in early April 1946. According to the Civil Rights Congress, "Negroes in the community stated that Collins' death was the third such incident since the establishment of the Navy Marine Base [sic] a few years previously. They declared that the city police carried on a veritable reign of terror against the Negro shore patrolmen; that on numerous occasions they swooped down on the Negro section, making searches and seizures without warrants."[253] Local inquiries during research for this volume revealed no further details on the Collins case or any similar slayings.

Elliot Brooks
June 1946; Gretna, LA

In its 1952 genocide petition to the United Nations, the Civil Rights Congress described this case as follows:

June—Elliott Brooks of Gretna, Louisiana, was killed by the Gretna chief of police because he "knew too much" about the disappearance of another Negro who was a prisoner, according to affidavits filed with the Gretna branch of the NAACP.[254]

My inquiries to local sources and the NAACP's national office went unanswered.

Samuel E. Hicks
July 17, 1946; Spokane, WA

Hicks was an 18-year-old member of the U.S. Army Air Force, assigned to Spokane's Geiger Field (now Spokane International Airport). On July 17, fighting and rock-throwing erupted on base after an interracial Golden Gloves boxing match. Colonel Eric Dougan, commanding Geiger, denied that the melee was racial in nature, but local newspapers stressed fighting between whites and blacks, with reports of black airmen stoning white motorists. At 10:30 p.m., military police found Hicks 100 yards from the boxing ring, near Geiger's administrative building, dying from a fractured skull. Postmortem tests attributed the injury to a "blow of a blunt instrument above his right ear." A white airman reported seeing two white civilians assaulting Hicks, but the investigation developed no suspects.[255]

Eugene Montenegro
July 21, 1946; Monterey Park, CA

Montenegro was a 13-year-old honor student at St. Alphonsus Catholic School in East Los Angeles. On Sunday night, July 21, a sheriff's deputy investigating a report of prowlers in Monterey Park, 10 miles east of L.A., shot Montenegro in the back, killing him instantly. The officer claimed he saw Montenegro—five feet three inches tall and unarmed—emerging from the window of a private residence, and that the youth ran when ordered to halt. The slaying was deemed justifiable homicide.[256]

Leon McTatie
July 22, 1946; Lexington, MS

A white man in West, Mississippi, accused McTatie of stealing a saddle. Accompanied by five others, the accuser seized McTatie and whipped him to death on July 22, dumping his corpse in a bayou near Lexington. The killers were indicted, but an all-white jury acquitted them after deliberating for only 10 minutes.[257]

Sutton Matthews
July 27, 1946; Moultrie, GA

Around 7:30 p.m., motorman R. V. Holt saw "an object" lying on the tracks before his Georgia Northern Railroad train, near the Hall Commission Company's yards in Moultrie. "At first," he said, "I thought it was a white piece of paper. As the car drew nearer I could see that it was a man. It was too late to stop. I applied the emergency brake and blew the whistle. It was about one car length before I could stop." Stepping down from the train, Holt was joined by black porter Lonnie Pope, who had not seen the man "until after the train had run over him." Pope declined to touch the corpse, but Hold did, finding that "it was already cold." Both men later testified that "there was no quiver about the body when they reached it."[258]

Colquitt County Coroner F. A. White reached the scene by 8 p.m., with Deputy Sheriff T. V. Beard, Jr. Holt explained that when first seen, the man was lying across the tracks with his head on the right-hand rail. The train had rolled him over, so that "when he reached it the man was face down." Deputy Beard confirmed that the body was cold.

All four witnesses noted "a wound back of the man's left ear," but none opined as to its cause, whether from impact with the train or other trauma. On July 29 a coroner's jury rendered its verdict that the African American man—"tentatively identified" as Sutton Matthews—"came to his death from an unknown cause."[259]

But was it murder? And if so, was that crime racially motivated? Six years later, in its historic genocide petition to the United Nations, the Civil Rights Congress declared that "Sutter Matthews" had been murdered with a blunt instrument, after which the unknown killers laid his body on the railroad tracks. Aside from misspelling his first name, that report also misstated the date of the coroner's verdict as July 31.[260] The crime, if crime it was, remains officially unsolved.

Harrison Johnson
July 29, 1946; Eatonton, GA

A white gunman pistol-whipped sharecropper Harrison Johnson, then shot him six times at close range, leaving his body on the shoulder of a rural highway. Putnam County's sheriff deemed the killing "self-defense" and filed no charges, although Johnson was unarmed.[261]

Willie Henry
July 31, 1946; Helena, AR

Willie Henry survived warfare in the Pacific Theater of World War II, released from service as a disabled veteran, only to meet violent death on the home front, a year after V-J Day. Visiting Arkansas from Chicago, he approached an agent of the Brocato Bus Line at Helena's depot, asking the price of a trip to a neighboring county. When the agent quoted two different ticket prices, Henry questioned the discrepancy. A white bystander, irrationally furious at Henry's "impertinence," struck Henry with a piece of metal pipe, knocking him down. When two other men tried to help him stand, Henry—dazed and mistaking their intentions—broke away and leaped into a nearby concrete ditch for cover. Patrolman J. C. White and his partner, identified only as Officer Jones, arrived to find Henry sitting in the ditch. They ordered him out, whereupon he replied, "I won't come up for you to beat me to death." The officers then reportedly fired two warning shots, before shooting Henry once in the left side, the bullet exiting at his right hip. He died three hours later.[262]

James Henry, Jr., wrote to NAACP attorney Thurgood Marshall from Detroit, requesting an investigation of his brother's death, suggesting that Willie was slain "in cold blood." His description of Willie's military discharge, placed in care of elder brother Ezra, suggests that Willie may have suffered from posttraumatic stress disorder, known in the 1940s as "shell shock" or "battle fatigue," contributing to his reaction when he was assaulted. The Rev. J. E. Shepard, president of the NAACP's Lee County chapter, referred headquarters to Henry's aunt in Arkansas for further details, but the sparse legal file suggests that no investigation was conducted.[263]

J. C. Farmer
August 3, 1946; Sims, NC

Army veteran J. C. Farmer was standing at a bus stop in Wilson, North Carolina, when Constable Fes Bissette assaulted him without apparent cause. When Farmer defended himself, Bissette drew his pistol but only managed to shoot himself in the hand. Farmer escaped to his mother's home in Sims, nine miles west of Wilson, where a vigilante posse of 20 to 25 whites soon appeared and shot him dead in the front yard, while his mother watched from the porch. Prosecutors filed no charges against the killers.[264]

John J. Gilbert
August 3, 1946; Gordon, GA

A passing motorist found Gilbert, a chalk mill worker, lying at roadside near his home, dead from gunshot wounds. Investigation revealed that he was a union activist, suggesting murder by whites—perhaps Ku Klux Klansmen—who hated blacks and labor unions equally. The case remains officially unsolved.[265]

John Cecil Jones
August 8, 1946; Minden, LA

On July 30, 1946, Webster Parish sheriff's deputies arrested 17-year-old Albert Harris, Jr., for trespassing on the property of white neighbor Sam Maddry, Jr., allegedly tampering with a window screen and frightening Maddry's pregnant wife. After several days in jail, Deputy Oscar Henry Haynes, Jr.—son of the parish sheriff—delivered Harris to a mob at Dixie Inn. The vigilantes bound and beat Harris until he agreed to name his cousin, honorably discharged war veteran John Jones, as the actual prowler.[266]

The mob released Harris, but Haynes and another deputy visited his home on August 3, breaking his father's jaw and leaving orders for Albert Jr., to surrender. This he did on August 4, along with Jones. In jail, both prisoners were beaten and interrogated by Sheriff Haynes and Sam Maddry, Sr., but they denied any wrongdoing. On August 8 Deputy Haynes released the inmates to another mob, waiting outside the county jail. The lynchers drove their captives to a private pond outside of Minden, where Jones and Harris were tortured with a blowtorch and other weapons. The mob left both for dead, but Harris survived and escaped to a relative's home, later fleeing to Chicago and Detroit.[267]

NAACP officials investigated the lynching, obtaining a mortician's statement that "Jones had been burned about the face and body with a blowtorch, that he was mutilated and that his wrists were gouged out with a cleaver and that his eyeballs had popped out of his skull." Harris identified several lynchers, and a federal grand jury indicted six defendants—including Deputies Haynes and Charles Edwards, with Minden Police Chief Benjamin Gantt—on October 16, 1946. U.S. Attorney Malcolm Lafargue dismissed Gantt's charges when the chief agreed to testify against his codefendants.[268]

John Cecil Jones, tortured to death by lynchers on August 8, 1946 (National Archives).

At trial, a jailhouse trusty testified that he saw Deputy Haynes and Sam Maddry, Sr., beat the two victims one day before their release to the mob. Chief Gantt accused Haynes of conspiring with the lynchers, while the parish coroner confirmed that "lewd photos," allegedly found on Jones's body, had been planted postmortem. Three witnesses confirmed that Jones was playing dominoes with friends during the supposed trespassing incident, but defense attorneys branded them, Alfred Jr., and his father as dupes of the NAACP, coached in their testimony by FBI agents. An all-white, all-male jury acquitted the five defendants.[269] The verdict discouraged FBI Director J. Edgar Hoover from pursuing further civil rights cases, noting in a bitter memo that "We had clear-cut, incontrovertible evidence of a multiple agency cover-up."[270]

Deputy Haynes later succeeded his father as sheriff, serving from 1964 to 1980, then entered private business, dying in December 1996. His son, Oscar H. Haynes III, served in various positions with the sheriff's office from 1973 to 2008, while grandson Oscar H. Haynes IV joined the Louisiana State Police.[271] Carrie Lee Jones sued Sheriff Haynes, Sr., for $50,000 in August 1947, charging that he failed to provide her husband with safekeeping, but the parish district court dismissed that case.[272]

James Walker, Jr.
August 12, 1946; Elko, SC

On the last day of his life, Walker quarreled with white gas station owner Bill Craig and some of Craig's friends. A short time later, Craig and company found Walker sitting on the porch steps of his father's home, killing him with an army-issue M1 Garand rifle from a range of 125 feet. Afterward, Craig claimed self-defense, saying Walker was armed with a shotgun. As noted by the *Pittsburgh Courier*, "No such weapon was in the Walker home at the time of the slaying and the dead man had just arrived from Charleston and had no weapon of any sort." Barnwell County Sheriff Jeff Black and civilian helpers searched for the mythical shotgun, "suspicious of an invention," but never found it. Nonetheless, a coroner's jury accepted Craig's self-defense plea and released him.[273] In its 1952 genocide petition to the United Nations, the Civil Rights Congress listed Walker's slaying twice—once in August 1946, omitting a specific date and dropping "Jr." from his name, later correcting the name but placing his death on August 11, 1947.[274]

Berry L. Branch, Sr.
September 20, 1946; Houston, TX

Branch, a 60-year-old barber, took his last bus ride in Houston on September 17, 1946. During that brief journey, the white driver shot him in the face for reasons unknown today. Berry died from his wounds three days later, at Jefferson Davis Hospital.[275] My inquiries to local sources uncovered Berry's death certificate, but no details about the slaying.

Walter Lee Johnson
September 27, 1946; Atlanta, GA

Johnson, a war veteran recently discharged from service, was standing on a downtown sidewalk when a streetcar stopped in front of him. Recognizing one of the passengers, he called out to his friend in a joking tone. The streetcar's white conductor, thinking the "disrespectful" remark was meant for him, left the car and shot Johnson where he stood. Police questioned and released the gunman. Prosecutors filed no charges.[276]

Jesse James Payne
October 12, 1946; Madison, FL

Payne argued with his white boss in early July 1946, threatening to expose the employer's illegal activities. To silence him, the boss accused Payne of trying to molest his daughter. A posse arrested Payne at Monticello on July 4, wounding him in he process, and Madison County's sheriff lodged him in Raiford State Prison to avert lynching. Returned to Madison for trial three months later, on a charge of assault with intent to rape, Payne was left unguarded at the county jail overnight. Lynchers equipped with keys removed him and killed him with multiple gunshots. Florida attorney general J. Tom Watson recommended the sheriff's suspension, but Governor Millard Caldwell refused. Two separate grand juries failed to return indictments.[277]

Noverta Robinson
October 17, 1946; Walnut, MS

Robinson, age 24, was walking home from work when he was stopped by a law enforcement officer named Wells, described in various accounts as a policeman or a sheriff. According to eyewitness reports collected by the NAACP, Wells beat Robinson on the street, then took him to jail, detaining him before releasing him on bail. Robinson died several hours later, whereupon his wife, Canana Gunn, asked a Dr. Tate in Ripley to perform an autopsy. Tate refused, but a Dr. Ford in Brownsville, 45 miles distant, agreed, locating four blood clots in Robinson's brain. A coroner's inquest in Tippah County found no one at fault for the slaying.[278] My inquiries to local libraries and newspapers revealed no further details on this case.

Jose Adrano Trujillo Seitas
November 1, 1946; Bunnell, FL

A Flagler County sheriff's deputy shot Trujillo Seitas as the young war veteran sat in his own car outside a Jim Crow café. He had protested the establishment's whites-only policy, which prompted the proprietor to call for help. The summary execution threatened an international incident—Trujillo Seitas was the adopted nephew of Rafael Trujillo, president of the Dominican Republic—but local authorities declined to discipline the officer, accepting his claim of "self-defense."[279]

George Hill
November 15, 1946; Toomsboro, GA

On this Friday, 70-year-old Sam Gilbert, a dairy farmer and retired mail carrier, drove with his 62-year-old wife Dora to the home of George Hill, a black tenant living on their property. Sam Gilbert left his car and something went terribly wrong. According to Hill's wife, he grabbed a shotgun and first blasted Sam Gilbert, nearly severing his landlord's arm, then turned the gun on Dora, killing her in the car. Next, he set fire to his own home and barn, as well as a nearby vacant house, before fleeing to a third empty dwelling with his shotgun. Wilkinson County Sheriff George Hatcher organized a 75-man posse and led it to the scene, where Hill fired on the new arrivals, then ran into some woods close by and died in a second exchange of gunfire.[280]

Afterward, Hatcher told reporters he "could learn no motive" for Hill's deadly outburst, concluding that Hill "apparently went amok, completely crazy." Hatcher stressed that "there was no racial ill will involved in the affair."[281] Sam Gilbert was still alive on November 16, but my research for this work disclosed no further reports on his condition.

William M. Daniel
December 21, 1946; Westfield, AL

A sharecropper's son, born in 1925, Daniel served with the U.S. Army in World War II, then settled in Fairfield, a Birmingham suburb, living with Calphus Newton's family and working as a coal miner for TCI—the Tennessee Coal, Iron and Company. He married in September 1946, looking forward to a better life than that of his farming parents.[282]

Four days before Christmas, Daniel, wife Ruby, and neighbor Joe Windham went shopping at TCI's commissary in Westfield. During their visit, a white female clerk at the store complained to her boss that Daniel had "insulted," touched, or "brushed up against" her (accounts differ). Seven decades later, witness George D. Thomas claimed a white youth shopping in the store had touched the clerk playfully, then ducked behind a nearby staircase, so that when she turned, "The only thing she see is this black man walking up the stairs." In any case, the commissary's outraged manager summoned TCI Deputy J. W. Vanderford, who ejected Daniel from the store and followed him outside.[283]

Stories diverge on what came next. Fairfield Police Chief E. L. Allman told the *Birmingham News* that Vanderford planned to question Daniel about the clerk's complaint, then fired his pistol when Daniel "put his hand in his pocket." Ruby Daniel and Joe Windham, alerted by another shopper to William's impending arrest, reached the door in time to see Vanderford shoot him multiple times. Both would deny that Daniel made any threatening moves. Shopper Robert Lamarr, arriving after the gunfire, saw Daniel lying on the sidewalk, crying out that he "had been shot for nothing, and that God would punish him [Vanderford] for it." Transported to the TCI Employees Hospital, Daniel died nine hours later.[284]

The Southern Negro Youth Congress, headquartered in Birmingham, launched an investigation of Daniel's slaying on December 22, hiring detective Frank Hunter to collect eyewitness statements. Most denied that Daniel reached into his pocket prior to being shot, though one confirmed it, and another—Tom Rudolph, a TCI employee who had known Vanderford for years—changed his story radically over time, first denying that Daniel made any threatening moves, later claiming he "jumped back" 10 to 12 feet, reaching into his shirt as if for a weapon. Decades later, Demetrius Newton (son of Calphus) told researcher Michelle Newman, "There were two or three rumors that the white folks side was saying that he was feeling on the white woman. The other one being that the white woman asked him something and he forgot to say 'yes, ma'am.'" TCI employee Henry Bradley claimed Vanderford told him "he was sorry that he had shot the boy, but did so when he was angry."[285]

Despite alleged intimidation by TCI personnel, the SNYC delivered seven witness statements to Bessemer's prosecutor, who declined to arrest Vanderford but presented the case to Jefferson County's grand jury on February 20, 1947. Two days later, that panel returned a "no bill" and Daniel's case abruptly dropped out of the press. Ruby Daniel remained in Fairfield, remarried, then died prematurely at age 26, in 1954.[286]

Matt McWilliams

January 5, 1947; Daleville, MS

At 8:30 a.m. on January 5, Kemper County Sheriff Arnold Harbour, accompanied by brothers Jesse and L. L. Wilkerson, went to evict 68-year-old Matt McWilliams and his wife, 73-year-old Nettie, from their lucrative timber farm, outside Daleville. No documents survive explaining the eviction, but Southern whites often sought to dispossess African Americans whom they regarded as too "big" or prosperous. That morning, Harbour had a warrant to arrest McWilliams for "trespassing" on land he had owned for decades. During the arrest, McWilliams allegedly told his wife "he was not going to jail," then tried to snatch Harbour's pistol. According to the *Kemper County Messenger*, Harbour shot McWilliams once during that struggle, then three more times as McWilliams tried to reach his own shotgun, finally killing him.[287] Curiously, a death certificate signed by Sheriff Harbour lists only one wound, a "gun shot in breast."[288]

Harbour faced a hearing on Monday morning, in DeKalb, before Justice of the Peace L. F. Hardy. Jesse Wilkerson described the shooting, calling McWilliams a "bad negro" who had once attacked him for no reason with an axe. Brother L. L. Wilkerson agreed, saying "he had had trouble with [McWilliams] also." Even Justice Shumate, sharing the bench with Hardy, chimed in, claiming "he also had had trouble with McWilliams when he was constable." District Attorney Red Brown told the court, "This killing was completely justifiable on ground of self-defense." He urged Harbour's release without bond, and the justices agreed, permitting the *Messenger* to report that "Mr. Harbour was thoroughly exonerated."[289]

No records presently disclose the disposition of McWilliams's land, but geographical discrepancies surround his death. The *Messenger* claimed he lived in Blackwater, south of DeKalb, while another report places his home in the county seat itself. McWilliams's death certificate says he was shot at home in Daleville, listed by two gazetteers as an unincorporated community in northern Lauderdale County, neighboring Kemper County to the south. Maps from those sources, however, appear to place Daleville squarely on the county line.[290] Whatever the precise location, Lauderdale County authorities took no interest in the slaying.

Willie Earle

February 17, 1947; Pickens County, SC

Earle, a 24-year-old African American, hired white cabbie Thomas Watson Brown to drive him from Greenville to Earle's mother's house in Pickens County on the night of February 15. Before midnight, police in Pickens found Brown stabbed and seemingly robbed. They identified Earle as Brown's last known fare and arrested him, lodging him in the county jail. When Brown died at St. Francis Hospital on February 16, Earle's charge was upgraded to murder.[291]

In the early hours of February 17, Greenville taxi drivers formed a convoy, descended on the jail, and demanded Earle's surrender from the solitary jailer, who complied. Driving Earle first to the Saluda Dam, the lynchers obtained his "confession," then rolled on toward Bramlett Road in Green County, where they beat Earle, stabbed and mutilated him, one lyncher breaking the stock of a shotgun over his head. Finally, point-blank shotgun blasts snuffed out the last spark of life. Departing, the killers phoned black mortician S. C. Franks to collect Earle's corpse.[292]

New governor Strom Thurmond sent a state constable to investigate Earle's murder, while FBI agents and a U.S. marshal examined federal issues. They quickly "exonerated" the jailer, then stayed to assist local officers in identifying the lynchers. By February 21, agents had questioned 150 suspects and charged 31, all but three of them cabbies. Twenty-six confessed, several naming Roosevelt Carlos Hurd as the mob's leader and

Earle's shotgun executioner. Trial convened in Greenville on May 5, covered by journalists including Dame Rebecca West for the *New Yorker*.[293]

The defense played openly to racial prejudice throughout the trial. At one point, an attorney for the lynchers said, "Willie Earle is dead and I wish more like him was dead." Dame West observed, "There was a delighted giggling, almost coquettish response from the defendants and some of the spectators. A more disgusting incident could not have happened in any court of law at any time."

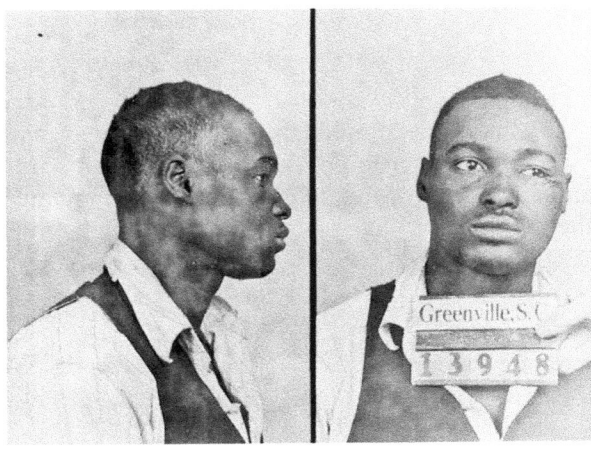

Police mug shot of Willie Earle, taken shortly before his February 17, 1947, lynching (National Archives).

One cabbie who refused to join the mob found nerve enough to testify against them. Later, he was beaten and run out of Greenville by "persons unknown." Relying on the all-white jury's racism, defense attorneys called no witnesses, nor was their faith misplaced. On May 21, the panel acquitted all 31 defendants. Furious, Judge J. Robert Martin left the courtroom without the customary thanks to jurors for their service.[294]

Willie Earle's killers and supporters celebrate their May 1947 acquittals (National Archives).

Charles White
April 23, 1947; La Junta, CO

White, a decorated Hispanic war veteran recently discharged from the U.S. Army, objected to exclusion of two other Mexican Americans from a public tavern. Anglos attacked him, and White died in the ensuing brawl. Authorities took no action against the bar's owner. Local inquiries in 2014 failed to disclose if anyone was charged with White's slaying.[295]

William Pittman
May 1947; Rocky Mount, NC

Passersby found the mutilated, decomposing corpse of black cab driver William Pittman beside a country road outside of town, with his taxi abandoned in the woods nearby. His skull was crushed, limbs severed, and his torso sliced open. An autopsy could not determine Pittman's date of death precisely. While local whites hushed up the crime, a report of it reached the National Negro Congress on May 27. The case, considered a possible lynching, remains unsolved today.[296]

Joe Nathan Roberts
May 1947; Sardis, GA

A 23-year-old army veteran, attending Philadelphia's Temple University on the GI Bill, Roberts was visiting relatives in Georgia when a white man reportedly shot him for failing to say "Yes, sir" in response to a question.[297] Inquiries to local sources, seeking further details, went unanswered.

Mary Lizzie Norris
May 4, 1947; Camp Hill, AL

The death of this victim—called "Mary Irvin," "Mary Mathews," and "Mary Noyes" in various accounts, listed as Mary Norris on her death certificate—resulted from a rampage initiated by racist Albert O. Huey. The trouble began when Huey confronted black war veteran Australia Farrow, demanding that Farrow surrender a cane he was carrying. Farrow refused, saying it belonged to his granddaughter, and Huey left in a rage, soon returning with a second white man, Charles Chester. This time, Huey pulled a knife on Farrow and a struggle ensued, during which Farrow struck Huey with the cane. Farrow then fled, pursued by Chester, while Huey left to retrieve a pistol. On his way home, Huey met policeman Otis Smith, announcing plans to "run all Negroes out of the streets because they had no damn business being there."[298]

Huey returned 30 minutes after sundown, prowling around Pecan Alley, Camp Hill's African American district, with several white companions, allegedly including both of Camp Hill's police officers. Huey assaulted women on their porches, pistol-whipping several, then invaded a diner and fired at its owner, chasing him outside. Next he moved on to the Veterans Café, a white establishment with segregated seating for blacks at the rear. Entering that section, Huey punched and pistol-whipped several diners, then shot Mary Norris, a 22-year-old mother of three who was five months pregnant. Norris staggered away to the home of a white woman, Mrs. Emory Reeves, who sent a friend to fetch Norris's family. By the time they returned, she was dead.[299]

Tallapoosa County sheriff's deputy Horace Aiken arrested Huey at 8 p.m., releasing him on $1,000 bond the next day. Meanwhile, the case took a strange turn as prosecutors charged Australia Farrow with attempted murder, for defending himself against Huey. Both men appeared at separate hearings on June 2, where Huey's murder charge was apparently dismissed. Officer Smith acknowledged Huey's threat against the black community, but said he failed to restrain Huey because "his arm was sore." No evidence exists today concerning disposition of Farrow's case. Norris's father, Tom Erwin (called "Truin" in some reports) hired attorney Nesbitt Elmore of Montgomery to sue Huey, but no record remains of that case. Huey died in May 1986, at age 82.[300]

Ernest Gilbert
May 24, 1947; Gretna, VA

Gilbert was a prosperous Pittsylvania County farmer, described in contradictory reports as being 65 or 68 years old. Around 8:30 p.m. on Saturday night, two white men knocked at his door while Gilbert, his wife, and their young grandson were in the living room. A son, age 16, was asleep in a nearby bedroom. The men first asked Gilbert if he had any whiskey, then one drew a pistol when Gilbert denied it, holding the three hostages at gunpoint while his partner crossed the hallway to a parlor where Gilbert kept a 400-pound safe. When Gilbert heard the safe rolling, he began to rise and was shot once, then grappled with the gunman, taking four more shots before he collapsed and died. While that occurred, an unseen accomplice was backing a vehicle up to the family's porch. The gunman's partner called outside for help, whereupon someone fired several shots through the window but did not enter. Finally, the two invaders rolled the safe outside, placed it in their vehicle, and fled.[301]

By May 30, Sheriff Arch Overbey's deputies had arrested three suspects—Calvin Coolige [sic] Haile (spelled "Hale" in a later report), Ray Peters, and Toby Smith—all "mountain men" from the neighborhood of Ferrum, in Franklin County. Overbey told reporters they all "seem to be about 25 years old," freely admitting that he was "not certain" of their guilt. The three were suspected moonshiners, and witnesses placed their car in Gretna on May 24, but lawyer Brady Allman secured their release on bail, on June 6, after presenting "perfect alibis."[302]

Part of the problem was a series of vague, conflicting stories told by Gilbert's widow. She denied seeing either of the home invaders previously, and despite witnessing her husband's death at close range, she could not describe either unmasked bandit's face. The gunman was, she said, "a stocky, medium heighth [sic] person," while his accomplice was shorter. As for the safe, never recovered, Gilbert's relatives all knew he kept money in it, but none knew the amount, offering estimates that ranged from $1,500 to $15,000. Sheriff Overbey opined that the killers had their plan "well worked out" in advance and "knew their way around the house."[303]

While the first three suspects vanished from the public record, Overbey charged another—23-year-old Elton Wheeler, also from Ferrum—with Gilbert's murder in late 1947. At trial in January 1948, Wheeler testified that he spent the whole night of May 24 at the Polecat Inn, a dive in Franklin County, but two girlfriends contradicted him, saying Wheeler left them alone for a two-hour period. Gilbert's widow testified for the prosecution, but her "conflicting testimony" concerned Judge Kennon Whittle, who charged jurors to return a "fair" verdict. The all-white panel deliberated for 25 minutes before acquitting Wheeler on January 21.[304] Gilbert's case remains officially unsolved.

Elijah Myles
July 1947; Orleans Parish, LA

Ferdinand J. Mohr, white foreman of the parish agricultural dump, killed 21-year-old Elijah Myles and claimed self-defense, although postmortem tests proved Myles was shot in the back. A grand jury refused to indict Mohr.[305] Local inquiries produced no further information.

Anguilla Stockade Massacre
July 11, 1947; Anguilla, GA

In 1947, Anguilla—12 miles northwest of Brunswick—was home to State Highway Camp No. 18, commonly called the Anguilla Stockade. It housed 75 African American inmates, assigned to work on road maintenance crews.[306] On July 11 of that year, stockade guards shot 13 prisoners, fatally wounding eight, under circumstances that remain disputed to this day.

The *New York Times* informed America of the Anguilla massacre on July 12, under a headline reading "Five convicts slain in break in Georgia." That article carried Warden H. G. Worthy's version of events, as follows:

> A group of new prisoners joined the camp yesterday and were sent out today to work on the Jesup Highway. The new men refused to work and were brought back to the camp about 4 p.m. They would not get out of the trucks when ordered and Warden Worthy called county police.
>
> Chief of Police Russell B. Henderson of Glynn County talked to the prisoners and told them to do what the warden ordered, "cut out that foolishness."
>
> The men left the trucks and were lined up in the prison enclosure. When the police chief finished talking to them they broke, ran to the barracks and dove under the building, which is about two feet off the ground. The prisoners crawled on under the building and ran toward the fence enclosure on the other side.
>
> Officers then opened fire with shotguns and rifles. Five were killed and eight were wounded. Fourteen prisoners came back and surrendered.[307]

Three more inmates died from their wounds over the next two days, while the local *Brunswick News* amended Warden Worthy's account of the shootings. According to that paper's coverage, Worthy "strode into a group of unruly negro convicts about 8:30 o'clock yesterday afternoon [*sic*]." Ringleader Willie E. Bell, "a long-timer and reported trouble-maker," cursed the assembled officers, prompting Worthy to remove him from the group. At that, Bell reportedly "lunged" at Worthy, whereupon the warden shot him in one leg. Six guards then opened fire with shotguns and pistols, as "the prisoners broke in all directions, men scrambling over the nearby bunk house." One scaled a 10-foot fence, only to fall dead on the other side. Fourteen inmates escaped injury, as they "crouched or lay still on the ground." Chief Henderson supported that account, while noting that he and his men, armed with submachine guns, did not fire on the prisoners.[308]

Coroner J. D. Baldwin convened an inquest, with attorney Vance Mitchell representing Warden Worthy, while Brunswick's NAACP chapter launched its own investigation of the slayings, led by attorney C. J. Cogdell. Judge Gordon Knox convened a grand jury, while conflicting stories of the massacre began to filter out of the stockade.[309] Survivor Willie Bell testified that Worthy was "half-drunk and wanted to kill me," a charge disputed by J. B. Hatchett, assistant director of the State Department of Corrections. On July 18 the grand jury exonerated Worthy and five of his guards, ruling the shootings justified.[310]

The story did not end there, however. Soon, reports from the NAACP revealed that Worthy's guards had "ordered the Negro prisoners into a ditch occupied by poisonous snakes," denying them protective boots. Those who protested, that report said, had been shot. Glynn County Commissioner Sam Levine told an August hearing of the State Board of Corrections, "There was no justification for the killings. The chief of county police and two policemen were there, but they didn't see any reason to shoot the prisoners. They had tear gas guns they could have used. I saw the Negroes where they fell. Two were killed where they crawled under the bunkhouse and two others as they ran under their cells. The only thing they were trying to escape was death. Only one tried to get over the fence." If the inmates wanted to escape, Levine explained, they "could have overpowered their two guards on the road instead of waiting until they were back in the barracks surrounded by guards and police all heavily armed."[311]

The Board of Corrections branded the July grand jury's verdict a "one-sided whitewash investigation," ordered a new examination of the evidence, and closed the Anguilla Stockade. In October 1947 a federal grand jury charged Worthy and four guards with violating eight dead inmates' constitutional right "to be secure in their person while in the custody of the State of Georgia and to be immune from illegal attack at the hands of officers and employees of the State of Georgia while in custody, and not to be subjected to punishment without due process of law." Trial convened on October 27, with multiple prisoners describing threats "made against prisoners engaged in road work after the convicts declined to work in ditches they said were filled with water and snakes." Defense attorney Mitchell countered by telling the all-white jury, "The men in the detail were rapists, murderers and burglars and all but one had escaped on previous occasions. The guards fired upon the convicts in defense of their own lives." Jurors agreed, deliberating for eight minutes before they acquitted all five defendants, on November 4.[312]

William Brown

July 17, 1947; Pointe Coupee Parish, LA

On the last day of his life, 83-year-old William Brown went hunting, as was his daily habit. This time, he met white game warden Charles Ventril, who noted Brown's lack of a hunting license. Directing Brown to the forest's edge, Ventril shot him in the back of the head, then approached a white sharecropper working nearby and said, "I just shot a nigger. Let his folks know." Ventril was exonerated, the parish coroner's report reading: "The Negro's gun was cocked; the killing was justified because the game warden shot in self-defense."[313]

Versie Johnson
August 1, 1947; Prentiss, MS

Johnson was arrested for raping a white woman, held at the crime scene, instead of being lodged at the Jefferson Davis County jail. According to the *Orlando Morning Sentinel*, a white mob gave the sheriff a deadline for obtaining Johnson's confession, but time ran out when Johnson allegedly grabbed for a highway patrolman's pistol, prompting a fatal barrage of gunfire.[314] In its 1952 genocide petition to the United Nations, the Civil Rights Congress reported three officers charged with manslaughter, subsequently acquitted.[315] Local inquiries failed to reveal the officers' names or any other details of the case.

Beverly Lee
October 12, 1947; Detroit, MI

Patrolman Louis Begin shot 13-year-old Beverly Lee on Pine Street without apparent cause. A witness, Mrs. Francis Vonbatten, described the patrol car approaching Lee and a companion who were walking on the sidewalk. Officer Begin shouted, "Stop, you little so-and-so"—profanity omitted from Mrs. Vonbattten's statement—then fired the shot that killed Lee. Coroner Lloyd K. Babcock ruled the slaying "justified."[316]

Amos Starr
October 25, 1947; Tallassee, AL

Around 3 p.m. on Saturday, Officer Cecil Orris Thrash claimed he saw Starr, age 35, selling whiskey to a pair unnamed men, a misdemeanor under Alabama law. Starr fled as Thrash approached, eluding him, but Thrash and two other officers found him at 5 p.m., talking to friends outside May's Café. Again, Starr ran, leading police on a chase that ended with gunfire. Since shooting misdemeanor suspects was illegal, Thrash claimed self-defense, saying that Starr first hurled a rock at the pursuing officers, then pulled a knife. Elmore County's sheriff soon arrived, stripped Starr's corpse at the scene, and pronounced him dead from a shot to the chest, ostensible supporting Thrash's story.[317] Starr's death certificate rubber-stamped that verdict, attributing death to a "gun shot wound of chest (shot by police)."[318]

Matters might have rested there but for Edgar Daniel Nixon, president of Montgomery's NAACP chapter, later a leading figure in that city's historic bus boycott. Suspicious of the hasty verdict in Starr's case, Nixon lobbied for an independent autopsy, finally performed on May 19, 1949. That examination proved Starr was shot from behind, the fatal bullet entering below his right shoulder blade and exiting through his chest near the right armpit. With that evidence in hand, a federal grand jury indicted Thrash on September 14, 1949, charging that he "wilfully [sic] shot and killed the said Amos Starr without cause" during a misdemeanor arrest.[319]

Momentum from that indictment spread statewide, with federal investigation and prosecution of five other police officers—including ex-Police Chief Thomas I. Gantt of Covington County—on civil rights charges in other, unrelated cases, but justice remained elusive for Starr's family. Thrash faced trial on November 3, 1949, and was acquitted the following day, after white jurors deliberated for a mere 22 minutes. Starr's slayer died in December 1989, nearly two decades prior to passage of the Till Act.[320]

Roland T. Price
November 6, 1947; Rochester, NY

Price, a 20-year-old military veteran, quarreled with a white bartender at the Royal Palm Restaurant after being shortchanged. The bartender drew a pistol and called police. Six officers responded to the call, five waiting on the street while Patrolman William Hamill entered the restaurant with gun drawn and ordered Price outside. There, all six policemen opened fire on Price, striking him 25 times and killing him instantly. Although Price was unarmed and offered no physical resistance, the shooting was deemed "justified."[321]

Raymond Couser and Charles Fletcher
November 16, 1947; Philadelphia, PA

Witnesses described Patrolman Frank Cacurro stalking black pedestrian Raymond Couser with a drawn pistol on Montrose Street. After trailing him for some distance, Cacurro shot Couser four times, killing him. Cacurro claimed he was sent to Couser's home to investigate a domestic disturbance and fired in the mistaken event that Couser was armed. Later on the same day, in a separate incident, Patrolman Manus McGettingan answered a prowler call and fatally shot unarmed pedestrian Charles Fletcher, a 10-year employee of the Exide Battery Company with no police record. Both slayings were ruled "justified."[322]

Charles Smith
November 23, 1947; Lillington, SC

White gunmen Wyatt Adams and Marvin Matthews carried out a reign of terror in the town's black community, killing Charles Smith and wounding Daniel Lee Brasford with drive-by gunshots, also trying to run down several other African Americans. At their murder trial, multiple witnesses described attacks by the pair during their rampage. A white jury deliberated for 27 minutes before acquitting both defendants of all charges.[323]

Elmore Bolling
December 4, 1947; Lowndesboro, AL

Elmore Bolling was a self-made man. Born in 1908, he entered school belatedly at age 13, then quit before completing first grade, embarrassed by the age disparity between his classmates and himself. He never learned to read or write, but succeeded without formal education, farming in "Bloody Lowndes" County by age 18, founding a livestock-hauling business five years later, with a Ford Model T converted into a truck. White friend Thomas Belvin Holley bought the vehicle and served as Bolling's front in business, furnishing registration papers in the name of a nonexistent "Bob Dickson." Later, other white farmers joined in the charade, providing forged bills of lading. Bolling prospered, buying a full-size semi trailer, hiring multiple drivers and providing them with lodging, all while running a successful general store in Lowndesboro.[324]

It was too much for certain white neighbors, who resented Bolling's success. On December 4, passersby found Bolling dead, 150 yards from his store, riddled with shotgun pellets and pistol slugs. Authorities jailed a white suspect, Producers Commission Company Union Stock employee Charles Luckie, who claimed Bolling had insulted his wife on the telephone. Initially released on $2,500 bond, Luckie never faced trial for the slaying.[325] Today, a wayside marker on the spot where Bolling died declares, "It is believed that more than one person figured in the murder.... Those who 'know' say Bolling has [sic] long been a 'marked man' since he was rated by whites here as 'too successful to be a Negro.'"[326]

Memorial plaque for murder victim Elmer Bolling outside Lowndesboro, Alabama (author's collection).

Charles Curry
December 17, 1947; Corsicana, TX

Off-duty Dallas policeman Nolan O. Ray, age 24, was riding a Corsicana streetcar when an African American man sat beside him. Ray ordered the man to move, prompting complaints from other black passengers. Ray then stood, drew his pistol, and ordered all blacks on the car to "take your hands out of your pockets," fatally shooting Charles Curry when Curry did not move fast enough to suit him. Ray claimed he "thought he saw" Curry pulling a knife, though none was found on the corpse. Other witnesses reported that Curry neither spoke nor moved during the confrontation. Police Chief Carl Hansen fired Ray on December 19.[327] A Navarro County grand jury indicted Nolan for "murder without malice," but an all-white jury acquitted him on October 5, 1949.[328]

James Harmon
January 28, 1948; Camden, NJ

Patrolmen James Hooven and William Yeager arrested 30-year-old construction worker James Harmon on charges of being drunk and disorderly. Officers held him incommunicado for 25 days, then delivered him to Lakeland General Hospital with obvious signs of prolonged, severe beating. When he died, police spokesmen initially blamed "heart disease," but postmortem testing attributed Harmon's death to blood poisoning. Relatives challenged the premise of his arrest, declaring that Harmon was a teetotaler. Prosecutors filed no charges.[329]

James Tolliver
February 1948; Little Rock, AR

Tolliver, age 40, saw a drunk white woman fall on a public sidewalk sometime in the last week of February. He was trying to help her up when a policeman named Blaylock approached from behind him, clubbing him over the head. Tolliver died at the scene with a fractured skull.[330] Local inquiries revealed no further information on this case.

Roy Cyril Brooks
February 27, 1948; Gretna, LA

After boarding a city bus and paying her nickel fare, an African American woman discovered she had picked the wrong bus and asked for her money back. The white driver refused, whereupon Roy Brooks, waiting to board, gave the woman a nickel and asked to ride on the fare she had already paid. Traffic policeman Alvin Bladsacker heard the driver shouting his refusal and rushed Brooks from behind, striking him in the back of his head, drawing blood. Pulling his pistol, Bladsacker prodded Brooks off the bus and began walking him toward the police station. When Brooks half-turned, saying he had done nothing wrong, Bladsacker shot him twice. Brooks died 40 minutes later, prompting Bladsacker's indictment for manslaughter, but prosecutors later dropped the charge and he returned to duty.[331]

Rayfield Davis
March 7, 1948; Mobile County, AL

White gunman Horace Miller shot 35-year-old Rayfield Davis during a "civil rights squabble." Although Davis was unarmed, the county grand jury accepted Miller's plea of self-defense and filed no charges.[332]

Ellis Hutson, Sr.
March 13, 1948; Nacogdoches, TX

Constable Travis Helpenstill had a savage reputation among black residents of Nacogdoches County. A former marine who had served in combat on Saipan and Iwo Jima, Helpenstill had no experience in law enforcement when he sought the constable's post in 1946, at age 21, running on the slogan "Old enough to know what to do, experienced enough to know how to do it, and young enough to do it." Elected as the youngest constable in Texas history, he took office on January 1, 1947. One month later, on February 2, he saw the Rev. Willie Lee Mergerson, a 41-year-old Baptist preacher and father of seven, walking home from Sunday services at his church. Helpenstill approached Mergerson aggressively, prompting the minister to flee, and fired shots as he ran, finally overtaking Mergerson when the minister stopped at a taxi stand to phone the county sheriff for help. Enlisting aid from several white youths, Helpenstill beat Mergerson there, and again at another location, stripping him of his clothes before white passersby arrived and demanded Mergerson's release. Hospitalized with a fractured skull that required insertion of a steel plate, suffering from brain damage that caused severe headaches for the remainder of his life, Mergerson reported the beating to FBI agents on February 5 and hired white attorney Arthur Lowery to sue Helpenstill.[333]

One day later, Helpenstill entered Mergerson's hospital room, waving his pistol, and "threatened to kill him if he attempted to take any step against him in any manner." On the same day, February 6, Helpenstill's father visited Mergerson's home, pressuring his wife and children to drop the lawsuit. They fled into hiding, while a county grand jury considered Helpenstill's case, indicting him for assault on May 28, 1947. Despite that formal charge, however, Helpenstill was never arrested, arraigned, or tried. His charge was dismissed on a motion from the state's attorney nearly two years later, on January 17, 1949. Mergerson filed a $20,000 civil suit against Helpenstill, but it was also dismissed. In 1956 the minister suffered a fatal car crash, physicians telling his family he would have survived but for the plate in his skull.[334]

Helpenstill's brutality sometimes spilled over to the white community, as when he recklessly fired shots into a white couple's car, wounding a woman in the back. Rumors also circulated that he killed a pregnant white woman by deliberately striking her with his car. Time and again he wriggled through the legal net, escaping punishment.[335]

On March 8, 1948, Helpenstill joined Police Chief M. C. Roebuck and other officers in removing black war veteran Turner White from his home, ostensibly to question him on his whereabouts two nights earlier. Repeatedly harassed by white police since his return from service in World War II, White reported on this occasion that Helpenstill beat him, then falsely charged him with public drunkenness. White pled guilty the next morning and obeyed Helpenstill's order to leave Nacogdoches, traveling to a veterans' hospital in Louisiana, where physicians treated him for injuries to his head, eyes, and legs. White's wife and children soon followed him, leaving Nacogdoches forever.[336]

Ellis Hutson, Sr., killed by Constable Travis Helpenstill on March 13, 1948 (Civil Rights Archive).

Four days later, on March 12, African American cousins Ellis Hutson, Jr., and Elree Littles, both 24 years old, were transporting a hog to a neighbor's farm for breeding, passing by a car that had sat abandoned in a roadside ditch for weeks. Near that vehicle, another car approached, bearing three white men: Constable Helpenstill was at the wheel, accompanied by Deputy Constable G. W. "Happy" Copeland and a civilian, Hal B. Stripling, Jr. Helpenstill questioned the cousins about the junk car and their pig, then drove on after Littles answered him. Moments later, the trio returned, Helpenstill ordering Hutson to approach his car. When Hutson complied, Helpenstill asked if Hutson knew who he was. Hutson replied in the negative, neglecting to call the 23-year-old lawman "Sir." Furious, Helpenstill leaped from the car, drew a pistol, and struck Hutson with it. Hutson fought back, at which time Helpenstill identified himself as "the law." Hutson fled on foot, but returned when Helpenstill threatened to kill Littles. The three whites then forced Hutson into their car and drove off, leaving Littles alone.[337]

Copeland drove as the group proceeded to Eggnog Branch, a nearby stream, while Helpenstill continued beating Hutson with his pistol in the car's backseat. Arriving at their destination, Helpenstill ordered Hutson to wash the blood from his face, then shoved him into the stream. Two of Hutson's neighbors, passing by on foot, witnessed that assault and heard Helpenstill telling Hutson to "take this pistol so I can kill you." Hutson refused and begged for his life, whereupon the white men dragged him back to their car and drove to the Nacogdoches County jail, Helpenstill continuing to beat and prod Hutson with his pistol, asking, "If I don't kill you, will you go to the FBI or go get you a colored lawyer, or will you plead guilty before the judge in the morning?" To save himself, Hutson agreed. En route to jail, Deputy Copeland tried without success to place a pistol in Hutson's hand, apparently to mark it with his fingerprints for a subsequent frame-up.[338]

Arriving at the county jail, Helpenstill and Sheriff Hagan Parmley placed Hutson in a cell, as NAACP lawyers later claimed, "without complaint, warrant of arrest, commitment or legal process of any kind." Later that night, Helpenstill returned with Chief Roebuck and Officer Pad Spradley, Roebuck beating Hutson and threatening to kill him while the others held him down. The next morning, Deputy Copeland escorted Hutson to court for arraignment on an assault charge, reminding Hutson of his promise to plead guilty. County Attorney Harlon Martin spoiled that plan, however, informing Hutson that no guilty plea was required, and in fact it might prove more expensive. Hutson therefore denied the assault charge, despite Copeland's warning that Helpenstill would be angry.[339]

At 10 o'clock that morning, after consulting attorney Arthur Lowery, Ellis Hutson, Sr., arrived at the jail with girlfriend Charlean Hudson to post bond for his son. Helpenstill arrived moments later, described by Justice of the Peace Hugh B. Davis as "agitated." First, Helpenstill phoned Lowery from Davis's office, challenging his legal advice to Ellis Jr., threatening the lawyer's life in the presence of Ellis Sr. and Ms. Hudson. Next, Helpenstill ordered Ellis Sr. to follow him from Davis's office, into a secluded hallway. Within seconds, Helpenstill shouted, "You tried to pull a knife on me!" and shot Ellis Sr. three times in the chest.[340]

A six-inch pocketknife lay beside Hutson's body, but Ms. Hudson swore that he neither owned nor carried one. Furthermore, autopsy results showed that Hutson was "standing at right angles" to Helpenstill when the constable shot him. Arthur Lowery, who had cautioned Ellis Sr. against taking any weapons to the courthouse, later testified that Hutson had "pulled out his pockets" to prove himself unarmed before leaving the lawyer's office. Ellis Jr. left jail 90 minutes after his father was killed, stayed in Nacogdoches for the funeral on March 17, then fled the county. Helpenstill also left town, entering a navy hospital in Houston for treatment of injuries from a year-old auto accident. Lawyer Lowery remained, telling NAACP investigators that he now feared being "shot in the back."[341]

Under pressure from the NAACP, a grand jury indicted Helpenstill for Hutson's murder on May 28, 1948. Returning from Houston on May 31, Helpenstill was arrested, then released on bond, resigning from his post and stating that he would not run for reelection. Helpenstill's trial before an all-white jury convened on June 8 and ended with acquittal on a plea of self-defense, two days later.[342]

On August 25, 1948, Ellis Hutson, Jr., filed a $22,500 civil lawsuit against Helpenstill, then settled out of court with an insurance company that bonded Helpenstill for $1,050 plus legal fees. On February 20, 1950, a federal grand jury indicted Helpenstill on two counts of conspiracy to violate Ellis Jr.'s civil rights. Helpenstill represented himself at trial, pleading *nolo contendere* to one count on October 2, 1950, while the other charge was dismissed. He received a 90-day suspended jail sentence, effectively evading punishment once more.[343]

Samuel Mason Bacon
March 15, 1948; Fayette, MS

A Mississippi native, born in 1897, Bacon moved to Akron, Ohio, in 1942, working for the Firestone Rubber Company and living with his eldest daughter. On March 12, 1948, he boarded a Greyhound bus en route to Natchez, Mississippi, hoping to visit relatives and reconcile with his estranged wife. By March 14 Bacon had reached Fayette, 23 miles northeast of Natchez, where Marshal Stanton D. Coleman arrested him for "disturbing the peace" and lodged Bacon in the Jefferson County jail.[344]

Stories differ as to why Bacon was jailed. The *Natchez Democrat* claimed he was "raising a disturbance and using abusive language," while the *Pittsburgh Courier* told readers he "refused to stand in the bus when vacant seats were available." More specifically, according to the *Chicago Defender*, seating in the rear section reserved for African Americans was full, while seats in the forward "white" section were vacant. Great-nephew Paul Bacon suggested that Samuel's very appearance may have troubled Mississippi whites. "When he got down this way," Paul told researcher Mary Nguyen, "wearing a shirt and tie, that gave him a title of what some would consider to be an 'uppity nigger.'" Samuel's family, waiting to meet him in Natchez, learned from other passengers that he had been arrested in Fayette. By the time brother Warrington reached Fayette to retrieve him, Samuel was dead.[345]

Marshal Coleman later told an FBI agent he visited the jail early on March 15, "to get some tools [he] had stored there and check on Bacon." Unknown to jailer Herbert Willison, he had placed Bacon in a cell where Coleman stored tools including an axe, rake, and broom. When Coleman opened Bacon's cell to remove the potential weapons, Bacon allegedly "came rushing out the door," armed with the axe. Coleman said he struck Bacon with a blackjack, then grabbed one of his feet and tried to drag Bacon back inside the cell, aided by 70-year-old janitor Bill Gray. During that struggle, Coleman claimed Bacon lashed out with his free leg, knocking Coleman "about six or seven feet away." Coleman drew his pistol and Bacon allegedly lunged for it, continuing the battle in which Bacon "picked [Coleman] up clear of the ground some two or three times attempting to get the gun." An accidental shot mortally wounded Bacon, Coleman claimed, saying, "I could not tell if this man was drinking, under the influence of dope, or what was wrong with him, if anything. He was very powerful, and active, more so than the average drunk man."[346]

Within days of the slaying, Attorney General Tom C. Clark received letters from the NAACP and the Southern Negro Youth Congress—which employed one of Bacon's daughters at its Birmingham headquarters—urging a "speedy and vigorous" federal investigation. The SNYC branded Coleman's tale of a conveniently forgotten axe a "transparent and clumsy coverup for barbaric cruelty."[347] The FBI assigned Agent George A. Gunter from New Orleans, known for his hostility toward African Americans and civil rights groups, to investigate the case.[348]

Immediately, whites closed ranks to paint Bacon in the worst possible light. Tri-State Coach Lines driver James H. Minninger claimed that when Bacon boarded his bus in Vicksburg, he shoved other passengers aside, saying in a loud voice that he was "the voice of Firestone." Agent Gunter claimed that Minninger "asked [Bacon] in a nice way to please keep quiet," but Bacon refused. En route to Fayette, Minninger stopped at Port Gibson,

Samuel Bacon, killed in jail by Marshal Stanton Coleman on March 15, 1948 (Civil Rights Archive).

where a white man boarded the bus and demanded Bacon's seat. Bacon's refusal further angered Minninger and his white passengers. One of those told Gunter Bacon had shoved his young daughter, declaring that "he would have shot [Bacon], himself, if he had a gun." Another claimed Bacon was ranting against bus drivers, convincing her he was a union activist who planned too "start trouble for non-union bus drivers." Other whites aboard claimed Bacon was drunk, high on drugs, or "possibly insane." Gunter accepted those statements, and Marshal Coleman's, at face value, advising headquarters that his inquiry "did not disclose any evidence of violation of any Federal law on part of the arresting officers and Town Marshal."[349]

Against that "evidence," the *Chicago Defender* quoted a witness who claimed Coleman said he planned to "kill the nigger because he didn't know his place."[350] That comment did not reach Jefferson County's all-white grand jury, which exonerated Coleman on September 23, based on testimony from Coleman and Bill Gray. The panel praised Coleman's "maintenance of law and order," noting for the record that it had only convened to refute "unfavorable publicity in Northern negro newspapers."[351]

Otis Newsome
March 27, 1948; Wilson, NC

Newsome, a 26-year-old father of two and war veteran-turned-funeral director, went shopping for brake fluid on March 27, with friend James Williams. Service station attendant U. C. Strickland provided the fluid, but refused to either install it in Newsome's car or loan Newsome a funnel, saying, "All I want from you is 85 cents for the fluid." Incensed, Newsome replied, "If I can't get it into the car I don't want it." Then, according to Williams, Strickland drew a pistol from beneath the counter and shot Newsome in the torso. Transported to Mercy Hospital, Newsome died a short time later.[352]

Police Chief A. A. Privette arrested Strickland on March 29, charging him with first-degree murder. Strickland pled not guilty on March 30, whereupon Recorder Charles B. McLean ordered him held without bail pending trial. Despite that order, the Wilson County's superior court released him on April 3, after friend J. L. Boykin posted $5,000 bond. A grand jury indicted Strickland for murder in May 1948, charging that he "feloniously, willfully and of his malice aforethought did kill and murder one Odis [*sic*] Newsome."[353]

Before his trial on that charge, Strickland was arrested once again, in July, for possessing untaxed liquor. Convicted on that charge, he paid a $150 fine and court costs, but his bail was not revoked in the Newsome case. Strickland's murder trial convened on September 8, 1948, with the defense producing white witness Robert Deans to contradict James Williams's account.[354] As reported in the *Wilson Daily Times*,

> Robert Deans told the jury that Strickland was attacked by Newsome, who at the time, was carrying a knife in his right pocket. Deans said that he recalled the shooting clearly because he saw Newsome put his hand into his pocket and withdraw an object which he at first thought was a gun. Deans said that Strickland shot Newsome and as he fell to the floor the knife came out of his pocket and also landed on the floor near his body.... Deans further testified that the knife was picked up by James Williams who left the local service station shortly after the shooting occurred. During the trial it was

also brought out that Deans left the store hurriedly saying, "I don't guess there's anything I can do so I'd better go. I gotta catch a bus."³⁵⁵

Similar tales of vanishing weapons were common in Dixie courtrooms, including the cases of Robert Hall (January 30, 1943, above), James Walker, Jr. (August 12, 1946, above), and Jonathan Daniels (August 20, 1965, in Part 1), among others.

After closing arguments, prosecutor George Fountain informed Judge Walter Bone that the state would only seek a conviction for second-degree manslaughter, rather than murder. On September 9, Judge Bone declared a mistrial, the *Daily Times* claiming "the jury could not reach a decision and remained hung on a six to six vote for [Strickland's] conviction or acquittal." The trial docket contradicts that report, stating that Bone declared the mistrial after he "ordered the withdrawal of a juror" on September 9.³⁵⁶

Otis Newsome with his wife, circa 1945 (Civil Rights Archive).

Strickland's retrial was postponed repeatedly between December 1948 and February 1949. Strickland was arrested April 13, 1949, detained by court order while jurors were selected, but his lawyer challenged that process on May 2, complaining that all farmers on the jury list had been dismissed. That practice was common in 1940s North Carolina, but Judge Paul Edmundson found that it violated state law, requiring selection of new potential jurors. Edmundson also authorized expenditure of $30 to retrieve James Williams from his new home in New York.³⁵⁷

Trial convened on May 9, with new twists in testimony from both sides. Williams now claimed that Newsome's right hand was injured and bandaged on the day he died, thereby preventing him from wielding nonexistent knives. Strickland, for his part, forgot the brake fluid dispute, claiming Newsome and Williams came looking for beer, threatening to search his store when Strickland denied having any in stock. Once again, the prosecution lowered its original charge from murder to second-degree manslaughter, but even that was too much for the new all-white jury, which acquitted Strickland after two hours' deliberation.³⁵⁸

Ike Madden
March 27, 1948; Birmingham, AL

Police shot unarmed 27-year-old Ike Madden for "resisting arrest." Investigators deemed the slaying "justifiable."[359] Local inquiries failed to produce any further information.

John Johnson
March 29, 1948; Birmingham, AL

Police killed their second African American victim in three days for "resisting arrest." Department administrators rule the shooting "justified," while local blacks described a reign of terror perpetrated by officers calling themselves the "Black Raiders."[360]

Almas Shaw
April 19, 1948; Birmingham, AL

Members of the Birmingham Police Department's "Black Raiders" squad attacked 42-year-old Almas Shaw, inflicting fatal injuries. Officers claimed Shaw fought with them, then fled, cracking his skull on the stone base of a building when tackled by Officer Windman. Investigators deemed Shaw's death accidental.[361]

Marion Franklin Noble
April 27, 1948; Birmingham, AL

Patrolman C. L. Borders shot the unarmed 19-year-old for "resisting arrest." Department spokesmen deemed the slaying "justified."[362]

Eugene Ward
April 30, 1948; Bessemer, AL

Patrolmen Lawton Grimes and Sam Montgomery shot Ward when he allegedly "resisted arrest and reached for a knife." No evidence proves he was armed.[363]

Hosea Carter
May 2, 1948; Sandy Hook, MS

Carter died from a shotgun blast to the chest. Marion County sheriff's deputy T. W. White reported that Carter, his brother Willie, and companion William Harris tried to enter a rural home uninvited, whereupon a white neighbor "whose name I don't remember" killed Hosea. In the deputy's opinion, "He did what any decent white man would have done." White jailed Willie Carter and William Harris on trespassing charges.[364]

Isaac Crawford

June 5, 1948; Augusta, GA

A city judge sentenced Crawford to the Richmond County stockade on April 22, 1948, for public drunkenness. One month later, on May 21, Crawford abandoned work in a swampy ditch, calling guard David L. Turner to shoot a rattlesnake. Turner refused and ordered Crawford back into the ditch. When Crawford hesitated, Turner attacked him with a stick, beating him until it broke, then continuing the assault with a length of rubber hose. Later that day, Crawford was admitted to Augusta's University Hospital, where he was examined and treated by Dr. Virgil Williams, the resident in charge of eye, ear, nose, and throat maladies.[365]

Dr. Williams, in an affidavit, described Crawford's severely swollen left eye—injured, prison guards claimed, when an officer "accidentally" struck Crawford with a shovel handle—and Crawford's own description of a protracted beating. Williams wrote, "On his sixth day in the hospital there was elevation of the patient's temperature. At the time he was suffering from obvious cardiac failure. It was on or about this date, June 2 that I ordered nasal oxygen to be started." Crawford died on June 5, "from reportedly natural causes while still under treatment."[366] Another patient's description of Crawford says that "his body was covered with welts on the arms, chest, back, sides, thighs, and hips and that his face was swollen beyond recognition."[367]

On June 18 J. B. Hatchett, deputy director of Georgia's Board of Corrections, announced an investigation into Crawford's case and other claims of brutality at the Richmond County stockade. Sheriff M. G. Whittle "strongly indicated he was not satisfied" with a coroner's verdict blaming Crawford's death on natural causes, citing an affidavit from Mrs. J. M. Adams, an Augusta resident who watched David Turner beat a black inmate to his knees in a ditch near her home. As reported in the press, "She said the beating was inhuman and made her so nervous and tore her up so badly she had to go to a doctor for treatment."[368]

On June 24 Sheriff Whittle arrested Turner on nine counts of assault and battery, including Crawford's fatal beating, but a grand jury convened on July 12 declined to indict Turner for homicide. While Turner faced charges of beating nine different inmates, the panel also indicted guard Alvin Jones on three assault charges and Horace "Doggie" Wingard for assaulting one convict.[369] Wingard pled *nolo contendere* on September 3, with sentencing set for "sometime in October," while Turner demanded a jury trial. Jones's trial was indefinitely postponed due to absence of his lawyer.[370]

If Turner counted on a racist jury to acquit him, he was disappointed. White jurors convicted him of all nine counts December 9, 1948, but he still escaped any meaningful punishment. City Court Judge Gordon W. Chambers ordered Turner to pay a $50 fine for the death of Isaac Crawford, then sentenced him to six months' parole for the other eight charges.[371]

Jesse Jefferson
June 12, 1948; Jackson, GA

The Civil Rights Congress, in its 1952 genocide petition to the United Nations, said Jefferson was killed on his farm "after two white men drove up behind his wagon and accused him of not giving them room to pass by."[372] My local inquiries elicited no further information, but the crime, as described, is strikingly similar to the murder of Malcolm Wright in Mississippi, one year later (see July 2, 1949, below).

James Burts
July 12, 1948; Greenville, SC

Patrolmen S. C. Kelly and R. C. Woddall beat 23-year-old James Burts with a blackjack and a nightstick before delivering him to General Hospital in what Dr. J. R. Bryson, Jr., called "pretty bad condition." Burts died soon after admission to the hospital, prompting manslaughter charges against the two officers. An all white jury acquitted them in November 1948.[373]

William Milton
July 14, 1948; Brooklyn, NY

Milton and his brother Jack (called "Joe" in some reports) met two friends at a neighborhood bar on July 14, after running various errands. The four finished one round of beers and ordered a second, whereupon white bartender Charles Kennefick told them, "Drink up and get the hell out." When the quartet took exception to that order, Kennefick called them "niggers," grabbed a weapon—described in published reports as an "ice churner"—and attacked his customers. Patrolmen Peter Kilcommons and John O'Neill arrived with the scuffle ongoing, prompting the Milton brothers and their friends to flee on foot. A witness, 11-year-old Leroy Goodwin, later told reporters:

> I saw the tall policeman—that's Peter Kilcommons—chasing Mr. Milton and his brother. He was shooting as he ran. John O'Neil, the other cop, was running and shooting too. But the bullets didn't hit Mr. Willie at first. They didn't get him until he turned into South First Street and reached his front stoop. The first bullet hit him in the back, just under his right armpit, as he was turning the knob of his door. Mr. Milton fell to his right knee. Then he got up and fell into the house. The cops kept on shooting through the door.[374]

Milton's wife and 13-year-old son witnessed his death on the threshold of their home. Afterward, Jack Milton was detained and beaten at the Bedford Avenue police station, in an unsuccessful attempt to make him confess starting the fight with Charles Kennefick.[375] Officers Kilcommons and O'Neil claimed they were only firing in the air, as a warning for the fugitives to halt, yet Milton was shot once in the back and twice in the chest, the latter shots at close range.

After the killing, Milton's widow told reporters officers had harassed her husband since early 1946, when he spoke out against execution-style police shootings in Freeport.

Long Island (see February 5, 1946, above). Milton was also a tenement activist, who led rent strikes against Brooklyn slumlords. After his death, another local activist, Simon Gerson, wrote: "He was lynched, my friends, lynched. What matter is it if a man is lynched by a hempen rope from a Georgia cottonwood tree or lynched by a police revolver in the trigger-happy hands of a Brooklyn cop?" Neither officer was charged with any crime or disciplined by the department.[376]

Joe W. Perkins
August 1948; Birmingham, AL

White police shot Perkins, claiming he was "trying to escape." Observers listed him as the ninth African American slain by lawmen since May.[377] My inquiries to local libraries and newspapers on this and other Birmingham police cases went unanswered.

Herman Burns
August 21, 1948; Los Angeles, CA

"Special officers" of the L.A. Police Department beat African American brothers Herman, John and Julius Burns outside the La Veda Ballroom on Vernon Avenue, killing Herman, hospitalizing John, and arresting Julius for possession of a small, rusty pocketknife. Herman Burns was an army veteran and father from a well-respected family. Departmental investigators cleared the officers of all charges.[378] The latest in a long series of brutal incidents brought a delegation of African Americans to confront Mayor Fletcher Bowron, demanding that he curb police mayhem. Bowron refused, branding all protests against the police "communistic," while a white ex-policeman branded Herman Burns "troublesome" and possessed of a "bad character."[379] On the day of that meeting, LAPD officers beat innocent victim Cecil Jones for loaning his car to a cousin and then truthfully denying the car was stolen.[380] Virginia Burns filed a $250,000 lawsuit against LAPD Chief Clement Horrall and Assistant Chief Joseph Reed for dereliction of duty, when they refused to suspend her husband's killers.[381] My inquiries to local libraries and newspapers revealed no disposition of that lawsuit, suggesting the case was dismissed.

Isaiah Nixon
September 8, 1948; Montgomery County, GA

Nineteen forty-eight was a momentous year in Georgia politics, with the white-supremacist States' Rights Democratic Party in rebellion against President Harry Truman's civil rights program, and a special gubernatorial election scheduled to resolve the state's "three governors controversy," sparked by the death of governor-elect Eugene Talmadge in December 1946. Favored in the latter contest was "Old Gene's" son, Herman Talmadge, who, like his father, was closely tied to the Ku Klux Klan.[382]

Against all odds in Jim Crow Georgia, Isaiah Nixon—a 28-year-old father of six—wanted to vote in September's Democratic primary election. The U.S. Supreme Court's

1944 ruling in *Smith v. Allwright* banned exclusion of African American voters from primary elections, but Georgia tradition and white vigilantes still maintained the color line in most counties. On September 8, Nixon approached Montgomery County's registrar, requesting a ballot. The official agreed that Nixon had the right to vote, but advised against it. Nixon persisted, casting the first vote of his life.[383]

That night, white brothers Jim and Johnny Johnson visited Nixon's home, outside Alston. They called Nixon out and ordered him to step down from the porch. When he refused, Jim Johnson shot him three times, with Nixon's wife and children looking on. Nixon died on September 10, at a hospital in Dublin.[384]

Sheriff R. M. McCrimon told reporters that Nixon was murdered for voting. The Johnson brothers, in custody, claimed they had offered Nixon a job and were surprised when he attacked them, forcing Jim to fire in self-defense. A grand jury indicted Jim Johnson for murder, charging Johnny as an accessory. An NAACP investigation revealed that the Johnsons had also attacked D. V. Carter, a civil rights activist who encouraged blacks in Montgomery County to vote. At trial, Jim told his tale of self-defense, winning acquittal from an all-white jury on November 5, 1948. Prosecutors then dropped the case against brother Johnny.[385]

Nixon's death left widow Sallie and their children impoverished and living in fear. In December 1948 the *Pittsburgh Courier* established a "Nixon Fund," soliciting donations nationwide to relieve the family's plight. By then, Sallie and her children were living with Isaiah's mother in Jacksonville, Florida, crowded into a two-bedroom house. A follow-up story in December 1954 found the Nixons leading "happy lives" in Jacksonville, Sallie remarried with a seventh child.[386]

Isaiah Nixon's family after his September 8, 1948, murder for voting in Georgia (Civil Rights Archive).

Hosea W. Allen
September 26, 1948; Tampa, FL

Tavern proprietor Victor Pinella shot Hosea Allen after Allen ordered a beer in his white's-only establishment. Justice of the Peace Joseph G. Spicola freed Pinella with no charges filed.[387]

Danny Bryant
October 10, 1948; Covington, LA

In 1952 the Civil Rights Congress included Bryant's case in its historic genocide petition to the United Nations, stating that Bryant "was shot to death by policeman Kinsie [sic] Jenkins after Bryant refused to remove his hat in the presence of whites."[388] A local newspaper, the *St. Tammany Farmer*, told a very different story, reporting that Bryant, a 37-year-old resident of Gulfport, Mississippi, employed at Covington's Delta Pine Products Corporation, died after attacking a young Boy Scout and a night porter at the Southern Hotel, around 1 p.m. on Sunday, October 10.[389]

According to the *Farmer*, Bryant entered the hotel through a side door used by bus passengers, then walked to the lobby and assaulted the young Scout without provocation. A black porter intervened trying to eject Bryant from the hotel, and a fight ensued, while the Scout ran outside to fetch a patrolman. Officer Kenzie Jenkins responded, finding Bryant and the porter grappling on the floor of a dead-end hallway.[390] The article goes on to say:

> When he separated the two Bryant turned on him and they fought for several minutes. He then warned the negro [sic] that he would shoot if the negro did not stop his crazed fighting. Bryant told him to shoot and then continued to try to fight him. Officer Jenkins then fired one shot into the air, thinking the negro would stop, but he only fought harder. Jenkins then fired three shots into the negro, one shot striking him in the right arm and two in the region of the heart.
>
> Even after being shot three times in a fatal spot the negro continued to try to get his grasp on Officer Jenkins. The two fought on down the main corridor into the lobby where the negro knocked Officer Jenkins through the front door of the lobby. Officer Jenkins stated he was then able to reach for his blackjack and as he rose from the floor he hit the negro several times on the head and knocked him unconscious.[391]

Sheriff Andrew L. Erwin, new to the office he would hold for 16 years,[392] soon arrived on the scene with Dr. E. H. Gatreaux, the parish coroner. Gatreaux found Bryant still alive and sent him off to a hospital in Bogalusa, 23 miles northeast of Covington in Washington Parish, but Bryant died before reaching help. Gatreaux told reporters "that the negro was apparently not drinking and that he felt the negro was insane or had been doped up in some manner."[393]

Robert C. Mallard
November 20, 1948; Toombs County, GA

At age 37, Robert "Duck" Mallard was unusually prosperous for an African American in postwar Georgia. A successful traveling salesman, light-skinned enough to "pass"

Robert Mallard with his wife and family, circa 1947 (Civil Rights Archive).

for white in some company, he shared a spacious home with wife Amy, a schoolteacher, and two-year-old son John on a farm fronting the Altamaha River. Mallard wore stylish clothes and drove a new Kaiser-Frazer sedan, enough in themselves to make white neighbors think he had "forgotten his place."[394]

Timing made Mallard's situation doubly dangerous. In 1948, white Georgians were caught up in racist fever, seething against the federal government's first halting steps toward equality for African Americans. In September's primary election, they chose Herman Talmadge—son of late racist demagogue Eugene Talmadge—as their new governor, suppressing black votes with a wave of Ku Klux terrorism that claimed at least one life (see September 8, 1948, above). It was a bad time, all around, to be black in Georgia.

Herman Talmadge was not merely a white supremacist, but also closely tied to the KKK. On November 18, 1946, he attended "grand dragon" Samuel Green's birthday party, telling assembled Klansmen that their order, "through its power and influence was of tremendous assistance in electing my father.... I believe in the Ku Klux Klan, and will fight for it and white supremacy with the last drop of my blood." Green returned the favor, calling governor-elect Eugene Talmadge "the only hope for white supremacy in Georgia."[395]

When "Old Gene" died three weeks short of inauguration, the Klan switched its support to Herman. At his triumph in September 1948, Green told his followers, "At last the Klan has a friend in the governor's chair. We're sitting on top of the world and nothing can stop us. Herman has assured me of his cooperation at all times, and has promised to go all the way down the road to protect the Klan. If you ever need anything from him, be sure to make it known that you are a friend of Sam Green's."[396]

Talmadge showed his gratitude for victory by making Green a "colonel" on his staff and naming Green's second in command, Atlanta policeman Sam Roper, to head the Georgia Bureau of Investigation (GBI). In Toombs County, Green boasted that Sheriff R. E. Gray and most other elected officials were Klansmen.[397]

On the night of November 20, Mallard attended a school function in Lyons, the county seat, with his wife, son, and two teenage cousins of Amy's, William and Angelina Carter. Driving home at 11 p.m., they found several cars blocking the road near the Providence Baptist Church, surrounded by a group of men in Klan robes and hoods, with masks folded back to bare their faces. According to Amy Mallard, one of the Klansmen shouted, "Hands up!" followed by a "volley of shots." Only Robert was hit, killed by a bullet to the chest.[398]

Most published accounts say Mrs. Mallard ran to the nearby home of white farmer Frank Brinson. First on the scene, Brinson would later testify that he found Robert Mallard on the ground, outside the Frazer, and that Amy asked him to put her husband back in the car. While doing so, he claimed, "a gun fell out on the dirt."[399] Mrs. Mallard told a rather different story.

> I got out of the car and found my husband lying on the ground with blood gushing out of his mouth. I sent the oldest boy in the car to get a doctor, and sent the little girl running to the house with the baby. A crowd had collected and someone looked at my husband, said he was gone. They went to get the state patrol, six miles away. After a while the deputy sheriff came with another man and two state patrolmen. They didn't even try to find the killers. All they did was search through my pocketbook and read all my personal letters, stalling around while the mob got away.[400]

Terrified, Mrs. Mallard took her son and cousins to Savannah. NAACP investigators entered the case on November 22, while Sheriff Gray denied any knowledge of Mallard's slaying until journalists asked him about it on November 24. At Mallard's funeral in Savannah, on November 27, GBI agents led by Lieutenant W. E. McDuffy arrested Amy Mallard for her husband's murder, transporting her to the Toombs County jail. Questioned by reporters, McDuffy said, "I think the Ku Klux Klan has been wrongfully accused in this case."[401] Samuel Green promptly declared that the Klan had been exonerated.[402]

Adverse publicity put more heat on Governor Talmadge. On November 29 he demanded capture of Mallard's slayers, no matter "what color they are or who they are," and warned GBI leaders, "I don't want any statements being issued through the Ku

Klux Klan or any other organization like that." Queried for details on the manhunt, Talmadge likened the investigation to "a military secret" and would say no more. In Lyons, Sheriff Gray reluctantly dropped Amy Mallard's murder charge.[403] As to Robert Mallard, Gray said, "This Negro was a bad Negro, as I have had dealings with him. I further know that this Negro was hated by all who knew him." In Atlanta, also on November 29, Patrolman John "Itchy Trigger Finger" Nash—a Klansman who bragged of killing 13 blacks "in the line of duty"—told fellow Kluxers that Talmadge had warned GBI officers "not to believe everything the niggers tell them" about Mallard's murder.[404]

Suggested motives for Mallard's killing vary. Amy recalled whites warning Robert not to vote in September, but no one claimed he had cast a ballot. Later, Mrs. Mallard said, she had honked their car's horn at a vehicle blocking the road outside Providence Baptist, forcing one of the church's white parishioners to move the car. Later, Mrs. Mallard said, "They started talking awful about my husband and said he ought to be lynched for letting me blow the horn." In a third incident, Mrs. Mallard had told white farmer William Lamar "Spud" Howell to get off her lawn—more than coincidence, perhaps, since she named Howell as one of Robert's killers.[405]

On December 3, 1948, private investigator Joseph Goldwasser delivered a list of suspects to Governor Talmadge, with supporting evidence. Talmadge passed the file to Sheriff Gray and Toombs County Solicitor W. L. Lanier, prompting five white men to surrender on December 4. Aside from Howell, those jailed were J. Roderick Clifton, Barney Sikes, Herschel Sikes, and James Spivey. Their attorney, reputed Klansman Thomas Ross Sharpe, called for a grand jury investigation. On the day that panel convened, December 10, arsonists destroyed most of the shops owned by blacks in Lyons.[406]

The grand jury indicted Clifton and Howell for murder, releasing the others without charges. Trial commenced on January 11, 1949, with Amy Mallard called as the prosecution's first witness. Before breaking down on the witness stand, she testified that the murder mob consisted of "about twenty men, wearing white stuff and all carrying pistols." She specifically identified Howell as one of the Klansmen, and Clifton's car as part of the roadblock. Cousins William and Angelina Carter also testified, but could not identify any suspects.[407]

Against that evidence, Howell told jurors he had spent the night of November 20 at home with friends, who corroborated his story. Frank Brinson repeated his tale of moving Mallard's body and seeing a pistol that later vanished. He also claimed that Mrs. Mallard pegged the number of gunmen at six to eight, saying she recognized none of them. Sheriff Gray's wife claimed that William Carter had told her Robert Mallard "fired the first shot and somebody else the other." Finally, attorney Sharpe called two jurors to testify as character witnesses for Howell, adding their opinions that Robert Mallard had carried a "bad reputation." Prosecutor Lanier raised no objection to jurors testifying for the defense, and Judge Robert H. Humphrey ruled the tactic "perfectly legal." In his summation, Sharpe injected anti–Semitism, saying of Joseph Goldwasser, "That roaring lion from Judea is a disgrace to the Jewish race. He wouldn't even make catfish bait in the Altahama River."[408]

Howell's trial was brief, lasting only seven hours, and white jurors needed barely 20 minutes to acquit him, their verdict greeted by applause. Lanier immediately dismissed Clifton's charges, telling Judge Humphrey that his case against Clifton was "by no means as strong as that against Howell."[409]

While the verdict was a victory for Klansmen, many bitterly resented Herman Talmadge's "desertion" of their cause. On July 4, 1949, arsonists—reportedly dressed in Klan regalia—burned the Mallard home. Sheriff Gray told reporters, "It was just an accident. That woman hasn't been back here to look after her property since she left." In fact, Amy Mallard and son John had settled in Buffalo, New York, beyond the reach of her husband's killers.[410]

Willie Vinson
1949/50; Oakland, FL

A late addition to this volume, discovered while researching another case, Willie Vinson should not be confused with a prior Texas lynching victim of the same name (see July 13, 1942, above). Three retrospective articles in the *Orlando Sentinel*, written over a span of 15 years by two different reporters, summarize his case in identical language.

> The Rev. Blaney Bennett of Oakland, who was sitting on his porch one Sunday morning in 1949, saw a car coming. In it were white men drinking beer and laughing. He saw a black man in the back seat. Offended by the drinking, Bennett headed toward the road to say so. Then, he heard a noise that sounded like an animal being hit by a car. It was Willie Vinson being thrown from the car's rear door. He died of a brain hemorrhage.[411]

Vinson's slayers were presumed to be Ku Klux Klansmen, in an era when that secret society dominated Orange County, claiming the sheriff and other elected officials as members. Accordingly, no serious investigation was conducted. Oddly, the Social Security Death Index lists Orange County's only Willie Vinson as dying in 1950, again with no specific date. Local inquiries to libraries and newspapers failed to reveal any further details.

Herman Glasper
January 1949; Bryan County, GA

Corporal Dee E. Watson of the Georgia State Patrol shot 30-year-old Herman Glasper, reportedly while trying to arrest him for stealing a pig, sometime during the week of January 2nd to 8th. Sheriff E. W. Miles called the shooting accidental, saying Watson fired his pistol after stumbling over some bushes.[412] Local inquiries revealed no further information on this case.

Charles Ferrell
January 10, 1949; Albany, NY

Police arrested Ferrell at his home, on a misdemeanor charge, beating him in front of his wife and two children as they took him away. Ten minutes after he was booked at the First Police Precinct, an officer "found" Ferrell dead, hanging in his cell. Authorities branded Ferrell's death a suicide.[413]

Charles Phifer
January 16, 1949; The Bronx, NY

Patrolman Eugene Stasiuk answered a call to the home of Mrs. Anne Phifer, who was engaged in a quarrel with her stepson. Stasiuk shot and killed Charles Phifer, claiming self-defense, although Phifer was shot in the back and unarmed. Investigators deemed the slaying "justified."[414]

George Waddell
February 18, 1949; Brooklyn, NY

Police raided Waddell's home in a supposed search for gambling equipment, although they had no search warrant. Waddell was unarmed when officers shot him in the back, killing him instantly. A departmental review deemed the shooting "justified."[415]

Unnamed Man
February 26, 1949; Manchester, GA

Manchester straddles the border between Meriwether and Talbot counties in western Georgia. According to the Civil Rights Congress, in its 1952 genocide petition to the United Nations, an unidentified black prisoner suffered three fatal gunshots to the back on February 26, 1949, while locked inside a room at the police station with several white officers.[416] Inquiries to local libraries and newspapers regarding this case went unanswered. Author Stuart Woods, a Manchester native, renamed his hometown "Delano" and used it as the setting for his first best-selling novel, *Chiefs* (1981), portraying racial tension and police brutality in small-town Georgia from 1919 to 1963.[417]

Hayes Kennedy
April 1949; Birmingham, AL

In its 1952 genocide petition to the United Nations, the Civil Rights Congress listed Kennedy, age 45, as a victim of fatal police brutality. He died in a hospital sometime during the week of April 10–16, after a jailhouse beating. According to the petition, "Police Sheriff [*sic*] Lacey Alexander claimed Kennedy fought with officers in the jail."[418] My inquiries to local sources went unanswered.

Willie Johnson
May 3, 1949; Brunswick, GA

City police shot 58-year-old Willie Johnson for "looking suspiciously at a house." Investigation revealed that Johnson was a Glynn County employee, a 14-year resident of Brunswick, and a deacon at St. Paul's Baptist Church. Departmental administrators deemed the slaying "justified."[419]

Caleb Hill, Jr.
May 30, 1949; Irwinton, GA

In the early hours of May 30, Wikinson County Sheriff George C. Hatcher responded to the stabbing of black victim Ned Burney at a local "juke joint." While he was questioning a witness, Hatcher later said, his pistol was snatched by Caleb "Picky Pie" Hill, a 28-year-old chalk miner, head of household for a family of nine. Hatcher subdued Hill, after a shot was fired, but lost his gun in the struggle, leaving without it when another patron drove him and Hill to the county jail—oddly located on the second floor of Hatcher's home. After locking Hill up with three other prisoners, Hatcher said he saw a mob forming outside his house, yet left his keys on the dining room table while he returned to the bar, searching for his pistol. In his absence, two unmasked white men entered the house, abducted Hill, and shot him three times. Passersby found his body next morning, three miles from Hatcher's home-cum-jail.[420]

Sheriff Hatcher and the Georgia Bureau of Investigation hoped to control the case, but FBI agents arrived in Irwinton on June 2. Two days later, GBI agents arrested suspects Malcolm "Mack" Vivian Pierce and Dennis Lamar Purvis. Judge George Carpenter convened a special grand jury on June 14, which disbanded the same day, refusing to indict the suspects. The FBI continued its investigation, questioning 165 persons, but local law enforcement officers refused to cooperate. Hill's former cellmates described Sheriff Hatcher beating Hill with broomstick, which broke during the assault, while McIntyre Police Chief J. A. Fountain beat Hill with a blackjack and threatened him with a rifle. Under FBI grilling, Hatcher finally admitted beating Hill, but claimed Hill was resisting imprisonment.[421]

All three surviving prisoners named Pierce and Purvis as Hill's abductors. One, Tom Carswell, saw

Caleb Hill, Jr. (front row, left), with his family, shortly before his slaying by Sheriff George Hatcher on May 30, 1949 (Civil Rights Archive).

Sheriff Hatcher outside, talking to Pierce and Purvis before the kidnapping. Nonetheless, agents reported finding "no information indicating that Sheriff George C. Hatcher (or other law enforcement) actively assisted in the lynching," although Hatcher "had reason to believe that [Hill] would be lynched and failed to take the necessary precautions to prevent it." U.S. Attorney John P. Cowart closed Hill's case on April 7, 1950, declaring that "casual or bare knowledge by Sheriff George Hatcher or other law enforcement officers that subjects intended to remove [Hill] is not sufficient for successful prosecution."[422]

Malcolm Wright
July 2, 1949; Chickasaw County, MS

Tenant farmer Malcolm Wright lived and worked with his family on a farm four miles from Houston, Mississippi. On his last Saturday, Wright embarked on a trip into town with wife Virginia and five of their seven children; the two oldest boys were already in Houston, working weekend jobs. Halfway to town on Thorn Road, a pickup truck approached Wright's mule-drawn wagon from the opposite direction, driven by 20-year-old James Moore, with passengers Eunice E. Gore, 22, and James "Red" Kellum, 23. Moore shouted from his window, calling Wright's family "niggers" and ordering them to "stop hogging the road." Noting that the car had ample room to pass, Wright replied, "I was not hogging the road." Moore drove on, then made a U-turn and came back, passing Wright's wagon a second time and stopping in the middle of the road, to block his progress.[423]

Wright warned his family to silence as the three whites left their truck, Moore pausing to grab a bumper jack. Approaching the wagon, Moore and his friends dragged Malcolm Wright from the driver's seat, throwing him to the ground, where Moore rained blows on Wright's head, shattering his skull. Afterward, Moore drove to Houston and confessed the killing to Deputy Sheriff T. A. Bryant. Driving to the murder scene with Houston town marshal Jim Alexander, a mortician, and the killers, Bryant professed himself shocked to find Wright's head "popped wide open. His skull was burst open clear down to his temple." Officers noted the position of Wright's wagon, clear from blocking traffic, and arrested all three assailants for murder.[424]

Malcolm Wright with his wife and children (Civil Rights Archive).

Wright's murder outraged Chickasaw County, where he was known as a "good Negro" and "a hardworking man who minded his own business." Jasper

Rich, Wright's white landlord, raised several thousand dollars for the prosecution led by District Attorney A. T. Patterson, aided by Mrs. Elmer Price, a lawyer from the Mississippi House of Representatives. A grand jury indicted Moore, Kellum and Gore for murder on October 10, afterward releasing them on bond. The defendants filed to sever their cases on October 15, and Moore's attorney, Bob Smith, secured a change of venue to Calhoun County two days later.[425]

Moore's trial began in tiny Pittsboro (2010 population 202), before Judge Taylor H. McElroy, on March 31, 1950. Kellum and Gore attended the proceedings, Moore sporting his airman's uniform, lately assigned to Keesler Air Force Base. Attorney Smith challenged prospective jurors, asking each, "Do you believe in the right of self-defense, in the right of a man to stand his ground and meet force with force?" As noted by the *Tupelo Daily Journal*, "juror after juror" was excused upon admitting that their judgment would be influenced by race. Virginia Wright was the state's first witness, followed by her daughter Mary, 15, and son Henry, 14.[426] Judge McElroy barred three other Wright children from testifying, also warning Henry, "You make sure you tell the truth and you refer to me as mister."[427] When Henry referred to the defendants by name, Judge McElroy rebuked him, demanding that he call his father's slayers "Mister."[428]

Newly married and testifying in his own behalf, Moore claimed he had politely asked Moore to clear the road, whereupon Moore replied, "You boys are drunk." Stopping to reprimand Wright for that insult, Moore alleged that Wright brandished a piece of iron, saying, "You white sons of bitches fixing to get it," then tried to strike Moore, forcing Moore to wield his bumper jack in self-defense. Gore and Kellum corroborated Moore's account, while other friends described his alleged wounds from the fight. Four police officers contradicted that testimony, denying that he had any visible injuries on July 2.[429]

In his final summation, Bob Smith urged jurors to ignore race, then said, "I still do not think that we're so jittery that we would convict a white man for killing a Negro simply because of this situation." Prosecutor Patterson replied, "The only question is: how much punishment for this defendant. You would indeed be doing violence to your conscience to find him guilty of manslaughter only. You cannot murder for pastime. Let's cut that out and we will save our reputation and our boys." Jurors disagreed, acquitting Moore. As usual in Dixie, charges against his codefendants were dismissed.[430]

Chrispin Charles
July 4, 1949; New Orleans, LA

Patrolmen E. Landry and E. Sahue arrested navy veteran Chrispin Charles during a family quarrel at his home, then shot him six times, killing him instantly. Witnesses testified that Charles was unarmed, shot after telling the officers, "I didn't do anything." Investigators ruled the slaying "justified."[431]

Frank Bates
July 18, 1949; New Orleans, LA

Police arrested Bates during their sweep for the unknown slayer of a white Catholic priest. Jailers subsequently "found" Bates dead in his cell, badly beaten, with eyes swelled shut and multiple broken ribs. A coroner's inquest blamed his death on "malnutrition." Detectives found no evidence linking Bates to the clergyman's murder.[432]

Ernest Thomas
July 26 1949; Taylor County, FL

Early on July 16, a Saturday, 22-year-old Willie Padgett approached a service station in Leesburg, bleeding from a scalp wound, telling the attendant four black men had stopped to "help" him when his car broke down, then knocked him out and kidnapped his wife, fleeing in a dark-colored Mercury sedan with Lake County license plates. Deputies LeRoy Campbell and James Yates took the call, driving Padgett 21 miles south to Groveland, a town of 600 whites and 400 African Americans. Cruising Groveland's black quarter, Padgett claimed to recognize the kidnap car outside James Shepherd's home. Shepherd told the officers his brother, Samuel, had borrowed the car Friday night, with friend Walter Irvin, both of whom were sleeping in the house. Facing Irvin, Padgett raged, "You little son of a bitch! You were there! You'd better get my wife or I'm going to kill you!"[433]

The deputies restrained Padgett, then arrested both Irvin and Shepherd, driving them to the county jail in Tavares. There, Deputy Yates locked them up with a stranger,

Sheriff Willis McCall (left) and jailer Reuben Harcher pose with Groveland rape defendants Samuel Shepherd, Walter Irvin, and Charles Greenlee (left to right) (National Archives).

16-year-old Charles Greenlee, arrested at 3:15 a.m. on Saturday while idling at a Groveland filling station with a pistol in his pocket. Meanwhile, 17-year-old Norma Padgett had appeared outside an Okahumpka dancehall, begging a ride to look for her husband in Groveland. En route she told of being kidnapped, beaten, and discarded overnight by four black men. No other crime was mentioned until she was reunited with Willie for a tearful, whispered conversation. Only then did Norma add the telling detail that she had been gang-raped by her kidnappers.[434]

Thus began Florida's most notorious rape case since the tragic events at Rosewood, in January 1923. Transported to jail for a lineup, Norma Padgett identified Irvin and Shepherd as two of her rapists, then added Greenlee, whom neither of the pair had met before they joined him in a cell that morning. Beatings and death threats ensued, during which the prisoners allegedly confessed, while Greenlee named a friend, 25-year-old Ernest Thomas—an alleged *bolita* gambling operator and all-around "troublemaker"—as the kidnap gang's fourth member. Lake County Sheriff Willis Virgil McCall returned from travels out of town in time organize a 1,000-man posse in search of Thomas, scouring the swampy countryside, tracking him 150 miles northwest into Taylor County, where he was cornered and riddled with bullets on July 26. McCall, present at he slaying, told reporters Thomas had been armed and "belligerent as the Devil." Postmortem tests could not determine which posse members dealt Thomas his fatal wounds.[435]

Back in Lake County, trial of the surviving "Groveland Boys" proceeded, using fabricated evidence, perjured testimony, and statements obtained under torture to convict Greenlee, Irvin, and Shepherd. While Irvin and Shepherd were sentenced to die, the court considered Greenlee's tender years and offered "mercy" in the form of a life sentence.[436] Ongoing legal machinations in that case would ultimately claim Sam Shepherd's life (see November 6, 1951, below)—and, many believe, would prompt the Christmas night murder of NAACP spokesman Harry Moore and his wife in Brevard County (see December 25, 1951, in Part 1).

George Westray
August 10, 1949; The Bronx, NY

Police arrested 31-year-old George Westray on unknown charges, beating him severely in custody and subsequently delivering him to Lincoln Hospital for emergency treatment. While there, Westray was shot and killed by Patrolman Daniel McEnery. Investigators ruled the unarmed prisoner's slaying "justified."[437]

James Perry
August 11, 1949; St. Louis, MO

At 4 p.m. a park watchman called police to help him evict 41-year-old unemployed war veteran James Perry and a female companion from a small park in the city's black ghetto, allegedly for stealing sodas from a soft-drink vendor. Four officers arrested Perry for larceny, fatally beating him in the process. A coroner's inquest listed the cause of death as "unknown," though hospital records blame an intracranial hemorrhage. The inquest proved Perry innocent of theft, when the soda vendor testified that children had stolen the soft drinks.[438]

David Hanley
September 1, 1949; Lexington, KY

Patrolmen William B. Foster and William Lewis shot Hanley, age 17, when he "tried to escape." Prosecutors charged the officers with murder, but an all-white jury acquitted them at trial.[439]

Holis Riles
September 3, 1949; Decatur County, GA

A prosperous farmer at age 59, Riles had persistent trouble with whites trespassing on his 200-acre farm near Bainbridge. Warned repeatedly to leave the county, he refused. On September 3 he confronted a group of white fishermen on his land and they shot him. Witness Jesse Gordon reported the killers departing in two cars, and Sheriff A. E. White described the murder as premeditated. Agents from the Georgia Bureau of Investigation failed to identify any suspects.[440]

Linwood Matthews
October 2, 1949; Baltimore, MD

White thugs attacked six members of an African American athletic club as they prepared to play football in Carroll Park. Initially chased off, the six returned to another section of the park and were attacked a second time. During that assault, 19-year-old Linwood Matthews suffered fatal stab wounds. Police made no arrests.[441]

Michael Rice
November 12, 1949; Walhallla, SC

White gunmen Roy Lawing and Leroy Parker shot Rice, a 69-year-old farmer, after robbing him of an estimated $400. Henry Davis, a 14-year-old African American, witnessed the murder and received orders to stay with Rice's body under pain of death. Oconee County's sheriff arrested the killers, and Parker reportedly confessed in custody.[442] Inquiries to local libraries and newspapers produced no further information on this crime or its outcome.

Eugene Jones
November 1949; Gretna, LA

According to the Civil Rights Congress, two deputy sheriffs beat ex-marine Eugene Jones to death at the Jefferson Parish jail, sometime during "the week of November 19."

Jones's widow said four officers had taken him from home without explanation, and that when she visited the jail to check on him next day, a deputy informed her he was dead.[443] The date is difficult to calculate, since November 19 was a Saturday, and normal English usage counts "the week of (date inserted)" from its Monday. My inquiries to local libraries and newspapers revealed no further information on this case.

Samuel Lee Williams
November 20, 1949; Birmingham, AL

White streetcar conductor M. A. Weeks shot Williams and two other unarmed African Americans when they objected to sitting in the car's Jim Crow section. Police declined to arrest or charge Weeks. Williams, age 28, died on November 28. Victims John Carlington III and Amos Crisby survived their wounds.[444]

Samuel Taylor
December 31, 1949; Ballsville, VA

Early on New Year's Day 1950, Ballsville resident Allen Ligon (called "Liggon" in some reports) found 35-year-old neighbor Samuel Taylor's corpse behind his—Ligon's—home, killed by what press reports called a small stab wound in the throat. Postmortem tests pegged the time of death between 4 and 5 p.m. on December 31. Powhatan County Sheriff F. W. Simpson arrested 28-year-old Frank Clayton, a white man, several hours later. A grand jury indicted Clayton for Taylor's murder on January 25.[445]

At trial in late February, Clayton admitted stabbing Taylor in a fight over money he owed Taylor as an employee of Clayton's illegal whiskey business, claiming self-defense. White jurors deliberated for two hours before convicting Clayton of second-degree murder, recommending a 20-year sentence. The judge overruled Clayton's motion to quash the verdict and imposed the recommended sentence.[446]

The Civil Rights Congress, in its 1952 genocide petition to the United Nations, presented Taylor's case in a very different light, calling him a "farm worker" and claiming he was "mutilated to death by a group of white whites." That document noted Clayton's arrest but ignored his conviction, adding: "Local reports charged that all the killers were known and that they included a woman."[447]

George West
January 1, 1950; Manhattan, NY

Patrolman James W. Beaman shot West in Harlem on New Year's Day. After a departmental hearing, Beaman was fired for "improper conduct," but prosecutors filed no charges.[448]

Mattie Debardeleben
January 1950; Birmingham, AL

In its 1952 genocide petition to the United Nations, the Civil Rights Congress listed Mattie Debardeleben as a victim of lethal police brutality. According to that report, she refused to sell chickens to three agents from the U.S. Bureau of Internal Revenue, accompanied by a Jefferson County sheriff's deputy. The four officers beat and arrested her, claiming that she died "of a heart attack" en route to jail. Local inquiries disclosed no further information on this case, and Debardeleben's name is not listed in the Social Security Death Index.[449]

Willie Boxter Carlisle
February 19, 1950; Lafayette, AL

A Lafayette native, born in 1931, Carlisle was six when his mother died, followed by his father nine years later. Little is known of his adolescent years, but by age 18 he worked at a gas station run by pro tem mayor Harrell Huguley, who recalled him as a "good boy" with a reputation for avoiding trouble. Carlisle found it nonetheless, five weeks before his 19th birthday.[450]

On Friday night, February 17, Carlisle attended a basketball game at the C. L. Café with three friends: 18-year-old Robert Holloway, 18-year-old Joe Junior Silmon, and 16-year-old Porter James Spence. A dance was scheduled afterward, and while other spectators cleared the establishment, Carlisle and his friends refused to leave. Proprietor C. L. Johnson called police to eject them and headquarters dispatched two officers—Doyle Mitcham, a 10-month rookie, and James R. Clark, a former Chambers County sheriff's deputy who joined the city force for higher pay. They removed the four youths without incident, but moments later found a tire on their cruiser deflated.[451]

Angry, assuming that the black teens were responsible, Mitcham and Clark searched for them the following night. They found Spence back at the C. L. Café, arrested Holloway at home, nabbed Silmon at a grocery store, and finally found Carlisle walking alone. Spence and Silmon later testified that Clark confiscated a knife from Carlisle before driving on to the county jail. Clark entered to retrieve a rubber hosepipe, then returned and Mitcham drove their captives to Lafayette's city jail.[452]

There began a round of vicious beatings, with the hosepipe and a walking stick, while Clark grilled the youths in an effort to learn who had flattened his tire. Willie Carlisle bore the brunt of it, beaten at least three times according to his friends and witness J. Frank Lambert, a disabled white man who stopped by the jail to get a ride home. At some point during the ordeal, Mitcham and Clark released Spence. "They had let me out," he later testified, "and they said I had better go home and I had better not know nothing and I had better not tell nothing. If I does, he was going to put that hose pipe on me."[453]

After driving Lambert home, the officers returned to find Carlisle in dire straits. Holloway and Silmon carried him to the patrol car, for the short drive to Lafayette's hospital. Nurses summoned the on-call physician, Dr. William G. Wood, shortly after 2 a.m., and he found Carlisle in "desperate condition," his head, hands, right shoulder, right hip and right thigh covered with bruises and abrasions. Carlisle's wounds prevented Dr. Wood from taking X-rays, but he later testified, "My impression was at the time he had a fractured skull or cerebral hemorrhage in addition to a severe concussion, brain concussion."[454]

Carlisle died at 5 a.m., whereupon Officer Clark called Joe Silmon's father—a local mortician—to fetch the body. While loading Carlisle onto a stretcher, Roy Silmon noted that the left side of the boy's skull felt "soft as a piece of cotton." Clark and Mitcham then returned Joe Silmon and Holloway to the city jail. En route, Silmon recalled, "They told us if they heard anything out of us they were going to send us to Four Spot [a reformatory]. Said they ought to do it now. Then they turned us loose and told us to go home."[455]

State toxicologist Paul E. Shoffiett performed Carlisle's autopsy on February 21, attributing his death to a severe concussion with multiple brain hemorrhages. Sheriff James R. Abney charged Clark and Mitcham with murder the following day. Lafayette's city council suspended both officers, while their boss, Chief W. A. Garrett, told reporters both admitted "whipping" Clark, though they claimed he died "in a fall in his cell." A grand jury indicted the pair on March 8, and both pled not guilty at their arraignment, two days later.[456]

At trial, Clark and Mitcham told jurors they only struck Carlisle when he pulled a knife at the jail and refused to enter his cell. During that struggle, they said, Carlisle "fell against the door to the cell block, probably hitting his head several times." White jurors deliberated for 80 minutes before acquitting both defendants, on March 27. One day later, at a city council meeting, Doyle Mitcham resigned. The council then fired Clark, because its members "felt that the city would incur much adverse publicity if the subjects were retained in the employ of the city."[457]

The case did not end there, however. FBI Director J. Edgar Hoover—normally hostile toward blacks and civil rights complaints—took a personal interest in Carlisle's slaying, sparked by reports that Sheriff Abney and Chief Garrett had refused to cooperate with state prosecutors "because of political reasons." In April 1950 Hoover ordered "a discreet, diplomatic" investigation by "mature and well-qualified Special Agents." Mitcham and Clark avoided interviews, but all in vain. A federal grand jury indicted both on September 19, for depriving Carlisle of his civil rights under the Fourteenth Amendment.[458]

Mitcham pled guilty on October 12, 1950, receiving a six-month sentence. Clark faced trial on October 30, represented by attorneys Jacob A. Walker and R. C. Wallace. White jurors convicted him he same day, after deliberating for 15 minutes. Judge Charles B. Kennamer sentenced Clark to 10 months in prison, then freed him on bond pending appeal, where the conviction was upheld.[459]

Booker Hill Massacre
February 28, 1950; Cairo, GA

In its 1952 genocide petition to the United Nations, the Civil Rights Congress reported this gruesome mass murder as follows:

March 2—Seventy-six-year-old James Turner, Negro Baptist minister, of Cairo, Georgia, was found slain in his bed and his three young children were also found dead—all with their heads smashed with an axe. His wife said that someone dressed in a white garment that looked like a gown ran after her. She escaped and went to the police.[460]

That brief description of a massacre in Cairo's all-black Booker Hill section, bearing an incorrect date, seems to hint at Ku Klux Klan involvement, but 32-year-old survivor Hattie Turner's story was confused. She woke, Hattie said, to someone grappling with her husband in bed, then fled the house and ran four blocks to the home of friends Arthur and Mamie Smith, who accompanied her to fetch authorities. At the sheriff's station, she required a sedative injection to quell her hysteria.[461]

When Deputy Sheriff H. L. Lunsford reached the Turner home, he found an even more disturbing scene that that depicted in the 1952 petition. Next door, 50-year-old neighbor John Harvey Arline lay dead, face blasted by a shotgun while he laid a fire in a wood-burning stove. In the Turner house, James had been slaughtered with 10-year-old daughter Jimmie Lou, eight-year-old son J. T., and four-year-old daughter Bobbie Joe. All had been bludgeoned with an axe, their throats slashed with a razor. Officers found the axe under the Reverend Turner's bed, beside a shotgun with two expended cartridges, recently fired. A towel had been forced into the Reverend Turner's mutilated throat, to stanch the flow of blood. Also found at the scene were a bloody straight razor and an ice pick.[462]

By the time Deputy Lunsford arrived, Geneva Arline—John's widow—had returned from her nursing job, having walked home from Grady County Hospital when John failed to meet her at midnight, as usual. Approaching the house, she heard furtive movement inside and asked, "Who is that?" A female voice replied, "It's me," immediately followed by a shotgun blast into the floor, inside the front door. The shooter pursued her, but Mrs. Arline managed to escape in the darkness, running to the home of another neighbor, also named Smith. They were en route to notify authorities when they met officers returning to the Turner house.[463]

By the time a coroner's jury convened on the afternoon of March 2, Hattie Turner was "calm and sane as anyone," repeating her original story. That panel named Hattie as the killer, recommending her detention on five counts of murder. A grand jury convened on March 6, voting five murder indictments against Hattie three days later. Prior to scheduling her trial, a judge ordered psychiatric tests at Milledgeville State Hospital. On March 10, on day before her scheduled departure, Hattie used a broken soft drink bottle to cut her own throat, bleeding to death in her cell. Authorities considered the murder case closed with her suicide, although Cliff Owsley, foreman of the coroner's jury, told reporters, "It is entirely within the realm of possibility that she had help in doing it."[464]

Thurmond Towns
May 8, 1950; The Bronx, NY

Police shot 19-year-old garment worker Thurmond Towns in St. Nicholas Park, claiming he ran when they tried to question him about the theft of a white woman's purse. Towns was unarmed, and further investigation revealed he was a union member and "substantial citizen," with a "large amount of money" in his bank account. Prosecutors ruled the slaying "justified."[465]

Unnamed Man
June 5, 1950; Washington, D.C.

In its 1952 genocide petition to the United Nations, the Civil Rights Congress included the following incident: *"June 5*—An unidentified Negro man was beaten to death in the Washington, D.C. penitentiary. Attested to by fellow prisoners. No mention of incident in press."[466]
Local inquiries produced no further information on this crime, if in fact it occurred.

Lorenzo Best
June 19, 1950; Anniston, AL

White police sergeant J. D. Thomas killed Best with four close-range gunshots, subsequently deemed "justifiable homicide." The Civil Rights Congress listed Best's slaying in its 1952 genocide petition to the United Nations, but offered no further details.[467] My inquiries to local sources went unanswered.

Morris Scott
October 1950; Linden, AL

Sometime in the first week of October, white home invaders George Baker and William R. Welch killed Scott in his home. Marengo County Sheriff T. Wilmer Shields refused to explain their motive, but told reporters Welch had confessed to firing the fatal shotgun blast.[468] My inquiries to local libraries and newspapers went unanswered.

Harvey Wilson
October 20, 1950; Vanndale, AR

Wilson purchased a small amount of coal oil from white vendor W. M. Stokes, and an argument ensued over he price, ending when Stokes shot Wilson. The Civil Rights Congress, in its 1952 genocide petition to the United Nations, claimed Stokes was charged with first-degree murder, but no disposition of the case was mentioned.[469] My local inquiries went unanswered in 2014.

Sam Jones
December 1950; San Pedro, CA

White police officers Richard W. Clare and James R. Graham attacked Jones, a 35-year-old construction worker, and 46-year-old companion Nathaniel Ray on a public street, beating both severely. After Jones died from his injuries, the officers claimed both men pulled knives on them during an arrest for drunkenness.[470] Local inquiries failed to reveal any further details of this case, including the date when it occurred.

John Derrick
December 7, 1950; Manhattan, NY

An army veteran recently discharged from Fort Dix, New Jersey, Derrick was shot and killed in Harlem by Patrolmen Basil Minakotis and Louis Palumbo. Despite testimony from multiple witnesses that Derrick died with empty hands raised overhead, a county grand jury deemed the slaying "justified."[471]

Robert J. Evans
December 12, 1950; Norfolk, VA

While searching for an unknown African American stabbing suspect, Patrolman E. M. Morgan shot and killed 86-year-old Robert Evans, afterward claiming that Evans threatened him with a knife. Although Evans was unarmed, authorities ruled the slaying "justified."[472]

Kelly Gist
December 20, 1950; Cedar Fork Township, NC

Gist, age 27, lived with his wife on Morrisville Route 1. His brother was visiting that morning, planning for Christmas, when a white man neither he nor Gist's wife recognized drove up to the house and "asked Kelly to go for a ride." It seemed Gist must have known the driver, though, since he entered the man's car without protest and the pair drove away. Less than half an hour later, Gist was dead.[473]

Raleigh's *News and Observer* reported that Gist died on Morrisville Carpenter Road around 12:30 p.m., "after spectators watched him writhe in agony for 20 minutes." He was shot once in the chest with a 20-gauge shotgun, damaging his heart beyond repair. According to Wake County Coroner L. M. Cheek, the fatal shot was fired at "very close range because the full charge entered Gist's chest and was concentrated in an area about the size of a 50 cent piece."[474]

Two hundred yards from the murder scene, sheriff's deputies found a car stuck in a roadside ditch. They traced it to white parolee N. G. "Little Nat" Williams, age 33, who matched descriptions of a man seen fleeing the murder scene. Manhunters led by Deputies Connie Holmes and Wiley Jones set off for High House Road, where Williams lived with his wife and six children, overtaking their man a mile and a half from his house.[475]

Williams seemed intoxicated, initially telling the officers, "I'm not going to talk," but on arrival at jail he outlined the incident for Apex police chief S. L. Bagwell. According to Williams, he was driving with Gist when his car slid into the ditch, whereupon they began walking. Soon they quarreled and, Williams said, Gist "called me a son of a bitch, and anyone who calls me that is going to die."[476] Two years later, the Civil Rights Congress included Gist's case in its historic genocide petition to the United Nations, reporting that Williams was held without bond on a murder charge.[477] No disposition of that case was mentioned, however, and my own inquiries to local sources in 2014 revealed no evidence that Williams ever went to trial.

Fred Prettyman
December 29, 1950; Birmingham, AL

Birmingham police killed their eleventh African American victim for 1950, shooting unarmed prisoner Fred Prettyman, age 28, as he "tried to escape." As in the other cases, Coroner Joe Hildebrand immediately ruled the slaying "justifiable homicide."[478]

Andrew Johnson
January 13, 1951; Chicago, IL

Police charged Johnson, age 19, with killing white barber Coleman Hairston during a robbery, despite testimony from Hairston's black employee, Sonny Porter, that Johnson bore no resemblance to the gunman. At Chicago's Central Station, Officers Edward Cagney and Joseph Corcoran used "third-degree" tactics in an effort to make Johnson confess. By 3:30 p.m. Johnson was dead from internal injuries, including a lacerated liver. Police insisted that he "just keeled over and died" in custody. Prosecutors filed no charges.[479]

Bobby Lee Joyner
January 19, 1951; La Grange, NC

Police Chief J. A. Wheeler and Officer W. E. Williford shot 17-year-old high school student Bobby Joyner seven times, killing him instantly. They claimed Joyner had tried to stab them, but the *Greensboro Record* and Raleigh's *News & Observer* accused the officers of murder, demanding prosecution. A grand jury convened and ruled the shooting justified.[480]

G. W. Batchelor, William Battle, Vonzella Battle and John Melvin
February 4, 1951; North Carolina

In its 1952 genocide petition to the United Nations, the Civil Rights Congress reported a disturbing case—or collection of cases—from neighboring counties in North Carolina. Although apparently concise, that report misstated the date and the sex of one victim, while leaving critical questions unanswered. It read:

> February 7—The bodies of four Negroes slain under mysterious circumstances were found in Edgecomb [sic] and Nash Counties, North Carolina. The body of John Melvin, 50, was found on a farm in Edgecomb. William Battle, 29, was found on his door steps. Both were nude and partially burned. The body of G. W. Batchelor, 80, was found in a corn crib. The one-year-old son of Tom George Battle was found dead in bed and Battle himself was shot in the arm.[481]

According to local newspaper reports, the deaths were actually discovered on Sunday morning, February 4. The trouble began at Tom Battle's home in Nashville, one block from police headquarters, at 1 a.m., when a visiting friend, James Cooper, shot Tom in the arm. Cooper and his wife were scheduled to baby-sit for Tom's nine or 10 children (reports differ), while Tom and his wife were away from home. Cooper told police Tom gave him the pistol for self-protection and it discharged accidentally. Family members found 18-month-old Vonzella Battle, a daughter, dead at home "several hours" after the shooting, with no evident cause.[482]

Two more bodies surfaced around 8 a.m. that Sunday. White farmer Otha Baker went to feed livestock on his property, 1½ miles south of Langley Crossroads in Nash County, and found 50-year-old tenant John Melvin's nude body near his—Baker's—home, "slightly burned," with scorched clothing either "scattered around" the corpse or "burned from the body." Police could not decide if Melvin died from his burns or from exposure overnight.[483]

Meanwhile, near Battleboro in neighboring Edgecombe County, friends found the corpse of 28-year-old tenant farmer William "Jack" Battle in his own front yard, between the doorstep and his car, one hand clutching the underside of the car's running board, his body displaying deep burns "from the chin to the shoe tops." If William was related to the Nashville Battles, no local reporter managed to discover any link between them. Sheriff Tom Bardin treated Battle's death as murder and started an immediate investigation.[484]

Sunday's last victim was elderly G. W. Batchelor, found in a corncrib on white farmer J. E. Earp's property, 12 miles south of Nashville. If his corpse bore any wounds, they were not reported, nor is any record presently available for Batchelor's cause of death. At 80, we are left to speculate about what killed him overnight, but it did not appear to be a homicide.[485] Vonella Battle's death, likewise, remains unsolved, Coroner Van B. Matthews listing "natural causes—unknown."[486] Friends of John Melvin, last seen alive around midnight on Saturday, told police that he was "drinking but not drunk." How his clothes may have ignited is unknown.[487]

William Battle's death seemed the most likely to be solved. African American witnesses Robert Brake and Nathaniel "Eddie" Pittman, both detained as suspects by Sheriff Bardin, said they were with Battle on Saturday night, lounging near the ABC Store in Battleboro when thy met a white man named Jim Williams and offered him a ride home. Instead, however, they drove to Battle's house, a half-mile distant, and drank a pint of whiskey Williams offered them, the black men dancing with Battle's wife by turns. At some point, Battle and his wife "scuffled," whereupon she left for her mother's house. Brake and Pittman soon left Battle drunk in bed, drove Williams home, then proceeded to Pittman's house. Passersby saw a car resembling Pittman's 1939 sedan at Battle's home, later that night, and one recalled flames in the yard but did not stop to investigate. Brake denied returning to Battle's house, but admitted borrowing Pittman's car around 10 p.m., "to go home and feed my stock." Returning to Pittman's place 60 to 90 minutes later, Brake found him asleep and spent the night there.[488]

Coroner J. G. Raby convened an inquest but uncovered little useful information. Rumors suggested that Brake and Battle's wife were "going together," though both denied it. Police believed Battle was doused with an accelerant but found none at his home, except for the gasoline in his car's fuel tank. Coroner Raby, finally, could not decide if Battle died from burns or was set afire after dying. Sheriff Bardin released Pittman on February 5, but said Brake would remain in custody for further questioning—and the rest is silence. No follow-up reports suggest that anyone was charged with any crime, much less mass murder committed for racist motives.[489]

April 2, 1951; May 11, 1951

Melvin Womack
April 2, 1951; Winter Garden, FL

The Ku Klux Klan ruled Florida's Orange County in the late 1940s and early 1950s, with members including Sheriff Dave Starr, Deputy Sheriff P. C. Coleman, Apopka Police Chief William Dunnaway, Winter Garden Justice of the Peace Pete Tucker, County Commissioner John Talton, Winter Park City Manager Earl Y. Harpole, Ocoee ex-councilman and marshal Mose Bryant, and Criminal Court clerk Charles Limpus, Sr. When the county's three "klaverns" turned to terrorism, they counted on protection from Governor Fuller Warren, himself an admitted Klansman.[490]

In early 1951 the Klan heard rumors that Luther Coleman, a black janitor at all-white Winter Garden Elementary School, had entered the girls' restroom unescorted. The school's principal denied it, but Klansmen tried to kidnap Coleman from a downtown street on February 6, beating him and shoving him toward their car for a trip to the Klan's "stomping grounds" on a red clay road outside town. Coleman broke free and ran, prompting one would-be kidnapper to shoot him, grazing his leg before they fled. Patrolman Willie Welch strolled by and ordered Coleman to stop bleeding on the sidewalk. When a bystander offered Welch the getaway car's license number, he refused to accept it.[491]

Dave Starr, Ku Klux Klan member and sheriff of Florida's Orange County (National Archives).

Frustrated, the Klan's "knights" tried again on March 31, unaware that Coleman had left town after having his wounds treated. Confusion or inebriation led them to the home of Coleman's brother-in-law, Melvin Womack, a 27-year-old fruit picker. Striking by night, they snatched Womack and drove him to their stomping ground, there beating and stabbing him, finally shooting him several times, with one round to the head. Passersby found him still breathing, but he died two days later. The *Orlando Sentinel-Star* failed to mention Womack's murder, and local lawmen saw no reason to investigate.[492]

Nearly two years later, on March 25, 1953, a federal grand jury published a 12-page "catalog of terror" listing crimes committed by Florida's Klan during recent years. The panel indicted seven Klansmen for perjury, but a judge later dismissed those charges, finding that the U.S. government lacked jurisdiction to investigate state crimes. Dave Starr went on to serve as sheriff until 1971.[493]

Lon G. Asman and Louis Passmore
May 11, 1951; Hawkinsville, GA

Asman and Passmore were army privates assigned to the 82nd Airborne Division at Fort Bragg, North Carolina. Both were listed as AWOL—absent without official leave—when Police Chief Thomas Bragg encountered them in Hawkinsville, Georgia. Bragg recognized Passmore as a Hawkinsville native whom he had jailed once before and delivered to military police. When he approached the soldiers this time, both admitted being AWOL and he took them into custody, intending to collect a reward of $25 per head the army offered for straying soldiers.[494]

As Bragg told the story, he handcuffed Asman and Passmore together, then decided on a whim to bring his six-year-old son along for the 50-mile drive to Robins Air Force Base, the nearest military post to Hawkinsville. He placed the boy in his backseat, while the soldiers sat up front with Bragg. When they were 15 miles from Robins, crossing a narrow bridge, Bragg said both soldiers "jumped" him, one clutching his throat while the other shouted, "Kill him! Kill him!" The shouter allegedly grabbed for Bragg's pistol, saying, "This is your last roundup. This is the end." Bragg shot them both at point-blank range and drove on to Robins, where both soldiers were dead on arrival.[495]

A coroner's jury readily accepted Bragg's self-defense plea, but county, state, and military officers pressed for a full grand jury investigation. On May 16, Solicitor General William M. West announced deferment of that hearing to July, a move that prompted Passmore's widow to swear out a murder warrant against Bragg. Held without bond, Bragg sat in jail until the grand jury convened and declined to indict him.[496]

Joseph Mann
May 29, 1951; Norfolk, VA

At age 38, the Rev. Joseph Mann served as pastor of two black congregations in Virginia: the Union Congregational Christian Church in Norfolk, and a Congregational Christian Church at Holland, in Nansemond County. Memories differ as to whether he was an NAACP member, but most who knew him agree that he was not an activist for civil rights.[497]

Around 9:30 p.m. on May 26, 1951, Mann was walking to a restaurant on Olney Road in Norfolk, when two white men in a car stopped him at the Landing Street intersection. After telling Mann they "wanted him to help them do a job," they forced him into the car at gunpoint and drove to the 700 block of Roswell Avenue. There, they cut wires securing a gate on an passageway between homes at 737 and 739, shoving Mann into the alley. Next, Mann later said, "he heard an explosion in the alley, a fire started, and the men tried to push him into it." With his clothes aflame, Mann fled the alley and collapsed on the sidewalk nearby. A neighbor smothered the flames in his clothing, while others doused a fire against the wall of No. 737.[498]

Police arrived, soon followed by an ambulance. At the same time, a man approached Sergeant L. L. Jones, introducing himself as Robert Simpson of 1112 Walker Street in nearby Berkley. Simpson said he had been visiting friends on Roswell and was leaving when he saw Mann on fire. He accompanied the officers and Mann to Norfolk Community Hospital, then slipped away while police were distracted and disappeared forever. Detectives later interviewed the real Robert Simpson in Berkley, residing at the given address, but he was not their man. The "witness" has never been identified.[499]

Mann suffered burns over most of his body, from face to knees. He survived until 1:59 a.m. May 29, but "was unable to give any reason for the attack on him." At the crime scene, police found oily rags and several chicken heads, none of which could be explained. They concluded that Mann had been doused with gasoline, flames from which also damaged an adjoining wall.[500]

At 10:30 a.m. on May 27, an anonymous caller telephoned the Norfolk *New Journal and Guide*, asking the reporter who answered, "Do you know the Rev. Joseph H. Mann? Was he connected with the NAACP? Has he ever made any radical speeches on the race problem in Norfolk?" Rumors soon spread in Brambleton, an integrated Norfolk neighborhood, that Mann's attackers told him "they wanted to run the Negroes out of Brambleton and he should help them." When interviewed, however, white Brambletonians "displayed no opposition" to blacks and claimed "a spirit of neighborliness" had developed between them.[501]

In its 1952 genocide petition to the United Nations, the Civil Rights Congress claimed Mann was slain "for preaching a sermon against segregation."[502] No evidence of that survives today, and the case remains unsolved.

Samuel Shepherd
November 6, 1951; Lake County, FL

The furor over Florida's Groveland rape case (see July 26, 1949, above) did not end with conviction and sentencing of defendants Charles Greenlee, Walter Irvin, and Samuel Shepherd. In April 1950 the *St. Petersburg Times* disputed Greenlee's presence at the alleged crime scene and challenged the entire trial's fairness. Lake County Sheriff Willis McCall produced a tape of Greenlee's confession, implicating the other "Groveland Boys." From prison, Greenlee claimed that he "confessed" while McCall held a gun to his head. NAACP attorneys pursued death row appeals for Irvin and Shepherd to the U.S. Supreme Court, which declared in April 1951 that their trial failed to meet "any civilized conception of due process of law." The court overturned both convictions and ordered a new jury trial.[503]

On November 6, Sheriff McCall drove from Tavares to the state prison at Raiford, retrieving Irvin and Shepherd for their second day in court. Deputy Sheriff James Yates—soon to be notorious for fabricating evidence in other cases—trailed McCall in a separate car, for security's sake. After nightfall, near Umatilla, McCall stopped his cruiser, ostensibly to let his handcuffed prisoners relieve themselves. McCall would later say the pair attacked him, forcing him to shoot them both in self-defense. Shepherd died immediately, but Irvin would survive his wounds to tell a very different story. In his version, McCall dragged both men from the car and shot them point-blank without warning. Deputy Yates soon arrived, Irvin said, and finding one man still alive, shot Irvin in the throat.[504]

A firestorm of publicity ensued. Governor Fuller Warren sent J. Jefferson Elliott—a Ku Klux Klansman and former bodyguard for Georgia governor Eugene Talmadge—to investigate the case, without result. Lake County's grand jury exonerated McCall, one local telling Northern reporters, "We're proud as all get out." Walter Irvin's second trial convened in February 1952, resulting in conviction and another death sentence.[505] Under pressure from the NAACP and other sources, Governor Leroy Collins reviewed Irvin's case in 1955, commuting his sentence to life imprisonment. Paroled in 1968, Irvin revisited Lake County two years later and was found dead in his car, allegedly from natural causes.[506]

Groveland defendants Walter Irwin and Samuel Shepherd, shot by Sheriff Willis McCall while handcuffed, on November 6, 1951 (National Archives).

Willis McCall continued his one-man reign of terror in Lake County for another 20 years, until his April 1972 indictment on second-degree murder charges, for the fatal beating of Tommy J. Vickers, a mentally retarded black inmate at the county jail. Governor Reuben Askew suspended McCall from office, and while white jurors took only 70 minutes to acquit McCall at trial, he lost his reelection bid that November. McCall died in April 1994, after telling a reporter, "I would hate to be remembered like some of them would like me to be remembered, as an old sonofabitch."[507]

John Lester Mitchell
November 19, 1951; Opelousas, LA

In autumn 1951, 33-year-old John Mitchell joined fellow African Americans Joseph Donatto and Jacob Joubert to register as voters. St. Landry Parish registrar George C. Blanchard rejected them, prompting a lawsuit from the NAACP. Federal judge Gaston Porterie was scheduled to hear their case on November 29, but Mitchell did not live to see his day in court.[508]

On November 19, St. Landry Parish Sheriff Clayton Guilbeau led a squad of deputies into the black section of Opelousas, surrounding an eatery called The Chicken

Snack, ordering its customers and passersby to "keep their voices down." Mitchell was present and objected, saying, "We may as well be in slavery if we can't speak out here on our side of town." Lawmen later said Mitchell was "boisterous" and "raising a disturbance," provoking a "scuffle" with Deputy David Lanclos. Despite the fact that Mitchell was unarmed and outnumbered, Lanclos emptied his revolver into Mitchell at point-blank range, killing him instantly.[509]

New York City's *Amsterdam News*, America's oldest black newspaper, suspected a conspiracy in Mitchell's death, asserting that "a Negro 'stool pigeon' was seen phoning someone under questionable circumstances," 30 minutes before Sheriff Guilbeau led his raid on The Chicken Snack.[510] A coroner's jury ruled his death "justifiable homicide," and Judge Porterie subsequently dismissed the lawsuit against registrar Blanchard.[511]

Della McDuffie

April 25, 1953; Alberta, AL

Although confined to a wheelchair at age 63, McDuffie helped her husband William—"Snowball," to his friends—run Della's Place, a café attached to their home in Alberta. Around midnight on April 25, notorious Wilcox County Sheriff Percy Columbus "Lummie" Jenkins entered Della's Place with two highway patrolmen, wielding a flexible weapon resembling a black rubber hose or cable. Jenkins struck several diners, also firing a pistol into the floor and ceiling, before he focused on Della McDuffie.[512]

Witness J. C Varner, McDuffie's nephew, later said of Jenkins, "So he walked in and hit her, told her, 'Get up old lady, go to bed.' So she told him she couldn't get up, so he hit her across her arm, on her knees, then he hit her on the head. And he shot down by her feet a couple of times, at her feet."[513] William McDuffie summoned Dr. Robert E. Dixon, but Della died within an hour of the beating. (Local rumors of a gunshot wound are unsubstantiated.) While no autopsy was performed, Dr. Dixon certified her death—falsely, relatives say—as caused by a cerebral hemorrhage resulting from longstanding arteriosclerosis. He specifically denied head trauma.[514]

Under pressure from the NAACP, FBI agents investigated McDuffie's case in July 1953, but ultimately filed no charges. William McDuffie kept agitating for a full investigation until his suspicious

Biography of Sheriff Percy "Lummie" Jenkins, posthumously lionized in print by his daughter (author's collection).

death in 1954. Thereafter, his surviving relatives fled Alabama in fear for their lives. Wilbur Williams, a McDuffie grandson, later said, "I found my grandfather and it had appeared that he had been killed by way of drowning. They killed him because of the intensity of this investigation. They tried to get him to change his mind and change his statements like everyone else did. He refused to do that. And they took care of it. The doctor as well as the sheriff were all in this together and they worked very hard to cover it up."[515]

Lummie Jenkins is remembered as a "character" in Wilcox County, where he served as sheriff from 1939 to 1971, his reputation largely dependent on the race of those recalling him. Ben Windham, writing for the *Tuscaloosa News* in 2012, called Jenkins a "master psychologist" who "never carried a gun," adept at extracting confessions from foolish suspects with cheap parlor tricks, such as foul-tasting "truth serum."[516] *Time* magazine, in 1976, quoted a courthouse hanger-on as saying, "Old Lummie had blacks so scared, all he had to do was pass the word he wanted some nigger in his office in the morning. Sure enough, that nigger'd be there—or he'd fled the county."[517] After 32 years in office, Jenkins lost his eighth reelection bid to Deputy Reginald Albritton, in 1970. He died at age 77, in December 1978.[518]

Corinne Hines
May 3, 1953; Atmore, AL

When FBI agents investigated the police slaying of Della McDuffie in Wilcox County (see April 25, 1953, above), they also examined the case of African American schoolteacher Corinne Hines, killed in Escambia County eight days later. A report in the *Chicago Defender* says Atmore police chief Clarence Bryars fatally injured Hines on May 3, beating and kicking her when she visited his jail to inquire about her husband's recent arrest. Hines died within an hour of the beating.[519] My inquiries to local libraries and newspapers failed to elicit any further information on this case.

Henry Randle
July 3, 1954; Holmes County, MS

An outdated Internet website lists African American Henry Randle as a Mississippi murder victim, killed sometime in July 1954.[520] Preliminary research for this volume revealed that while Randle was indeed shot without provocation by Holmes County Sheriff Richard F. Byrd, he survived the wound, prompting a local newspaper investigation and a libel suit.

Byrd was a car salesman and Scoutmaster before he won election as sheriff in 1952, running on a promise to end bootlegging, gambling, and cattle rustling. Beyond that, his campaign rested on the slogan "Just ask the Boy Scouts about me." Upon inauguration, Byrd indeed cracked down on gin mills—then allowed them to reopen if they bought their booze from one of his close friends. Slot machines, likewise, first vanished, then flourished in new settings, while the sheriff got his cut. Meanwhile, presumably unknown to Scout leaders and most of Holmes County's all-white electorate was Byrd's nocturnal passion for terrorizing blacks with random acts of violence, a rage exacerbated by the U.S. Supreme Court's May 1954 ruling on school desegregation.[521]

Two months after that announcement, on July 3, Sheriff Byrd went on an epic rampage, accompanied by three other lawmen. He attacked multiple victims on his rounds, beating at least seven victims, breaking a black teacher's glasses in one incident, leaving his own flashlight shattered from clubbing people in another. Finally, at a rail spur near Tchula, he spied several young blacks talking and approached them, knocking one to the ground and telling the rest to "get goin.'" As they fled, Byrd shot young Henry Randle from behind, drilling his thigh, then drove away and left him at the roadside.[522]

Crusading newspaper editor Hazel Brannon Smith, the first woman to receive the Pulitzer Prize for Editorial Writing, had already clashed with Byrd over his corrupt alliance with gangsters. Now she interviewed Randle and "decided that, if I didn't print this story, I was just as guilty of shooting that Negro as Richard was."[523] Her scathing editorial called for Byrd's resignation, saying that Byrd "has violated every concept of justice, decency and right in his treatment of some of the people of Holmes County."[524]

Journalist Hazel Brannon Smith risked her life to challenge brutal Mississippi sheriff Richard Byrd (Library of Congress).

Byrd retaliated with a libel suit. At trial in October 1954, Deputy I. C. Farmer said that Randle was actually shot by Constable Bob Gillespie, who in turn refused to testify. A fourth police witness, Highway Patrolman J. A. Love, claimed ignorance of who had fired the shot. A white jury found in Byrd's favor, awarding him $10,000, but Smith appealed that verdict and it was reversed by Mississippi's Supreme Court on November 7, 1955.[525]

Howard Bromley

November 5, 1955; Heathsville, VA

Bromley, age 23, entered a store owned by Ira D. Hinton, Jr., on Saturday, November 5, and struck up a conversation with Hinton's brother Meade. The "friendly" chat turned ugly after Bromley put his arm around Meade's shoulders, prompting the Hinton brothers to order him out of the store. Before the quarrel got violent, Ira telephoned Northumberland County Sheriff T. T. Bouldin, reporting "trouble" at the store. The Hintons later claimed that Bromley was drunk and "attacked" them, whereupon Ira fired a warning shot into the floor, then shot Bromley by accident during a "tussle" for Ira's pistol. Black witness Camright King disagreed, saying he saw Bromley drop while fleeing the store, shot from several feet away. An autopsy revealed three bullet wounds in Bromley's back.[526]

A special grand jury including two African Americans indicted Ira Hinton for murder on November 25. When his trial opened on December 20, two black attorneys from Richmond assisted Commonwealth's Attorney Walter Johnson for the prosecution. White jurors acquitted Hinton deliberated for 21 minutes prior to acquitting Hinton on December 22, explaining the "slow" vote by saying that one juryman was initially missing.[527]

H. Johnson
December 7, 1955; Gonzales, TX

Brief news reports named Johnson—no first name provided—as a local NAACP leader found beaten to death, adding that authorities denied any racial motive.[528] My inquiries to local libraries and newspapers added nothing to that sparse account.

Beulah Melton
December 22, 1955; Tallahatchie County, MS

Following the murder of her husband, Clinton (see December 3, 1955, in Part 1), Beulah Melton divided her time between caring for her four young children and pursuing evidence against Clinton's killer, Elmer Kimball. That research was not far advanced, a mere 19 day's after Clinton's death, when Beulah swerved her car into a bayou near Glendora. She drowned when the car sank, but a relative passing by chance

Beulah Melton, with her children, is interviewed by Medgar Evers concerning her husband's murder in December 1955. She died in a suspicious car crash days later (Library of Congress).

arrived in time to save two children—daughter Deloris and son Clinton Jr.—from the stagnant water. County officials blamed the crash on careless driving, but Melton's surviving daughter, now Deloris Melton Gresham, disputed that finding in a 2005 interview with author Susan Klopfer. "Later," she said, "a relative told me that was not true, that everyone knew she was run off the road."[529] Six decades after the fact, evidence of drive-by murder is impossible to find.

William King
January 6, 1956; Eufala, AL

Mississippi's *Clarion-Ledger* newspaper lists a "Richard King" among forgotten race murder victims of the 1960s.[530] Research for this volume identified the victim as William King, a father of eight shot without apparent cause by a one-armed white gunman. Unlike most other cases in this volume, King's murder was solved with the arrest of suspect O. B. Mann. White jurors convicted Mann of first-degree murder and sentenced him to life imprisonment, despite testimony from his wife, father-in-law, and several neighbors that Mann was at home when King was shot.[531]

Milton Russell
January 21, 1956; Belzoni, MS

Russell was a 25-year-old truck driver from Greenville, known as a "good Negro" who worked hard and paid his bills on time, while avoiding trouble with police. On January 21 he traveled 30 miles southeastward from home, to sing with a quartet called the Lovely Brothers in Belzoni. Russell never made it home that night, found bludgeoned in a house on Cain Street, his clothing doused with kerosene and set afire, spreading a blaze that nearly consumed the small dwelling. Relatives surmised that he was murdered for $100 that he carried when he left Greenville, but police seemed so indifferent that Hodding Carter II, editor of Greenville's *Delta Democrat-Times*, complained that they were treating Russell's death as "just another Negro killing." Belzoni coroner J. W. Wampler sent Russell's corpse to Jackson for autopsy, promising an inquest, but that panel never convened and the case remains unsolved.[532]

While Carter surmised that Russell may have been slain by a member of his own race, "Bloody Belzoni" had a savage reputation among African Americans, lately including the murder of civil rights activist George W. Lee (see May 7, 1955, in Part 1) and the near-fatal shooting of Gus Courts, cofounder with Lee of Belzoni's NAACP chapter, on November 25, 1955.[533] Medgar Evers and others suspected Russell was murdered by whites, but no suspects were identified.[534]

Edward Duckworth
January 27, 1956; Smith County, MS

Duckworth, age 25, worked for George Luckey at a sawmill four miles north of Mize, on Highway 35. On Friday, January 27, he allegedly borrowed $10 from Luckey "to carry his child to the hospital," then returned drunk and entered Luckey's store, adjacent to the mill, asking Luckey's wife for another $5. (Sheriff G. R. Nobles told a different story to reporters, claiming Duckworth was "hanging around" the store all day.) Mrs. Luckey refused, then called her husband when Duckworth became irate. Luckey told Duckworth to leave, saying he "had no business" in the store, whereupon Duckworth supposedly replied, "You're going to have some business with me right now." According to the *Smith County Reporter*, Duckworth then "reached in his shirt as if to draw a gun, and Luckey fired five shots into his body killing him almost instantly."[535]

Or did he?

Someone at the scene called Duckworth's brother, Wadell, who placed him in a car and rushed off toward a hospital in Magee, 11 miles distant. En route, he "swerved and overturned" the vehicle, prompting District Attorney Bill Little to blame Duckworth's death on a broken neck from the crash. In Magee, two white physicians and black mortician Allen Reed claimed they could not decide whether that injury or gunshot wounds claimed Duckworth's life. Reed further claimed that Duckworth had only two bullet wounds, both "near the shoulder." Based on that, the *Galveston Daily News* reported Duckworth was "shot twice during a gunfight"—though, in fact, he was unarmed.[536] An autopsy, ordered by prosecutor Little, determined that Duckworth died from a gunshot to the heart.[537]

Grover Luckey faced a preliminary hearing on January 30 and was released on $5,000 bond pending action by the next grand jury, but authorities did not pursue the case. Decades later, a researcher from Northeastern University's School of Law interviewed a witness to the slaying, Judge McLauren, who told a very different version of events. Fridays were payday at the Luckey mill, McLauren said, and Duckworth bought his boss a beer as a gesture of friendship. When he reached inside his shirt to get the bottle, Herman Luckey shouted to his brother, "Grover, he's got a gun," whereupon Grover shot Duckworth five times at close range.[538]

Charles H. Baldwin
April 22, 1956; Huntsville, AL

The Rev. Baldwin, age 70 or 73 (reports differ), was leading a cow across a street when a convertible occupied by four white men passed by, one of the passengers hurling a 10-pound stone. The rock struck Baldwin's leg, knocking him down. His skull cracked on impact with the pavement, and he died while en route to a local hospital. Madison County Sheriff L. D. Wall arrested four men—driver Charles Connally, 31; Doc Hill, 22; Walter Thompson, 20; and William Walling, 22—all from New Hope, 17 miles southeast of Huntsville.[539]

Sheriff Wall said one suspect had confessed to hurling the rock at Baldwin. When asked the motive, Wall told reporters, "Pranking, I reckon."[540] He soon released Connally and Walling, while charging Hill and Thompson with murder, then dismissed Thompson's charge in exchange for his testimony against Hill at trial. District Attorney Glenn Manning presented the state's case, spanning four days, and white jurors compromised by convicting Hill of manslaughter, resulting in a one-year sentence to "hard labor."[541]

Taplin Family
June 1956; Centreville, MS

Author Anne Moody, in her 1968 memoir *Coming of Age in Mississippi*, describes an arson fire that killed nine members of a family named Taplin, sometime in June 1956. As Moody reconstructs he case, a local racist group she calls "The Guild"—probably referring to the Citizens' Council, formed two years earlier—suspected one Mr. Banks, "a high yellow man of much wealth," was romancing and financially supporting a single white mother of three whose husband had deserted her. Guild members planned to kill Banks but torched his next-door neighbor's house by accident, annihilating the Taplin family. Banks soon fled Centreville, as did his white lover. Three years later, Moody claimed, murder victim Samuel O'Quinn (see August 14, 1959, in Part 1) was killed because he "supposedly knew all the facts underlying the Taplin burning and other mysterious killings in and around Centreville and Woodville."[542]

That story has enthralled Moody's readers for decades, but now a major part of it appears to be erroneous. While writing a history of Mississippi's Ku Klux Klan, I pursued the Taplin case and found no public record of any such fire. Two years later, Samuel Kennedy-Smith, a researcher with Northeastern University's Civil Rights and Restorative Justice Project, shared information gathered while investigating O'Quinn's death, stating his belief that a fatal house fire did occur in June 1956, "but under substantially different circumstances than Moody recounted in her book." Although "nothing panned out on the Moody/Taplin story," Kennedy-Smith pieced together a grim alternative version.[543]

In that tale, the arsonist—name withheld—was the "bad apple" of a large African American family based in Centreville, some of whom were active in civil rights work. As described by Kennedy-Smith, he "was for lack of a better description the town or area pimp. He would set black women up with white men." In summer 1956 one of his working girls rejected a certain white client, whereupon the pimp burned her home in reprisal, killing everyone present. "On a side note," Kennedy-Smith wrote, "one thing that comes to mind is that maybe there was not as many people killed as Moody believed, which may have helped muddy the waters in figuring out what actually happened." According to Kennedy-Smith, local rumors also linked the killer pimp to Samuel O'Quinn's unsolved murder—one version claiming a deathbed confession that named an accomplice still living in 1968.[544] As this book went to press, inquiries to sources suggested by Kennedy-Smith had turned up no new information.

Mrs. M. A. Rigdon
October 6, 1956; Newton, GA

A white gunman reportedly shot Mrs. Rigdon.[545] My inquiries to local libraries and newspapers revealed no record of the crime.

James Peterson
December 1, 1956; Blaine, MS

On the last night of his life, 38-year-old tenant farmer James Peterson dined at the One Minute Café with his wife, sister, and brother-in-law in Blaine, a small village near Ruleville. Peterson became embroiled in an argument with three other men, prompting the proprietor to summon night marshal W. B. "Bill" Townsend.[546] Townsend later said he arrived to find several black men "fighting over a gun." They surrendered it upon demand, but when Townsend tried to arrest Peterson on some unspecified charge, Peterson allegedly "whirled on him," causing the marshal to shoot him three times in the chest and right side.[547]

On December 5, Justice of the Peace H. L. Pearson convened a preliminary hearing on Peterson's death, questioning several witnesses from the café. Sunflower County Sheriff Ed Williams told reporters that those witnesses all concurred with Townsend's version of events. Apparently, none claimed that Peterson was armed. Pearson pronounced the slaying self-defense and filed no charges against Townsend.[548]

D. Moore
February 7, 1957; Jackson, MS

This case ranks among the most enigmatic of "forgotten" racist slayings, with literally nothing known about the victim or the crime beyond the alleged date and location. Author Susan Klopfer calls the victim "D. Moore," citing a "list of lynched black people in the Delta collected by Joyce Russer of Bolivar County," while other websites present the name as "O. Moore."[549] From the latter listing, it is tempting to suggest confusion with victim Oneal Moore (see June 2, 1965, in Part 1), but that presumes an eight-year discrepancy, plus transposition of a Louisiana homicide to Mississippi. My inquiries to local libraries and to award-winning *Clarion-Ledger* journalist Jerry Mitchell produced no records of D. (or O.) Moore's alleged murder. Attempts to contact Mss. Klopfer and Russer proved fruitless.

Alvin N. Palmer
March 11, 1957; Chicago, IL

A mob of young whites attacked 17-year-old Alvin Palmer at the corner of 59th Street and Kedzie Avenue, fracturing his skull. He died at Holy Cross Hospital on March 12. That same day, police arrested eight suspects, including three unnamed juveniles, two of them girls. Those named were Stephen Brooks, 18; Jerry Floyd, 17; Fred Gumn, 17; Joseph D. Kramer, 18; and Gerald O'Mara, 18. The teens admitted being present at the crime scene and described their roles in Palmer's death.[550] On March 13 police announced that a new suspect, 17-year-old Joseph Schwartz, had confessed to striking Palmer with a hammer.[551]

By March 14 authorities had 15 suspects in custody, with State's Attorney Benjamin Adamowski and a coroner's jury recommending execution for all as "equally guilty."

New additions to the list included James Adams, 17; Lawrence Adas, 16; James Bandyk, 18; Andrew Budz, 17; Donald Duchak, 16; Edward Fron, 17; Edward Gorski, 18; Raymond Kozlowski, 17; Frank Nowobielski, 18; Lawrence Pavlik, 16; Ronald Rybka; Thomas Trybula, 16; Ronald White, 17; and Alan Zureki, 19. Police found the murder weapon in Bandyk's garage.[552] Coroner Walter McCarron denounced parents of the accused when most left their sons to face the March 14 inquest alone.[553]

On March 15, Cook County's grand jury indicted Adams, Adas, Budz, Duchak, Fron, Gorski, Kozlowski, Nowobielski, Pavlik, Rybka, Schwartz, Trybula, and Zureki on charges of murder and conspiracy. Bandyk and White were charged as accessories after the fact, for hiding the murder weapon.[554] Threats from other prisoners placed Bandyk, Gorski, Schwartz and Zureki is protective isolation at Cook County's jail on March 16.[555] The defendants pled not guilty before Criminal Court Chief Justice Wilbert F. Crowley on March 27.[556]

Confessed killer Joseph Schwartz waived trial by jury, trusting his fate to Judge Crowley—who convicted him on June 26, 1957, imposing a 50-year sentence. Trial for 11 more defendants began the same afternoon, again without a jury, while the case of James Adams was severed for separate trial.[557] On June 30, Judge Crowley convicted Adas, Budz, Fron, Gorski, Kozlowski, Rybka and Trybula, while acquitting Duchak, Nowobielski, Pavlik and Zurek.[558] On August 1 the convicted defendants received prison terms ranging from 14 to 20 years.[559] My inquiries in Chicago revealed no further information on James Adams and his pending case.

Juliette Hampton Morgan
July 16, 1957; Montgomery, AL

Born in 1914, Morgan was a teacher, librarian, and a rare white Alabama "liberal," a seventh-generation southerner who sacrificed her social standing and her life for racial justice in the Cotton State. In the early 1940s she joined activist groups including the Alabama Council on Human Relations, the Fellowship of the Concerned, and the Southern Conference Educational Fund. By 1946 she was involved with an interracial women's prayer group that met in black churches, when no white congregations would tolerate it. In 1952, four years before Montgomery's famous bus boycott propelled Martin Luther King, Jr., to national prominence, Morgan began personal protests against white bus drivers' offensive treatment of African Ameri-

Memorial for Juliette Hampton Morgan in Montgomery, Alabama (author's collection).

can passengers. That same year, she drew widespread attention with a letter to the *Montgomery Advertiser*, condemning the city's segregation laws.[560]

Ostracized by "friends" and threatened by Mayor William A. Gayle with dismissal from her post as superintendent of Montgomery's libraries, Morgan tempered her criticism for a time, but broke her silence in January 1957, with a letter congratulating Buford Boone, editor of the *Tuscaloosa News*, on his public stand against racist violence. On July 15, 1957, Ku Klux Klansmen burned a cross on Morgan's lawn. She resigned her post the following day, and apparently committed suicide that night, with an overdose of sleeping pills. Montgomery's library desegregated five years later, without incident. On March 3, 2005, Morgan was inducted into the Alabama Women's Hall of Fame in Marion. Eight months later, Montgomery's City-County Library Board and the Montgomery County Commission voted unanimously to rename the city's central library on High Street the Juliette Hampton Morgan Memorial Library.[561]

Betty Butler
August 1957; McComb, MS

On August 23, 1957, a black minister in McComb, the Rev. Hollis N. Turner, penned a nine-page letter to Lieutenant Governor Carroll Gartin, describing recent crimes against African Americans in Pike County. One recent incident, undated, was the death of Betty Butler, murdered near Overhead Bridge, linking State Street and Pearl River Avenue in downtown McComb, "by a sixteen-year-old white boy because she resisted his sex advances." Gartin ignored the letter, which also described two other rapes, one by a white man who confessed his crime but was nonetheless acquitted by an all-white jury.[562]

Unnamed Woman
November 1957; Ringgold, GA

An outdated, untitled website listing race-related murders in America from 1940 through 1965 includes the following brief item: "1 unidentified black woman (wife of civil rights activist) murdered Ringgold Georgia November 1957."[563] Research fails to reveal any such incident from Ringgold during 1957, suggesting that the citation may be a garbled reference to the bombing murder of victim Mattie Green in May 1960 (see Part 1). The confusion may have arisen from an article on Southern racist bombings, published in 1963, listing explosions from Ringgold in November 1957 and May 1960, without any reference to fatalities.[564] No evidence exists linking Green's husband to the civil rights movement.

Willie V. Dunigan
November 17, 1957; Lomax, AL

Despite the public assurance of Chilton County Deputy Sheriff Floyd Porter that "we have no racial trouble in this county and do not anticipate any," Lomax was a hotbed of Ku Klux Klan activity in the latter 1950s, including reports of drive-by shootings at African American homes, largely ignored by white police.[565] Those incidents—and a cross-burning outside Lomax on November 14, 1957—sparked an outburst of violence two days later, apparently caused by a case of mistaken identity.[566]

On Saturday night, November 16, a group of deputies embarked on a tour of Lomax's black neighborhood. Someone apparently thought they were Klansmen and fired at their car, whereupon the officers returned fire. Four deputies suffered minor wounds in the ensuing series of hit-and-run skirmishes, while one African American, 33-year-old Willie Dunigan, died in what newspapers called a 30-minute "pitched battle" at his home, shot several times in the chest. On Sunday morning, Sheriff Hugh Champion echoed Deputy Porter, denying any racial animosity within his county. "Some people were extremely reckless with firearms last night," Champion told reporters, "but the incidents have no bearing on race."[567]

James Henry Ellison
September 21, 1958; Chattanooga, TN

Throughout the troubled 1950s and '60s, Chattanooga was a center of Ku Klux Klan activity and racial violence, including multiple bombings. On September 21, 1958, two white couples driving through a racially mixed neighborhood "had words" with African Americans on the street and gunfire erupted, leaving 21-year-old black bystander James Ellison dead on the pavement. Homicide detective R. E. Cornish told reporters Ellison was standing a street corner "minding his own business" when a bullet cut him down. Officers found three 9mm shell casings at the scene, one beneath Ellison's body.[568]

Police traced the two white couples, none of whom were armed when they were arrested for questioning. Their stories conflicted with those of black witnesses, but prosecutors finally charged a black man, 27-year old Walter Graves, with Ellison's murder. According to the official story, Graves fired at the white motorists but missed their car, striking Ellison in the back with one shot. On September 22, District Attorney Edward Davis told reporters that Graves had confessed to the slaying.[569] The placement of a cartridge under Ellison's corpse, as if he were shot at extremely close range, remains unexplained.

Jonas Causey
May 10, 1959; Clarksdale, MS

The slaying of Jonas Causey, 70, presents another case wherein black witnesses and white authorities told strikingly different stories. Elnora Causey, speaking to the press after her husband's death, described incidents of harassment by two white men, Orville Bailey and Bunion W. Knight, culminating on the night of Saturday, May 9, when the pair arrived at Causey's home "cursing and shooting," sparking a battle that continued past dawn on Sunday.[570] As Mrs. Causey described the incident:

> A bullet from one of the guns wounded me in my right thigh. When my husband discovered I was shot he came enraged and fired on Mr. Bailey shooting him in the face.

This was done in self-defense as Mr. Bailey was advancing and trying to kill both my husband and me. Mr. Bailey immediately turned around to the truck. He fell before he reached the truck and my husband also fired on the truck from which Mr. Knight was shooting.[571]

Clarksdale police first learned of the incident at 11:15 a.m. on May 10, when a Mrs. Catalina phoned headquarters from her home on Highway 62, two miles south of town. Bunion Knight was at her door, she said, "all bloody and he seemed to be intoxicated." Knight said Jonas Causey had killed Orville Bailey, and a police dispatcher notified Coahoma County Sheriff Leighton Miller. Both departments mobilized, sending a total of 15 officers to surround Causey's home.[572]

On arrival, the officers fired tear gas into Causey's house, flushing out his wife. Jonas—a former mental patient at Whitfield State Hospital—remained inside, at one point having a loud, one-sided conversation with President Dwight Eisenhower. As Sheriff Miller later explained, "We did a lot of yelling for him to come out, but he wouldn't and finally we just all shot in there and killed him."[573] Six officers who stormed the house found Causey mortally wounded, reportedly clutching a shotgun with "a hot barrel" and three rounds in its magazine. He died moments after police dragged him out the backdoor.[574]

While local NAACP leader Aaron Henry argued in vain for an FBI investigation, local lawmen carefully ignored the reason for Bailey's and Knight's presence at the Causey home, and the report of Knight's intoxication. They stressed Jonas Causey's mental history and dismissed his widow's statements as "contradictory," claiming that her observations did not match "what we found at the scene." An unnamed Clarksdale doctor told reporters Mrs. Causey visited him around 4 p.m. on Sunday, seeking treatment for a "small nick" on her leg that "could have come from anything." Sheriff Miller insisted that she fled the house during the "battle," shouting to police, "He's crazy!"[575] The FBI did not investigate.[576]

Horace G. Bell
May 23, 1959; Dallas County, AL

Born in 1859, the Rev. Horace Bell was a civil rights activist and member of the Montgomery Improvement Association led by Martin Luther King, Jr., a group targeted for Ku Klux violence during its boycott of segregated city buses in 1956–57.[577] On Saturday, May 23, 1959, he joined other black residents of Montgomery to visit Dallas Public Lake, opened by the Alabama Department of Conservation three days earlier, 13 miles south of Selma. The day passed without incident, blacks and whites fishing on opposite shores of the 100-acre reservoir, but Bell never returned to his Montgomery home. The following day, white mobs attacked three black men at the lake, beating them severely, breaking one's arm, and chasing them out of the county.[578]

Bell's family called W. L. Allen, chief investigator for the Alabama Highway Patrol, offering to organize a massive search by African Americans, but he refused, turning instead to Dallas County Sheriff Jim Clark. On May 29, the Rev. King wrote to Governor John Patterson, elected with Klan support in 1958, requesting an investigation of Bell's disappearance, but officers found Bell's corpse that same day, at the lake.[579]

Confusion still surrounds Bell's death. Two sources claim it was attributed to drowning; two others blame it on a heart attack.[580] King biographer Jim Bishop provides the most detail, writing that sheriff's deputies found Bell with fishing pole in hand, summoning Dr. Carl J. Rehling from the State Toxicologist's Office and an "anatomical expert named Van Pruitt, who was not a physician," to perform a lakeside autopsy, reporting death from myocardial infarction.[581] Even so, suspicion of foul play persists and one anonymous website lists Bell as having been "murdered [in] Selma Alabama May 29 1959."[582]

Tommy Dwight
June 13, 1959; Dalton, GA

Dwight, 11 years old, was attending a fish fry at his uncle's home when drive-by shooters killed him on this Saturday. Eight days later, Whitfield County Sheriff Donald McArthur arrested four whites—18-year-old Herschell Elkins, 23-year-old Leroy Gentry, 18-year-old Kermit Pritchett, Jr., and 17-year-old Billy Joe Rolen—on murder charges.[583] According to McArthur, the suspects admitted firing shots but claimed they were unaware of hitting anyone until the following day.[584] My inquiries to local libraries and newspapers revealed no further information on the case.

William Joe Lee Person
June 13, 1959; Wake County, NC

White farmer Roger Earl Williams shot Person in the back with a .22-caliber rifle, while Person ran through a field two miles east of Wake Forest. The shooting occurred near a store owned by Person's employer, Buck Cooley. On the day he died, Person was supposed to work for Williams, by arrangement with Cooley, but he disliked that idea. As Deputy Sheriff Jake T. Turner later testified, "Person had said he wasn't going to work that day for Williams. He said he was going to run when he saw Williams coming."[585]

That, in fact, is what happened when Williams came to fetch Person at midday. Watching Person flee, Williams said Person could run faster if someone was shooting at him. Aiming the rifle—borrowed from Cooley to kill hogs—Williams fired twice "in the air." One bullet struck Person, who ran another 56 feet before collapsing. Williams then put Person in his pickup truck and drove off to seek help, but Person died before reaching Dr. George Corbin's office in Rolesville.[586]

Williams told authorities that he was "horse playing" with Person and did not intend to harm him. A magistrate released Williams without charges, but a county grand jury indicted him for manslaughter on July 13. At trial in August, Deputy Turner—the prosecution's only witness—declared his belief that the shooting was accidental. District Solicitor Lester V. Chalmers, Jr., dubbed the charge "a technical case of manslaughter," and Judge William Bicket agreed, saying, "It was no accident that he got the gun out and pulled the trigger. It was an accident that he aimed wrong."[587]

Williams pled *nolo contendere* on August 25, receiving a three-to-five-year prison term. Judge Bicket suspended that sentence, on condition that Williams "remain of good behavior and law abiding," while paying widow Rosa Mae Person and her four young children $2,750 ($22,750 today) over the next two years. Rosa's attorney, Herman Taylor, told reporters she had agreed to the settlement.[588]

Cleveland Holmes
January 30, 1960; Brandon, MS

Holmes was an imposing man by any standards: six feet seven inches tall, 285 pounds, a successful farmer and landowner, father of 15 children. Around 8:30 p.m. on Saturday, January 30, Officers Grady Cook and Oscar Cook arrested Holmes and a friend, Leon Hooker, ostensibly for being drunk in public. At the Rankin County jail in Brandon, they were placed in a cell with a third black inmate. Jailers reportedly found Holmes dead in his cell on Sunday morning, the *Brandon News* telling its readers: "Other prisoners reported that they heard Holmes fall out of bed during the night and, considering him thoroughly drunk, thought no more of the incident." Justice of the Peace Walter Ratcliff held an inquest, ruling that Holmes died from "natural causes."[589]

Once he was freed from custody, Leon Hooker told a different story. His affidavit, collected by Mississippi NAACP leader Medgar Evers, stated that while en route to jail, "Oscar Cook struck Cleve Holmes repeatedly over the head with a black jack, because as Mr. Oscar Cook said later: 'His talking back made me mad.'"[590] Inez Holmes, one of Cleveland's daughters, later told researchers from Northeastern University's School of Law that Grady Cook held a gun to Hooker's head, forcing Hooker to beat Holmes as well. Additionally, Hooker said both Cooks and two Rankin County sheriff's deputies had beaten Holmes overnight, in his jail cell, leaving him facedown "in a pool of blood." An "investigation" by the Rankin County Sheriff's Department upheld the official verdict of death by natural causes.[591]

Louis Stapleton
August 5, 1960; Clarksdale, MS

Stapleton, age 42, traveled from Chicago to Clarksdale for a relative's funeral. While there, he was arrested for drunk driving and possession of an illegal firearm disguised as a fountain pen, receiving a 30-day jail sentence. Assigned to an inmate road crew run by the Coahoma County Board of Supervisors, Stapleton fell ill on August 2, whereupon white overseer Pat Williams beat him and forced him to continue working. Another bout of illness prompted a second beating on August 5, this time with Williams leaving Stapleton unconscious in a roadside ditch for over an hour, while work continued around him. Stapleton died in jail later that day, photos of his corpse displaying lacerations on his back and buttocks.[592]

Sheriff L.A. Ross convened a coroner's jury, which could not decide if Stapleton died from heat exhaustion or his final beating. Some reports claim a grand jury also investigated the case, but if so, no records remain. Sheriff Ross also requested an investigation by the Mississippi State Sovereignty Commission, whose report spells Stapleton's first name as "Lover."[593] The Board of Supervisors fired Williams, but otherwise he was never punished. NAACP spokesman Aaron Henry warned black travelers that

"Illinois, New York or a Michigan license plate is an invitation to insult by the highway patrol" in Mississippi.[594]

David Jackson
December 14, 1961; McDuffie County, GA

On the morning of December 14, 1961, two young boys exploring woodlands near Augusta, Georgia, found the corpse of an African American man hanging by the neck from a tree. They alerted local police, who summoned an agent from the Georgia Bureau of Investigation to the scene. That agent took one photograph and instantly declared the death a suicide, supporting his snap judgment with a statement that the dead man's hands were not bound. Officers subsequently identified the dead man as David Jackson, a "trusty" inmate from McDuffie County's prison farm. Thirty years after the fact, one of the boys who found Jackson's body disputed the GBI's verdict in a televised interview, insisting that Jackson's hands were bound when he discovered the corpse.[595]

Police manipulated evidence in the death of David Jackson to support a "suicide" verdict (Library of Congress).

Otis Nash
May 1962; Neshoba County, MS

Otis Nash was a troubled 27-year-old, suffering from epilepsy and erratic mood swings that led to three years' confinement at Whitfield State Hospital, a mental facility 15 miles southeast of Jackson, Mississippi. In May 1962, living with his family in Philadelphia, Nash quarreled violently with relatives, causing his brother to suspect that Nash's "mind had gone bad again." Without consulting father Levie Nash, the brother called Neshoba County Sheriff Ethel "Hop" Barnett to collect Otis. Barnett arrived with two deputies, arrested Otis, and took him to the county jail. Next morning, Levie signed commitment papers for Whitfield, offering to ride along and keep his son calm on the journey, but Barnett refused.[596]

Levie Nash had reason to fear for his son's life in custody. During his son's last trip to Whitfield, he said, Sheriff Barnett had threatened, "If I ever get that nigger in my car again I'm going to kill him." And so it was that day in May. As told by Barnett and Deputy Lawrence Rainey, they had only traveled a few miles when Nash, although handcuffed in the backseat, tried to grab a pistol from the car's glove compartment, forcing Barnett to fatally shoot him in "self-defense." Some residents of Philadelphia believed Rainey had done the shooting, and that Barnett lied to cover his deputy's growing reputation for racist brutality. In either case, a coroner's jury ruled the shooting to be "justifiable homicide."[597]

Rainey was elected to replace Barnett as sheriff in 1963. In 1967 both officers were indicted on federal charges of conspiring to kill civil rights activists James Chaney, Andrew Goodman, and Michael Schwerner (see June 21, 1964, in Part 1). White jurors acquitted Rainey, while failing to reach a verdict on Barnett. Later that year, voters elected Barnett to succeed Rainey as sheriff. He died on January 7, 1989, followed by Rainey on November 8, 2002.

Hattie Carroll
February 9, 1963; Baltimore, MD

A prominent member of Baltimore's African American community and mother of 11, 51-year-old Hattie Carroll was working the bar at the Emerson Hotel's annual Spinster's Ball on February 8, 1963, when William Devereux Zantzinger, 24-year-old son of

William Devereux Zantzinger, slayer of Hattie Carroll, in police custody (National Archives).

a wealthy tobacco-farming family, came in drunk and spoiling for a fight, already quarreling with his wife. Zantzinger ordered a drink, and when Carroll moved too slowly to please him, he called her a "black son of a bitch" and struck her on the head and shoulders with a 25-cent toy cane, moving on from there to assault his wife and at least three hotel employees. Of the five, only Carroll was badly injured, dying from a brain hemorrhage at 9 a.m. on February 9.[598]

Prosecutors initially charged Zantzinger with murder, then reduced the charge to manslaughter when Baltimore's coroner deemed Carroll's death stress-induced, rather than a direct result of blunt-force trauma. Zantzinger, who admitted being drunk but denied any memory of the attack, also faced a charge of disorderly conduct. Jurors convicted him on both charges, on August 28, 1963, resulting in a six-month jail term and a $500 fine. Zantzinger also paid Carroll's family $25,000, though researchers from Northeastern University School of Law found "some question as to whether the money was truly a settlement to stave off a civil case or given in exchange for the family's silence."[599]

Few Americans knew anything of Carroll's case until folk singer Bob Dylan issued his third album, *The Times They Are A-Changin'*, in January 1964, including a song titled "The Lonesome Death of Hattie Carroll." Critics still debate the accuracy of Dylan's song, pointing to discrepancies between his lyrics and the court record, while William Zantzinger branded the song "a damn lie."[600] After serving his county jail time, Zantzinger returned to the family plantation, later branching out into real estate. He died at age 69, on January 3, 2009.[601]

Willie Joel Lovett
June 30, 1963; Tchula, MS

Confusion surrounds the poorly reported death of 20-year-old Willie Lovett. An account published by Student Nonviolent Coordinating Committee (SNCC) activists in early 1964 says that a local policeman shot Lovett at his (Lovett's) home, around 6:30 p.m. on June 30, noting that Town Marshal W. O. Moore "declined to say who fired the fatal shot."[602] Two days after the shooting, a brief story in the *Delta Democrat-Times* quoted Holmes County Chief Deputy Andrew Smith as saying that Moore himself shot Lovett "in self-defense."[603] Nothing more is known about the case today, beyond author Susan Klopfer's assertion that SPLC spokesmen list Lovett among suspected "victims of racially motivated murders."[604] In fact, however, Lovett's name does not appear on the SPLC's list of "forgotten" civil rights martyrs.[605]

Clyde Kennard
July 4, 1963; Chicago, IL

Six years before James Meredith made global headlines for integrating the University of Mississippi, Clyde Kennard struggled to crack racial barriers at the all-white University of Southern Mississippi (USM). The end result was false imprisonment and death.

Born in Hattiesburg, in 1927, Kennard moved to Chicago at age 12 to help a disabled sister. He graduated from high school there, joined the army, and served as a paratrooper in the Korean War. Back in civilian life, he completed three years at the University of Chicago before returning to Mississippi in 1955. Kennard bought a farm at Eatonville and taught Sunday school at Mary Magdalene Baptist Church while preparing his assault on the bastion of white supremacy at USM in Hattiesburg. Administrators rejected his applications in 1956, 1957, and 1959, when Governor James P. Coleman offered free tuition to any black college in Mississippi. Kennard declined that offer, citing the Supreme Court's 1954 school desegregation order in *Brown v. Board of Education of Topeka*.[606]

Enter Zack Van Landingham, an investigator for the shady Mississippi State Sovereignty Commission, who teamed with white Hattiesburg attorney Dudley Connor to silence Kennard. Commission files reveal that state officials considered bombing Kennard's car or staging a fatal auto accident, before deciding to frame him on criminal charges instead. On September 15, 1959, Constables Charlie Ward and Lee Daniels arrested Kennard for "reckless driving," then told Justice of the Peace T. C. Hobby that they found five pints of moonshine in his car. Convicted in that case and fined $600, Kennard next found himself the target of a white boycott that threatened his livelihood as a farmer.[607]

Police arrested Kennard a second time on September 25, 1960, charging him with theft of chicken feed valued at $25 from the Forrest County Cooperative warehouse. Alleged accomplice Johnny Lee Roberts testified for the prosecution, and an all white jury deliberated for 10 minutes before convicting Kennard of burglary on November 21. For his supposed crime, Kennard received a seven-year sentence at maximum-security Parchman Penitentiary. NAACP spokesman Medgar Evers called Kennard's trial "a mockery of judicial justice," for which he was fined $100 and sentenced to 30

Advertisement for a 2013 commemoration of Clyde Kennard's struggle against Mississippi segregation (author's collection).

days in jail. The state supreme court overturned that conviction, but years would pass before Johnny Roberts recanted his false testimony, admitting that "Kennard did not ask me to steal, Kennard did not ask me to break into the co-op, Kennard did not ask me to do anything illegal."[608]

Kennard was diagnosed with colon cancer in 1961, and while state authorities permitted surgery at the University of Mississippi Medical Center—by then allowing black physicians to attend postgraduate classes—they ignored recommendations that Kennard remain at the hospital for further care. Returned to Parchman as a laborer, Kennard became a *cause célèbre*, bringing great embarrassment to Mississippi. Governor Ross Barnett granted Kennard an "indefinite suspended sentence" in January 1963, whereupon Kennard returned to Chicago for further medical treatment. Two more operations failed to halt his cancer, and he died 10 days after the second surgery, on July 4.[609]

Crusading journalist Jerry Mitchell broke the story of Johnny Roberts's perjured testimony in December 2005, launching a movement to obtain a pardon for Kennard. Governor Haley Barbour rejected that petition in 2006, but he did designate March 30 as Clyde Kennard Day, in honor of Kennard's "determination, the injustices he suffered, and his significant role in the history of the civil rights movement in Mississippi." Finally, in May 2006, Judge Bob Helfrich in Hattiesburg dismissed Kennard's 1960 burglary conviction. Governor Barbour termed that action the "appropriate, constitutional way for this innocent man to be exonerated."[610]

Reinaldo Colon Rodriguez
July 5, 1963; Fort Meade, MD

Colon Rodriguez was an army private, born in Puerto Rico, assigned as a mess hall cook at Fort Meade. On July 3, with African American soldiers Connis L. Hubbard and Robert Wiley, he attempted to enter Barrattini's Bar and Package Goods Store on Annapolis—a stretch of saloons known as "Boomtown"—in Odenton, near Fort Meade. Owner Pearl Barrattini later told reporters that she welcomed all customers, "but not many Negroes come in." On July 3 a waitress told Hubbard and Wiley that state law forbade her from serving them. As the trio left, a group of five whites shouted after them to leave Boomtown, adding, "If you ever come back again, nigger, we'll kill you."[611]

More courageous than wise, Hubbard and Colon returned to Boomtown on July 4, with black serviceman John A. Pettiford. They bought a bottle of liquor and parked at a gas station, where Pettiford says he passed out and missed the ensuing events.[612] While he dozed, a jeering crowd of white toughs gathered, then a carload of whites cruised past, its occupants lobbing stones. As that vehicle fled, another pulled up, driven by William H. Warfel, a 21-year-old shipyard worker previously arrested for harassing demonstrators at a segregated restaurant in April 1962. A judge fined him $25 in that case, then suspended the fine.[613]

Warfel tried to trap Hubbard's car in the parking lot, but Hubbard swerved around him and raced back toward Fort Meade. Jerry W. Robbins, 17, was among 12 whites who joined the chase, later saying, "It was like a madhouse then, with everyone running around, jumping into two cars to go down the main street in Odenton."[614] The pursuit continued onto Fort Meade, where Hubbard parked between two barracks buildings and prepared to fight when whites leaped from one of the chase cars, attacking a black soldier passing by on foot. "I got out of my Caddy," Hubbard testified, "and saw them beating up on this soldier when that man there [Warfel] asked me if I knew he had a sawed-off shotgun. He kicked me then, and then Ray opened my car door and he just wheeled and shot him down."[615]

Warfel fled the scene, tossing his gun into some bushes as he drove through Meade Heights, then hid his car, intending to report it stolen—all in vain, as Anne Arundel County officers arrested him within a half mile of Fort Meade.[616] A 14-year-old boy soon found the gun and gave it to authorities.[617] Colon died from his wounds at 12:30 p.m., at Fort Meade's hospital, and army spokesmen notified his pregnant widow at her home in Portsmouth, Virginia.[618]

FBI agents charged Warfel with murder on federal property, holding him without bond pending a hearing on July 10.[619] Deputy U.S. Attorneys Robert J. Carson and Robert W. Kernan were assigned to prosecute, while the court appointed lawyers Robert R. Bair and Luke Marbury to defend Warfeld.[620]

At trial in November 1963, Hubbard admitted having two tire irons in his car after the threats made on July 3, but said he approached his white pursuers empty-handed, intending to help a fellow soldier in trouble. Four possible weapons—the tire irons and two small knives—were found in his car, untouched, after the fatal shooting. Warfel, testifying on his own behalf, told a confused story, claiming he only took the shotgun from his car after Hubbard approached with a tire iron. "I kicked at Hubbard," he said, "and then swung back around. I thought it was pointed in the air when it went off."[621]

After pleading self-defense, Warfeld's attorneys added a suggestion that his shotgun was inoperable on the day Colon died. To counter that assertion, an FBI agent displayed the weapon's operating mechanism for the jury, and witness Douglas H. Woods testified that Warfel let him fire the gun on July 3, boasting that he "kept it for niggers" beneath his car's dashboard.[622] Jurors deliberated for nearly six hours on November 21, convicting Warfel of voluntary manslaughter. He received a 10-year prison term from Judge Harrison L. Winter on December 6.[623]

Colon's widow remarried. Their son, Ray McCarthy, grew up believing his father died in a car accident, only learning the truth in 2010, when Colon's name was added to the SPLC's Civil Rights Memorial in Montgomery, Alabama.[624]

Unnamed Woman
August 1963; Columbus, MS

In 1964 civil rights activists reported the fatal shooting of an unnamed African American woman near the Columbus Air Force Base. According to that report, the shooter, white Technical Sergeant Rotha R. Ayers, said he was "shooting at a stray dog that had been bothering the neighborhood and the bullet apparently ricocheted, hitting the woman in the chest." On August 29, 1963, a Lowndes County coroner's jury ruled the shooting accidental.[625] Despite that verdict, some websites still list the case as a civil rights–related murder, incorrectly citing the date of the coroner's ruling as the date of the shooting.[626]

John Coley
September 4, 1963; Birmingham, AL

On September 4 Ku Klux Klansmen bombed the home of African American attorney and civil rights activist Arthur Shores for the second time in 16 days. Rioting erupted in the black Birmingham neighborhood nicknamed "Dynamite Hill," and one of those present was 20-year-old John Coley. Police blasted Coley with shotguns, and he was dead on arrival at University Hospital. Officers later claimed they shot Coley when he "burst from a house firing a gun," but scores of witnesses insisted Coley was unarmed, a victim of promiscuous police gunfire.[627]

Witnesses to Coley's shooting noted his striking resemblance to longtime activist Rev. Fred Shuttlesworth, 20 years Coley's senior, surmising that police may have killed him in a case of mistaken identity while trying to assassinate Shuttlesworth. Other officers *did* assault Shuttlesworth at the bombing scene, as he tried to quell the riot, but he escaped without major injury. The nearest officer to Coley when he fell was Fred C. Garrett, a nephew of Klansman and serial bomber Robert Chambliss. Garrett denied being armed with a shotgun that night, but as author Diane McWhorter notes, "Garrett would lie about that shotgun in connection with a future bombing."[628] Since shotgun pellets bear no rifling marks, the officer or officers responsible for Coley's death remain unidentified.

Klansmen bombed the home of attorney Arthur Shores on September 4, 1963, sparking a riot in which police killed John Coley (Library of Congress).

Lula Mae Anderson, Eli Jackson and Dennis Jones
December 1963; Woodville, MS

Confusion surrounds the death of these three African Americans, including one website that lists them as "unidentified" while moving the date of their deaths to February 1964.[629] In fact, they were found dead in December 1963, in a car parked near Poor House Road in Woodville.[630] An early newspaper report claimed the trio had fallen asleep in their vehicle with engine running, dying from suffocation by carbon monoxide, but later accounts claimed two were shot, while one suffered a broken neck.[631] A memoir penned by civil rights activist Joseph Schwartz identifies the three as "movement activists," asserting that they were "summarily executed in their car."[632] Suspected Ku Klux Klan victim Clifton Walker was shot and killed near the same Woodville location (see February 28, 1964, in Part 1). My inquiries to local sources in 2014 produced no further information on this troubling case.

Romie Harris
December 30, 1963; Tupelo, MS

A white man, identified in published reports as Calvin Deaton, shot Harris and claimed self-defense. No other information was available on this case as *Justice Denied* went to press.[633]

Unidentified Man
March 1964; Natchez, MS

Author Susan Klopfer cites this case in one of her Internet blogs on civil rights–related murders, reporting: "Unidentified black man shot to death in car, Natchez, March 1964."[634] My inquiries to local sources failed to uncover any such case, but Klopfer may have confused information from the near-fatal shooting of victim Richard Joe Butler from Kingston, Mississippi.

Butler, an African American laborer, was 25 years old in 1964. On March 11 of that year, two weeks after Clifton Walker's murder (see February 28, 1964, in Part 1), two carloads of white men tried to run Butler and his wife off the Pretty Creek Bridge, in the Homochitto National Forest southeast of Natchez. Police interviewed Butler about that incident but arrested no suspects. On Sunday, April 5, after working on a Kingston farm owned by Hayward and Louisa Drane, Butler was confronted by two white men wearing hoods and armed with shotguns. The gunmen told him they "wanted to kill a smart nigger." Butler tried to flee on foot and was shot four times. Mrs. Drane heard the shots and Butler's cries for help, finding him badly wounded, with no sign of his attackers. She drove him to a Natchez hospital, where Butler recovered under police guard. As in the first attack, officers made no arrests.[635]

Unnamed Victim
June 22, 1964; Brandon, MS

Sketchy media reports describe an unidentified "Negro youth" killed by a white hit-and-run driver during Mississippi's "freedom summer." Police deemed the incident accidental, while African Americans suspected murder.[636]

Research conducted for this volume identified the victim as 14-year-old H. T. Thompson, struck while riding his bicycle on Highway 468, shortly before 7 a.m. on June 22. According to the *Rankin County News*, there was no hit-and-run. Rather, as described by Highway Patrol investigators, one car passed Thompson, after which he "cut back into the highway" and was struck by a second vehicle, driven by James B. Bassett, Jr., a white resident of Philadelphia, Mississippi, employed at the state hospital in Whitfield. Police filed no charges.[637]

Wayne Yancey
August 1, 1964; Holly Springs, MS

A native of Tennessee, born in 1943, Yancey graduated from high school in Chicago and joined the local chapter of SNCC, becoming a civil rights activist. The announcement of Mississippi's "freedom summer" brought him south again, and he became a well-

Wayne Yancey (standing), with Charles Scales and two unidentified civil rights activists, shortly before a car crash killed him and injured Scales on August 1, 1964 (Civil Rights Archive).

known figure among local African Americans and Northern volunteers. On August 1, Yancey rode from Memphis to Holly Springs with SNCC colleague Charlie Scales. A few miles short of their destination, their car struck another vehicle head-on.[638]

What happened next remains a matter of some controversy. One website claims Yancey "died after being denied admission to [a] white hospital."[639] SNCC activist Cleveland Sellers, Jr., arrived at the local hospital, later writing: "We were shocked to find Wayne's body lying in the back of the ambulance/hearse with blood dripping into a puddle underneath. We could not tell how long the body had been there or if Wayne had died at the scene or while still in the ambulance waiting for medical attention." Scales was admitted to the hospital, but he received no treatment before police arrived, seeking to arrest him for vehicular homicide. Two hours of tense negotiation secured his release, whereupon he was driven to Memphis, then flown to Chicago, where physicians saved his life.[640]

Reporters Allen Breed and Sharon Cohen termed the highway crash "suspicious."[641] Scales supported that contention, telling other volunteers in Holly Springs that "as he was lying on the ground immediately after the wreck, some white men walked over to him and said, 'Stay still or you will get the same as your buddy.' Charlie assumed that they might have been responsible for not allowing the car to return to the appropriate lane."[642] My inquiries to local libraries and newspapers revealed no further information on the crash, beyond descriptions of the second driver as "a local man."

Curtie Watts
January 25, 1965; Forest, MS

Author Susan Klopfer includes Watts on a list of persons "suspected by [the] SPLC as victims of racially motivated murders."[643] Unfortunately, she provides no further details, and his name does not appear on the SPLC's published list of presumed civil rights victims.[644] My inquiries to local libraries and newspapers revealed no information on this case.

Perry Small
August 27, 1965; Hale County, AL

An anonymous, obsolete website lists African American Perry Small as being lynched at Greensboro on August 27.[645] Further research confuses matters, as the *Tuscaloosa News* calls the 87-year-old victim Perry "Smaw," reporting that he died in a Greensboro hospital at 9 a.m. on August 27, from injuries suffered at his farmhouse outside town on the night of August 21. Neighbors found Smaw—or Small, as rendered by author Thomas Parker in 1974[646]—lying in the doorway of his home on Sunday, August 22, with his "head battered and his tongue cut out." On August 26, Deputy Sheriff David Holloway announced a "major development" in the case, telling reporters, "Things are looking mighty good."[647]

In what seemed a coup for segregationists, Holloway reported the arrest of two unnamed black men, one of them allegedly jailed during local civil rights protests in late July. Holloway quoted "other Negroes," likewise anonymous, as saying Smaw had criticized black activists, presumably inciting one or more to silence him. Gilbert Flay, third vice president of the Hale County Improvement Association, did not know Smaw personally, but denied that the assault stemmed from a denunciation of protesters. "It's a false statement," he said, "that this man has spoken out against the movement." Flay also denied that either man detained by sheriff's officers was active in local protests.[648]

And indeed, the case advanced by Deputy Holloway soon ran out of steam. By the time Small or Smaw died on August 27, one alleged suspect had been released from custody, while the other was held on an "open" charge.[649] My inquiries to local libraries and newspapers revealed no evidence of anyone being indicted or tried for the brutal slaying.

Yoeman Julius Jones
September 4, 1965; Laurel, MS

Susan Klopfer's Internet blog lists "Julius Y. Jones" among persons "suspected by [the] SPLC as victims of racially motivated murders from 1954 to 1968," citing the date of his death at September 4, 1965.[650] However, no such name appears on the SPLC's published list of "forgotten" civil rights martyrs.[651] According to the *Laurel Leader-Call*, 23-year-old Yoeman Julius Jones, a local resident, was struck and killed by a passenger train at 4 a.m. on September 4, while walking along railroad tracks near Harrison Boulevard. Patrolmen John Gatlin, R. L. Keyes, and Hub Wells investigated the incidents, and Justice of the Peace Tony Parker convened a coroner's jury that pronounced the death accidental.[652] That said, it is worth noting that Laurel served as headquarters for America's most violent Ku Klux Klan faction of the mid–1960s, linked to multiple murders. It comes as no surprise, therefore, that local African Americans may have suspected Jones was murdered.

Eddie Cook
November 7, 1965; Detroit, MI

Cook, a 53-year-old sanitation worker, was walking home from work in black east side neighborhood when drive-by gunmen blasted him with a 16-gauge shotgun. Bystanders rushed Cook to a hospital, but doctors were unable to revive him. Witnesses described the shooters as three or four white men in their early twenties. Homicide Investigator Hiram Phipps told reporters that a "neighborhood informer" blamed the shooting on gang rivalry. Earlier in the evening, young African Americans had thrown bottles at a passing carload of whites, who later returned for vengeance. Cook, Phipps said, was an innocent victim of circumstance.[653] My inquiries to local libraries and newspapers revealed no follow-up reports concerning suspects.

Lillie Dell Powers
November 1965; Oktibbeha County, MS

Our sketchy information on this case comes from two newsletters issued by the Mississippi Freedom Democratic Party in December 1965, preserved by the Mississippi

State Sovereignty Commission and later cited on various websites. The first bulletin, labeled "Key List Mailing #4" and covering the period from December 6 to 14, says that Lillie Dell Powers was shot by Starkville police on November 29, while riding with other MFDP workers in a car. Surviving passengers said the car's driver "didn't do anything wrong. The police just began to follow them, and then shot directly into the window, killing the girl."[654]

The second bulletin, released on December 20, calls the victim Lillie *Bell* Powers, lists her age as 14 years, and says she died at Jackson's University Hospital on November 10. According to that report, the shooting occurred on Highway 82, eight miles outside Starkville and the officers' legitimate jurisdiction, with four other persons in the target vehicle. Internet websites generally drop the final "s" from Lillie's surname without explanation, while claiming she was shot on November 10.[655]

The shooting occurred during an MFDP voter registration drive in Oktibbeha County, accompanied by other acts of white violence. While the party's first report says that "local people plan action," no follow-up accounts suggest what form it may have taken. If state or federal agents investigated the killing, no record of their inquiries survives today.[656]

Lee Edward Culbreath
December 5, 1965; Portland, AR

Culbreath, age 14, was delivering Sunday newspapers when drive-by gunmen shot him from his bicycle. Arkansas State Police officers charged white brothers Ed and James Vail with murder, recording admissions of Ku Klux Klan membership from both (later denied in court).[657] A 12-man jury, including one African American, convicted triggerman Ed Vail of second-degree murder on February 26, 1966, finding that his intoxication ruled out premeditation. Brother James, named as driver of the murder vehicle, was scheduled for trial at a later date, but Ashley County's prosecutor subsequently *nol prossed* his indictment.[658] Despite obvious collusion between the Vail brothers, and their probable Klan membership, FBI agents took no visible interest in Culbreath's slaying.

David B. Colston, Sr.
January 23, 1966; Camden, AL

Colston, age 32, was active in Wilcox County protests against disfranchisement of African Americans. On Sunday, January 23, he planned to attend a civil rights meeting with his family, at Camden's Antioch Baptist Church. As he pulled into the parking lot, a pickup truck driven by white farmer Jim Reeves struck Colston's car, some say deliberately. Both men stepped from their vehicles, Reeves drawing a pistol and shooting Colston in the head at close range, before dozens of witnesses. Police soon arrived, taking Reeves into "protective custody."[659] Witness Cynthia Cooper recalls that when ambulance attendants retrieved Colston's corpse, "they threw his splattered brains in the bushes."[660]

The Rev. Frank Smith and SCLC spokesman Daniel Harrell pressed on with he scheduled meeting, adding a eulogy for Colston and planning a protest march for the following day. Dr. Martin Luther King led that solemn procession on July 24. Prosecutors charged Reeves with murder, but a white jury acquitted him despite eyewitness testimony.[661]

Colston's son, David Jr., graduated from high school in Camden, afterward earning a bachelor of science degree in criminal justice from Alabama and Faulkner Universities in Montgomery. He served six years as a military policeman with the Alabama National Guard, and another 12 with the state's Department of Public Safety, before winning election to the Alabama House of Representatives in 2010. He did not seek reelection in 2014.[662]

Donald Ray Sims
March 11, 1966; Bogalusa, LA

A website listing "forgotten" civil rights martyrs includes an entry for "Donald Ray Simes," allegedly killed in Bogalusa, Louisiana, on March 11, 1966.[663] In fact, that notation is wrong on two counts: the victim's name and the claim that "Simes" died.

Captain Donald *Sims*, a six-year U.S. Army veteran on active duty, was indeed shot in Bogalusa, while home on leave from Germany. He was using a gas station's public telephone, conversing with his brother in Los Angeles, when four bullets shattered the station's front window, one striking Sims in the shoulder and angling up into his neck. The station's white attendant—who claimed he neither saw nor heard the shooting—tried to help Sims, reporting that a black couple refused to transport Sims for medical aid. Sims finally drove himself to the Washington–St. Tammany Charity Hospital (now Washington–St. Tammany Regional Medical Center), where doctors stabilized him and passed him on to the U.S. Public Health Service Hospital in New Orleans.[664] Sims survived and returned to full duty, embarking on a combat tour in Vietnam.

Police Chief Claxton Knight arrested 43-year-old sheet metal worker Thomas Bennett on March 12, reporting that Bennett confessed to the shooting without stating a motive, and that a .22-caliber pistol found in his home matched the bullets fired at Sims. Charged with attempted murder, Bennett was freed on March 13, his $10,000 bond signed by local racists including Saxon Farmer, Louisiana "grand titan" of the Original Knights of the Ku Klux Klan, and Klansman Ernest R. McElveen, himself free on $25,000 bond pending trial for the murder of a black deputy sheriff (see June 2, 1965, in Part 1). Ironically, the "grand dragon" of a competing Klan faction, Jack Helm of New Orleans, had offered a $1,000 reward for the arrest and conviction of Sims's attacker.[665]

The shooting's circumstances prompted widespread indignation. Southern political cartoonist Clifford "Baldy" Baldowski published a cartoon depicting an army officer delivering a telegram to an African American woman. The wire read "Regret to inform you that your son Capt. Donald Sims was shot," while Baldowski's caption said: "Not in Vietnam, mam.... In a Bogalusa phone booth!"[666] Bennett's trial was twice postponed, then apparently forgotten. Sims won two Silver Stars for valor in Vietnam, the second awarded by President Lyndon Johnson in November 1967. With no prospect of hometown justice in sight, Sims told reporters on that occasion, "I still have faith in my fellow man and faith in America."[667]

James Eddie Keglar
April 1966; Charleston, MS

Tragedy brought 38-year-old James "Sonny Boy" Keglar home to Tallahatchie County from military service in early 1966. Ten days after New Year's, his mother and a close friend, both civil rights activists, had died in a suspicious car crash (see January 11, 1966, in Part 1). Convinced that they were murdered, Keglar began a private investigation, aided by his married daughter Alma Chism in Memphis. Chism later told author Susan Klopfer, "My grandmother's death really changed James. He became very angry and outspoken, and he wanted to know who did this to his mother. I know that Sonny Boy was trying to get answers and had even gone to Washington, D.C., about my grandmother's murder."[668]

That agitation had a price in 1960s Mississippi. One April weekend, Charleston police arrested Keglar for auto theft. He denied the charge and phoned his brother Robert from jail, asking him to contact FBI agents. "I could tell he was scared," Robert Keglar told Susan Klopfer. Robert phoned the FBI's office in Clarksdale, but no agents responded. Robert continues: "James got out of jail and went straight on to a house party. Early that Sunday morning at about 6 a.m., the police came to my house and said that James was dead. They would not tell me what happened to him. Later, I was told by others that 'a hired killer' had murdered him. I know that he had been hit on the head and a fire was started that burned down his house. He died in the fire." Alma Chism shares that memory, saying, "My father, James Keglar, was hit on the head before the fire was started. I know his death was not an accident."[669]

Local authorities disagreed. As with the "accidental" death of Keglar's mother, no investigation worthy of the name was carried out. My inquiries to Tallahatchie County failed to peg the date of Keglar's death, but April's Sundays that year fell on the 3rd, 10th, 17th, and 24th.

Eddie Wallace Sallis
June 1, 1966; Waterloo, IA

Half a century ago, Eddie Sallis would have been termed "a police character." He had a lengthy record of arrests, including one for auto theft, with three accomplices, on February 3, 1966. In that case, he was caught while changing a flat tire on the hot car—clearly, no gangland mastermind.[670] Four months later, at age 23, police arrested him once more, with companion Howard Calvin Saunders, but this time, Sallis would not have to worry about raising bail. Soon after he was booked, jailers allegedly found him hanged in his cell, ruling his death a suicide.[671] A report from the Iowa Civil Rights Commission, announced in July 1966, confirmed the suicide judgment.[672]

Relatives of Sallis, and many others in Waterloo's African American community, refused to accept that verdict. Ghetto rioting ensued, and 29 plaintiffs joined in filing a $200,000 federal lawsuit against the city on July 17, demanding remedies for "unequal and discriminatory practices existing in the area of municipal and quasi-municipal services, and to promulgate all appropriate ordinances, regulations and directives to assure all residents Freedom of Residence in the purchase, sale, leasing and use of property."[673] Judge Edward J. McManus dismissed part of that lawsuit on July 6, 1967, while directing that other portions must be filed "personally" against individual city officers no later than July 20.[674] The lawsuit was refiled but failed to satisfy McManus, who dismissed it for the last time on June 17, 1968.[675]

Clarence Triggs
July 30, 1966; Bogalusa, LA

Triggs, a 24-year-old Vietnam War veteran and bricklayer, moved to Bogalusa from Jackson, Mississippi, with wife Emma in early July 1966. They found the town in turmoil, members of CORE protesting segregation in the face of police violence and mayhem by the local Ku Klux Klan, regarded as one of Louisiana's strongest, most militant chapters. Triggs attended CORE meetings and joined in some of its demonstrations, the last a few days before his murder.[676]

On July 30 police found Triggs dead, shot through the head at roadside, near an abandoned car. Officers refused to let Emma identify her husband's body at the scene, but they retrieved fingerprints from the auto's steering wheel and from a broken bottle nearby, leading them to arrest white suspects John W. Copling, Jr., and Homer Richard Seale on murder charges. Police Chief Claxton Knight hastened to tell reporters that the slaying was "definitely not racial," but he failed to offer any other motive.[677] Perhaps coincidentally, Seale shared his surname with a notorious family of Mississippi Klansmen, one of whom was later convicted of kidnapping two murdered African Americans (see May 2, 1964, in Part 1).

Coping faced trial first, acquitted by white jurors who deliberated for less than an hour before pronouncing him not guilty. That verdict spared Seale from a trial, his charges dismissed by the parish prosecutor.[678] The case remains officially unsolved.

Lester Mitchell
September 1, 1966; Dayton, OH

Mitchell, age 39, was sweeping the sidewalk outside his West Dayton home at 3 a.m., when a pickup truck with three white occupants passed by, one of the men firing a shotgun blast that struck Mitchell in the face, killing him instantly. Neighbors in West Dayton—96 percent black and mired in poverty—rioted for two nights in response to Mitchell's murder, prompting Governor James Rhodes to dispatch 1,000 National Guardsmen at the request of Mayor Dave Hall. More than 130 looters were arrested, with a second black man shot by whites who accused him of throwing rocks at their home. Troops remained in place until September 6, when order was restored.[679]

Decades later, *Dayton Daily News* reporter Amelia Robinson boosted Mitchell's age to 49, writing that he "supposedly was a bootlegger and his stash of liquor was the first place looted by rioters after his death." His early-morning sweeping, she said, was occasioned by "a very loud dice game in the alley behind his house (called trash alley)." According to Robinson, Mitchell "was shot in both eyes, and police said he was looking directly at his assailants when the shots were fired."[680] At last report, his slayers remained unidentified.

Dayton police guard vandalized stores during riots that followed the drive-by murder of Lester Mitchell (Library of Congress).

Anthony Shelton
January 19, 1967; Jefferson County, AL

Anthony Shelton, age 27, drove from Detroit to Birmingham in January 1967 to visit relatives and his ex-wife, with whom he hoped to reconcile. On January 19, State Trooper Mickey Shell stopped Shelton on U.S. Route 11, between Birmingham and Bessemer, accusing him of driving while intoxicated. Shelton's brother Mack disputed that claim, noting that Anthony was en route to visit his mother-in-law and, therefore, "he wasn't about to be drunk." Moments after Shell stopped him, Shelton lay fatally wounded beside Shell's patrol car—left to bleed for an hour, witnesses said, before an ambulance arrived and carried him to Birmingham's University Hospital, where physicians pronounced him dead.[681]

Colonel C. W. Russell, commander of Alabama's Department of Public Safety, defended Shell's actions in old-school terms, telling reporters that Shell "arrested the nigra for DWI" and placed him in Shell's cruiser. Then, Russell said, "the nigra broke and run," after which "the nigra jumped the trooper and actually got the gun away from the trooper." Finally, "the nigra hit him and knocked him down an embankment. That's when he shot him."[682]

Predictably, the shooting sparked black protests in Jefferson County. The Rev. C. W. Woods told a January 23rd meeting of the Alabama Christian Association that failure to act in Shelton's case guaranteed that "they'll just get bolder and bolder. Understand me, I don't condone the Negro that does wrong. But white folks talk back to cops. Why don't they get shot and killed for it?"[683]

Robert Lacey
January 28, 1967; Birmingham, AL

Lacey, a 40-year-old father of six, died because a neighbor complained about his dog. The neighbor claimed it bit her son; Lacey's family said the injured boy harassed their pet, reaching through the fence of a pen containing it. When Jefferson County's Health Department ordered a rabies test, the Laceys ignored it, saying they had no car to transport the large pet downtown. Matters came to a head on a Saturday night, when two sheriff's deputies called at the house—not for the dog, but to arrest Robert on some unspecified charge.[684]

According to Lacey's mother, the officers found him fresh out of the shower, ordering him to dress and accompany them. When Robert asked, "Why don't you just take the dog?" one of the deputies replied, "The dog's not our business. Get dressed." They followed Robert to his bedroom, where he was handcuffed and frisked. Then, Mrs. Lacey said, the deputies began to shove him back and forth, causing one to trip and fall. At that point, Deputy M. L. Wood drew his pistol and shot Robert in the leg. As Robert collapsed, his mother begged the officers to hold their fire, adding, "That's when they shot him through the head."[685]

Neighbor Sylvester Brown came running at the sound of shots and screams. He later told reporters, "There wasn't a sign of not even a scuffle in that bedroom." Stranger still, he said, the deputies ordered him and other bystanders to move Lacey's corpse "before the coroner came, before any kind of investigation, just plain destroying evidence as far as I can see."[686]

Sheriff's lieutenant F. A. Smith had a different opinion. "The man was resisting arrest," he said. "It's that simple. And he was big. Just because there wasn't any sign of a scuffle, that doesn't mean there wasn't a scuffle. We say he lunged. And as far as having the body moved before the coroner got there, who says that's destroying evidence?"[687] Clearly not the county's grand jury, which declined to investigate the slaying. Lacey was the second African American killed by police in Jefferson County over a span of nine days.[688]

Lillian Corine Briley
January 29, 1967; Atlanta, GA

On Saturday evening, January 28, during special services at the James Avenue Church of God in Christ, a congregation member noticed smoke seeping underneath the door of the Rev. George Briley's private study. Rushing to investigate, parishioners found a burning wad of cotton, soaked in kerosene, and doused it with fire extinguishers. Police logged a report of the arson attempt but found no useful clues.[689]

In the predawn hours of Sunday, the Rev. Briley was at home in bed, sleeping with his wife Lillian and their three-year-old grandson, when the doorbell rang. Lillian, age

53, rose to answer it, leaving her husband and the child asleep. Moments later, a gunshot roused the minister and he ran to investigate, finding his wife just inside the front door, stuck in the chest by a close-range shotgun blast. She died en route to a nearby hospital.[690]

The crime remains unsolved today—no useful evidence, no suspects—and it seems a curious omission from the DOJ's list of cold cases, especially since Atlanta hosted two of the decade's most violent Ku Klux Klan factions. While no contemporary news reports link the Brileys to civil rights activities, an ecumenical service held in May 2011 honored George, deceased in the late 1970s, as a minister who "led positive changes in Atlanta's urban communities."[691]

Charles Henry Rasberry
February 16, 1967; Prattville, AL

On February 14, 43-year-old Charles "Buttercup" Rasberry answered a call for help from his next-door neighbor, James Huffman, engaged in a shootout with three white men. The leader of the trio, William Cranmore—accompanied by brothers J. D. Parrish and William Parrish—was Huffman's former employer and had sold him a used car, then later "nagged at him" for payment, in the words of an acquaintance. Both Huffman and Cranmore were wounded that Valentine's Day, Cranmore fatally. When he died, Prattville police charged Huffman and Charles Rasberry with murder, then apparently decided to release Rasberry that same night. As he prepared to leave the jail, however, he was shot from behind by Deputy Police Chief Kenneth Hill. Before he died on February 16, Rasberry spoke to relatives and friends, telling them "they [the police] said he was free to go, but "as he was leaving, he was shot in the back."[692]

Police Chief O. C. Thompson told a different story, claiming Hill shot Rasberry as they were walking between the jail and courthouse. "They say he was trying to escape," Thompson told reporters. "He hit Hill and knocked him down twice." Unconvinced, the Rev. K. L. Buford, Alabama field secretary of the NAACP, sent a telegram to the DOJ in Washington, complaining of the "violation of both men's [Rasberry's and Huffman's] civil rights." In Prattville, protestors called for Hill's dismissal and Autauga County Sheriff Phillip Wood's resignation, also demanding appointment of African Americans to Prattville's all-white police force.[693]

The DOJ announced an investigation of the case in March 1967 but filed no charges.[694] A year later, white jurors astounded African Americans by acquitting James Huffman of Cranmore's murder, despite testimony from the Parrish brothers that he called them "dirty names" and fired the gunfight's first shot.[695]

James E. Small
February 17, 1967; Birmingham, AL

Patrolman R. G. Holtam and his partner were on their normal rounds at 2 a.m. when they found a window pried open at Albert Martin Elementary School, separating to circle the building in search of a suspect. Holtam saw a figure running and fired his gun, as he later said, "to apprehend a fleeing felon." Soon afterward, the officers found

18-year-old James Small lying dead, just off campus. Detective Albert Wallace called Small's home after 9 a.m., asking Small's mother if James was there. When she said he was missing and asked his whereabouts, Wallace advised her to collect him from a local mortuary.[696]

Small's mother was an active member of the Alabama Christian Movement, and his sister, Charlena Fortune, had participated in 1961's freedom rides, later joining Dr. Martin Luther King, Jr.'s March on Washington in August 1963. James, by contrast, was a troubled youth, described by his mother as having "a very violent temper, and he don't like white people." Police Chief Jamie Moore alluded to Small's "lengthy juvenile record and FBI records," but provided no details.[697]

On the night he died, Charlena Fortune said she gave her brother money for a pack of cigarettes and saw him leave their home at 1:30 a.m. Thirty minutes later, officers reported finding no cash on his body, but told Small's mother she could retrieve his hat and a new pack of smokes from police headquarters.[698] The fatal shooting—Birmingham's 10th in 14 months—sparked angry protests led by longtime civil rights activist, the Rev. Fred Shuttlesworth. "Every time you turn around," he said, "some Negro's been killed by some trigger-happy policeman in Birmingham. Every time one of your sons is accused of some crime, a policeman's bullets serve as judge, jury, and courts. I think we ought to start tonight, letting the city know we don't like it—hell no, we don't like it!"[699]

Willie James King
April 8, 1967; Union Springs, AL

Bullock County Sheriff C. M. Blue, Jr., claimed that his only black deputy, Tom "Preacher" Tolliver, accidentally shot and killed Willie King while trying to arrest another man. When local African Americans called for Tolliver's dismissal, Sheriff Blue retaliated, leading his son and Tolliver to arrest Ernest Pugh for "cursing" at a public protest meeting. During that arrest, Blue unplugged the group's sound system and challenged the crowd, saying, "Who don't like it? Who wants to do something about it?" Justice of the Peace L. L. Reeder fined Pugh $27.50. "I wasn't cursing," Pugh insisted, "but I guessed I'd better go along."[700]

Critics of Granada County's sheriff included H. O. Williams, who lost his 1966 race against Blue by a few hundred votes. Calling King's death a "legal lynching," he raged, "Every one of you who voted for white people helped pull that trigger." Activists Rufus Huffman blamed "the laxity of county officials in putting a gun into the hand of an individual whose conception of enforcing the law is to kill, and to kill only one group of people—Negroes." Observers noted that when King was killed, Tolliver wore a badge marked "Private Watchman" and drove an old car with a damaged red light. Afterward, he sported a regular deputy's badge and a new patrol car. "It's just like they rewarded him," said Huffman. "They're saying, 'You killed one. Now you have the privilege to kill another.' Unless we stop this now, eventually they will say, 'Let's kill a lot of them.'"[701]

David Wheeler
April 21, 1967; Grenada, MS

On Friday night, April 21, Constable Pat Lott stopped a car occupied by four black Grenada residents: 29-year-old David Wheeler; brother-in-law Earl Hines; Charles Pigdons; and an unnamed female friend. Approaching the car, Lott asked, "Where's the liquor?" Informed that they had none, he searched the vehicle and asked the female passenger if she was carrying a knife. Finding no booze or weapons, Lott nonetheless arrested all four and crammed them into his patrol car. When Pigdons asked why they were being arrested, Lott replied, "Shut up."[702]

As they entered Grenada proper, Wheeler asked Lott, "I haven't said a word since I've been in the car have I?" Again, the answer was, "Shut up." At that point, Hines said, Wheeler called Lott by his name, omitting the obligatory "Sir." "After he said that," Hines recalled, "he [Lott] just reached out and grabbed him and slowed down. Then Dave grabbed the keys from the car, and somehow the car door on the left side opened, and they both got out almost at the same time." While the driverless car rolled on to strike a telephone pole, Hines heard a gunshot. Looking back, he saw "Dave down in the street. It looked like he was trying to get up, but then I saw him fall back. They say there was a second shot but I didn't hear it, I guess because the girl was screaming so." Returning to his vehicle, Lott told the other prisoners, "Don't move. I'll shoot you too, if you try to get out of the car."[703]

Lott charged the three survivors with public drunkenness, while local African Americans called for his dismissal. The Rev. S. T. Cunningham, president of the Grenada County Freedom Movement, told reporters, "He uses his position to express his hatred and dislike of Negroes. We feel it would be better if he would be replaced." Authorities declined to comment and took no action against Lott. The following week, Wheeler's relatives said they had still not been formally notified of his death.[704]

Bobby Thomas
May 20, 1967; Birmingham, AL

Officer Paul A. Price shot Thomas, a 20-year-old father of two, allegedly while trying to arrest him for breaking into a liquor store. Like three other African Americans slain by local officers since January, Thomas was unarmed when Price shot him in the back. Laid off from his last workplace a month earlier, Thomas was scheduled to start a new job on the morning he died. Officers raided Thomas's home on May 21, searching "for tools," but found nothing to implicate him in any burglaries.[705]

Police chief Jamie Moore told reporters that Officer Price saw three men standing inside the W&W Beverage Company at 2 a.m. and called for them to halt, whereupon the ran for the backdoor. Price's first shot wounded J. C. Barnes in the leg, while Thomas and Henry Smith escaped under fire. Police found Thomas dead, several hours later, a block and a half from the store. Smith, freed on bond, denied robbing the shop and said he heard Price shout "something, I don't know what," before he opened fire. Chief Moore noted that Thomas had a prior record of arrests for burglary and grand larceny, further noting that his men were authorized to shoot any fleeing subject, armed or otherwise.[706]

Aaron Lee
June 11, 1967; New Orleans, LA

The Jackson *Clarion-Ledger* lists Aaron Lee among "forgotten" martyrs of the civil rights movement, but little is known today of his death.[707] Blogger Jake Adam York reports that a hit-and-run driver stuck Lee on Gentilly Road, in New Orleans East, leaving him dead at the scene, several miles from his home. Today the rundown neighborhood is largely abandoned, and York found no police files on the incident during his 2008 investigation.[708]

Carl Cooper, Aubrey Pollard and Fred Temple
July 25, 1967; Detroit, MI

In the predawn hours of July 23, police raided an unlicensed "blind pig" tavern on Detroit's Near West Side, sparking a mob scene that swiftly escalated into Motor City's worst-ever riot, leaving 43 persons dead, 1,189 injured, 7,231 jailed, and 2,509 buildings burned. Governor George Romney dispatched National Guardsmen, aided by members of the U.S. Army's 82nd Airborne Division, finally quelling the riot on July 27.[709]

In the midst of chaos, nine black men and two white women holed up for safety at the seedy Algiers Motel, on Woodward Avenue. Shortly after midnight on July 25,

Detroit's former Algiers Motel, scene of a police triple slaying on July 25, 1967 (National Archives).

someone fired a blank starter's pistol from a balcony at the Algiers, prompting National Guard Warrant Officer Theodore Thomas to report sniper fire. Guardsmen swarmed the motel, accompanied by city and state police. Finding no snipers present, officers beat the black men present and stripped the women, dragging Michael Clark and Roderick Davis into separate rooms, firing shots as they lay on the floor to simulate executions. When that tactic failed to identify the nonexistent sniper, violence intensified. By dawn, unarmed victims Carl Cooper, Aubrey Pollard, and Fred Temple lay dead from close-range police gunfire.[710]

State troopers and Guardsmen fled the Algiers, leaving city police with 26-year-old private security guard Melvin Dismukes to prepare alibis. Police initially claimed that Cooper, Pollard and Temple were snipers killed in a firefight, but forensic evidence soon proved that story false. On July 30, one Algiers victim accused Dismukes of beating him. On August 2 prosecutors secured warrants charging Officers Ronald August and Robert Paille with murdering Pollard and Temple, respectively. Both officers made statements in custody, August claiming he shot Pollard in self-defense, after Pollard tried to grab his shotgun.[711]

Dismukes was arraigned on August 4, held over for trial on a charge of felonious assault. Ten days later, Judge Robert E. DeMascio convened a preliminary hearing on August and Paille. A third murder suspect, Officer David "Snake" Senak, testified at that hearing, admitting that he killed two other black men on July 24, before reaching the Algiers, but denied firing any shots inside the motel. On August 17, Judge DeMascio ruled Paille's statement inadmissible on constitutional grounds, while holding August over for trial.[712]

Dissatisfied with that decision, on August 23 prosecutor William Cahalan charged August, Paille, and Senak with conspiracy to commit a legal act in an illegal manner. Specifically, the indictment charged that "the defendants in their effort to put an end to the sniping entered the motel to locate the sniper and his weapon. In seeking informative leads they herded the occupants of the motel from their rooms into a line-up facing a wall and then engaged in a course of conduct which unmistakably exhibited and demonstrated a concert of action to commit and condone the commission of unlawful acts."[713]

Judge Robert Schemanski, known among defense attorneys as "terribly police-prone," presided over the defendants' preliminary hearing, begun on September 16. On December 1, he threw out the conspiracy charge, finding that none of the Algiers victims had furnished credible testimony. On February 20, Judge Gerald Groat denied Cahalan's appeal to reinstate the conspiracy charges. Seven weeks later, on March 28, Judge Geraldine Ford ordered Judge DeMascio to reopen preliminary hearings on Robert Paille's murder charge.[714]

On May 3, 1968, U.S. Attorney Lawrence Gubow announced a federal indictment charging August, Dismukes, Paille, and Senak with conspiracy to violate the civil rights of 11 Algiers Motel victims. Dismukes faced trial on his assault charge four days later, acquitted by an all-white jury after 13 minutes of deliberation.[715]

Ronald August came next, after winning a change of venue from Detroit to the Lansing suburb of Mason, in Ingham County. White jurors acquitted him of murder on June 10, 1969, after defense attorney Norman Lippitt told them, "Some call it a riot. It was not a riot. It was a war! A war where every police officer, every Guardsman and every soldier was working in a battleground. Ronald August is guilty of working under

Algiers Motel defendants (from left) David Senak, Ronald August, Robert Paille and private guard Melvin Dismukes at their federal conspiracy trial on February 25, 1970 (National Archives).

these conditions. Guilty of working days and nights with little or no rest. Guilty of standing idle while looting and firebombing and sniping was going on. Guilty of being shot at in the street. Guilty for not being allowed to shoot criminals. This is what happened in those first days of that war in Detroit, while the mayor and the governor and the president were indecisive."[716]

On May 15, 1969, following a change of venue to Flint, Michigan, defendants August, Dismukes, Paille, and Senak faced trial in federal court before another all-white jury. Defense attorneys stressed the fact that their clients were charged only with conspiracy, rather than assault, coercion, intimidation or murder. The panel acquitted all four on February 25, 1970, prompting the suspended officers to say they would seek reinstatement, with back pay dating from 1967. Fred Temple's mother said, "I wasn't surprised or shocked over it. I could see it coming day by day in the way the judge was acting." Assistant U.S. Attorney Kenneth McIntyre was more philosophical, telling journalists, "I would have loved to have had a conviction, but people don't like to convict police officers for what they do during a riot."[717]

Joseph Thomas
September 9, 1967; New Orleans, LA

Thomas appears on the Jackson *Clarion-Ledger*'s list of "forgotten" civil rights martyrs, but information on his death is sparse today.[718] Thanks to blogger Jake Adam York, we know that police found Thomas dead in his own backyard, in the former St. Bernard Community, killed by a gunshot through one nostril. Detectives found no clues at the scene and developed no suspects. Today, the crime scene is a vacant field, wiped clean by Hurricane Katrina in 2005.[719] The case remains officially unsolved.

Robert Elwood Barbee
September 17, 1967; Dayton, OH

At 12:45 a.m. on Sunday, vice squad detectives Robert S. Collier and David L. Michael were conducting surveillance on a Shriners convention in downtown Dayton. They observed Robert Barbee, a 41-year-old, light-skinned African American, exiting a car outside a restaurant and glimpsed "a dark colored object" tucked into his waistband. The officers left their unmarked vehicle, dressed in plainclothes and Shriners hats, shouting for Barbee to stop. Perhaps fearing a robbery, he ran, and Collier shot him twice in the back, killing him outright. The suspected weapon proved to be a smoking pipe, so Collier rushed home, retrieved a "throwaway" pistol, and planted it on Barbee's corpse, filing a false report with his superiors.[720]

Dayton's African American community, already rocked by riots in September 1966 and June 1967, seethed at news of the latest shooting. Civil rights leader and state legislator Clarence Josef McLin, Jr., told reporters, "This is murder. It just slaps us right in the face. The mayor and city manager should immediately conduct a full, open hearing."[721] A protest rally, held on September 19, degenerated into further rioting, with 30 persons arrested and police reporting "a few slight injuries."[722]

Meanwhile, Detective Collier confessed his crude attempt to frame a dead man and was charged with manslaughter on September 18. Investigation of Barbee's background identified him as a former Dayton resident with a master's degree in psychology, onetime head of a West Dayton civic improvement association, currently a field representative for the U.S. Social Security Administration.[723] Several observers later testified that Barbee's skin tone was so light, they did not recognize him as an African American until his corpse was formally identified on September 18.[724]

Robert Collier faced trial on January 16, 1968. After six days of testimony, jurors deliberated for four hours on January 22, then acquitted him of manslaughter. Police Chief Robert Igleburger told reporters that Collier still faced charges of filing a false report and planting the gun on Barbee's body.[725] Local inquiries revealed no disposition for that case.

John Arthur Langdon
November 5, 1967; Selma, AL

On the night of November 5, black residents of Southside, a rural ghetto outside Selma, reported shots fired into their homes from passing automobiles. Morning's light brought news that one Southside resident, John Langdon, had been killed overnight. Police charged three white defendants—James J. Reeves, Jr., Donald Meeks and Bernard E. Steward—with murder and other charges for the shooting spree, citing a .22 Magnum rifle owned by Steward as the weapon that killed Langdon. The trio claimed Langdon was shot in a scuffle, when he approached their truck on the highway.[726]

Steward faced trial first, in January 1968. Dallas County prosecutors Virgis Ashworth and Lee Pilcher recused themselves from the case, leaving special state prosecutor Lewey Stephens of Elba to face father-son defenders McLean and Henry Pitts, both attorneys for the city of Selma and Dallas County. The prosecution's case rested chiefly on testimony from state toxicologist Guy Purnell and Deputy Archibald Riley, an FBI agent for 22 years prior to joining the Dallas County Sheriff's Department. Purnell said that powder burns on Langdon's clothing indicated a shot fired from eight feet, thereby ruling out a struggle described by the three defendants, and he added that Langdon's blood revealed enough alcohol to render him "staggering drunk."[727]

Deputy Riley described his arrest of the three defendants. Steward, he said, had handed him the murder weapon, saying, "I'm glad to go with you. I'm glad to get it off my chest." Meeks, Riley said, admitted it was he who fired "toward" one black family's home on November 5, adding, "We did all we could to stop Steward from shooting in those houses and killing that Negro."[728] Meeks denied both statements when he testified for the defense.

The Pitts team presented an unabashed racist defense of their client, presenting a small, everyday pocket knife found in Langdon's trousers as proof of his aggression, falsely calling it "a switchblade without the switch." Dallas Co. Probate Judge B. A. Reynolds testified for the defense, reporting that Langdon had spent 20 days at Searcy Mental Hospital in 1966, a revelation that prompted Henry Pitts to brand the victim a "drunken lunatic nigra." Conversely, despite his record of arrests for assault and battery, petty larceny and disorderly conduct, character witnesses called on Steward's behalf agree that he boasted "a good reputation." In his closing argument, Henry Pitts asked jurors, "What is the interest served by a trial such as this?" His father concurred, railing, "It's not proper to use a jury to satisfy an element of the nigra people. They will never be satisfied."[729]

The all-white, all-male jury nearly agreed, deliberating for over 24 hours on the weekend of January 20–21, finally convicting Steward of second-degree manslaughter, deemed by one courthouse observer as "one step above an accident." Judge William Craig sentenced Steward to one year in the county jail. Eleven days later, Steward and Meeks pled guilty to charges of firing shots into an occupied dwelling. Judge Craig handed both the maximum sentence, one year at hard labor, noting their "willful disregard for the life and safety of other people."[730] Meeks and Reeves still faced trial on murder charges, but no further record remains of their case.

Earnest Richmond
November 26, 1967; Holly Springs, MS

Acquaintances claimed that Richmond was "not a civil rights person," but he did work for a federally sponsored legal services program in Marshall County. Two years before his death, he filed a $1 million federal lawsuit against Sheriff J. M. "Flick" Ash and two deputies, William Hurst and Virgil Lindsay, charging that they beat him during a 1965 traffic arrest, breaking his jaw and causing Richmond to suffer persistent headaches. Coworker Lizzie Mae Mitchell later told reporters that Richmond was offered $25,000 to drop the case but he persevered, looking forward to trial in spring of 1968 and vowing to "go through with it even if he didn't get a dime."[731]

On November 26, 1967, Richmond hitched a ride out of town with friend Jacob Johnson. Johnson explained that Richmond "asked me to take him out to Gene Laney's place. He had been trying to get him on welfare. Then, after we passed the Tyson's place on top of the hill, he told me to let him out, that he would walk back." Soon afterward, a passing motorist found Richmond dead beside the highway, with visible head injuries. Osborne Bell, an African American mortician recently elected as the county's coroner, identified Richmond's corpse and ordered an autopsy "because there was a hole almost between the eyes, but they couldn't find anyplace a bullet could have come out the back of his head."[732]

Investigators from the Mississippi Highway Patrol ruled Richmond a hit-and-run victim but identified no suspects. In January 1968, new sheriff Johnny Taylor denied possessing any records of the case. "The ex-sheriff has all that," he said. "We just took office on January 1."[733] Richmond's case remains officially unsolved.

Clayton Pitts
December 9, 1967; Loachapoka, AL

Pitts, a 20-year-old farm worker, left home on Saturday to spend time with friends at the Hatchet Place, a café on Highway 14, one mile west of Loachapoka. Hours later he was dead, shot by State Trooper Howard Bass of Opelika. Major John Cloud, chief of Alabama's Highway Patrol and leader of the troopers who beat civil rights marchers on Selma's Edmund Pettus Bridge in March 1965, told reporters Bass had fired in self-defense. As Cloud explained, Bass had arrested Pitts for drunk driving around 10:30 p.m. "He didn't have any trouble with him at the time of the arrest," Cloud said, "and he thought he had searched the boy pretty thoroughly." Nonetheless, Cloud said that Pitts—who should have been handcuffed—pulled a knife in the patrol car and slashed Bass three or four times across the abdomen before Bass shot him. "They weren't deep cuts," Cloud added, "but the trooper's shirt was cut everywhere the knife went."[734]

Bass was examined at the Lee County Hospital in Opelika and released. T. E. Peterson, director of the mortuary that received Pitts's body, said Pitts had been shot "five times in the chest and stomach area." Major Cloud explained: "The first two shots didn't stop the boy, so he kept firing. We're sorry it happened, but a man's got a right to defend himself. I wouldn't anticipate any charges being filed. It was justifiable homicide."[735]

Friends of Pitts disputed Cloud's account of the arrest. Gordon Willis, Jr., whose family owned the Hatchet Place, said Pitts was one of 70-odd customers on Saturday evening. Willis said Pitts planned to test drive a friend's car around 10:30 p.m., but he saw Trooper Bass parked across the road and came back inside, since Pitts had no driver's license. Moments later, according to Willis, Bass entered the café and ordered Pitts to get in his patrol car. "Bass said, 'You're under arrest,'" Willis told reporters. "The boy wanted to know for what. The state trooper refused to tell him for what." Pitts followed Bass to the patrol car, standing outside it until Bass "pulled out one of them long kind of sticks. So Pitts got in. They didn't exchange no words. The state trooper didn't even search or handcuff him."[736]

Willis added that Pitts was "a nice guy. If you say to him, 'Clayton, you're wrong,' he would apologize. He wouldn't get mad. I don't believe he'd do something like that, knife somebody for no cause." Trooper Bass, by contrast, was described by local African

Americans as having "a reputation for beating folkses."[737] Major Cloud's prediction was correct: the shooting was indeed deemed "justifiable."

Clarence Causey
April 23, 1968; Soledad, CA

A Louisiana native, born in 1933, Causey moved to Los Angeles with his family as a child. He joined a street gang, with the nickname "Dopey Dan," and engaged in petty crime until conviction on an October 1955 burglary conviction earned him a sentence of six months to 15 years in prison. Authorities paroled Causey on July 6, 1959, then revoked his parole five months later, on December 3, sending him to the maximum-security prison at Soledad. There, he became affiliated with the Black Guerilla Family, a politicized gang founded in 1966 by inmates George Jackson and W. L. Nolen. BGF members enlisted for self-defense against racist inmates and espoused revolutionary causes similar to those of he Black Panther Party.[738]

White guards at Soledad and other California prisons despised the BGF and branded Causey in particular as a "troublesome nigger." On April 23, 1968, Causey suffered fatal stab wounds, allegedly while attacking six members of a rival gang. BGF members claimed that racist white guards deliberately opened Causey's cell for the assassins, said to be members of the neo-Nazi Aryan Brotherhood. Causey's death set off a chain-reaction of racial violence at Soledad and San Quentin prisons, claiming the lives of multiple inmates, guards, and outsiders through summer of 1970.[739]

Carol Marie Jenkins
September 16, 1968; Martinsville, IN

Martinsville, the seat of Morgan County, was a stronghold of the Ku Klux Klan during the 1920s, when hooded terrorists controlled the Hoosier State from local city councils and police departments to the governor's mansion. That racist reputation still lingered four decades later, when 21-year-old Rushville native Carol Jenkins tried her hand at selling Collier's encyclopedias door-to-door. Her first night on the route, she asked one homeowner to call police, because two white men in a car were trailing her. Officers responded and found nothing. At 8:45 p.m., witnesses saw Jenkins walking along Morgan Street, through the heart of town. Moments later, neighbors heard a scream and glimpsed a car speeding away, while Jenkins lay sprawled on the sidewalk, stabbed in the heart with a screwdriver.[740]

Devoid of leads, the investigation quickly stalled. It was ice-cold by June 2000, when Elizabeth Jenkins received an anonymous phone call from a woman claiming she had witnessed Carol's murder as a child. Mrs. Jenkins hired a private detective, who in turn persuaded the Indiana State Police to launch a cold case investigation. In November 2001, an unsigned letter fingered Klansman Kenneth Clay Richmond as the killer, naming his daughter Shirley as a witness. Officers soon located Shirley McQueen, then 40 and married, extracting her tale of the murder. McQueen said she was riding with her father and another man she did not know when they shouted racial slurs at Jenkins, then left the car to attack her, Richmond stabbing Carol while his partner pinned her arms. Afterward, the men came back laughing and saying, "She got what she deserved." Richmond gave Shirley seven dollars, with orders to keep his secret. Years later, she told the story to sister-in-law Connie McQueen, who penned the anonymous letter.[741]

Police arrested Richmond on May 8, 2002, but he cheated justice in the end, dying from bladder cancer at Larue D. Carter Memorial Hospital on August 31, at age 70.[742] As for his still-unnamed accomplice, Carol's stepfather, 74-year-old Paul Davis, still hoped for belated justice. "There is still another man out there who was involved in Carol's murder," he told *People* magazine. "I won't rest until I find out if he's dead or alive."[743]

James Sanders
November 30, 1968; Birmingham, AL

Patrolman L. E. Blackwell shot 22-year old James "Soap" Sanders, allegedly as Sanders attacked Blackwell with a knife in Birmingham's all-black Ensley district. Aside from the supposed attempted stabbing, department spokesmen said Sanders was fleeing the scene of a store burglary, bearing an armload of stolen clothes which, they asserted, was found in the street near the spot where he died.[744]

Witness Levi Brown of Fairfield told a very different story to a protest meeting held on December 2 at the Metropolitan Christian Methodist Episcopal Church, chaired by the Rev. L. H. Wheeler, president of Ensley's NAACP chapter, and attorney U. W. Clemmons. According to Brown, he was driving slowly north on Avenue E, when Sanders ran in front of his car, pursued by the white officer. "If I didn't have good brakes," he said, "I would have run over both of them." After they dodged hiss car, Brown said, "they runs across the street and into an alley. There was plenty of light, and I seen the young man raise his hands, you know, like he was surrendering. Here's the thing that kills me. The cop shot him while his hands were up in the air."[745]

Prosecutors took no action in the case, maintaining that police have the right to shoot any fleeing suspect. African Americans, for their part, questioned why that right seemed only to be exercised against black targets.

Alprentice Carter and John J. Huggins
January 17, 1969; Los Angeles, CA

Carter and Huggins were members of the Black Panther Party, targeted for "neutralization" by the FBI's covert and illegal "COINTELPRO" (*Counterintelligence Program*) network after J. Edgar Hoover declared the small organization "the greatest threat to the internal security of the country." Aside from helping local police frame various Panthers on false criminal charges or lure them into deadly ambushes with aid from mercenary *agents provocateur*, FBI headquarters also did everything within its power to promote violent feuds between Panthers and rival militant organizations or street gangs. To that end, FBI agents mailed anonymous death threats, bankrolled groups hostile to the Panthers, and gloated in private memos—later released under the Freedom of Information Act—whenever FBI-promoted violence claimed Panther lives.[746]

One organization used by—some say *created* by—the FBI in Southern California, was "U.S.," variously interpreted as "United Slaves" or a more prosaic "U.S. black people vs. THEM." Founder Ronald McKinley Everett was a doctoral student at the University of California, Los Angeles (UCLA) when the Watts riot erupted in 1965. Switching allegiance from CORE and SNCC to black nationalism, Everett changed his name to Maulana Ndabezitha Karenga (Swahili-Arabic for "master teacher") and began recruiting disciples. Initially, U.S. worked in concert with Panthers on neighborhood patrols and other programs, but animosity grew between them, encouraged in large part by the FBI and the Los Angeles Police Department's Intelligence Division.[747]

Alprentice Carter, murdered by rival black militants with official collusion on January 17, 1969 (Civil Rights Archive).

Scholars still debate whether Karenga—inventor of the previously nonexistent "African" holiday Kwanzaa in 1966—was a conscious agent of COINTELPRO or merely another hapless victim of government machinations, but the end result was identical. On January 17, 1969, as Panthers Alprentice "Bunchy" Carter and John Huggins addressed a Black Student Union meeting at UCLA's Campbell Hall, five members of Karenga's *Simba Wachuka* ("Young Lions") opened fire on them, killing both men. Huggins, dying and firing in self-defense, wounded one of the attackers, thus permitting journalists and COINTEL-

Ronald McKinley Everett, aka Maulana Karenga, founder of the US militant group, in 1966. Subsequently, Karenga invented the "African" Kwanzaa holiday (National Archives).

PRO agents to describe the ambush as a "battle" in the midst of a militant "turf war." Three of the assassins were captured, while two more escaped. Brothers George and Larry Steiner received life prison terms; a juvenile gunman was confined as a youthful offender.[748]

Karenga's reputation took another hit in 1971, when L.A. jurors convicted him of felonious assault and false imprisonment, for torturing his estranged wife and another female U.S. member. The charges arose from Karenga's paranoid delusion the women were conspiring to poison him. Sentenced to prison for one to 10 years, Karenga was paroled in 1975. U.S. dissolved in his absence, but was later reestablished and exists today. Karenga received his Ph.D. in 1976 from United States International University (now Alliant International University), and received a second Ph.D. from the University of Southern California in 1996. As this book went to press, he was chairman of the Africana Studies Department at California State University, Long Beach.[749]

Edwin T. Pratt
January 26, 1969; Shoreline, WA

A Florida native, born in 1930, Pratt earned a master's degree in social work from Atlanta University (now Clark Atlanta University), before joining the National Urban League, serving its offices in Cleveland, Ohio, and Kansas City, Missouri. In 1956 he moved to Seattle, as the local Union League's community relations secretary, promoted to serve as executive director five years later. Pratt's achievements include the Triad Plan for desegregation of Seattle's public schools and an equal housing opportunities initiative.[750]

Around 9 p.m. on January 26, 1969, Pratt and wife Bettye heard a sound like a snowball striking a car outside their home in Shoreline, 10 miles north of Seattle. Stepping out the front door to investigate, Pratt was killed by a shotgun blast to the face. Bettye Pratt, watching from a nearby window, saw two men fleeing the family's carport. Neighbors watched them jump into a Buick Skylark, driven by a third man, and speed

Shoreline, Washington, home of Edwin Pratt, where he was shot from ambush on January 26, 1969 (National Archives).

away from the scene. Darkness prevented witnesses from giving clear descriptions of the killers, or even guessing their race.[751]

Rewards totaling $10,500 dollars failed to crack the case, nor were FBI agents able to locate suspects. Freelance journalist David Newman launched a personal investigation in 1994, while King County authorities kept certain pieces of evidence secret. Captain Dan Richmond, the county's homicide commander, told reporters, "The only reason for not opening it up is the chance that someone might confess. It's one or two items the perpetrator might know. It's not much. It's nothing that would solve the case, but it's something that would keep the wrong person from admitting to it." Newman's lawsuit to reveal that evidence failed in 1997.[752]

There matters rested until May 2011, when *Seattle Weekly* author Rick Anderson claimed to have solved the mystery. According to Anderson, snow forced Pratt to cancel a date with his white secretary/mistress on January 26. Soon afterward, Bettye Pratt received an anonymous phone message, the female caller warning, "If Ed doesn't shut up, he'll end up like Medgar"—a reference to NAACP leader Medgar Evers, shot in the driveway of his Jackson, Mississippi, home in 1963. Next came the snowball barrage and the shooting that snuffed out Pratt's life. (FBI agents ruled out the mistress and her brother, a Washington state trooper, as suspects.)[753]

Anderson, citing interviews conducted by the *Seattle Post-Intelligencer* in 1995, named Pratt's slayer as Tommy Kirk, a "violent street thug" born in 1944. His companion in the carport, 28 years Kirk's senior, was named as drug dealer Texas Barton Gray. Michael Lee Jordan allegedly drove the getaway car, his own Buick. All three were white, all deceased by 2011. As for motive, Anderson wrote, "Someone probably paid for the hit," to the tune of $25,000 ($164,000 today).[754]

Who was responsible? According to Anderson, "Cold-case detectives think a rabble-rousing black contractor named Henry Roney, who can be circumstantially connected to Tommy Kirk through a supposed association with the Black Panthers, is most likely the man who paid for the shooting." Detective Scott Thompson told Anderson, "No one had a greater motive. When you look at the evidence, it's very compelling." Roney, dead since 1996, cannot speak for himself, but his ex-attorney called the charges false.[755]

So did Danella Jordan, widow of the alleged wheelman, who agreed with Anderson's list of suspects but denied any murder contract. Danella was with her husband, Kirk, and Gray prior to Pratt's murder, recalling Kirk's expressed desire to kill "a 'rich nigger.'" She called Pratt's murder "a monumental hate crime," committed by Kirk with Gray and her husband as pawns. An FBI report from 1995 confirms that Tommy Kirk "was superprejudiced about blacks and fearful of being killed by blacks."[756]

Tommy Kirk, named by his ex-wife as Edwin Pratt's killer in 1995 but never charged with that crime (National Archives).

Alfred Daniel William King
July 21, 1969; Atlanta, GA

The younger brother of Martin Luther King, Jr., commonly known as A. D. King, followed family tradition by training for the ministry and serving as pastor to various African American churches in several states. While overshadowed by his famous sibling, King also joined in the civil rights movement and was targeted for death by Ku Klux bombers in Birmingham, Alabama, on May 11, 1963. Following Martin's assassination in April 1968, King struggled alcohol and with depression, while continuing work with the SPLC. Nine days before his 39th birthday, King's daughter found him dead in their swimming pool. Authorities ruled the death an accidental drowning, but conspiracy theories persist. In his 1980 autobiography, King's father wrote, "Alveda [King's daughter] had been up the night before, she said, talking with her father and watching a television movie with him. He'd seemed unusually quiet ... and not very interested in the film. But he had wanted to stay up and Alveda left him sitting in an easy chair, staring at the TV, when she went off to bed.... I had questions about A. D.'s death and I still have them now. He was a good swimmer. Why did he drown? I don't know—I don't

A. D. King with his father and brother, Martin Luther King, Sr., and Jr. Police called King's July 21, 1969 drowning an accident; relatives believe it was murder (Library of Congress).

know that we will ever know what happened."⁷⁵⁷ King's widow, Naomi, was more direct. In 2014 she wrote:

> When the body was found in the pool a paramedic tried a compression technique and found there to be no water in his lungs, which meant he was dead before he hit had ever hit the water. Witnesses at the scene even reported him saying: "There's no water in his lungs. He was dead when he hit the water!"
>
> I believe that my husband was killed. Many others have come to the same conclusion. When I examined his body at the mortuary before he was released for burial, I clearly saw that he had rings around his neck and bruises on his head and stomach. He was found in the fetal position at the bottom of the pool with no water in his lungs. I am convinced that he was murdered because they could not live with the power of the two Kings, ML and AD, walking this earth; dreaming the same dream; demanding the freedom that didn't just belong to them—it belonged to us all.⁷⁵⁸

Lillie Belle Allen
July 21, 1969; York, PA

Longstanding racial tension boiled to the surface York, Pennsylvania, during the summer of 1969, following six years of black protests against police brutality and discrimination at City Hall. On July 17 a black youth who burned himself while playing with lighter fluid falsely blamed the accident on members of a racist white gang, the Girarders. That same day, an unknown gunman wounded 17-year-old Taka Nii Sweeney while police detained her and several other African Americans for a curfew violation. Random fighting and sniping continued in York over the next two weeks, claiming the

Troops patrol York, Pennsylvania's, riot zone in July 1969 (Library of Congress).

lives of black visitor Lillie Belle Allen on July 21 and white rookie policeman Henry Schaad on August 1.[759]

Allen, a 27-year-old resident of Aiken, South Carolina, was riding through York in a car driven by her sister, Hattie Dickinson, with their parents in the backseat. When Dickinson turned onto North Newberry Street, seeking a grocery store, multiple Girarders and members of another racist gang, the Newberry Street Boys, opened fire on her car. More than 100 shots were fired in all, fatally wounding Allen with bullets from several different weapons. Governor Raymond Shafer declared a state of emergency in York on July 22, sending 200 National Guardsmen to quell the riots.[760]

A task force including four prosecutors and four detectives spent two years trying to solve Allen's murder, met with a wall of silence from York's white community. Lead detective Thomas Chatman, Jr., told reporters, "It was tougher than pulling teeth. There were witnesses. But no one wanted to tell you anything. People took sides according to race and didn't want to cooperate." York County deputy prosecutor Tom Kelley reopened the case in 1999, focusing on the Newberry Street Boys. By then, three suspects had committed suicide, but a fourth, dying of cancer, confessed his role in the crime and named another shooter as Donald Altland. Altland stonewalled police but confessed to his wife on the night of his interrogation, then shot himself, leaving a taped confession and a note reading "Forgive Me, God."[761]

On April 27, 2001, York's grand jury indicted brothers Arthur and Robert Messersmith for criminal homicide in Allen's slaying. A second indictment, on May 10, charged two former Girarders, Rick Lynn Knouse and Gregory Harry Neff. On May 18 the panel indicted ex-policeman Charles Robertson, then York's mayor, based on a statement from Rick Knouse that Robertson had given him rifle ammunition used to kill Allen, with instructions to "kill as many niggers as you can." Amidst public demands for his resignation, Robertson canceled plans to seek a second term as mayor.[762]

Before the grand jury disbanded, it indicted 10 defendants in Allen's murder. In August 2002, seven pled guilty to reduced charges of criminal conspiracy and agreed to testify against their cohorts. Defendants Neff, Robertson, and Robert Messersmith stood trial in October 2002, with Neff and Messersmith convicted on October 18, while Robertson was acquitted.[763] In November 2002 six of the defendants who pled guilty received prison terms ranging from 18 months to 23½ months. On December 18, Robert Messersmith received a sentence of nine to 19 years, while Neff was sentenced to 4½ to 10 years in prison.[764] A tenth defendant, Ezra T. Slick, pled no contest to attempted murder and conspiracy in May 2003, receiving a sentence of two to five years.[765]

Allen's family sued the city of York and several policemen for malfeasance, settling their case for $2 million in December 2005.[766] The true number and identify of Allen's slayers may never be known.

Mark Clark and Fred Hampton
December 4, 1969; Chicago, IL

Born in 1948, Fred Hampton was a gifted student and athlete who graduated from high school with honors in 1966, then enrolled at Triton Junior College as a pre-law student, simultaneously joining the NAACP and rising to lead its Maywood youth council. By 1967 he was a SNCC member, soon shifting to the Black Panther Party, where he forged alliances with other militant groups including the National Young Lords, Students or a Democratic Society, the Brown Berets, and the Red Guard Party. Hampton called that collection the "rainbow coalition," a phrase later adopted and popularized by the Rev. Jesse Jackson.[767]

Hampton's involvement with the Panthers made him a target for Chicago police and FBI agents, collaborating to destroy the party under the Bureau's "COINTELPRO" campaign. Between 1967 and 1969, FBI agents collected 4,000 pages of information on Hampton, illegally tapping his mother's phone in February 1968 and adding his name to the FBI's "Agitator Index" in May, marking Hampton as a "key militant leader for Bureau reporting purposes." At the same time, felon William O'Neal infiltrated the Chicago Panthers as a paid informer and *agent provocateur*, soon rising to serve as the chapter's security director and Hampton's personal bodyguard.[768]

Fred Hampton, murdered in his sleep by Chicago police with FBI collusion on December 4, 1969 (National Archives).

On April 2, 1969, O'Neal instigated an armed clash between Panthers and a dangerous street gang, the Blackstone Rangers. On May 26 jurors convicted Hampton of stealing ice cream bars valued at $71, a peculiar charge that recalls other frame-ups engineered against political dissenters by the FBI and Chicago police. Hampton received a two-to-five-year prison term, but remained free on bond pending appeal. On July 16 a shootout with police left one Chicago Panther dead and six more jailed on felony charges. On November 13, another battle killed one Panther and two policemen. A *Chicago Tribune* editorial raged against the Panthers, under the headline "No Quarter for Wild Beasts."[769]

Between those firefights, in October, Hampton rented an apartment on West Monroe Street with pregnant girlfriend Deborah Johnson. O'Neal told the FBI, falsely, that the flat contained a cache of illegal weapons. He also furnished agents with a floor plan of Hampton's new home, including the location of Hampton's bed. G-men passed that information to Cook County State's Attorney Edward V. Hanrahan, who organized a 14-member raiding team.[770]

Shortly after midnight on December 4, O'Neal prepared a meal at Hampton's flat for Hampton, Johnson, and seven other Panthers: Blair Anderson, Harold Bell, Verlina Brewer, Mark Clark, Brenda Harris, Ronald "Doc" Satchell, and Louis Truelock. O'Neal left without dining, after he spiked Hampton's beverage with the powerful barbiturate secobarbital sodium, found in his blood during autopsy. At 1:30 a.m., Hampton fell asleep in mid-sentence, while talking to his mother on the telephone.[771]

Hanrahan's team stormed the apartment at 4:45 a.m., first killing Mark Clark, assigned to stand watch with a shotgun in the front room. Shot through the heart, Clark triggered one blast toward the ceiling, in what pathologists later termed a reflexive death convulsion. Clark's single shot was the only one fired by Panthers during the raid, while police fired at least 82 rounds (some reports say 99), many targeting Hampton's bedroom. Survivor Harold Bell later recalled an exchange between the raiders:

"That's Fred Hampton."
"Is he dead? Bring him out."
"He's barely alive.
"He'll make it."

Bell then heard two more shots, before an officer said, "He's good and dead now." Officers dragged Hampton's corpse to the bedroom doorway, presumably to disguise the fact that he died while sleeping, but Hampton's blood-soaked bed told the story, as did two point-blank bullet wounds in his skull.[772]

With Hampton dead, police fired on the remaining Panthers, seriously wounding Anderson, Bell, Brewer, Harris and Satchel, finally beating all present before they were shoved and dragged to the street. Hanrahan charged the survivors with aggravated assault and the attempted murder, each held in lieu of $100,000 bond (later dismissing the false charges on May 8, 1970). At a press conference on December 5, police spokesmen praised the raiders for their "remarkable restraint," "bravery," and "professional discipline" for only killing two Panthers. FBI agent Gregg York later told colleague M. Wesley Swearingen, "We expected about 20 Panthers to be in the apartment when the police raided the place. Only two of those black niggers were killed, Fred Hampton and Mark Clark."[773]

In 1972, while pursuing reelection without Democratic Party support, Edward Hanrahan was indicted with 13 other defendants on conspiracy charges related to the Hampton raid. Jurors acquitted all 14, but Hanrahan lost the November election, followed by two defeats in mayoral campaigns and a failed race for Chicago's city council.[774] Survivors of Clark and Hampton sued the city, state, and federal governments in June 1970, seeking $47.7 million in damages. That case went to trial before Judge Joseph Sam Perry in 1976, ending with a directed verdict for the defense in June 1977, when jurors deadlocked in deliberations. The People's Law Office appealed that ruling, saw it overturned by the Seventh Circuit Court of Appeals, and successfully defended that verdict before the U.S. Supreme Court. Finally, after 13 years, the defendants settled out of court for $1.85 million.[775]

Ex-informer William O'Neal committed suicide in January 1990, by running into traffic in Maywood, where Fred Hampton launched his career in civil rights activism. Ten months later, Chicago's city council passed a resolution declaring December 4 to be Fred Hampton Day. A swimming pool in Maywood, the Fred Hampton Family Aquatic Center, is named in his honor. When admirers of Hampton's charity work proposed naming a street for him, in March 2006, Chicago's chapter of the Fraternal Order of Police opposed the suggestion.[776]

Cleveland Edwards, Alvin Miller and W. L. Nolen
January 13, 1970; Soledad, CA

The murder of Soledad Prison inmate Clarence Causey (see April 23, 1968, above) set off an unprecedented chain-reaction of racial violence inside that institution and beyond, claiming an estimated 40 lives by its bloody climax in August 1971. In the summer of 1969, five African American inmates led by W. L. Nolen, 26-year-old cofounder of the Black Guerrilla Family, filed civil litigation against Soledad warden Cletus J. Fitzharris, five guards, and the California Department of Corrections, charging that officials knew of "existing social and racial conflicts" and that they deliberately encouraged violence by "direct harassment and in ways not actionable in court," such as leaving black inmates' cells open to attack by white inmate "confederates" of the guards, thereby "willfully creating and maintaining situations that creates and poses dangers [*sic*] to the plaintiffs."⁷⁷⁷

(From left) "Soledad Brothers" John Clutchette, George Jackson, and Fleeta Drumgo with unidentified prison guards in 1970 (National Archives).

While that case wound its slow way through the courts, Soledad's embattled "O-Wing" remained under virtual lockdown, with inmates released singly into the exercise yard for short periods—until January 13, 1970. According to later testimony from a white prison trusty, the officer in charge of O-Wing activities, Sergeant R. A. Maddix, planned to solve the "racial vendetta war" by releasing black and white enemies into the yard together, "and if there was trouble kill a couple of those black bastards over there."[778]

To supervise the experiment, Maddix placed white guard Opie G. Miller in the yard's gun tower, armed with a .30-caliber carbine, overlooking a concrete pen 40 yards wide by 150 yards long, surrounded by high walls. On the appointed day, 15 prisoners entered the yard—nine black, six white—and the inevitable happened, with racial jibes degenerating into combat. From his tower, Miller shouted, blew a whistle, then fired four precisely aimed shots into the killing pen. His bullets fatally wounded W. L. Nolen, 21-year-old Cleveland Edwards, and 23-year-old Alvin Miller. The only white convict injured, 23-year-old Billy D. Harris, lost a testicle but would survive.[779]

Thomas Meneweather, a black survivor of the fusillade, testified that he tried to help Alvin Miller, carrying him to get medical aid. "I started to walk toward the door through which we had entered the yard," he said, "but the tower guard pointed the gun at me and shook his head. Then I started forward with tears in my eyes, expecting to be shot down every minute, but the tower guard told me, 'That's far enough.'"[780] In all, Meneweather and others insist, guards stalled for 20 minutes before providing any help, thereby ensuring the deaths of Nolen, Edwards and Miller.[781]

Ellsworth Ferguson, administrative assistant to Warden Fitzharris, told reporters that Officer Miller—unnamed in early reports—fired only "when it appeared that two downed men were in danger of being beaten to death." Those inmates, both white, escaped with minor injuries, leaving officials to "surmise" that the brawl had been racially motivated.[782] Whether by accident or design, Sergeant Maddix's prediction was fulfilled—but it failed to ease tension at Soledad.

On day after the shooting, 13 black O-Wing inmates launched a hunger strike, calling for segregated facilities and "psychiatric examinations by a black psychiatrist for all gun tower guards."[783] On January 17, white guard John Vincent Mills was murdered. A note left with his corpse read "One down, two to go." Authorities charged black inmates John Clutchette, Fleeta Drumgo, and George Jackson—cofounder with W. L. Nolen of the BGF—with that crime and moved them to San Quentin Prison pending trial.[784] Jurors acquitted Clutchette and Drumgo, while Jackson was killed—some say assassinated—by San Quentin guards during a prison riot on August 21, 1971.[785] Meanwhile, an all-white Marin County grand jury exonerated Opie Miller of any wrongdoing. None of January's six black shooting survivors were allowed to testify at that hearing.[786]

Ralph Featherstone
March 9, 1970; Bel Air, MD

A dedicated SNCC activist, Featherstone is described in contradictory accounts as a victim of white racist violence and a terrorist who accidentally killed himself. Born in 1939, Featherstone was at the forefront of 1960s civil rights campaigns in Birmingham and Selma, Alabama, also helping to establish 41 "freedom schools" in Mississippi

Ralph Featherstone (second from left) with William Porter, Ella Baker (third from left), and Cynthia Washington at a SNCC meeting in Waveland, Mississippi, in November, 1964 (Civil Rights Archive).

during 1964–65. Another of his Mississippi projects was a "catfish farm," from which poor rural African Americans processed food and fertilizer for commercial sale. In the latter 1960s, Featherstone joined militants H. Rap Brown and Stokeley Carmichael in the "Black Power" movement, then moved to Washington, where he ran a black bookstore, the Drum and Spear, while serving as chief lieutenant to future mayor Marion Berry's Free D.C. Movement.[787]

Somewhere along that path, white police maintain, Featherstone turned to violence. Mississippi officers suspected him of bombing Clay County's courthouse, in West Point, on January 25, 1970, one day after nightriders burned the Clay County Community Development Corporation's office. Moments after the courthouse blast, black drive-by gunmen also wounded Billy Wilson, a white storekeeper who boasted of participating in Emmett Till's murder (see August 28, 1955, in Part 1) and who had married confessed killer Roy Bryant's ex-wife. No evidence linked Featherstone to either crime, but Sheriff Virgil Middleton arrested six other suspects—then released them when a hired informer recanted his false testimony.[788]

On March 9, 1970, Featherstone and a companion were driving on U.S. Route 1 south of Bel Air, Maryland, heading toward Washington, when a "tremendous" explosion shattered their car, killing both men instantly. Police quickly identified Featherstone, while recognition of his passenger was delayed by the fact that he carried I.D. in five different names. Initially believed to be Rap Brown, scheduled for trial in Bel Air on riot charges the following day, Featherstone's passenger was later named as William "Che" Payne, a former member of Alabama's Lowndes County Freedom Organization that popularized the black panther as a symbol of militancy.[789]

Investigators determined that a powerful bomb had exploded on or under the front floorboard of Featherstone's car. FBI agents and Maryland state police claimed Featherstone and Payne planned to bomb the Bel Air courthouse, while SNCC colleagues insisted the bomb was planted without the victims' knowledge, perhaps hoping to catch Rap Brown in the vehicle. Brown disappeared for 18 months after the bombing, captured by New York City police after a shootout in October 1971. He received a 15-year prison term in that case and was never tried on the Maryland charges.[790]

H. Rap Brown in 1967 (Library of Congress).

Featherstone's death remains officially unexplained today. A statement released by SNCC soon after the blast read: "He was murdered by the powerful forces in America that in their fear have decided to behead the black militant movement.... Officials are committing the final obscenity of suggesting that the explosives that killed him were intended for someone else. Again they are blaming the victim for the crime, still acting as if thy can blot out ugly truth by destroying the people who speak it."[791]

Rainey Pool
April 12, 1970; Louise, MS

Seven drunken whites attacked Pool—a one-armed, 54-year-old sharecropper, outside a honky-tonk tavern on Sunday night, beating him for 15 minutes before they tossed him into a pickup truck, drove him away, and dumped him into the Sunflower River. Police found Pool's corpse on April 14. Dr. David Steckler conducted an autopsy, blaming Pool's death on drowning. Detectives arrested four suspects, one of whom allegedly confessed, and Humphreys County's grand jury indicted the men, but the state circuit court, acting on a prosecutor's request, *nolle prossed* the charges in July.[792]

There matters rested until 1998, when Pool's family pressed authorities to reopen the case. By then, two suspects were deceased, but a grand jury indicted five more. Jurors acquitted Dennis Newton on June 30, 1999. Joe Oliver Watson pled guilty to manslaughter on August 2 and agreed to testify against the remaining defendants:

Charles Ernie Caston, his brother James "Doc" Caston, and their half-brother Harold Spivey Crimm. Those three faced trial before an integrated jury, which convicted them of manslaughter on November 13, 1999. Judge Jannie M. Lewis imposed the maximum 20-year sentence on each defendant.[793] Mississippi's Supreme Court affirmed the convictions on May 23, 2002.[794]

Phillip Lafayette Gibbs and James Earl Green
May 15, 1970; Jackson, MS

America's invasion of Cambodia on April 29, 1970, sparked protests nationwide. The most famous occurred at Ohio's Kent State University, where National Guardsmen shot 13 unarmed students, killing four, on May 4. Ten days later, demonstrations began at Mississippi's Jackson State College, merging antiwar sentiment with anger at racial discrimination and harassment of students by white motorists passing through campus on J. R. Lynch Street. At 12:50 a.m. on May 15, city police and highway patrolmen sought to disperse students outside Alexander Hall, a women's dormitory, firing at least 140 rounds from shotguns and carbines over a span of 28 seconds. That barrage shattered every dormitory window facing Lynch Street, wounding 14 people. Two of those—20-year-old Jackson State junior Phillip Gibbs and 17-year-old high school student James Green—died at the scene.[795]

Police said they were under sniper fire, reporting glimpses of a gunman at dormitory windows. After the fact, three officers claimed minor injuries from flying glass, most likely caused by bullet-shattered windows overhead. An FBI review found no evidence of sniper fire, and the President's Commission on Campus Unrest declared that "the 28-second fusillade from police officers was an unreasonable, unjustified overreaction.... A broad barrage of gunfire in response to reported and unconfirmed sniper fire is never warranted." The state's case suffered further from public airing of a police radio broadcast reporting "dead niggers" on campus.[796]

No officers were charged in the Jackson State shootings, and the incident fell outside the Till Act's

Damage from police gunfire at Jackson State College on May 15, 1970 (National Archives).

1969 time limit, disappointing relatives of the slain students. James Green's sister, Gloria Green-McCray, told reporters in 2014, "We've never really got any closure because of the investigation not being thorough and everything just being kicked out. It was like, 'Just another black person dead. I mean, so what?'"[797] Today, Jackson State's Gibbs-Green Plaza commemorates the slayings, as do bullet holes still visible at Alexander Hall.

Leon Mercer Jordan
July 15, 1970; Kansas City, MO

Leon Jordan was a longtime politician and civil rights activist in Kansas City. Elected as a Democratic Party committeeman for the 14th Ward in 1958, he co-founded Freedom, Inc. four years later, to increase political awareness among African-Americans in Kansas City, organized mass voter registration drives, and promoted black candidates for office, electing seven of eight nominated in 1964. Jordan was among the victors, winning the first of three terms in the Missouri House of Representatives. By 1970, campaigning for a fourth term at age 65, he was known as "one of the most influential African Americans in Kansas City's history" and the "state's most powerful black politician."[798]

In the early hours of July 15 Jordan left his Kansas City tavern and was killed by shotgun blasts. Police recovered the weapon (stolen from an Independence hardware store in 1966) and the killer's getaway car, with partial fingerprints, and grilled eyewitnesses to the shooting, all in vain. Sergeant Lloyd DeGraffenreid, Sr., assigned to the investigation, told reporters, "I can't remember a case with less information, more blind alleys, more possible motives and more possible suspects. It's totally baffling."[799] Three associates of the Black Mafia crime syndicate were charged with Jordan's murder, but jurors acquitted one and prosecutors dropped charges against the others.[800]

Activist Leon Jordan, murdered in Kansas City on July 15, 1970 (Library of Congress).

Kansas City Star reporters Mike McGraw and Glenn Rice reopened Jordan's case in 2010, discovering that the murder weapon and suspect fingerprints had disappeared. The shotgun, it turned out, had been refurbished and was being used as a police patrol weapon, but the fingerprints were lost for good.[801] The *Star* team concluded that North End mobster "Shotgun Joe" Centimano supplied the shotgun and recruited Black Mafia members as the assassins, but motive remained obscure. One informant said Jordan's slaying had elements of both a contract killing and a murder for revenge, while another claimed it was "all about politics," planned by 1970 rival candidate Lee Bohannon, a black activist with the Social Action Committee of 20.[802]

By the time McGraw and Rice went to work, all principal suspects in Jordan's death were deceased. Police captain Rich Lockhart told the reporters that "without any new information, we will not be reopening the investigation."[803] The crime remains officially unsolved today.

John Thomas, Jr.
August 15, 1970; West Point, MS

West Point, in Mississippi's Clay County, was a target for SNCC organizers during 1964's "Freedom Summer." While "boss" John Bryant, Jr.'s meat packing plant dominated the town, black residents rallied in 1969 to join the Clay County Development Corporation, founded by Ralph Featherstone (see March 9, 1970, above) to build a operate a co-op catfish cannery. West Point mayor Charles Ivy died in June 1970, with 18 months remaining on his term, and a special election to replace him was scheduled for August 4. Acting mayor Barnes Marshall sought election to a full term, contested by three other white candidates and John Buffington, a former SNCC activist from 1964's "freedom summer."[804]

John Thomas, Jr.—a 38-year-old African American father of 11 children, known as "one of the best liked black men" in West Point—joined Buffington's campaign staff and became one of its most active workers. On August 4, more than 300 black voters had been turned away from the polls on election day, rejected on grounds of improper registration after white registrars failed to record their signatures in Clay County's registration book. Even so, Buffington placed second behind Marshall, with 590 votes to the leader's 790. Since neither scored a clear majority, prompting a runoff vote to be scheduled for August 18.[805]

In that tense atmosphere, John Thomas went shopping with his wife on Saturday, August 15, at the Southern Grocery on Highway 50. He was sitting in the Buffington campaign's sound truck, outside, when white factory worker Seth P. "Sonny" Stanley, age 49, approached the vehicle on foot at 1:30 p.m. Despite the relatively early hour, Stanley was intoxicated and had been cut off by the bartender in a nearby tavern, subsequently engaging in a loud quarrel with his wife in a shop adjoining Southern Grocery. Two eyewitnesses later told police that Stanley approached the campaign truck, drew a pistol from his pocket, and fired three shots into the cab. John Thomas then "dived" through the truck's open window and fell to the pavement, where Stanley—a vague acquaintance of Thomas—shot him twice more. Thomas was dead on arrival at a local hospital.[806]

Police charged Stanley with murder, District Attorney Harvey Buck telling reporters that despite its racial overtones, the crime would "be handled like any other criminal case."[807] Its outcome was an echo of countless other Dixie homicides spanning prior decades. On October 11, 1970, despite the fact that Thomas died unarmed and did not leave his vehicle until he had been shot three times, an all-white jury accepted Seth Stanley's self-defense plea, acquitting him of all charges.[808]

Rubén F. Salazar
August 29, 1970; Los Angeles, CA

Born in Mexico, in 1928, Salazar immigrated to Texas as a child, graduated from high school in El Paso, and served two years in the U.S. Army before enrolling at Texas Western College, where he earned a journalism degree in 1954. First employed at the now-defunct *El Paso Herald-Post*, Salazar posed as a vagrant to document abuses in the county jail. From there, he moved to California, working for various papers until he landed his last job with the *Los Angeles Times*, as a Latin American correspondent from 1959 to 1968, then as a columnist reporting on the local Hispanic community.[809]

Salazar left the *Times* in January 1970 to serve as news director for the local Spanish-language television station KMEX. There, he investigated allegations of police brutality—including six suspicious Chicano "suicides" at the East Los Angeles sheriff's station—and reports of officers planting evidence to frame Hispanic defendants. In March 1970, KMEX aired footage of L.A. officers beating Chicano students. Four months later, on July 16, police killed two unarmed Mexican nationals, Gilardo and Guillermo Sanchez, while raiding their apartment in search of a nonexistent fugitive. Despite egregious overkill in that case, leading a federal grand jury to indict seven officers, all were acquitted at trial.[810]

Rubén Salazar, killed by Los Angeles County sheriff's deputies on August 29, 1970 (Library of Congress).

KMEX coverage of the Sanchez case prompted two undercover officers to visit Sanchez, as they later said, "to express their concern" with unfavorable coverage of the L.A. Police Department. In fact, Salazar wrote, the detectives warned him that his investigations were "dangerous in the minds of barrio people."[811] Six weeks later, Salazar was dead.

On August 29, 1970, some 25,000 persons joined a National Chicano Moratorium Committee march from Belvedere Park to Laguna Park, protesting the Vietnam War and its high mortality rate for American soldiers of color. The demonstration was peaceful, yet Los Angeles County sheriff's deputies attacked the closing rally, disrupting it with tear gas. Panic and rioting ensued, during which officers killed two unarmed demonstrators, Angel Diaz and 15-year-old Lynn Ward. When that mayhem erupted, Salazar had stopped for a beer with two friends at the Silver Dollar Bar near Laguna Park. Sheriff's deputies surrounded the tavern, allegedly searching for a man armed with a rifle, who was actually captured several hours earlier. Deputy Tom Wilson fired a 10-inch tear gas projectile into the bar, striking Salazar in the head and fracturing his skull. Witnesses report that officers left Salazar where he fell for several hours, while he died without medical aid.[812]

A sheriff's deputy fires into the Silver Dollar Bar where Rubén Salazar died (National Archives).

An inquest into Salazar's death convened on September 10 and continued through October 5, 1970. Sheriff's Department spokesmen grudgingly admitted that tear-gassing the Silver Dollar was inappropriate, but no criminal charges or disciplinary action resulted. Many Chicanos still believe Salazar was targeted for assassination, an attitude exacerbated by law enforcement's refusal to open its files on the case. In March 2010, Los Angeles County Sheriff Lee Baca refused a *Los Angeles Times* request that eight boxes of "classified" reports be released under the California Public Records Act. A report from the Office of Independent Review, aired in February 2011, summarized those documents and blamed Salazar's death on "deputies' mistakes," rather than malicious homicide. Salazar, the document maintained, was simply "in the wrong place at the wrong time." Still the sheriff's reports remained hidden until December 2012, when a lawsuit filed against Baca by the Mexican American Legal Defense and Educational Fund forced their release.[813]

Notes

Introduction

1. Bill Summary & Status, 110th Congress (2007–2008), H.R.923, http://thomas.loc.gov/cgi-bin/bdquery/z?d110:H.R.923. Retrieved October 17, 2014.
2. *Ibid.*
3. Emmett Till Unsolved Civil Rights Crime Act of 2007, http://www.gpo.gov/fdsys/pkg/PLAW-110publ344/pdf/PLAW-110publ344.pdf; Emmett Till Unsolved Civil Rights Crime Act, http://nuweb9.neu.edu/civilrights/emmett-till-act. Both retrieved October 17, 2014.
4. Emmett Till Unsolved Civil Rights Crime Act, http://nuweb9.neu.edu/civilrights/emmett-till-act.
5. *Attorney General's First Report.*
6. *Attorney General's Second Report.*
7. *Attorney General's Third Report.*
8. *Attorney General's Fourth Report.*
9. *Attorney General's Fifth Report.*
10. Anonymous, "Civil rights cold cases: 'We are writing to inform you...'"
11. Breed and Mohr, "FBI says the end is near."
12. *Ibid.*
13. Reeves, "Despite disappointment."

Part 1

1. Cox, *The Claude Neal Lynching.*
2. *Ibid.*
3. *Ibid.*
4. *Ibid.*
5. *Ibid.*
6. *Fifth Attorney General's Report*, p. 10.
7. Barry, "Killing"; Minor, "Answers."
8. Newton, *White Robes*, p. 90.
9. Barry, "Killing"; Minor, "Answers."
10. Barry, "Killing."
11. FBI letter dated April 12, 2010.
12. *Fifth Attorney General's Report*, p. 11.
13. Montado, "The lynchings"; 1946 Georgia lynchings.
14. *Ibid.*
15. 1946 Georgia lynchings.
16. *Ibid.*
17. *Ibid.*
18. *Ibid.*
19. Mathiowetz, "Lynching reenactment."
20. Montado, "The lynchings."
21. 1946 Georgia lynchings.
22. Bluestein, "Ga. authorities."
23. *Fifth Attorney General's Report*, pp. 9–10.
24. Newton, *Invisible Empire*, pp. 130–5.
25. Harry Tyson Moore.
26. Newton, *Invisible Empire*, pp. 130–5.
27. *Ibid.*
28. *Ibid.*
29. *Ibid.*
30. Crist, *The Christmas 1951 Murders.*
31. FBI letter dated July 15, 2011.
32. *Fifth Attorney General's Report*, p. 10.
33. SPLC, "The Forgotten."
34. *Attorney General's Fifth Annual Report*, p. 8.
35. FBI letter dated April 28, 2010.
36. "Workman dies after being severely beaten with chain."
37. *Attorney General's Fifth Report*, p. 11.
38. FBI press release, https://www2.fbi.gov/wanted/seekinfo/civilrightsnextofkin.htm.
39. *Attorney General's Fifth Report*, p. 8.
40. Isadore Banks (Murder of).
41. *Ibid.*
42. Leveritt, "A Georgia ruling."
43. Isadore Banks (Murder of).
44. Hadad, "After 57 years."
45. *Ibid.*
46. *Fifth Attorney General's Report*, p. 8.
47. SPLC, "The Forgotten."
48. FBI Seeking Victims [sic] Next of Kin.
49. *Attorney General's Fifth Report*, p. 10.
50. Beito, "Grim and overlooked anniversary."
51. *Ibid.*
52. Mendelsohn, *Martyrs*, pp. 4–10.
53. *Ibid.*
54. *Ibid.*, pp. 15–19.
55. *Fifth Attorney General's Report*, p. 9.
56. Lamar Smith, http://nuweb9.neu.edu/civilrights/lamar-smith.
57. *Ibid.*
58. FBI letter dated April 12, 2010.
59. Lamar Smith, http://nuweb9.neu.edu/civilrights/lamar-smith.
60. *Fifth Attorney General's Report*, p. 11.
61. FBI letter dated April 12, 2010.
62. Till-Mobley and Benson, pp. 36–38; Younge, "Justice at last?"
63. FBI File, "Emmett Till."
64. *Ibid.*
65. *Ibid.*
66. Huie, "The Shocking Story."
67. FBI File, "Emmett Till"; People & Events: Clarence Strider.
68. FBI File, "Emmett Till."

69. *Ibid.*; People & Events: Clarence Strider.
70. Whitfield, *Death in the Delta,* p. 117.
71. *Ibid.*, pp. 119–20.
72. Anderson, "Widow of Emmett Till killer dies"; Younge, "Justice at last?"
73. Breed, "End of Till case"; *Fifth Attorney General's Report,* p. 11.
74. John Earl Reese, http://nuweb9.neu.edu/civilrights/john-earl-reese.
75. The Trouble I've Seen, http://archives.nbclearn.com/portal/site/k-12/flatview?cuecard=65676.
76. Undated FBI letter.
77. John Earl Reese, http://nuweb9.neu.edu/civilrights/john-earl-reese.
78. *Ibid.*; Undated FBI letter.
79. *Fifth Attorney General's Report,* p. 10.
80. Undated FBI letter.
81. Halberstam, "Tallahatchie County acquits."
82. *Ibid.*; Clinton Melton, http://nuweb9.neu.edu/civilrights/clinton-melton.
83. Halberstam, "Tallahatchie County acquits."
84. *Ibid.*
85. *Ibid.*
86. *Attorney General's Fifth Report,* p. 10.
87. FBI letter dated April 12, 2010.
88. Evers-Williams, *Autobiography,* p. 45.
89. *Attorney General's Fifth Report,* p. 9.
90. "Negro fatally shot."
91. *Fifth Attorney General's Report,* p. 10.
92. FBI letter dated May 24, 2010.
93. Lloyd, "Thomas Brewer (1894–1956)."
94. *Ibid.*
95. "A Doctor's Death."
96. *Fifth Attorney General's Report,* p. 8.
97. *Attorney General's Fifth Report,* p. 10.
98. "FBI studying 3 deaths in N.C."
99. Bessie McDowell, http://nuweb9.neu.edu/civilrights/bessie-mcdowell.
100. *Ibid.*
101. *Fifth Attorney General's Report,* April 9, 2010.
102. "Mother slain for 'sassing'"; Maybelle Mahone, http://nuweb9.neu.edu/civilrights/maybelle-mahone.
103. *Attorney General's Fifth Report,* p. 10.
104. Greenhaw, *Fighting the Devil,* pp. 11–16.
105. Nossiter, "Murder, memory, and the Klan."
106. *Ibid.*
107. *Fifth Attorney General's Report,* p. 9.
108. SPLC, "The Forgotten."
109. FBI press release, http://www2.fbi.gov/wanted/seekinfo/civilrightscoldcases.htm; *Attorney General's Fifth Report,* p. 10.
110. "Young physician killed."
111. *Ibid.*
112. *Attorney General's Fifth Report,* p. 11.
113. Undated FBI letter.
114. *Congressional Record* Vol. 153, No. 104 (June 26, 2007), p. E1414.
115. *Attorney General's Fifth Report,* p. 9.
116. FBI letter dated April 16, 2010.
117. Fleming, "Midnight visitors."
118. *Ibid.*
119. Fleming, " Voices from a Cleveland park."
120. *Fifth Attorney General's Report,* p. 9.
121. "FBI seeking victims [*sic*] next of kin."
122. *Attorney General's Fifth Report,* p. 10.
123. Mississippi Civil Rights Martyrs.
124. FBI press release, https://www2.fbi.gov/wanted/seekinfo/civilrightsnextofkin.htm.
125. Mississippi Civil Rights Martyrs.
126. *Attorney General's Fifth Report,* p. 9.
127. Allen, "The Unsolved Civil Rights Murder."
128. *Ibid.*
129. *Ibid.*; James Brazier, http://nuweb9.neu.edu/civilrights/james-brazier; SPLC, "The Forgotten."
130. Browning, "A chief, a coach, a killer."
131. *Attorney General's Fifth Report,* p. 8; FBI letter dated April 6, 2009.
132. Ed Smith, http://nuweb9.neu.edu/civilrights/mississippi/ed-smith.
133. *Attorney General's Fifth Report,* p. 10.
134. Undated FBI letter.
135. *Ibid.*
136. *Attorney General's Fifth Report,* p. 8.
137. Blytheville (AR) *Courier News,* August 9, 1958.
138. *Ibid.*
139. Browning, "A chief, a coach, a killer."
140. *Attorney General's Fifth Report,* p. 9.
141. FBI letter dated April 6, 2009.
142. Sessions, "First witnesses"; Noel, "Sheriff Treloar."
143. "Mississippi sheriff acquitted."
144. Sessions, "First witnesses"; Noel, "Sheriff Treloar."
145. Noel, "Sheriff Treloar."
146. *Ibid.*
147. "Mississippi sheriff acquitted"; Mississippi Civil Rights Martyrs.
148. Roberts and Kilbanoff, "On the race beat."
149. Woodrow Wilson Daniels, http://nuweb9.neu.edu/civilrights/woodrow-wilson-daniels.
150. Social Security Death Index.
151. *Fifth Attorney General's Report,* p. 9.
152. Undated FBI letter.
153. *Ibid.*
154. *Attorney General's Fifth Report,* p. 9.
155. "FBI seeking victims [*sic*] next of kin."
156. *Attorney General's Fifth Report,* p. 9.
157. FBI letter dated May 2, 2010.
158. *Ibid.*
159. *Attorney General's Fifth Report,* p. 9.
160. Dray, *At the Hands,* pp. 434–43.
161. *Ibid.*
162. *Ibid.*
163. *Ibid.*
164. *Ibid.*
165. Older, "FBI reopens."
166. *Fifth Attorney General's Report,* p. 10.
167. Grady, "Paying the ultimate price"; Greenberg, "Legacy."
168. Greenberg, "Legacy."
169. Moody, *Coming of Age,* pp. 27, 137–9, 203.
170. Greenberg, "Legacy."
171. *Fifth Attorney General's Report,* p. 10.
172. Booker T. Mixon, http://nuweb9.neu.edu/civilrights/booker-t-mixon.
173. Booker T. Mixon, http://bookertmixoncivilrights.blogspot.com.
174. *Fifth Attorney General's Report,* p. 10.
175. "2 more join list"; Myers, "'59 police shooting."
176. Evers, *For Us,* pp. 211–12.
177. "2 more join list"; Myers, "'59 police shooting."

178. Luther Jackson, http://nuweb9.neu.edu/civilrights/luther-jackson; Cagin and Dray, *We Are Not Afraid*, p. 253.
179. Evers, *For Us*, p. 213.
180. Myers, "'59 police shooting."
181. FBI letter dated April 16, 2010.
182. The Murder of William Roy Prather, http://mscivilrightsproject.org/index.php?option=com_content&view=article&id=759:the-murder-of-william-roy-prather&Itemid=11.
183. *Attorney General's Fifth Report*, p. 10.
184. "State offers reward"; Catherwood and Richardson, "Mattie Green."
185. *Ibid*.
186. Catherwood and Richardson.
187. *Ibid*.
188. *Ibid*.
189. *Ibid*.
190. Jonnson, "Feds turn up heat"; *Fifth Attorney General's Report*, p. 9.
191. SPLC, "The Forgotten."
192. *Attorney General's Fifth Report*, pp. 9–10.
193. SPLC, "The Forgotten."
194. *Attorney General's Fifth Report*, p. 10.
195. "FBI studying three deaths in N.C."
196. *Attorney General's Fifth Report*, p. 9.
197. Herbert Lee, http://nuweb9.neu.edu/civilrights/herbert-lee; Martyrs Remembered: Herbert Lee; E. H. Hurst.
198. *Ibid*.
199. *Fifth Attorney General's Report*, p. 9.
200. FBI letter dated April 10, 2010.
201. SPLC, "The Forgotten."
202. *Fifth Attorney General's Report*, p. 8.
203. Roman Ducksworth Jr., http://nuweb9.neu.edu/civilrights/roman-duckworth-jr.
204. *Fifth Attorney General's Report*, p. 9.
205. FBI letter dated April 12, 2010.
206. SPLC, "The Forgotten."
207. *Attorney General's Fifth Report*, p. 9.
208. Doyle, *American Insurrection*, pp. 186–7; Mitchell, "Ole Miss declared."
209. Doyle, pp. 162–6.
210. *Fifth Attorney General's Report*, p. 9.
211. Undated FBI letter.
212. *Ibid*.
213. *Ibid*.
214. A. C. Hall, http://nuweb9.neu.edu/civilrights/a-c-hall.
215. Undated FBI letter.
216. *Attorney General's Fifth Report*, p. 9.
217. Mississippi Civil Rights Martyrs.
218. FBI letter dated May 2, 2010.
219. *Ibid*.
220. *Attorney General's Fifth Report*, p. 10.
221. Stanton, *Freedom Walk*, pp. 5–6.
222. *Ibid*., pp. 66–9, 74.
223. *Ibid*., pp. 76–9, 214–15.
224. Newton, *White Robes*, p. 152; Stanton, *Freedom Walk*, p. 202.
225. *Fifth Attorney General's Report*, p. 10.
226. Andrew Lee Anderson, http://nuweb9.neu.edu/civilrights/andrew-lee-anderson.
227. "Shooting of Arkansas Negro."
228. *Fifth Attorney General's Report*, p. 8.
229. Johnson, "Johnny's death."
230. *Ibid*.
231. FBI letter dated April 28, 2010.
232. Johnson, "Johnny's death."
233. *Attorney General's Fifth Report*, p. 10.
234. Virgil Ware, http://nuweb9.neu.edu/civilrights/virgil-ware.
235. FBI letter dated March 28, 2011.
236. *Attorney General's Fifth Report*, p. 11.
237. SNCC, *Chronology of Violence*, pp. 15–17.
238. *Attorney General's Fifth Report*, p. 9.
239. Mississippi Civil Rights Martyrs.
240. *Attorney General's Fifth Report*, p. 8.
241. Undated FBI letter.
242. Louis Allen, http://nuweb9.neu.edu/civilrights/louis-allen.
243. *Ibid*.
244. *Ibid*.
245. *Ibid*.
246. Schaeffer, "A brave man."
247. Louis Allen, http://nuweb9.neu.edu/civilrights/louis-allen.
248. *Fifth Attorney General's Report*, p. 8.
249. Clifton Walker Case, http://coldcases.org/cases/clifton-walker-case; Greenberg, "Decades after slaying."
250. Greenberg, "Decades after slaying."
251. *Ibid*.
252. *Ibid*.
253. *Ibid*.
254. *Ibid*.; *Fifty Attorney General's Report*, p. 11.
255. "FBI gets Miss. murder list."
256. Erle Johnston Jr. report dated March 6, 1964, http://mdah.state.ms.us/arrec/digital_archives/sovcom/result.php?image=images/png/cd04/029642.png&otherstuff=2|72|2|71|1|1|29115|#.
257. FBI letter dated May 2, 2010; *Fifth Attorney General's Report*, p. 8.
258. "Johnnie Mae Chappell."
259. *Ibid*.
260. Murphy, "Seeking justice."
261. *Ibid*.
262. "Lawyer: JSO conspired."
263. "President wants 1964 racial slaying reviewed."
264. "Man convicted in 1964."
265. *Fifth Attorney General's Report*, p. 8.
266. "Klunder, Bruce W.," Encyclopedia of Cleveland History.
267. *Ibid*.
268. Martyrs Remembered: Bruce Klunder.
269. "Stephen E. Howe Elementary," Cleveland Historical, http://clevelandhistorical.org/items/show/254.
270. Undated FBI letter to Klunder's survivors.
271. *Fifth Attorney General's Report*, p. 9.
272. Mudhar, "Cracking a very cold case."
273. "Reported as dead."
274. *Ibid*.
275. Wagster Pettus, "Reputed Klansman."
276. *Second Attorney General's Report*, pp. 11–13.
277. *United States v. Cecil Price, et al.*, 383 U.S. 787, 86 S. Ct. 1152; 16 L. Ed. 2d 267.
278. "Statement asking for justice."
279. Dewan, "Ex-Klansman guilty."
280. Mitchell, "Two-thirds of 124 civil rights cold cases closed."
281. *Fifth Attorney General's Report*, pp. 9–10.
282. Breed and Mohr, "FBI says the end is near."
283. *Fifth Attorney General's Report*, p. 9.

284. Undated FBI letter.
285. Nelson, "Whatever happened?"
286. *Ibid.*
287. Nelson, "Klansman's son recalls."
288. *Fifth Attorney General's Report*, p. 9.
289. Harlem riot of 1964.
290. *Ibid.*
291. *Fifth Attorney General's Report*, p. 10.
292. Mississippi Civil Rights Martyrs.
293. *Fifth Attorney General's Report*, p. 11.
294. Neimiah Montgomery, http://nuweb9.neu.edu/civilrights/neimiah-montgomery.
295. *Fifth Attorney General's Report*, p. 10.
296. SPLC, "The Forgotten."
297. FBI letter dated April 28, 2010.
298. *Attorney General's Fifth Report*, p. 10.
299. FBI letter dated April 12, 2010.
300. *Ibid.*; Hubert Orsby [*sic*], http://nuweb9.neu.edu/civilrights/hubert-orsby.
301. *Attorney General's Fifth Report*, p. 10.
302. Talbott, "FBI may reopen."
303. *Attorney General's Fifth Report*, p. 8.
304. Nelson, "Deputy DeLaughter Seen"; Nelson, "Silver Dollar Group may have targeted."
305. Nelson, "Deputy DeLaughter Seen."
306. "Cold Case: Five motives"; "Cold Case: Subject in Frank Morris arson dies"; Nelson, Silver Dollar Group linked."
307. "Cold Case: Five motives."
308. "Cold Case: Subject in Frank Morris arson dies"; Nelson, "Encounters"; Nelson, "Rayville man implicated."
309. *Fifth Attorney General's Report*, p. 10.
310. FBI letter dated June 4, 2011.
311. *Attorney General's Fifth Report*, p. 8.
312. FBI letter dated June 4, 2011.
313. Brasted, "6 civil rights-era murder cases."
314. *Attorney General's Fifth Report*, p. 10.
315. FBI letter dated May 2, 2010.
316. *Fifth Attorney General's Report*, p. 11.
317. Mississippi Civil Rights Martyrs.
318. FBI Seeking Victims [*sic*] Next of Kin.
319. *Attorney General's Fifth Report*, p. 11.
320. FBI letter dated April 28, 2010.
321. *Attorney General's Fifth Report*, p. 8.
322. Fleming, "The death of Jimmie Lee Jackson."
323. *Ibid.*
324. Fleming, "Former state trooper."
325. *Fifth Attorney General's Report*, p. 9.
326. Mitchell, "FBI investigating former Alabama trooper."
327. Willie Henry Lee, http://nuweb9.neu.edu/civilrights/willie-henry-lee.
328. *Ibid.*
329. *Ibid.*; Mississippi Civil Rights Martyrs.
330. *Fifth Attorney General's Report*, p. 9.
331. Donald Rasberry, http://nuweb9.neu.edu/civilrights/donald-rasberry; Mississippi Civil Rights Martyrs.
332. *Fifth Attorney General's Report*, p. 10.
333. "James Reeb," Encyclopedia of Alabama.
334. *Ibid.*; Helman, "Letter from Selma."
335. "James Reeb."
336. Helman, "Letter from Selma"; Mendelsohn, *Martyrs*, pp. 172–4.
337. *Ibid.*
338. May, *The Informant*, pp. 159–60.
339. *Fifth Attorney General's Report*, p. 10.
340. FBI letter dated June 1, 2011.
341. "Namon Hoggle," Bizapedia, http://www.bizapedia.com/people/NAMON-HOGGLE.html.
342. FBI letter dated June 28, 2011.
343. *Ibid.*
344. Kevin Connolly, "White House sorry for Shirley Sherrod 'racism' firing." *BBC News*, July 21, 2010.
345. *Fifth Attorney General's Report*, p. 10.
346. FBI letter dated June 28, 2011.
347. Serrano, "Answers Elusive."
348. *Ibid.*
349. *Ibid.*; Keller, "Deputy sheriff's murder."
350. Serrano, "Answers Elusive."
351. *Fifth Attorney General's Report*, p. 10.
352. FBI Seeking Victims [*sic*] Next of Kin.
353. SPLC, "The Forgotten."
354. *Attorney General's Fifth Report*, p. 11.
355. FBI letter dated June 1, 2011.
356. *Attorney General's Fifth Report*, p. 11.
357. FBI letter dated June 1, 2011.
358. William Piercefield, http://www.zoominfo.com/p/William-Piercefield/1871497267.
359. *Attorney General's Fifth Report*, p. 10.
360. Shapiro, "Justice."
361. *Ibid.*
362. *Ibid.*
363. *Ibid.*
364. *Ibid.*
365. *Fifth Attorney General's Report*, p. 10.
366. Mississippi Civil Rights Martyrs; Klopfer, "Murders around Mississippi."
367. *Fifth Attorney General's Report*, p. 11.
368. FBI Seeking Victims [*sic*] Next of Kin; SPLC, "The Forgotten."
369. *Fifth Attorney General's Report*, p. 9.
370. FBI letter dated May 27, 2011.
371. Woodham, "Jonathan Myrick Daniels."
372. Newton, *Ku Klux Terror*, pp. 156–7.
373. *Ibid.*, p. 157.
374. *Ibid.*, pp. 157–8.
375. Thomas, "Thomas Coleman."
376. Leadership Gallery: Jonathan Daniels, http://www.episcopalarchives.org/Afro-Anglican_history/exhibit/leadership/daniels.php.
377. *Fifth Attorney General's Report*, p. 9.
378. FBI letter dated April 26, 2011.
379. Fleming, "Thad Christian's death."
380. *Ibid.*
381. *Ibid.*
382. *Fifth Attorney General's Report*, p. 9.
383. FBI letter dated April 8, 2011.
384. FBI Seeking Victims [*sic*] Next Of Kin.
385. Mississippi Civil Rights Martyrs.
386. *Fifth Attorney General's Report*, p. 9.
387. Undated FBI letter.
388. Mississippi State Sovereignty Commission, http://en.wikipedia.org/wiki/Mississippi_State_Sovereignty_Commission.
389. Robert McNair, http://nuweb9.neu.edu/civilrights/robert-mcnair.
390. Undated FBI letter.
391. *Attorney General's Fifth Report*, p. 10.
392. Forman, *Sammy Younge, Jr.*
393. Summerlin, "Samuel Younge Jr."
394. *Ibid.*
395. Gale, "Was Segrest aiming."

396. Gale, "The trial."
397. *Ibid.*
398. *Fifth Attorney General's Report,* p. 11.
399. FBI letter dated March 28, 2011.
400. Breed and Mohr, "FBI says the end is near"; Klopfer, "Murders around Mississippi."
401. The Legacy of Birdia Keglar; Klopfer, "Murders around Mississippi"; Civil Rights Cold Cases.
402. Breed and Mohr; Klopfer, "Murders around Mississippi."
403. Klopfer, "Murders around Mississippi."
404. *Ibid.*; Civil Rights Cold Cases; Hamlett, "My great-grandmother Adlena Hamlett."
405. Civil Rights Cold Cases; *Attorney General's Second Report,* p. 15.
406. FBI letters dated May 27, 2011.
407. *Ibid.*
408. Breed and Mohr; Civil Rights Cold Cases.
409. *Fifth Attorney General's Report,* p. 9.
410. Mitchell, "FBI investigating former Alabama trooper."
411. *Fifth Attorney General's Report,* p. 9.
412. *Congressional Record,* Vol. 153, No. 104 (June 26, 2007), p. E1413.
413. March Against Fear, http://en.wikipedia.org/wiki/March_Against_Fear.
414. *Attorney General's Fifth Report,* p. 9.
415. Newton, *White Robes,* p. 157.
416. Mitchell, "The last days."
417. *Ibid.*
418. Bragg, "Last cry"; "Ernest Avants."
419. *Fifth Attorney General's Report,* p. 11.
420. Eddie James Stewart, http://nuweb9.neu.edu/civilrights/mississippi/eddie-james-stewart.
421. "Negro widow files $20 million suit."
422. *Fifth Attorney General's Report,* p.11.
423. FBI letter dated May 27, 2011.
424. *Ibid.*
425. *Ibid.*
426. *Attorney General's Fifth Report,* p. 9.
427. "White man held"; Smith, "Jury convicts."
428. *Ibid.*
429. Supreme Court of Georgia. *James v. State.*
430. Hulet M. Varner, Jr., https://scholarblogs.emory.edu/emorycoldcases/hulet-m-varner-jr.
431. *Fifth Attorney General's Report,* p. 11.
432. Lottman, "Negro man dies."
433. Lottman, "Witness saw blood."
434. *Ibid.*
435. *Fifth Attorney General's Report,* p. 10.
436. FBI letter dated April 28, 2010.
437. SPLC, "The Forgotten."
438. *North & South* (December 1966), http://www.crmvet.org/docs/sclc/6612_sclc_ns.pdf.
439. Bruce Hartford, "Weekly Watts Report—Grenada, Miss.," http://www.crmvet.org/docs/gren03.pdf.
440. FBI letter dated April 12, 2010.
441. *Fifth Attorney General's Report,* p. 9.
442. Wharlest Jackson Case, http://coldcases.org/cases/wharlest-jackson-case.
443. *Ibid.*
444. Nelson, "The night Wharlest Jackson was murdered."
445. Nelson, "SDG leader 'Red' Glover."
446. *Ibid.*
447. *Ibid.*
448. *Fifth Attorney General's Report,* p. 9.
449. Benjamin Brown, http://nuweb9.neu.edu/civilrights/benjamin-brown.
450. *Ibid.*
451. *Ollie Mae Brown and Margaret Brown v. Allen C. Thompson,* 430 F.2d 1214 (1970).
452. Benjamin Brown, http://nuweb9.neu.edu/civilrights/benjamin-brown.
453. *Fifth Attorney General's Report,* p. 8.
454. Fleming, "A more complete picture."
455. Rodell Williamson, http://nuweb9.neu.edu/civilrights/rodell-williamson.
456. Wilcox, "Man found in Wilcox."
457. *Ibid.*
458. "FBI to probe mystery death."
459. FBI letter dated May 2, 2010.
460. *Ibid.*
461. Brasted, "6 civil rights-era murder cases."
462. *Attorney General's Fifth Report,* p. 8.
463. Talbott, "FBI may reopen."
464. *Attorney General's Fifth Report,* p. 11.
465. South Carolina State University, http://en.wikipedia.org/wiki/South_Carolina_State_University.
466. Bass, "Documenting"; Orangeburg massacre, http://en.wikipedia.org/wiki/Orangeburg_massacre.
467. *Ibid.*
468. *Ibid.*
469. Cleveland Sellers, http://en.wikipedia.org/wiki/Cleveland_Sellers.
470. Bass, "Orangeburg Massacre."
471. "FBI will not reinvestigate."
472. *Fifth Attorney General's Report,* pp. 9–11.
473. Lollar, "Mother grieves."
474. *Ibid.*; undated FBI letter to Payne's mother.
475. *Ibid.*
476. Lollar, "Mother grieves."
477. *Fifth Attorney General's Report,* p. 10.
478. FBI Seeking Victims [*sic*] Next of Kin.
479. *Attorney General's Fifth Report,* p. 11.

Part 2

1. "Rex Scott is hanged."
2. *Ibid.*; "Three held."
3. "Perry jurors charge."
4. "Seven men indicted,"
5. "Troy Combs removed"; Wright, *Racial Violence in Kentucky,* p. 211.
6. "Lynching cases on trial"; Wright, p. 211.
7. "Lee Gibson is found not guilty."
8. Walter. "'A blot on Tampa's history.'"
9. *Ibid.*
10. "Lynching mob strings up 2 In Mississippi."
11. "Hang, shoot, drag Negro."
12. "Eight men on trial."
13. Ames, *Changing Character,* p. 48.
14. *Ibid.,* p. 41.
15. *Ibid.,* p. 43.
16. *Ibid.,* p. 43.
17. Newton, *Racial,* p. 408.
18. "Home is castle."
19. *Ibid.*
20. "No matter how humble."
21. "Mississippi mob lynches Negroes."
22. Ames, *Changing Character,* p. 34; "Accosts three white girls."

23. Bond, *Star Creek Papers,* pp. 6–129.
24. Ames, *Changing Character,* p. 42.
25. Payne, *I've Got the Light,* p. 8.
26. McMillen, *Dark Journey,* p. 247.
27. Payne, *I've Got the Light,* p. 9.
28. Newton, *Racial,* p. 410.
29. Stalking the Angel; Rubin Stacy [*sic*], http://spartacus-educational.com/USACstacy.htm.
30. Shapiro, *White Violence,* p. 246.
31. Newton, *Racial,* p. 409.
32. Payne, *I've Got the Light,* pp. 8–9.
33. Ames, *Changing Character,* p. 44.
34. *Ibid.*
35. "2 are lynched in Mississippi by white mob."
36. "Negro is lynched by mob in Florida."
37. Ames, *Changing Character,* p. 36.
38. *Ibid.,* p. 46.
39. *Ibid.,* p. 44.
40. *Ibid.,* pp. 43–4.
41. *Ibid.,* p. 38; "Lynch colored man arrested for drinking."
42. Ames, *Changing Character,* p. 38.
43. *Ibid.,* p. 42.
44. *Ibid.,* p. 48.
45. Wolff, "Justice and injustice."
46. Ames, *Changing Character,* p. 49.
47. *NAACP Annual Report,* p. 6.
48. *Ibid.,* p. 7.
49. Ames, *Changing Character,* p. 38; *NAACP Annual Report,* p. 7.
50. *NAACP Annual Report,* p. 7.
51. *Ibid.;* Ames, *Changing Character,* p. 35.
52. *NAACP Annual Report,* p. 7.
53. *Ibid.;* Ames, *Changing Character,* p. 39.
54. Ames, *Changing Character,* p. 36.
55. *Ibid.,* p. 39; *NAACP Annual Report,* p. 8.
56. *NAACP Annual Report,* p. 8; Payne, *I've Got the Light,* p. 9.
57. Ames, *Changing Character,* p. 39.
58. *Ibid.,* p. 34.
59. Roosevelt Townes and Robert "Bootjack" McDaniels, http://nuweb9.neu.edu/civilrights/mississippi/roosevelt-townes-and-robert-bootjack-mcdaniels.
60. *Ibid.*
61. *Ibid.*
62. *Ibid.*
63. Ames, *Changing Character,* p. 39.
64. *Ibid.,* p. 37.
65. *Ibid.,* p. 48.
66. Newton, *Racial,* pp. 413–14.
67. Ames, *Changing Character,* p. 37.
68. Washington Adams, http://nuweb9.neu.edu/civilrights/mississippi/washington-adams.
69. Guzman and Hughes, "Lynching," p. 10; Payne, *I've Got the Light,* p. 9.
70. J. W. Lipscomb to R. W. Whitfield, letter dated July 4, 1938.
71. Willie McDonald, http://nuweb9.neu.edu/civilrights/mississippi/willie-mcdonald.
72. "Mob burns slain man twice"; "Sharkey County posse kills Negro slayer."
73. Ames, *Changing Character,* p. 39.
74. "Second suspect held."
75. *Ibid.;* "Lynching goes underground."
76. *Ibid.*
77. *Ibid.;* Claude Banks death certificate, http://nuweb9.neu.edu/civilrights/wp-content/uploads/Banks_death-certificate.pdf.
78. "Lynching goes underground."
79. Ames, *Changing Character,* p. 37.
80. "Negro, 19, is lynched by Louisiana mob."
81. "No arrests for Louisiana lynching."
82. Wilder McGowan, http://nuweb9.neu.edu/civilrights/mississippi/wilder-mcgowan.
83. *Ibid.;* Ames, *Changing Character,* p. 44.
84. "Mob uses attack rumor"; Payne, *I've Got the Light,* pp. 10–11.
85. Ames, *Changing Character,* pp. 30, 37.
86. Payne, *I've Got the Light,* pp. 12–13.
87. O'Dee Henderson, http://nuweb9.neu.edu/civilrights/henderson.
88. *Ibid.*
89. Elbert Williams, http://nuweb9.neu.edu/civilrights/elbert-williams.
90. *Ibid.*
91. Ekanem, "Injustice unveiled."
92. *Ibid.*
93. *Ibid.*
94. Ames, *Changing Character,* p. 40.
95. Bruce Tisdale death certificate.
96. Personal communication from Patti Burns, Nov. 3, 2014.
97. *NAACP Annual Report,* p. 8.
98. Ames, *Changing Character,* p. 40.
99. Jean, "'Warranted lynchings,'" p. 140.
100. Bob White, http://nuweb9.neu.edu/civilrights/texas/bob-white.
101. *White v. State,* 1938.
102. *White v. State,* 1939; *White v. Texas,* 1940.
103. Bob White, http://nuweb9.neu.edu/civilrights/texas/bob-white.
104. "'My husband shot like dog.'"
105. Capeci, *The Lynching of Cleo Wright,* pp. 13–37.
106. *Ibid.,* pp. 38–108.
107. "Secret burial"; "Suppressed story."
108. *Ibid.*
109. "City patrolman shoots"; "Seek to avert violence."
110. *Ibid.*
111. Thomas Foster, http://nuweb9.neu.edu/civilrights/arkansas-2/thomas-foster.
112. Guzman and Hughes, "Lynching," p. 4; World War II, http://www.tshaonline.org/handbook/online/articles/npwnj.
113. "Posses search."
114. "Find body."
115. "13 accused."
116. "8 in posse give bond"; "Ex-sheriff's hearing set"; "12 enter pleas."
117. "9 farmers fined."
118. Ernest Green and Charles Lang, http://nuweb9.neu.edu/civilrights/ernest-green-and-charles-lang-3-2.
119. *Ibid.*
120. Atkins, "Shubuta bridge's toll,"
121. *Ibid.*
122. Ernest Green and Charles Lang.
123. Payne, *I've Got the Light,* p. 14.
124. Urofsky, *100 Americans,* pp. 180–2; Waldrep, *Lynching,* p. 241.
125. Urofsky.

126. *Ibid.*
127. *1961 Commission on Civil Rights Report,* p. 6; Whitehead, *FBI Story,* p. 255.
128. *1961 Commission on Civil Rights Report,* p. 8.
129. *Ibid.,* p. 6.
130. *Ibid.,* pp. 6–7.
131. Urofsky.
132. *Screws v. United States,* 325 U.S. 91 (1945).
133. Urofsky.
134. Lee, *United States Army in World War II,* pp. 366–70.
135. *Ibid.*
136. *Ibid.*; William Walker, http://nuweb9.neu.edu/civilrights/mississippi/william-walker.
137. Lee, *United States Army in World War II,* pp. 366–70.
138. "Race riot feared."
139. *Ibid.*
140. Lee, *United States Army in World War II,* pp. 366–70.
141. *Ibid.*
142. Case, *The Slaughter.*
143. Suro and Fletcher, "Mississippi massacre."
144. Muhammad, "Did the U.S. Army massacre."
145. *Harrison v. State.*
146. *Ibid.*; "Report a Negro clubbed to death."
147. "Accused Negro is lynched"; "Murder of a murderer"; "Negro taken out."
148. Cellos Harrison, http://nuweb9.neu.edu/civilrights/cellos-harrison.
149. Willie Lee Davis, http://nuweb9.neu.edu/civilrights/georgia/willie-lee-davis.
150. Joe Stokes affidavit, http://nuweb9.neu.edu/civilrights/wp-content/uploads/Joe-Stokes-Affidavit.pdf.
151. *Ibid.*
152. Death certificate, http://nuweb9.neu.edu/civilrights/wp-content/uploads/Willie-Davis-Official-Death-Certificate.pdf.
153. Willie Lee Davis; "Justice Dept. files charges."
154. "Justice Dept. files charges."
155. "U.S. drops case."
156. Camp Ellis, http://en.wikipedia.org/wiki/Camp_Ellis.
157. Guzman and Hughes, "Lynching," p. 4.
158. Willie James Howard, http://nuweb9.neu.edu/civilrights/willie-james-howard.
159. *Ibid.*
160. Affidavit of A. P. Goff et al., January 2, 1944.
161. Lula Howard affidavit, March 19, 1944.
162. Dunn, "Justice for Willie James."
163. King, "Florida's history."
164. Burch, "60 years later."
165. Gordet, "Rev. Isaac Simmons."
166. Isaac Simmons, http://nuweb9.neu.edu/civilrights/rev-isaac-simmons.
167. *Ibid.*
168. Affidavit of Eldridge Simmons, dated August 1, 1944.
169. *Ibid.*
170. Gordet, "Rev. Isaac Simmons."
171. *Ibid.*
172. 42 U.S. Code § 252—Medical examination of aliens.
173. Gordet, "Rev. Isaac Simmons."
174. Henry Hauser, http://nuweb9.neu.edu/civilrights/louisiana/henry-hauser.
175. "Brutal beating by cops blamed for man's death."
176. Henry Hauser death certificate, dated March 27, 1944.
177. Henry Hauser, http://nuweb9.neu.edu/civilrights/louisiana/henry-hauser.
178. Tony Bonn, "Meet crime lord Tom Clark," http://theamericanchronicle.blogspot.com/2013/09/meet-crime-lord-tom-clark.html.
179. Joshua Collins, http://nuweb9.neu.edu/civilrights/mississippi/joshua-collins.
180. "Jackson detective kills Negro."
181. Joshua Collins.
182. Jose Davila, http://nuweb9.neu.edu/civilrights/jose-davila.
183. *Ibid.*
184. *Ibid.*
185. Daly, "Libel?"
186. Jose Davilla.
187. *Ibid.*
188. Marland Littiebrant (1903–1970), http://www.ancientfaces.com/person/marland-littiebrant/53442417.
189. Cohen, "The lynching of James Scales."
190. *Ibid.*; James Scales, http://nuweb9.neu.edu/civilrights/james-scales.
191. Cohen.
192. *Ibid.*; "17-year-old boy lynched."
193. James Scales; Cohen; Fields, "Murder on the mountain."
194. Fields; Lucas, "'Valley folk' silent"; Cohen; James Scales.
195. Fields.
196. "Judge frees streetcar operator."
197. *Ibid.*
198. "Grand jury fails."
199. Patterson, *We Charge Genocide,* pp. 58–9.
200. "Aged Negro found."
201. Adams, "The Ones Left Behind."
202. "Negro is killed."
203. Adams, "The Ones Left Behind."
204. *Ibid.*
205. LeFlore, "Mobile cop kills innocent youth."
206. Adams, "The Ones Left Behind."
207. Patterson, *We Charge Genocide,* p. 63; Clark, "Klan buster."
208. "Slaying linked to reborn Klan."
209. Kennedy, *Klan Unmasked,* pp. 206–12.
210. Patterson, *We Charge Genocide,* p. 59.
211. *Ibid.*
212. Blume, "'Not In New Orleans Anymore.'"
213. Albert Bell affidavit.
214. Blume, "'Not In New Orleans Anymore.'"
215. *Ibid.*
216. "Forgets 'Yes, sir,' Miss. boy, 17, shot."
217. Blume, "'Not In New Orleans Anymore.'"
218. Patterson, *We Charge Genocide,* p. 59.
219. *Ibid.,* pp. 59–60.
220. "Court reverses Crews decision."
221. Patterson, *We Charge Genocide,* p. 60.
222. *Ibid.,* p. 60.
223. *Ibid.*; "Probes GI death at hands of officer."
224. "Murder on bus."
225. "Man bound over."
226. "Grand jury fails."
227. Patterson, *We Charge Genocide,* p. 60.
228. Weiss, *Vigilante Terror,* pp. 6–8.
229. *Ibid.,* p. 8.

230. *Ibid.*, pp. 9–13.
231. *Ibid.*, p. 16.
232. *Ibid.*
233. *Ibid.*, p. 17.
234. Patterson, *We Charge Genocide*, pp. 60–1.
235. Into a burning house: representing segregation's death. http://www.thefreelibrary.com/Into+a+burning+house%3a+representing+segregation%27s+death.-a0194963508.
236. Patterson, *We Charge Genocide*, p. 61.
237. *Ibid.*
238. Biondi, *To Stand and Fight*, pp. 61–2.
239. *Ibid.*
240. Patterson, *We Charge Genocide*, p. 61.
241. Biondi, p. 62; Patterson, p. 61.
242. Patterson, p. 61.
243. Biondi, p. 64.
244. Patterson, *We Charge Genocide*, p. 61.
245. *Ibid.*, p. 62.
246. *Ibid.*, pp. 62–3.
247. Columbia Race Riots; "Columbia Race Riot, 1946."
248. *Ibid.*; Fields, "Murder on the mountain."
249. *Ibid.*
250. *Ibid.*
251. *Ibid.*
252. *Ibid.*
253. Patterson, *We Charge Genocide*, p. 63.
254. *Ibid.*, pp. 63–4.
255. *Ibid.*, p. 64; Mack, *Black Spokane*, pp. 51–2.
256. Devon G. Pena, Mexmigration, http://mexmigration.blogspot.com/2014/03/acuna-nailing-latinao-political-class.html.
257. Payne, *I've Got the Light*, p. 15; Patterson, *We Charge Genocide*, p. 64.
258. "Train hits Negro."
259. *Ibid.*
260. Patterson, *We Charge Genocide*, p. 64.
261. *Ibid.*, pp. 64–5.
262. Willie Henry, http://nuweb9.neu.edu/civilrights/arkansas-2/willie-henry.
263. NAACP legal file, http://nuweb9.neu.edu/civilrights/wp-content/uploads/NAACP-Papers.pdf.
264. Patterson, *We Charge Genocide*, p. 65.
265. *Ibid.*
266. John Jones, http://nuweb9.neu.edu/civilrights/louisiana/john-jones; "John Cecil Jones," http://en.wikipedia.org/wiki/John_Cecil_Jones.
267. *Ibid.*
268. "John Cecil Jones."
269. *Ibid.*
270. "O. H. Haynes, Jr.," http://en.wikipedia.org/wiki/O._H._Haynes,_Jr.
271. *Ibid.*
272. "John Jones."
273. "Seek gun in Elko lynching."
274. Patterson, *We Charge Genocide*, pp. 65, 68.
275. *Ibid.*, p. 65; Berry Branch death certificate.
276. Patterson, *We Charge Genocide*, p. 65.
277. "This week in black history"; Patterson, *We Charge Genocide*, p. 59; Guzman and Hughes, "Lynching," p. 4.
278. Noverta Robinson, http://nuweb9.neu.edu/civilrights/mississippi/noverta-robinson.
279. Patterson, *We Charge Genocide*, pp. 65–6.
280. "Berserk slayer is hunted down."
281. *Ibid.*

282. Newman, "'They shot me for nothing.'"
283. *Ibid.*
284. *Ibid.*
285. *Ibid.*
286. *Ibid.*; Social Security Death Index.
287. "Clear sheriff in JP court."
288. Matt McWilliams death certificate, http://nuweb9.neu.edu/civilrights/wp-content/uploads/Death-Certificate-2.pdf.
289. "Clear sheriff in JP court."
290. *Ibid.*; Matt McWilliams death certificate; USA Place Names, http://www.placenames.com/us; Daleville, Mississippi, http://en.wikipedia.org/wiki/Daleville%2C_Mississippi.
291. Tollison, "And then there were 14."
292. *Ibid.*; Whitehead, *FBI Story*, p. 258.
293. Whitehead, pp. 258–9; Moredock, "The good fight."
294. Moredock, "The good fight."
295. Newton, *Racial*, p. 423; Mexican-American Soldiers during the Second World War, http://server2.research-assistance.com/essays/MEXICAN-AMER—SOLDIERS-IN-WWII.html.
296. Patterson, *We Charge Genocide*, p. 67.
297. *Ibid.*, p. 66.
298. Mary Lizzie Noyes [sic], http://nuweb9.neu.edu/civilrights/alabama-2/mary-lizzie-noyes.
299. *Ibid.*
300. *Ibid.*
301. "Sheriff is making every effort"; Patterson, *We Charge Genocide*, p. 67.
302. "Sheriff is making every effort"; "Gretna shooting remains unsolved."
303. "Sheriff is making every effort."
304. "Franklin youth freed."
305. Patterson, *We Charge Genocide*, p. 67.
306. "Six Negro convicts killed."
307. "Five convicts slain."
308. "Six Negro convicts killed."
309. *Ibid.*
310. The Anguilla Prison Camp Massacre, http://www.usprisonculture.com/blog/2012/12/23/the-anguilla-prison-camp-massacre.
311. *Ibid.*
312. *Ibid.*
313. Patterson, *We Charge Genocide*, p. 68.
314. "Negro shot to death."
315. Patterson, *We Charge Genocide*, p. 68.
316. *Ibid.*
317. Amos Starr, http://nuweb9.neu.edu/civilrights/alabama-2/amos-starr.
318. Amos Starr death certificate, http://nuweb9.neu.edu/civilrights/wp-content/uploads/Amos-Starr-Death-Certificate1.pdf.
319. Amos Starr, http://nuweb9.neu.edu/civilrights/alabama-2/amos-starr.
320. *Ibid.*
321. Patterson, *We Charge Genocide*, p. 68.
322. *Ibid.*
323. *Ibid.*, pp. 68–9.
324. The Elmore Bolling Foundation, http://bollingfoundation.weebly.com.
325. *Ibid.*; Patterson, *We Charge Genocide*, p. 69.
326. Elmore Bolling—Lowndesboro, AL, U.S.A., http://www.waymarking.com/waymarks/WMJT2D_Elmore_Bolling_Lowndesboro_AL_USA.
327. Patterson, *We Charge Genocide*, p. 69.

328. "Ex-cop acquitted."
329. Patterson, *We Charge Genocide*, p. 69.
330. *Ibid.*, p. 70.
331. *Ibid.*, pp. 69–70.
332. *Ibid.*, p. 70.
333. Rosen, "The Murder of Ellis Hutson."
334. *Ibid.*
335. *Ibid.*
336. *Ibid.*
337. *Ibid.*
338. *Ibid.*
339. *Ibid.*
340. *Ibid.*
341. *Ibid.*
342. *Ibid.*
343. *Ibid.*
344. Nguyen, "Law enforcement involvement."
345. *Ibid.*
346. *Ibid.*
347. "SNYC asks probe."
348. Nguyen, "Law enforcement involvement."
349. *Ibid.*
350. *Ibid.*
351. "Marshal absolved."
352. Nevins, "The murder of Otis Newsome."
353. *Ibid.*
354. *Ibid.*
355. *Ibid.*
356. *Ibid.*; "Mistrial ordered."
357. Nevins.
358. *Ibid.*; "Kills Carolina funeral director"; "Strickland freed."
359. Patterson, *We Charge Genocide*, p. 70.
360. *Ibid.*
361. *Ibid.*
362. *Ibid.*
363. *Ibid.*
364. *Ibid.*
365. Isaac Crawford, http://nuweb9.neu.edu/civilrights/georgia/isaac-crawford-2.
366. "New affidavit sheds more light."
367. Isaac Crawford, http://nuweb9.neu.edu/civilrights/georgia/isaac-crawford-2.
368. "Probe of reported brutalities promised."
369. "Guards indicted."
370. "Wingard facing assault sentence."
371. Isaac Crawford, http://nuweb9.neu.edu/civilrights/georgia/isaac-crawford-2.
372. Patterson, *We Charge Genocide*, p. 71.
373. *Ibid.*
374. Historical Moments of Police Violence.
375. Patterson, *We Charge Genocide*, p. 71.
376. Historical Moments of Police Violence.
377. Patterson, *We Charge Genocide*, p. 71.
378. *Ibid.*
379. "Mayor won't act."
380. "Police beat man."
381. Patterson, *We Charge Genocide*, p. 71.
382. Three Governors Controversy, http://www.georgiaencyclopedia.org/articles/government-politics/three-governors-controversy.
383. "Says Georgia Negro slain for voting."
384. *Ibid.*
385. *Ibid.*; Isaiah Nixon, http://nuweb9.neu.edu/civilrights/isaiah-nixon.
386. Anderson, "Courier call"; Williams, "Isaiah Nixon's family."
387. Patterson, *We Charge Genocide*, p. 71.
388. *Ibid.*
389. "Crazed Negro shot and killed by police officer."
390. *Ibid.*
391. *Ibid.*
392. St. Tammany Parish Sheriff's Office History, http://www.stpso.com/about/history.
393. "Crazed Negro shot and killed by police officer."
394. Warren, "Duck."
395. *Ibid.*
396. *Ibid.*
397. *Ibid.*
398. "Howell acquitted."
399. Warren, "Duck."
400. *Ibid.*
401. *Ibid.*
402. "Talmadge demands."
403. *Ibid.*
404. Warren, "Duck."
405. *Ibid.*
406. *Ibid.*
407. *Ibid.*
408. *Ibid.*; "Howell acquitted."
409. "Howell acquitted."
410. "Two face jail"; Warren, "Duck."
411. Clark, "Klan in Orange County"; Andrews, "County's history"; Andrews, " Klan entrenched."
412. Patterson, *We Charge Genocide*, p. 72.
413. *Ibid.*
414. *Ibid.*
415. *Ibid.*
416. Patterson, *We Charge Genocide*, p. 72.
417. Manchester, Georgia, http://en.wikipedia.org/wiki/Manchester,_Georgia.
418. Patterson, *We Charge Genocide*, p. 72.
419. *Ibid.*
420. Ibeabuchi, "Lyching Death."
421. *Ibid.*
422. *Ibid.*
423. Sanderman, "Legal history."
424. *Ibid.*
425. *Ibid.*
426. "Chickasaw Countian on trial"; "Slain Negro's widow."
427. The Trouble I've Seen.
428. Sanderman, "Legal history."
429. *Ibid.*
430. *Ibid.*
431. Patterson, *We Charge Genocide*, p. 73.
432. *Ibid.*
433. Newton, *Invisible Empire*, pp. 119–20.
434. *Ibid.*
435. *Ibid.*, p. 123.
436. *Ibid.*, pp. 122–4.
437. Patterson, *We Charge Genocide*, p. 73.
438. *Ibid.*
439. *Ibid.*
440. *Ibid.*
441. *Ibid.*, pp. 73–4.
442. *Ibid.*, p. 74.
443. *Ibid.*
444. *Ibid.*
445. "Murder charge filed."
446. "Court convicts man."
447. Patterson, *We Charge Genocide*, p. 74.

448. *Ibid.*
449. Social Security Death Index, http://www.socialsecuritydeathindex-search.com.
450. Kates, "Search for a Just Prosecution."
451. *Ibid.*
452. *Ibid.*
453. *Ibid.*
454. *Ibid.*
455. *Ibid.*
456. "Clark and Mitcham charged"; "Mitcham and Clark plead."
457. "Mitcham and Clark are acquitted"; Kates.
458. Kates; "Federal grand jury indicts."
459. Kates; "Clark and Mitchum [*sic*] draw sentences."
460. Patterson, *We Charge Genocide*, p. 75.
461. "Gruesome murder weapons."
462. *Ibid.*
463. *Ibid.*
464. "Grand jury indicts"; "Hattie Mae Turner commits suicide"; "Suicide closes murder mystery."
465. Patterson, *We Charge Genocide*, p. 75.
466. *Ibid.*
467. *Ibid.*
468. *Ibid.*
469. *Ibid.*
470. *Ibid.*, pp. 75–6.
471. *Ibid.*, p. 76.
472. *Ibid.*
473. Rankin, "Negro slain."
474. *Ibid.*
475. *Ibid.*
476. *Ibid.*
477. Patterson, *We Charge Genocide*, p. 76.
478. *Ibid.*
479. *Ibid.*
480. *Ibid.*
481. *Ibid.*, p. 77.
482. "Twin counties probe deaths"; "Still mysterious."
483. "Nash Negro found burned"; "Twin counties probe deaths"; "No foul play."
484. "Edgecomb coroner's jury."
485. "Twin counties probe deaths."
486. "Still mysterious."
487. "Nash Negro found burned."
488. "Edgecomb coroner's jury."
489. *Ibid.*
490. Clark, "The Klan in Orange County."
491. *Ibid.*
492. *Ibid.*; Newton, *Invisible Empire*, p. 129.
493. Santich, "A tale of citrus and secrets"; Andrews, "Klan entrenched."
494. "Two handcuffed soldiers"; "Jury probe delayed."
495. "Police chief slays."
496. "Jury probe delayed"; "Take no action."
497. Dabney, "Found on fire"; "Five years later."
498. "Five years later."
499. *Ibid.*
500. *Ibid.*
501. *Ibid.*, Dabney, "Found on fire."
502. Patterson, *We Charge Genocide*, pp. 173–4.
503. Newton, *Invisible Empire*, p. 124.
504. *Ibid.*
505. *Ibid.*, p. 125.
506. Groveland Case, http://en.wikipedia.org/wiki/Groveland_Case.
507. John Hill, "A Southern sheriff's law and disorder," *St. Petersburg Times*, November 28, 1999.
508. John Mitchell, http://nuweb9.neu.edu/civilrights/louisiana/john-mitchell.
509. "Killing of man may be Dixie plot."
510. *Ibid.*
511. John Mitchell, http://nuweb9.neu.edu/civilrights/louisiana/john-mitchell.
512. Della McDuffie: http://nuweb9.neu.edu/civilrights/alabama-2/della-mcduffie; "FBI probe murder."
513. The Trouble I've Seen.
514. Della McDuffie: http://nuweb9.neu.edu/civilrights/alabama-2/della-mcduffie.
515. *Ibid.*; The Trouble I've Seen.
516. Windham, "Wilcox County sheriff."
517. "A flying sheriff."
518. Fleming, *In the Shadow*, p. 223; P. C. Lummie Jenkins, Ancestry.com.
519. "FBI probe murder."
520. http://www.oocities.org/colosseum/base/8507/NLDates3.htm.
521. Kempton, "What have they got."
522. *Ibid.*
523. *Ibid.*
524. Newman, "Hazel Brannon Smith," p. 224.
525. *Smith v. Byrd* 225 Miss. 331 (1955), 83 So. 2d 172.
526. Hunter, "Hinton slaying trial"; Hunter, "Jury out"; Shires, "Storekeeper's murder trial."
527. "Shopkeeper indicted"; Hunter, "Hinton slaying trial"; Shires, "Shopkeeper is acquitted."
528. Newton, *Racial*, p. 436.
529. Klopfer, "Murders around Mississippi."
530. "Johnnie Mae Chappell and the forgotten others."
531. Undated newspaper clippings, provided by Evelyn Screws, Eufala Carnegie Library, Nov. 3, 2014.
532. "Justice for all"; "Belzoni coroner promises."
533. Mendelsohn, *The Martyrs*, pp. 1–20.
534. Evers, *For Us the Living*, p. 204.
535. "Order autopsy"; "Edward Duckworth slain."
536. "Order autopsy"; "Negro may have died."
537. Edward Duckworth, http://nuweb9.neu.edu/civilrights/mississippi/edward-duckworth.
538. *Ibid.*
539. Rev. C. H. Baldwin, http://nuweb9.neu.edu/civilrights/rev-c-h-baldwin.
540. "Four Ala. men held."
541. Rev. C. H. Baldwin, http://nuweb9.neu.edu/civilrights/rev-c-h-baldwin.
542. Moody, pp. 142–6, 203.
543. Personal correspondence with the author, January 5 and 7, 2012.
544. *Ibid.*, January 7, 2012.
545. Newton, *Racial*, p. 439.
546. James Peterson, http://nuweb9.neu.edu/civilrights/mississippi/james-peterson.
547. "Blaine JP rules."
548. *Ibid.*
549. Klopfer, "Murders Around Mississippi"; http://www.oocities.org/colosseum/base/8507/NLDates3.htm.
550. "Police seize 8."
551. "Youth admits slaying."
552. "15 held."
553. "Many parents let sons."
554. "Vote to indict."

555. "Threaten four."
556. "15 enter plea."
557. Foree, "50 years."
558. "7 Palmer slayers."
559. "13 get new date."
560. Juliette Hampton Morgan, http://www.encyclopediaofalabama.org/face/Article.jsp?id=h-1581.
561. Ibid.
562. Klopfer, "Murders around Mississippi."
563. http://www.oocities.org/colosseum/base/8507/NLDates3.htm.
564. Barbara Patterson, "Defiance and dynamite," New South 18 (May 1963): 8–11.
565. "4 Deputies Wounded."
566. "Shooting spree kills Negro."
567. Ibid.
568. "Negro man shot down."
569. "Negro held on murder charge."
570. "Clarksdale NAACP urged FBI."
571. Clarksdale police report, http://mdah.state.ms.us/arrec/digital_archives/sovcom/result.php?image=images/png/cd01/001890.png&otherstuff=2|9|0|127|1|1|1|1846|#.
572. Jonas Causey, http://nuweb9.neu.edu/civilrights/jonas-causey.
573. Sovereignty Commission Online.
574. Clarksdale police report.
575. "Clarksdale NAACP urged FBI."
576. Jonas Causey, http://nuweb9.neu.edu/civilrights/jonas-causey.
577. Carson, Papers of Martin Luther King, p. 216.
578. Ibid.; Thornton, Dividing Lines, p. 408.
579. Carson, Papers, p. 216; Jackson, Becoming King, p. 172.
580. Thornton, Dividing Lines, p. 408; Bishop, The Days, 198–9.
581. Bishop, The Days, 198–9.
582. http://www.oocities.org/colosseum/base/8507/NLDates3.htm.
583. "Hold youths for slaying."
584. "Hold four in slaying ff Negro."
585. Croswell, "Wake man to pay."
586. Ibid.
587. Ibid.
588. Ibid.
589. "Puckett Negro found dead."
590. Leon Hooker affidavit.
591. Cleveland Holmes, http://nuweb9.neu.edu/civilrights/mississippi/cleveland-holmes.
592. Louis Stapleton, http://nuweb9.neu.edu/civilrights/louis-stapleton.
593. Sovereignty Commission Online, http://mdah.state.ms.us/arrec/digital_archives/sovcom/result.php?image=images/png/cd03/024362.png&otherstuff=2|62|1|13|2|1|1|23883|.
594. Louis Stapleton, http://nuweb9.neu.edu/civilrights/louis-stapleton.
595. Simon, Pedagogy of Witnessing, p. 57.
596. Evers, For Us, pp. 213–14.
597. Cagin and Dray, We Are Not Afraid, pp. 253–4.
598. Hattie Carroll, http://nuweb9.neu.edu/civilrights/hattie-carroll.
599. Slade, "True lies."
600. Hattie Carroll, http://nuweb9.neu.edu/civilrights/hattie-carroll.

601. Ibid.
602. SNCC, A Chronology of Violence, p. 15.
603. Delta Democrat-Times, July 2, 1963.
604. Klopfer, "Murders around Mississippi."
605. SPLC, "The Forgotten."
606. Clyde Kennard, http://en.wikipedia.org/wiki/Clyde_Kennard.
607. Ibid.
608. Ibid.
609. Ibid.
610. Ibid.
611. Lotito, "Slaying linked."
612. Ibid.; Hendricks, "Witness cue"; "Testimony ends."
613. "Court is told of brawl."
614. "Victim's friend testifies."
615. Hendricks, "Defendant in murder case."
616. "Murder jury hears boy."
617. Hymes, "Ship worker charged."
618. Ibid.; "Man is charged."
619. "New jury list."
620. "Will show self-defense."
621. Hendricks, "Defendant in murder case."
622. "Gun clicked before jury."
623. Hendricks, "Warfel is guilty"; "Warfel gets 10 years."
624. SPLC, "Murder victim's son."
625. Student Nonviolent Coordinating Committee. A Chronology of Violence and Intimidation, p. 15.
626. Klopfer, "Murders around Mississippi."
627. McWhorter, Carry Me Home, pp. 499–500.
628. Ibid.
629. Klopfer, "Murders Around Mississippi."
630. Greenberg, "Cold-case list omits many names."
631. Payne, I've Got the Light of Freedom, pp. 298–9.
632. Schwartz, "A White Boy Goes to Mississippi," p. 13.
633. SNCC, Chronology of Violence, p. 18.
634. Klopfer, "Murders Around Mississippi."
635. Greenberg, "A Deep South Cold Case Goes Frigid."
636. Newton, Racial, p. 467.
637. "Negro youth killed."
638. Sellers, "Killed."
639. Mississippi Civil Rights Martyrs.
640. Sellers, "Killed."
641. Breed and Cohen, "50 years ago."
642. Sellers, "Killed."
643. Klopfer, "Murders around Mississippi."
644. SPLC, "The Forgotten."
645. http://www.oocities.org/colosseum/base/8507/NLDates3.htm.
646. Parker, Violence, p. 101.
647. "Mutilation victim dies."
648. Ibid.
649. Ibid.
650. Klopfer, "Murders around Mississippi."
651. SPLC, "The Forgotten."
652. "Negro killed, hit by train."
653. "Detroit Negro slain."
654. Sovereignty Commission Online, http://mdah.state.ms.us/arrec/digital_archives/sovcom/result.php?image=images/png/cd07/054194.png&otherstuff=2|165|5|51|1|1|1|53452|#.
655. Sovereignty Commission Online, http://mdah.state.ms.us/arrec/digital_archives/sovcom/re

sult.php?image=images/png/cd07/053920.png&otherstuff=2|165|5|16|4|1|1|53180|#.
  656. Lillie Dell Power, http://nuweb9.neu.edu/civilrights/lillie-dell-power.
  657. "Suspect in murder called Klansman."
  658. "Mechanic is guilty."
  659. Gitin, "In memory."
  660. Wilcox County Freedom Fighters, http://thislittlelight1965.wordpress.com/2013/06/28/wilcox-county-al-civil-rights-timeline-june-1965.
  661. Gitin, "In memory."
  662. "Colston seeks House District 69 seat," *Selma Times-Journal*, November 10, 2009; David Colston, http://ballotpedia.org/David_Colston.
  663. "Johnnie Mae Chappell and the forgotten others."
  664. "Man accused of shooting Negro."
  665. *Ibid.*; "Officer Shot."
  666. http://dlg.galileo.usg.edu/baldy/jpgs/chb233lo.jpg.
  667. "Medal given to soldier."
  668. Klopfer, "Murders around Mississippi."
  669. *Ibid.*
  670. "Accuse four of larceny of vehicle," *Waterloo Daily Courier*, February 4, 1966.
  671. Waterloo Crisis, http://www.iowa.gov/government/crc/docs/annual66waterloo.html.
  672. "Report on Sallis."
  673. "Sallis suit."
  674. "Judge throws out."
  675. "Dismisses bias suit."
  676. Gallagher and Lippard, *Race and Racism*, p. 271.
  677. "Arrest two Bogalusa men."
  678. Gallagher and Lippard, *Race and Racism*, p. 271.
  679. Fair or Not, https://cathymong1229.wordpress.com/2013/12/16/fair-or-not; Why I Am American Baptist: Part 1, http://abcnyexecutiveminister.blogspot.com/2014/10/why-i-am-american-baptist-part-1.html.
  680. Robinson, "A timeline."
  681. "Visitor shot by trooper."
  682. *Ibid.*
  683. *Ibid.*
  684. "Another shooting in Birmingham area."
  685. *Ibid.*
  686. *Ibid.*
  687. *Ibid.*
  688. "Ala. deputies kill Negro in fuss over dog."
  689. "Fire attempt failed"; "Wife of Negro minister shot to death."
  690. *Ibid.*
  691. Honoring Ministerial Mentors who led positive changes in Atlanta's Urban Communities, http://www.prlog.org/11463710-honoring-ministerial-mentors-who-led-positive-changes-in-atlantas-urban-communities.html.
  692. Reisig, "Citizens protest Rasberry death."
  693. *Ibid.*
  694. "Justice Dept. investigates possible Ala. lynching."
  695. Labarre, "White jury frees Negro."
  696. Clark, "Negro youth, 18, shot by police."
  697. *Ibid.*
  698. *Ibid.*
  699. Clark, "'Hell no, we don't like it.'"
  700. Rubin, "Another fatal arrest."
  701. *Ibid.*
  702. Rubin, "Another fatal arrest."
  703. *Ibid.*
  704. *Ibid.*
  705. Reisig, "Another B'ham killing."
  706. *Ibid.*
  707. "Johnnie Mae Chappell and the forgotten others."
  708. York, Ambient Witness.
  709. 1967 Detroit Riot, http://en.wikipedia.org/wiki/1967_Detroit_riot#Arrests.
  710. Anarchy at the Algiers.
  711. Hersey, *Algiers Motel*, pp. 245–330.
  712. *People v. Paille*.
  713. Hersey, *Algiers Motel*, pp. 245–330.
  714. *Ibid.*
  715. *Ibid.*
  716. A Moment Of Insanity.
  717. Schroeder, "Jury finds Detroit police innocent."
  718. "Johnnie Mae Chappell and the forgotten others."
  719. York, Ambient Witness.
  720. "Manslaughter charges filed"; "Officer found innocent."
  721. "Manslaughter charges filed."
  722. *Ibid.*
  723. "Dayton police battle riot."
  724. "Officer found innocent."
  725. *Ibid.*
  726. Wilcox, "One year for Selma killing."
  727. *Ibid.*
  728. *Ibid.*
  729. "One year for shots."
  730. *Ibid.*
  731. Rubin, "Holly Springs death is still mystery."
  732. *Ibid.*
  733. *Ibid.*
  734. Gale, "Lee youth killed."
  735. *Ibid.*
  736. *Ibid.*
  737. *Ibid.*
  738. Black Guerilla Family, http://www.assatashakur.org/forum/carriers-torch/47661-black-guerilla-family-black-liberation-army-black-militant-front-peoples-army.html.
  739. *Ibid.*
  740. Hewitt and Slania, "Slow justice."
  741. *Ibid.*
  742. "Indiana man held."
  743. Hewitt and Slania, "Slow justice."
  744. Phillips, "'B'ham cop shot him while his hands were in the air.'"
  745. *Ibid.*
  746. O'Reilly, *"Race Matters,"* pp. 293–324.
  747. *Ibid.*; Maulana Karenga, http://en.wikipedia.org/wiki/Maulana_Karenga.
  748. O'Reilly, *"Race Matters,"* pp. 293–324.
  749. Maulana Karenga, http://en.wikipedia.org/wiki/Maulana_Karenga.
  750. Edwin T. Pratt, http://en.wikipedia.org/wiki/Edwin_T._Pratt.
  751. Trescases, "Edwin Pratt is murdered."
  752. *Ibid.*
  753. Anderson, "He killed Edwin Pratt."
  754. *Ibid.*

755. *Ibid.*
756. *Ibid.*
757. King, *Daddy King,* p. 192.
758. King, *AD and ML King,* pp. 52–3.
759. 1969 York Race Riot, http://en.wikipedia.org/wiki/1969_York_Race_Riot.
760. *Ibid.*
761. *Ibid.*
762. *Ibid.*
763. "6 get prison terms for roles in '69 York, Pa., slaying."
764. "2 guilty in '69 race riot death get prison."
765. 1969 York Race Riot.
766. "$2M settlement reached for '69 race-riot killing."
767. Fred Hampton, http://en.wikipedia.org/wiki/Fred_Hampton.
768. *Ibid.*
769. *Ibid.*
770. *Ibid.*
771. *Ibid.*
772. *Ibid.*; Gregory, "The Black Panther raid."
773. Churchill and Vander Wall, Agents of Repression, pp. 69–70.
774. Fred Hampton; Swearingen, *FBI Secrets.*
775. Edward Hanrahan, http://en.wikipedia.org/wiki/Edward_Hanrahan.
776. Blau, "Panther informant death ruled suicide"; Fred Hampton.
777. Yee, "Death on the yard."
778. *Ibid.*
779. *Ibid.*; "Day 652."
780. Marin County courthouse incident, http://en.wikipedia.org/wiki/Marin_County_courthouse_incident.
781. "Day 652."
782. "Guard kills 3 prisoners"; Marin County courthouse incident.
783. Marin County courthouse incident.
784. *Ibid.*
785. San Quentin Six, http://en.wikipedia.org/wiki/San_Quentin_Six#Fleeta_Drumgo.
786. Marin County courthouse incident.
787. Bernstein, "Bomb blast victim."
788. Umoja, *We Will Shoot Back,* p. 179.
789. *Ibid.,* p. 180; Jay, "Car blast kills 2."
790. Jay, "Car blast kills 2"; H. Rap Brown, http://en.wikipedia.org/wiki/H._Rap_Brown.
791. Umoja, *We Will Shoot Back,* p. 180.
792. Brown, "Trial begins"; Rainey Pool, http://nuweb9.neu.edu/civilrights/rainey-pool.
793. "3 Guilty."
794. *Caston v. State.*
795. Mississippi Civil Rights Martyrs; Jackson State Killings, http://en.wikipedia.org/wiki/Jackson_State_killings.
796. *Ibid.*
797. Reeves, "Despite disappointment."
798. McGraw and Rice, "Unsolved killing."
799. *Ibid.*
800. McGraw and Rice, "Evidence points."
801. McGraw, "The missing gun."
802. McGraw and Rice, "Evidence points." McGraw and Rice, "Unsolved killing."
803. McGraw and Rice, "Unsolved killing."
804. "John Thomas was killed 'fer nothin'."
805. *Ibid.*
806. *Ibid.*; "Mississippi Civil Rights Martyrs."
807. "West Point election today."
808. Newton, *Hate Crime in America,* p. 22.
809. Rubén Salazar, http://en.wikipedia.org/wiki/Rub%C3%A9n_Salazar.
810. Tovar, "History timeline"; del Olmos, "Perspective."
811. del Olmos, "Perspective"; Rubén Salazar, http://en.wikipedia.org/wiki/Rub%C3%A9n_Salazar.
812. Tovar, "History timeline"; Chicano Moratorium.
813. Tovar, "History timeline"; Chicano Moratorium; Lopez, "No evidence."

Bibliography

Books

Ames, Jessie Daniel. *The Changing Character of Lynching: Review of Lynching 1931–1941*. Atlanta: Commission on Interracial Cooperation, 1942.

Ball, Howard. *Justice in Mississippi: The Murder Trial of Edgar Ray Killen*. St. Lawrence: University Press of Kansas, 2006.

_____. *Murder in Mississippi: United States v. Price and the Struggle for Civil Rights*. St. Lawrence: University Press of Kansas, 2004.

Bass, Jack, and Jack Nelson. *The Orangeburg Massacre*. Macon: Mercer University Press, 1992.

Biondi, Martha. *To Stand and Fight: The Struggle for Civil Rights in Postwar New York City*. Cambridge: Harvard University Press, 2009.

Bishop, Jim. *The Days of Martin Luther King, Jr.* New York: G. P. Putnam's Sons, 1971.

Bond, Horace Mann. *The Star Creek Papers: Washington Parish and the Lynching of Jerome Wilson*. Athens: University of Georgia Press, 2011.

Branch, Taylor. *At Canaan's Edge: America in the King Years, 1965–68*. New York: Simon & Schuster, 2006.

_____. *Parting the Waters: America in the King Years, 1954–63*. New York: Simon & Schuster, 1989.

_____. *Pillar of Fire: America in the King Years, 1963–65*. New York: Simon & Schuster, 1998.

Bullard, Sara. *Free At Last: A History of the Civil Rights Movement and Those Who Died in the Struggle*. New York: Oxford University Press, 1993.

Cagin, Seth. *We Are Not Afraid: The Story of Goodman, Schwerner, and Chaney, and the Civil Rights Campaign for Mississippi*. New York: Macmillan, 1988.

Capeci, Dominic J. Jr. *The Lynching of Cleo Wright*. Lexington: University Press of Kentucky, 1998.

Carson, Clayborne, ed. *The Papers of Martin Luther King, Jr. Vol. V: Threshold of a New Decade, January 1959-December 1960*. Berkeley: University of California Press, 2005.

Case, Carroll. *The Slaughter: An American Atrocity*. Magnolia, MS: First Biltmore Corporation, 1998.

Churchill, Ward, and Jim Vander Wall. *Agents of Repression: The FBI's Secret Wars Against the Black Panther Party and the American Indian Movement*. Boston: South End Press, 1988.

Cox, Dale. *The Claude Neal Lynching: The 1934 Murders of Claude Neal and Lola Cannady*. Bascom, FL: Old Kitchen Books, 2012.

Dittmer, John. *Local People: The Struggle for Civil Rights in Mississippi*. Urbana: University of Illinois Press, 1994.

Doyle, William. *An American Insurrection: The Battle of Oxford, Mississippi, 1962*. New York: Doubleday, 2001.

Dray, Philip. *At the Hands of Persons Unknown: The Lynching of Black America*. New York: Modern Library, 2007.

Eagles, Charles. *Outside Agitator: Jon Daniels and the Civil Rights Movement in Alabama*. Montgomery: University Alabama Press, 2000.

_____. *The Price of Defiance: James Meredith and the Integration of Ole Miss*. Chapel Hill: University of North Carolina Press, 2009.

Evers, Myrlie, and William Peters. *For Us, the Living*. New York: Doubleday, 1967.

Evers-Williams, Myrlie, and Manning Marable, eds. *The Autobiography of Medgar Evers: A Hero's Life and Legacy Revealed Through His Writings, Letters, and Speeches*. New York: Basic Books, 2006.

Fleming, Cynthia Griggs. *In the Shadow of Selma: The Continuing Struggle for Civil Rights in the Rural South*. Lanham, MD: Rowman & Littlefield, 2004.

Forman, James. *Sammy Younge, Jr.: The First Black College Student to Die in the Black Liberation Movement*. New York: Grove Press, 1968.

Gallagher, Charles, and Cameron D. Lippard, eds. *Race and Racism in the United States: An Encyclopedia of the American Mosaic*. Santa Barbara: ABC-CLIO, 2014.

Green, Ben. *Before His Time: The Untold Story of Harry T. Moore, America's First Civil Rights Martyr*. New York: Free Press, 1999.

Greenhaw, Wayne. *Fighting the Devil in Dixie: How Civil Rights Activists Took on the Ku Klux Klan in Alabama*. Chicago: Chicago Review Press, 2011.

Howlett, Duncan. *No Greater Love: The James Reeb Story*. New York: Harper & Row, 1966.

Hudson-Weems, Clenora. *Emmett Till: The Sacrificial Lamb of the Civil Rights Movement*. Bloomington: AuthorHouse, 2006.

Jackson, Troy. *Becoming King: Martin Luther King, Jr. and the Making of a National Leader*. Lexington: University Press of Kentucky, 2008.

Jean, Susan. "'Warranted lynchings': Narratives of mob violence in southern white newspapers, 1880–1940," in *Lynching Reconsidered: New Perspectives in the Study of Mob Violence*. New York: Routledge, 2014.

Kennedy, Stetson. *The Klan Unmasked*. Boca Raton: Florida Atlantic University Press, 1954.

King, Gilbert. *Devil in the Grove: Thurgood Marshall, the Groveland Boys and the Dawn of a New America*. New York: Harper, 2012.

King, Martin Luther Sr., and Clayton Riley. *Daddy King: An Autobiography*. New York: William Morrow & Co., 1980.

King, Naomi Ruth Barber. *AD and ML King: Two Brothers Who Dared to Dream*. Bloomington, IN: AuthorHouse, 2014.

Lord, Walter. *The Past That Would Not Die*. New York: Harper & Row, 1965.

Mack, Dwayne A. *Black Spokane: The Civil Rights Struggle in the Inland Northwest*. Norman: University of Oklahoma Press, 2014.

MacLean, Harry N. *The Past Is Never Dead: The Trial of James Ford Seale and Mississippi's Struggle for Redemption*. New York: Basic Civitas Books, 2009.

May, Gary. *The Informant: The FBI, the Ku Klux Klan, and the Murder of Viola Liuzzo*. New Haven: Yale University Press, 2005.

McGovern, James R. *Anatomy of a Lynching: The Killing of Claude Neal*. Baton Rouge: Louisiana State University Press, 1982.

McMillen, Neil R. *Dark Journey: Black Mississippians in the Age of Jim Crow*. Champaign: University of Illinois Press, 1990.

McWhorter, Diane. *Carry Me Home: Birmingham, Alabama: The Climactic Battle of the Civil Rights Revolution*. New York: Simon & Schuster, 2001.

Melanson, Philip H. *The Martin Luther King Assassination: New Revelations on the Conspiracy and Cover-Up, 1968–1991*. New York: Shapolsky Publishers, 1994.

Mendelsohn, Jack. *The Martyrs: Sixteen Who Gave Their Lives for Racial Justice*. New York: Harper & Row, 1966.

Minor, Robert. *Lynching and Frame-Up in Tennessee*. New York: New Century Publishers, 1946.

Moody, Anne. *Coming of Age in Mississippi*. New York: Doubleday, 1968.

National Association for the Advancement of Colored People. *NAACP Annual Report*. New York: NAACP, 1937.

Newman, Mark. "Hazel Brannon Smith (1914–1994): Journalist under siege," in *Mississippi Women: Their Histories, Their Lives*, Volume 1. Athens: University of Georgia Press, 2003.

Newton, Michael. *The FBI and the KKK: A Critical History*. Jefferson, NC: McFarland, 2009.

_____. *The Invisible Empire: The Ku Klux Klan in Florida*. Gainesville: University Press of Florida, 2001.

_____. *Hate Crime in America, 1968–2013: A Chronology of Offenses, Legislation and Related Events*. Jefferson, NC: McFarland, 2014.

_____. *The Ku Klux Klan: History, Organization, Language, Influence and Activities of America's Most Notorious Secret Society*. Jefferson, NC: McFarland, 2006

_____. *The Ku Klux Klan in Mississippi: A History*. Jefferson, NC: McFarland, 2010.

_____. *Ku Klux Terror: Birmingham, Alabama, from 1866-Present*. Atglen, PA: Schiffer Publishing, 2013.

_____. *Racial and Religious Violence in America: A Chronology*. New York: Garland Publishing, 1991.

_____. *White Robes and Burning Crosses: A History of the Ku Klux Klan from 1866*. Jefferson, NC: McFarland, 2014.

O'Reilly, Kenneth. *"Racial Matters": The FBI's Secret File on Black America, 1960–1972*. New York: Free Press, 1989.

Parker, Thomas F., ed. *Violence in the U.S. Volume 1, 1956–67*. New York: Facts on File, 1974.

Patterson, William L., ed. *We Charge Genocide: The Historic Petition to the United Nations for Relief from a Crime of the United States Government Against the Negro People*. New York: Civil Rights Congress, 1951.

Payne, Charles M. *I've Got the Light of Freedom: The Organizing Tradition and the Mississippi Freedom Struggle*. Berkeley: University of California Press, 2007.

Romano, Renee C. *Racial Reckoning: Prosecuting America's Civil Rights Murders*. Cambridge: Harvard University Press, 2014.

Schwartz, Joseph. "A White Boy Goes to Mississippi," in *Terror Within and Without: Attachment and Disintegration: Clinical Work on the Edge*. London: Karnac Books, 2013.

Shapiro, Herbert. *White Violence and Black Response: From Reconstruction to Montgomery*. Amherst, MA: University of Massachusetts Press, 1988.

Simon, Roger I. *Pedagogy of Witnessing: Curatorial Practice and the Pursuit of Social Justice*. Albany: SUNY Press, 2014.

Simpson, Mark. *In Search of Justice: Examining Efforts to Obtain Convictions in Unsolved Civil Rights Era Murders in Mississippi*. Bloomington, IN: iUniverse, 2006.

Smead, Howard. *Blood Justice: The Lynching of Mack Charles Parker*. New York: Oxford University Press, 1988.

Spofford, Tim. *Lynch Street: The May 1970 Slayings at Jackson State College*. Kent: Kent State University Press, 1989.

Stanton, Mary. *Freedom Walk: Mississippi or Bust*. Oxford: University Press of Mississippi, 2010.

_____. *From Selma to Sorrow: The Life and Death of Viola Liuzzo*. Athens: University of Georgia Press, 1998.

Student Nonviolent Coordinating Committee. *A Chronology of Violence and Intimidation in Mississippi Since 1961*. Atlanta: SNCC, 1964.

Swearingen, M. Wesley. *FBI Secrets: An Agent's Expose*. Boston: South End Press. 1995.

Till-Mobley, Mamie, and Christopher Benson. *Death of Innocence: The Story of the Hate Crime That Changed America*. New York: One World/ Ballantine, 2004.

Thornton, J. Mills. *Dividing Lines: Municipal Politics and the Struggle for Civil Rights in Montgomery, Birmingham, and Selma.* Tuscaloosa: University of Alabama Press, 2002.

Tuck, Stephen G. N. *Beyond Atlanta: The Struggle for Racial Equality in Georgia, 1940–1980.* Athens: University of Georgia Press, 2003.

Umoja, Akinyele Omowale. *We Will Shoot Back: Armed Resistance in the Mississippi Freedom Movement.* New York: NYU Press, 2013.

Urofsky, Melvin I., ed. *100 Americans Making Constitutional History: A Biographical History.* Thousand Oaks, CA: CQ Press, 2004.

Waldrep, Christopher, ed. *Lynching in America.* New York: NYU Press, 2006.

Waldron, Lamar, and Thom Hartmann. *Legacy of Secrecy: The Long Shadow of the JFK Assassination.* Berkeley: Counterpoint Press, 2013.

Weiss, Myra Tanner. *Vigilante Terror in Fontana: The Tragic Story of O'Day H. Short and His Family.* Los Angeles: Socialist Workers Party, 1946.

Wexler, Stuart, and Larry Hancock. *The Awful Grace of God: Religious Terrorism, White Supremacy, and the Unsolved Murder of Martin Luther King, Jr.* Berkeley: Counterpoint Press, 2012.

Whitehead, Don. *The FBI Story: A Report to the People.* New York: Random House, 1956.

Whitfield, Stephen J. *A Death in the Delta: The Story of Emmett Till.* Baltimore: Johns Hopkins University Press, 1991.

Wright, George C. *Racial Violence in Kentucky, 1865–1940: Lynchings, Mob Rule, and "Legal Lynchings."* Baton Rouge: Louisiana State University Press, 1996.

Articles and Other Media Reports

"Accosts three white girls; Alabama Negro lynched." *Chicago Daily Tribune*, August 24, 1934.

"Accused in 1964 Mississippi race slayings wrote hate letter." Canadian Broadcasting Corporation, March 9, 2007.

"Accused Negro is lynched in north Florida." *Sarasota Herald Tribune*, June 16, 1943.

"Aged Amite Negro slain Sunday morning at his home, near Berwick." *Southern Herald*, March 30, 1944.

"Aged Negro found slain near still." *Selma Times-Journal*, July 2, 1945.

"Ala. deputies kill Negro in fuss over dog." *Jet*, February 16, 1967.

Anderson, Devery. "Widow of Emmett Till killer dies quietly, notoriously." *Clarion-Ledger*, February 27, 2014.

Anderson, Rick. "He killed Edwin Pratt." *Seattle Weekly*, May 24, 2011.

Anderson, Trezzvant W. "Courier call gets results." *Pittsburgh Courier*, January 1, 1949.

Andrews, Mark. "County's history includes dark chapters of KKK terror." *Orlando Sentinel*, May 9, 1999.

———. "Klan entrenched in Orange County before bombings." *Orlando Sentinel*, August 17, 2006.

"Angry miners lynch him." *Hope Star*, January 25, 1934.

"Another shooting in Birmingham area." *Southern Courier*, February 4–5, 1967.

"Armed mob force jail, lynch Negro held for slugging." *Daily Illlini*, January 25, 1934.

"Arrest two Bogalusa men in slaying of a war vet." *Pittsburgh Courier*, August 13, 1966.

Atkins, Walter. "Shubuta bridge's toll stands at six lynch victims, but span is doomed." *Chicago Defender*, November 7, 1942.

Barnidge, Matthew. "Connected by vice: the Longs, Marcello & Concordia." *Concordia Sentinel*, July 9, 2009.

Barry, Dan, Campbell Robertson, and Robbie Brown. "When cold cases stay cold." *New York Times*, March 16, 2013.

Barry, Dan. "Killing and segregated plaque divide town." *New York Times*, March 18, 2007.

Bass, Jack. "Documenting the Orangeburg Massacre." *Nieman Reports* 57 (Fall 2003): 8–11.

"Believe Miss. death was 'lynching.'" *Pittsburgh Courier*, November 21, 1959.

"Belzoni coroner promises jury on mysterious death." *Delta Democrat-Times*, February 1, 1956.

Bernstein, Adam. "William Zantzinger; infamous after Dylan song 'Hattie Carroll.'" *Washington Post*, January 10, 2009.

Bernstein, Carl. "Bomb blast victim was a noted civil rights activist." *Washington Post*, March 11, 1970.

Bernstein, Victor H. "Folks in Dixie 'lynch town' don't care about FBI probe." *Pittsburgh Courier*, October 31, 1942.

"Berserk slayer is hunted down, killed by posse." *Weekly Moultrie Observer*, November 22, 1946.

"B'ham justice: Tougher on bricks than bullets or bombs." *Jet*, April 16, 1964.

"Blaine JP rules marshal shot in self defense." *Delta Democrat-Times*, December 6, 1956.

Blau, Robert. "Panther informant death ruled suicide," Chicago Tribune, January 18, 1990.

Bluestein, Greg. "Ga. authorities probe 1946 unsolved lynchings." *USA Today*, July 2, 2008.

"Boy left for dead by lynchers tells how he fled to the North." *PM*, August 30, 1946.

Boyack, James Edmund. "U.S. hints action in Ga. lynch case." *Pittsburgh Courier*, January 8, 1949.

Bradley Hobbs, Tamika. "'Hitler is here': Lynching in Florida during the era of World War II." Ph.D. dissertation, Florida State University, 2004.

Bragg, Rick. "Last cry for justice in Mississippi as U.S. trial revisits '66 killing." *New York Times*, January 26, 2003.

Breed, Allen G. "End of Till case draws mixed response." *Boston Globe*, March 3, 2007.

Breed, Allen G., and Sharon Cohen. "50 years ago, 'Freedom Summer' changed South, US." Associated Press, June 16, 2014.

Breed, Allen G., and Holbrook Mohr. "FBI says the end is near for investigations into civil rights-era cold cases." *Huffington Post*, November 5, 2011.

Brinkerhoff, Noel. "FBI still working on 108 civil rights murder cold cases." AllGov, November 21, 2009.

———. "Why is the FBI still hiding information about the assassination of Martin Luther King?" AllGov, January 19, 2010.
Brown, Timothy R. "Trial begins in 1970 death of black man." *Amarillo Globe-News*, November 12, 1999.
Browning, Michael. "Who was Harry T. Moore?" *Palm Beach Post*, August 16, 1999.
"Brutal beating by cops blamed for man's death." *New Orleans Informer & Sentinel*, May 6, 1944.
Burch, Audra D. S. "60 years later: A cry for justice in Fla. killing." *Baltimore Sun*, December 10, 2006.
"Cases the FBI re-investigated as part of its Civil Rights Cold Case Initiative." *Baltimore Sun*, June 1, 2013.
"Chain Arkansas farmer to tree, set him afire." *Chicago Defender*, June 26, 1954.
"Chained to tree, burned to death." *Pittsburgh Courier*, June 19, 1954.
"The Carol Jenkins slaying: Suspect dies before trial in 1968 Martinsville stabbing." *Indianapolis Star*, September 1, 2002.
Chandler, D. L. "Sammy Younge killed for using whites-only bathroom on this day in 1966." NewsOne.com, January 3, 2014.
"Charred body is still a mystery." *Arkansas State Press*, June 18, 1954.
"Chickasaw Countian on trial today in death of Negro, 45." *Tupelo Daily Journal*, March 31, 1950.
"City patrolman shoots Negro soldier." *Chicago Defender*, March 24, 1942.
"Civil rights cold cases: 'We are writing to inform you...'" *New York Times*, March 16, 2013.
"Civil rights: We are dedicated." *Time*, April 17, 1964.
Clark, James C. "Klan buster." *Orlando Sentinel*, July 7, 1991.
———. "The Klan in Orange County." *Orlando Sentinel*, October 17, 1991.
Clark, Joan. "'Hell no, we don't like it.'" *Southern Courier*, February 25–26, 1967.
———. "Negro youth, 18, shot by police." *Southern Courier*, February 25–26, 1967.
"Clark and Mitcham charged with murder in death of Negro." *Lafayette Sun*, February 22, 1950.
"Clark and Mitchum [sic] draw sentences in civil rights case." *Lafayette Sun*, November 1, 1950.
"Clarksdale NAACP urged FBI to investigate slaying of Negro." *Jackson Advocate*, May 22, 1959.
"Clarksdale NAACP urged FBI to investigate slaying of Negro." *Jackson Advocate*, May 23, 1959.
"Clear sheriff in JP court." *Kemper County Messenger*, January 9, 1947.
Cohen, Andrew P. "The lynching of James Scales: How the FBI, the DOJ, and state authorities 'whitewashed' racial violence in Bledsoe County, Tennessee." *Texas Journal on Civil Liberties & Civil Rights* 19 (2014): 285–334.
"Cold case: Five motives for Morris' murder." *Concordia Sentinel*, November 13, 2008.
"Cold case: Subject in Frank Morris arson dies." *Concordia Sentinel*, May 8, 2013.
"Court convicts man of murder, gives sentence." *Pulaski Southwest Times*, March 5, 1950.

"Court is told of brawl in soldier death." *Washington Post and Times-Herald*, November 7, 1963.
"Court reverses Crews decision." Associated Press, March 18, 1947.
"Courts lacked evidence; lynch mob didn't need it." *Afro-American*, July 24, 1943.
Cox, Major. "Justice still absent in bridge death." *Montgomery Advertiser*, March 2, 1999.
"Crazed Negro shot and killed by police officer." *St. Tammany Farmer*, October 15, 1948.
Croswell, Jack. "Wake man to pay $2,750 to family of Negro victim in playful killing." *News and Observer*, August 25, 1959.
"Crowds pack courtroom as five Minden suspects go to trial." *Pittsburgh Courier*, March 1, 1947.
Dabney, Thomas L. "Found on fire in street, man dies in hospital." *New Journal and Guide*, June 2, 1951.
———. "2,000 gather for rites for Rev. Joseph H. Mann." *New Journal and Guide*, June 9, 1951.
Daly, Pete. "Libel? A defender of the downtrodden is put on trial." *Michigan History Magazine*, July 1, 2010.
Davies, Nick. "The deadly secrets of a small town in Texas." *The Guardian* (London), February 1, 1991.
"Dayton police battle riot in 12-block area." *Chicago Tribune*, September 20, 1967.
"Defiant Dixie in poll tax rout, lynches 2, forms vigilantes." *Amsterdam Star-News*, October 17, 1942.
"Detroit Negro slain; seek white youths." *Chicago Tribune*, November 8, 1965.
Dewan, Shaila. "Ex-Klansman guilty of manslaughter in 1964 deaths." *New York Times*, June 22, 2005.
———. "Push to resolve fading killings of rights era." *New York Times*, February 3, 2007.
———. "Scant progress in effort on old racial killings." *New York Times*, August 23, 2010.
"Dismisses bias suit vt. [sic] city." *Waterloo Courier*, June 18, 1968.
"Dual lynching condemned by nation." *Winona Times*, April 16, 1937.
Dunn, Martin. "Justice for Willie James." *Tampa Tribune*, November 18, 2007.
"Edward Duckworth slain near Mize." *Smith County Reformer*, February 2, 1956.
"8 in posse give bond in shooting." *Commercial-News*, July 13, 1943.
"Eight men on trial for slaying of Negro farm hand on June 24, 1934." *Manchester Times*, September 6, 1934.
"Ernest Avants, 72, plotter against Dr. King." *New York Times*, June 17, 2004.
"Ex-cop acquitted." *Corsicana Daily Sun*, October 5, 1949.
"Ex-sheriff's hearing set at Terre Haute." *Commercial-News*, July 17, 1943.
"Farmer convicted in barmaid's death." *New York Times*, June 28, 1963.
"FBI gets Miss. murder list." *Chicago Defender*, July 16, 1964.
"FBI men move into Mississippi." *Pittsburgh Courier*, October 24, 1942.

"FBI probe murder of Ala. woman." *Chicago Defender*, July 25, 1963.
"FBI studying 3 deaths in N.C." *Fayetteville Observer*, March 5, 2007.
"FBI to probe mystery death of Alabama Negro." *Jet*, June 15, 1967.
"FBI will not reinvestigate Orangeburg Massacre." *Times and Democrat*, December 1, 2007.
"Federal grand jury indicts Clark and Mitchum [*sic*] in Negro death." *Lafayette Sun*, September 27, 1950.
"15 enter plea of innocent in Palmer death." *Chicago Daily Tribune*, March 28, 1957.
"15 held for teen murder." *Chicago Daily Tribune*, March 15, 1957.
"Find body of Negro sought by posse." *Terre Haute Tribune,*, November 28, 1942.
"Fire attempt failed, Atlanta cleric's wife killed." *Jet*, February 16, 1967.
"Five convicts slain in break in Georgia." *New York Times*, July 12, 1947.
"Five years later Norfolk still asks: Who killed Rev. Mann?" *New Journal and Guide*, May 26, 1956.
Fleming, John. "A more complete picture of a forgotten, long ago, death." *Anniston Star*, February 17, 2008.
_____. "Another forgotten found." *Anniston Star*, March 25, 2007.
_____. "Author: Killen was indifferent to killings but in '76 interview, he denied complicity." *Clarion-Ledger*, August 19, 2005.
_____. "Cold cases challenge the search for civil rights-era justice." *Anniston Star*, August 7, 2010.
_____. "Families of those slain during civil rights movement meet in Atlanta." *Anniston Star*, April 23, 2010.
_____. "Former state trooper, 77, gets six month sentence for civil rights-era slaying." *Anniston Star*, November 17, 2010.
_____. "Midnight visitors: The short life and troubled times of Rogers Hamilton." *Anniston Star*, December 13, 2010
_____. "Thad Christian's death still raises questions 45 years later." *Anniston Star*, September 6, 2010.
_____. FBI investigating former Alabama trooper *Anniston Star*, March 6, 2005.
_____. "The deputy comes calling." *Anniston Star*, December 14, 2010.
_____. "Voices from a Cleveland park." *Anniston Star*, December 13, 2010.
_____. "Waiting for justice: Jury selection begins Monday in civil right-era killing." *Anniston Star*, November 14, 2010.
"Florida prisoner killed." *New York Times*, June 16, 1943.
"A flying sheriff." *Time*, September 27, 1976.
Foree, Jim. "50 years for Palmer killer." *Daily Defender*, June 27, 1957.
"Forgets 'Yes, sir,' Miss. boy, 17, shot." *Chicago Defender*, October 6, 1945.
"Four Ala. men held in rock death of cleric." *Daily Defender*, April 25, 1956.
"4 Deputies Wounded." *The News*, November 18, 1957.

Fox, Margalit. "Willie Louis, who named the killers of Emmett Till at their trial, dies at 76." *New York Times*, July 24, 2013.
"Franklin youth freed in Gilbert murder." *Virginia Tribune*, January 23, 1948.
Fraser, Amy. "The formative years of Jonathan Daniels, civil rights martyr." *Keene Sentinel*, June 16, 2002.
Frazier, Ian. "Life after a lonesome death." *The Guardian* (London), February 25, 2005.
Gale, Mary Ellen. "Case stalled in Tuskegee." *Southern Courier*, April 6–7, 1968.
_____. "Killing of rights worker jolts Tuskegee students." *Southern Courier*, January 8–9, 1966.
_____. "King buried in Bullock County." *Southern Courier*, April 22–23, 1967.
_____. "Lee youth killed." *Southern Courier*, December 16–17, 1967.
_____. "Segrest's attorneys ask switch." *Southern Courier*, October 29–30, 1966.
_____. "The trial and after." *Southern Courier*, December 17–18, 1966.
_____. "Was Segrest aiming at Negro rights worker?" *Southern Courier*, December 10–11, 1966.
"Governor appoints special prosecutor in 1964 civil rights murder." WJXT Channel 4, January 9, 2006.
Grady, Marie. "Paying the ultimate price for respect." *The Union-News*, January 7, 2002.
"Grand jury fails to indict in two streetcar slayings." *Atlanta Daily World*, May 7, 1946.
"Grand jury indicts Hattie Mae Turner on five counts." *Cairo Messenger*, March 10, 1950.
Greenberg, Benjamin T. "Decades after slaying, Mississippi family seeks justice." *Clarion-Ledger*, July 21, 2012.
_____. "Investigations force feds to revisit murders of civil rights era." *Colorlines*, January 12 2011,
_____. "The legacy of a murder." *Colorlines*, March/April, 2008.
_____. "Traitor town: The unsolved slaying of Clifton Walker." *Clarion-Ledger*, July 22, 2012.
Gregory, Ted. "The Black Panther raid and the death of Fred Hampton," *Chicago Tribune*, September 30, 2014.
"Gretna shooting remains unsolved; officers on case." *The Star*, June 6, 1947.
"Gruesome murder weapons include ice pick and axe." *Cairo Messenger*, March 3, 1950.
"Guard kills 3 prisoners in California." *Milwaukee Journal*, January 14, 1970.
"Guards indicted as prisoner beaten to death in Georgia." *Los Angeles Sentinel*, July 8, 1948.
"Gun clicked before jury." *The Sun*, November 13, 1963.
Hadad, Chuck. "After 57 years, break in civil rights era cold case." AC360°, March 4, 2011.
Halberstam, David. "Tallahatchie County acquits a peckerwood." *The Reporter*, April 19, 1956.
"Hang, shoot, drag Negro." *New York Times*, June 22, 1934.
"Hattie Mae Turner commits suicide by cutting throat." *Cairo Messenger*, March 11, 1950.
"Hattie Mae Turner denies any knowledge of crime." *Cairo Messenger*, March 4, 1950.

Helman, Scott. "Letter from Selma." *Boston Globe Magazine*, July 17, 2011.
Hendricks, Theodore W. "Defendant in murder case says gun was aimed in air." *The Sun*, November 19, 1963.
———. "GI testifies in shooting." *The Sun*, November 6, 1963.
———. "Warfel is guilty in Meade killing." *The Sun*, November 22, 1963.
———. "Witness cue missed by GI." *The Sun*, November 7, 1963.
Hewitt, Bill, and John Slania. "Slow justice: Three decades after a racist murder, an eyewitness IDs the alleged killer: her father." *People*, July 15, 2002.
"Hold four in slaying of Negro." *Delta Democrat-Times*, June 25, 1959.
"Hold youths for slaying." *Daily Chronicle*, June 22, 1959.
"Home is castle, Mississippi court rules." *Afro-American*, June 23, 1934.
"Hosie Miller: Shirley Sherrod's dad, and a casualty in a forgotten war." *Philadelphia Inquirer*, July 21, 2010.
Howard, Walter. "'A blot on Tampa's history': The lynching of Robert Johnson." *Tampa Bay History* 6 (Fall/Winter 1984): 5–18.
"Howell acquitted in Mallard case." *Lyons Progress*, January 13, 1949.
Huie, William Bradford. "The shocking story of approved killing in Mississippi." *Look*, January 24, 1956.
Hunter, Jack R. "Hinton slaying trial opens at Heathsville." *Richmond Times-Dispatch*, December 21, 1955.
———. "Jury out for 21 minutes frees Hinton in shooting." *Richmond Times-Dispatch*, December 21, 1955.
Hymes, Donald. "Ship worker charged in slaying of Ft. Meade soldier after chase." *Washington Post and Times-Herald*, July 6, 1963.
"Indiana man held in woman's 1968 slaying dies of cancer." *Los Angeles Times*, September 1, 2002.
"Investigation of 1964 civil rights murder comes to end." WJXT Channel 4, May 9, 2006.
"It was a dark day in Mississippi history." *Desoto Times Tribune*, February 12, 2009.
"Jackson detective kills Negro at Capitol, Farish." *Clarion-Ledger*, July 26, 1944.
"Jackson: death of a movement solider." *Southern Patriot*, June 1967.
Jay, Peter A. "Car blast kills 2 near trial of Rap Brown." *Washington Post*, March 11, 1970.
"Jesse Thornton found dead in Patasaliga." *Luverne Journal*, July 3, 1940.
"John Thomas was killed 'fer nothin'." *Daily Iowan*, September 11, 1970.
Johnson, Carrie. "Johnny's death: The untold tragedy in Birmingham." National Public Radio, September 15, 2010.
Jonnson, Patrik. "Feds turn up heat to solve cold cases of civil rights days." *Christian Science Monitor*, April 4, 2007.
"JP sees no cause to hold man who shot Negro friend." *News & Observer*, June 17, 1959.

"Judge frees streetcar operator in killing of veteran." *Atlanta Daily World*, April 19, 1946.
"Judge throws out case against city." *Waterloo Courier*, July 7, 1967.
"Jury probe delayed in chief's slaying of handcuffed GIs." *Chicago Tribune*, May 17, 1951.
"Justice Dept. files charges in Dublin court." *Atlanta Daily World*, Oct. 11, 1944.
"Justice Dept. investigates possible Ala. lynching." *Jet*, March 9, 1967.
"Justice for all." *Delta Democrat-Times*, February 1, 1956.
Keller, Larry, "Deputy sheriff's murder still unsolved." SPLC *Intelligence Report* 134 (Summer 2009).
"Killing of man may be Dixie plot." *Amsterdam News*, November 4, 1951.
"Kills Carolina funeral director over 85 cents." *Pittsburgh Courier*, April 10, 1948.
"Kimbell loses bid for freedom on bond." Associated Press, December 28, 1955.
King, Gilbert. "Florida's history of failed justice." *The Root*, April 2, 2012.
Klibanoff, Hank. "The glacial pace of justice." *Washington Post*, August 9, 2010.
"Kluxers burn Mallard home," *Chicago Defender*, October 22, 1949.
Labarre, Bob. "White jury frees Negro." *Southern Courier*, March 30–31, 1968.
"Law firm takes up case of 1964 civil-rights killing." WJXT Channel 4, October 11, 2005.
"Lawyer: JSO conspired to cover up 1964 racial slaying." WJXT Channel 4, June 6, 2003.
"Lee Gibson is found not guilty." *Hazard Herald*, May 24, 1934.
LeFlore, John. "Mobile cop kills innocent youth." *Chicago Defender*, July 28, 1945.
Leveritt, Mara. "A Georgia ruling highlights the civil rights abuses ingrained in the West Memphis case." DK2, June 12, 2011.
Lollar, Michael. "Mother grieves son's death, overshadowed by King slaying." *Commercial Appeal*, March 28, 2008.
Lopez, Robert J. "No evidence Ruben Salazar was targeted in killing, report says." Los Angeles Times, February 19, 2011.
Lotito, Ernest. "Slaying linked to race clash." *Washington Post and Times-Herald*, July 7, 1963.
Lottman, Michael S. "Negro man dies in jail two hours after arrest." *Southern Courier*, November 26–27, 1966.
———. "Witnesses saw 'blood all over' but the jury set Harvey Connor free." *Southern Courier*, April 29–30, 1967.
Lucas, Robert. "'Valley folk' silent as hills on boy's lynchers." *Chicago Defender*, December 2, 1944.
"Lynch colored man arrested for drinking." *Chicago Tribune*, September 29, 1935.
"Lynched: Accused of attacking aged woman." *Hattiesburg American*, November 21, 1938.
"Lynched boy's kin win suit against sheriff." *Washington Post*, May 22, 1936.
"Lynching cases on trial today." *Hazard Herald*, May 17, 1934.
"Lynching goes underground: A report on a new

technique." Library of Congress Manuscript Collection, January 1940.

"Lynching mob strings up 2 In Mississippi." *Daily Illini,* June 9, 1934.

MacAskill, Ewan. "'Dead' Klansman on trial over 1964 deaths." *The Guardian* (London), May 28, 2007.

"Man accused of shooting Negro released on bond." *Montana Standard-Post,* March 14, 1966.

"Man bound over for grand jury for slaying on bus." *Atlanta Daily World,* December 1, 1945.

"Man convicted in 1964 killing denies involvement." WJXT Channel 4, March 26, 2003.

"Man is charged in killing GI." *The Sun,* July 6, 1963.

Mann, Simon. "Old wounds, new hope." *The Age,* June 14, 2010.

"Manslaughter charges filed against cop." *Sandusky Register,* September 18, 1967.

"Many parents let sons face inquest alone." *Chicago Daily Tribune,* March 15,, 1957.

"Marshal absolved in slaying of Negro." *Biloxi Daily Herald,* September 24, 1948.

Martin, Douglas. "W. D. Zantzinger, subject of Dylan song dies at 69." *New York Times,* January 9, 2009.

Mathiowetz, Dianne. "Lynching reenactment spurs demand for justice." *Workers World,* August 3, 2007.

"Mayor won't act in Burns killing delegation told." *California Eagle,* October 14, 1948.

McGraw, Mike, and Glenn E. Rice. "Evidence points to mob associate's involvement in Jordan killing." *Kansas City Star,* October 31, 2010.

_____. "Unsolved killing of Leon Jordan echoes civil rights era." *Kansas City Star,* September 9, 2010.

McGraw, Mike. "The missing gun turns up—in use by the police." *Kansas City Star,* September 9, 2010.

McLaughlin, Michael. "Roman Ducksworth family claims Department of Justice overlooked evidence in 1962 killing." *Huffington Post,* March 8, 2013.

"Mechanic is guilty in death of Negro." *New York Times,* February 27, 1966.

"Medal given to soldier who got taste of Viet in Bogalusa." *Afro-American,* November 21, 1967.

Meyers, Debbie Burt. "'59 police shooting among FBI's re-opened civil rights cold cases." *Neshoba Democrat,* April 1, 2009.

Minor, Elliott. "Answers sought in 1946 Ga. killing." *Washington Post,* February 13, 2007.

_____. "Ga. county declines to act on '46 death." Associated Press, February 13, 2007.

"Mississippi mob lynches Negroes." *St. Petersburg Times,* August 14, 1934.

"Mississippi mob murders insurance man: White posses terrorize citizens in new Mississippi lynching wave." *Chicago Defender,* July 30, 1938.

"Mississippi sheriff acquitted in Negro's death." *Jet,* August 21, 1958.

"Mistrial ordered after jury fails to reach decision." *Wilson Daily Times,* September 11, 1948.

"Mitcham and Clark are acquitted of murder in Carlisle case." *Lafayette Sun,* March 29, 1950.

"Mitcham and Clark plead innocent to first degree murder." *Lafayette Sun,* March 15, 1950.

Mitchell, David J. "1933 Labadieville lynching receiving new scrutiny." *The Advocate,* October 13, 2013.

Mitchell, Jerry. "FBI investigating former Alabama trooper for another killing." *Clarion-Ledger,* November 22, 2010.

_____. "FBI to reopen investigation into 1965 beating death of minister." *Clarion-Ledger,* March 11, 2011.

_____. "Killen claims God is on his side." *Clarion-Ledger,* March 1, 2010.

_____. "Lawsuit over '64 deaths settled." *Clarion-Ledger,* July 13, 2010.

_____. "Ole Miss declared national historic site." *Clarion-Ledger,* April 14, 2010.

_____. "Re-examining Emmett Till case could help separate fact, fiction." *Clarion-Ledger,* February 19, 2007.

_____. "Report: Half of FBI's civil rights-era cold cases are closed." *Clarion-Ledger,* August 2, 2010.

_____. "Researchers: Cold-case list too short." *Clarion-Ledger,* February 15, 2009.

_____. "The last days of Ben Chester White." *Clarion-Ledger,* February 23, 2003.

_____. "Two-thirds of 124 civil rights cold cases closed." *Clarion-Ledger,* November 7, 2011.

_____. "Unsolved 'others' etched in stone and in memory." *Clarion-Ledger,* February 5, 2007.

"Mob burns slain man twice." *Kansas City Plaindealer,* July 15, 1938.

"Mob uses attack rumor as excuse to slay man who wouldn't 'knuckle.'" *Chicago Defender,* December 17, 1938.

Montaldo, Charles. "The lynchings at Moore's Ford." *About News,* http://crime.about.com/od/unsolved/a/moores_ford.htm.

Montgomery, Ben. "Spectacle: The lynching of Claude Neal." *Tampa Bay Times,* October 20, 2011.

Moredock, Will. "The good fight: The last lynching." *Charleston City Paper,* February 14, 2007.

"Mother slain for 'sassing.'" *Daily Defender,* December 10, 1956.

Mudhar, Raju. "Cracking a very cold case." *Toronto Star,* January 26, 2007.

Muhammad, Charlene. "Did the U.S. Army massacre Black soldiers during WWII?" *The Final Call,* October 6, 1998.

"Murder charge filed against Powhatan man." *Kingsport News,* January 26, 1950.

"Murder jury hears boy, 14." *The Sun,* November 8, 1963.

"Murder of a murderer." *Tampa Morning Tribune,* June 18, 1943.

"Murder on bus evokes grave concern here." *Atlanta Daily World,* November 30, 1945.

Murphy, Dennis. "Seeking justice for a racial killing, 40 years later." *Dateline NBC,* September 7, 2005.

"Mutilation victim dies of injuries." *Tuscaloosa News,* August 27, 1965.

"'My husband shot like dog,' sobs Mrs. White at bier of slain mate." *Indianapolis Recorder,* June 21, 1941.

"Mysterious slaying baffles detectives." *Rome News-Tribune,* January 30, 1967.

"NAACP probes Alabama 'lynching.'" *Chicago Defender,* May 23, 1953.

"Nash Negro found burned." *Evening Telegram,* February 5, 1951.

"Negro fatally shot resisting arrest at night spot." *Yazoo City Herald,* January 26, 1956.

"Negro father of 6 is slain: FDP asks feds investigate." *Clarion-Ledger,* November 8, 1965.

"Negro held on murder charge." *Biloxi Daily Herald,* September 23, 1958.

"Negro in Arkansas is killed in chase," *New York Times,* July 18, 1963.

"Negro is killed by Mobile police." *Press-Register,* July 10, 1945.

"Negro is lynched at Marianna." *Evening Independent,* June 16, 1943.

"Negro is lynched by mob in Florida." *New York Times,* July 20, 1935.

"Negro killed, hit by train." *Laurel Leader-Call,* September 4, 1965.

"Negro man shot down on street." *Kingsport News,* September 22, 1958.

"Negro may have died of broken neck, DA reports." *Galveston Daily News,* January 29, 1956.

"Negro mother slain." *New York Times,* December 7, 1956.

"Negro, 19, is lynched by Louisiana mob." *New York Times,* October 14, 1938.

"Negro shot to death at scene of attack." *Orlando Morning Sentinel,* August 2, 1947.

"Negro slayer killed by mob in Pikeville: killer attacks wife, slays daughter of school head." *Nashville Banner,* Nov. 23, 1944.

"Negro taken out of Marianna jail beaten to death." *St. Petersburg Times,* June 17, 1943.

"Negro widow files $20 million suit." *Chicago Defender,* August 27, 1966.

"Negro youth killed Monday on Highway 468." *Rankin County News,* June 25, 1964.

"Negro's death is believed murder." *Crittenden County Times,* June 12, 1954.

Nelson, Stanley. "A drowning, a kiss triggered Joseph Edwards murder." *Concordia Sentinel,* May 5, 2010.

_____. "Beckwith recalls terrifying late night threat after Morris murder: 'You're next.'" *Concordia Sentinel,* March 4, 2010.

_____. "Bloody '64: Klan suspected in murders, assaults, and bombings." *Concordia Sentinel,* July 3, 2008.

_____. "Civil rights' group, rogue Klansmen blamed for Morris arson." *Concordia Sentinel,* January 8, 2009.

_____. "Connected by violence—the Mafia, Klan & Morville Lounge." *Concordia Sentinel,* July 16, 2009.

_____. "Daughters say top FBI informant—Coonie Poissot—lived for the chase." *Concordia Sentinel,* March 31, 2010.

_____. "Deputy DeLaughter seen with stranger in green car on night of Morris fire." *Concordia Sentinel,* March 11, 2010.

_____. "Did finger discovered in shop rubble belong to Frank Morris?" *Concordia Sentinel,* July 5, 2012.

_____. "Encounters with Concordia sheriff's deputy Frank DeLaughter in 1960s." *Concordia Sentinel,* June 4, 2009.

_____. "FBI adds Joseph Edwards to unsolved 1960s cold case list." *Concordia Sentinel,* August 4, 2010.

_____. "FBI interviewed three IP workers for December 1964 murder of Frank Morris." *Concordia Sentinel,* November 26, 2008.

_____. "FBI's Lancaster sought 'dying declaration' from Frank Morris." *Concordia Sentinel,* May 21, 2009.

_____. "Feds shift gears in Morris probe; some witnesses 'untruthful.'" *Concordia Sentinel,* May 7, 2009.

_____. "Grand jury probing Frank Morris murder." *Concordia Sentinel,* February 9, 2011.

_____. "In 1967, Klan leader E. L. McDaniel linked four men to 1964 Frank Morris murder." *Concordia Sentinel,* January 28, 2010.

_____. "J. Edgar Hoover's interest in Frank Morris murder." *Concordia Sentinel,* May 22, 2008.

_____. "James Ford Seale: A sheriff's election, nine deaths and a silver dollar." *Concordia Sentinel,* October 22, 2009.

_____. "Justice eluded Exerlena Jackson-Vanison after 1967 car bomb murder of her husband." *Concordia Sentinel,* August 5, 2009.

_____. "Klansman's son recalls Shamrock, Silver Dollar Group, meeting Joe Edwards." *Concordia Sentinel,* January 15, 2009.

_____. "Klansmen 'took great pride' in refining bombing skills." *Concordia Sentinel,* January 22, 2009.

_____. "Rayville man implicated in civil rights-era killing of Frank Morris." *Concordia Sentinel,* January 12, 2011.

_____. "Morris' granddaughter says FBI $10,000 reward gives her new hope." *Concordia Sentinel,* December 10, 2008.

_____. "Morris' best friend—James White Sr.—shot Klansman during shootout in 1964." *Concordia Sentinel,* March 24, 2010.

_____. "Morville Lounge owner caught in Klan, Mafia crossfire." *Concordia Sentinel,* April 21, 2010.

_____. "SDG leader 'Red' Glover was lead suspect in Wharlest Jackson murder." *Concordia Sentinel,* September 3, 2009.

_____. "Silver Dollar Group linked to attacks—Edwards, Morris, Jackson, Metcalfe." *Concordia Sentinel,* December 27, 2007.

_____. "Silver Dollar Group may have targeted Morris." *Concordia Sentinel,* December 6, 2007.

_____. "The day a dying ex–Klansman gave God his 'untold story.'" *Concordia Sentinel,* June 10, 2009.

_____. "The night Wharlest Jackson was murdered—Feb. 27, 1967." *Concordia Sentinel,* June 4, 2008.

_____. "Was Frank Morris killed over deputy's cowboy boots?" *Concordia Sentinel,* February 4, 2010.

_____. "Was shoe shop arson done by Tallulah

wrecking crew?" *Clarion-Ledger*, February 11, 2010.

———. "Whatever happened to Joseph Edwards?" *Concordia Sentinel*, December 13, 2007.

"New affidavit sheds more light on death of Negro convict here." *Augusta Herald*, June 20, 1948.

"New jury list due for murder case." *The Sun*, November 1, 1963.

"9 farmers fined $1,800 in killing." *Commercial-News*, December 9, 1946.

"No arrests for Louisiana lynching." *Carolina Times*, October 29, 1934.

"No foul play in death of child." *Evening Telegram*, February 6, 1951.

"No matter how humble." *Kentucky New Era*, June 23, 1934.

Noel, Ed. "Sheriff Treolar gives his story." *Clarion-Ledger*, August 7, 1958.

Norris, Michelle. "Indiana town: From racist past to primary present." National Public Radio, April 30, 2008.

Nossiter, Adam. "Murder, memory and the Klan: A special report; widow inherits a confession to a 36-year-old hate crime." *New York Times*, September 4, 1993.

"Officer found innocent in Dayton slaying." *Toledo Blade*, January 23, 1968.

"Officer shot, man arrested." *Traverse City Record-Eagle*, March 14, 1966.

Older, Patricia. "FBI re-opens Mack Charles Parker lynching." *Picayune Item*, May 9, 2009.

"One year for shots." *Southern Courier*, February 10–11, 1968.

"Order autopsy in death of Negro shot by employer." *Delta Democrat-Times*, January 19, 1956.

"Perry jurors charge seven men with part in lynching Rex Scott." *Hazard Herald*, February 8, 1934.

Phillips, Benjamin T. "'B'ham cop shot him while his hands were in the air.'" *Southern Courier*, December 7–8, 1968.

"'Playful' shot by white man kills Negro at Wake Forest." *News & Observer*, June 14, 1959.

"Police and guards calm JSC riot." Associated Press, May 12, 1967.

"Police beat man for denying he stole own car." *California Eagle*, October 14, 1948.

"Police chief slays GI pair." *Geneva Daily Times*, May 12, 1951.

"Police seize 8 in slaying of teen-ager." *Chicago Daily Tribune*, March 13, 1957.

"Posses search state line area for Negro menacing homes." *Paris Daily Beacon-News*, October 12, 1942.

"Preacher slain, tongue cut out." *New Orleans Informer and Sentinel*, June 24, 1944.

"President wants 1964 racial slaying reviewed." WJXT Channel 4, December 4, 2002.

"Probe of reported brutalities promised." *Atlanta Daily World*, June 19, 1948.

"Probes GI death at hands of officer." *Pittsburgh Courier*, November 24, 1945.

"Puckett Negro found dead in county jail." *Brandon News*, February 4, 1960.

"Race riot feared as sheriff slays soldier: Asks removal of regiment." *Cleveland Plain Dealer*, June 2, 1943.

Rankin, Jim. "Negro slain near Morrisville; parolee jailed." *News and Observer*, December 21, 1950.

Reeves, Jay. "Despite disappointment, backers of civil rights 'cold case' law want it expanded." *U.S. News & World Report*, September 21, 2014.

Reisig, Robin. "Another B'ham killing." *Southern Courier*, May 27–28, 1967.

———. "Citizens protest Rasberry death." *Southern Courier*, February 25–26, 1967.

"Relatives of slain youth accept judge's apology." *New York Times*, November 11, 1997.

"Report a Negro clubbed to death." *Milwaukee Journal*, June 16, 1943.

"Report on Sallis reset." *Waterloo Courier*, June 21, 1966.

"Reported as dead, suspect in '64 killings turns up alive." Associated Press, September 24, 2005.

"Retired cops answer subpoenas on 1964 racial murder, welcome inquiry." WJXT Channel 4, September 28, 2005.

"Rex Scott is hanged to tree near Sassafras at 8:30 o'clock last night." *Hazard Herald*, January 25, 1934.

"Richard headed group of four who took Thibodaux from bed to Bayou Bridge." *Louisiana Weekly*, November 11, 1933.

"Riot victims file suit." Associated Press, May 11, 1968.

Roberts, Gene, and Hank Kilbanoff. "On the race beat." *AJR*, December 2006/January 2007.

Robinson, Amelia. "A timeline: Black history in the Miami Valley 1798 to 2001." *Dayton Daily News*, February 22, 2013.

Rubin, Mertis. "Constable shoots Grenada man." *Southern Courier*, April 22–23, 1967.

———. "Holly Springs death is still mystery." *Southern Courier*, January 13–14, 1968.

———. "'We can't leave and do nothing.'" *Southern Courier*, May 27–28, 1967.

"Sallis suit against city is filed." *Waterloo Courier*, July 18, 1966.

Sanborn, Karen. "Remembering Jonathan Daniels: Part 1." *Keene Sentinel*, August 11, 2005.

———. "Remembering Jonathan Daniels: Part 2." *Keene Sentinel*, August 12, 2005.

Santich, Kate. "A tale of citrus and secrets." *Orlando Sentinel*, April 7, 2002.

"Say Mississippi youth murdered in cold blood." *New Journal*, October 6, 1945.

"Says Georgia Negro slain for voting." *New York Times*, September 12, 1948.

Schaeffer, Ward. "A brave man." *Jackson Free Press*, December 3, 2008.

Schroeder, Ken. "Jury finds Detroit police innocent of conspiracy," *Daily Republic*, February 26, 1970.

Schwabauer, Barbara A. "The Emmett Till Unsolved Civil Rights Crime Act: The cold case of racism in the criminal justice system." *Ohio Law Journal* 71 (2010): 653–98.

"Second suspect held while third is at large." *Daily Clarion-Ledger*, July 22, 1938.

"Secret burial held for Tex. mob victim." *Afro-American*, October 24, 1942.
"Seek gun in Elko lynching." *Pittsburgh Courier*, September 7, 1946.
"Seek to avert violence after cop kills soldier." *Chicago Defender*, March 28, 1942.
Serrano, Richard A. "Answers elusive in 1965 slaying." *Los Angeles Times*, June 26, 2002.
Sessions, Cliff. "First witnesses tell of beating at Yalobusha jail today." *Delta Democrat-Times*, August 5, 1958.
"Seven men indicted for lynching granted bonds after hearing." *Hazard Herald*, February 15, 1934.
"7 Palmer slayers await sentences." *Daily Defender*, July 1, 1957.
"17-year-old boy lynched by Tenn. mob: cook opens jail door for ring leaders; shot 4 times." *Chicago Defender*, Dec. 2, 1944.
Shapiro, Joseph. "Justice in the segregated South: A new look at an old killing." National Public Radio, May 3, 2013.
"Sharkey County posse kills Negro slayer of planter, then burn body." *Delta Democrat-Times*, July 7, 1938.
"Sheriff blamed in Minden death." *Chicago Defender*, September 14, 1946.
"Sheriff is making every effort to solve robbery; three suspects arrested." *The Star*, May 30, 1947.
Sherrod, Shirley. "We can't yield—not now, not ever." *Huffington Post*, August 17, 2010.
Shires, Carl. "Shopkeeper is acquitted in Heathsville murder trial." *Richmond News Leader*, December 22, 1955.
———. "Storekeeper's murder trial under way." *Richmond News Leader*, December 20, 1955.
———. "Testimony is completed in Heathsville murder trial." *Richmond News Leader*, December 21, 1955.
"Shooting of Arkansas Negro is ruled justifiable by jury." *New York Times*, July 19, 1963.
"Shooting sprees kill Negro, injure deputies." *Montana Standard*, November 18, 1957.
"Shopkeeper indicted in Va. slaying." *Chicago Defender*, November 26, 1955.
Singer, Mark. "Who killed Carol Jenkins?" *The New Yorker*, January 7, 2002.
"Sister tells about race riot murder." *Pittsburgh News*, October 1, 2002.
"Six dead after church bombing." *Washington Post*, September 16, 1963.
"6 get prison terms for roles in '69 York, Pa., slaying." *Los Angeles Times*, November 14, 2002.
"Six Negro convicts killed at local camp." *Brunswick News*, July 12, 1947.
"60 years later, a cry for justice in Fla. killing." *Baltimore Sun*, December 10, 2006.
"Slain Negro's widow is first witness today as white youth faces trial jury." *Tupelo Daily Journal*, April 1, 1950.
"Slain Washington Parish deputy to be honored." WDSU Channel 6, March 18, 2013.
"Slaying linked to reborn Klan after boasts." *Chicago Daily Tribune*, June 8, 1946.
Smith, Adam C. "Remembering Mama." *St. Petersburg Times*, April 5, 2000.
Smith, Jim. "Jury convicts Atlanta man of murdering Negro boy." *Southern Courier*, February 11–12, 1967.
"SNYC asks probe of jail slaying." *Afro-American*, March 27, 1948.
"Soldiers, FBI move in to halt 4th lynching." *Amsterdam Star-News*, October 24, 1942.
"SPLC gives FBI case files on civil rights-era killings." *Decatur Daily*, February 24, 2007.
"State offers reward in bomb death." *Atlanta Constitution*, May 20, 1960.
"Statement asking for justice in the June 21, 1964, murders of James Chaney, Andrew Goodman and Michael Schwerner." *Neshoba Democrat*, June 24, 2004.
"Still mysterious." *Rocky Mount Telegram*, February 7, 1951.
"Strickland freed of murder count here yesterday." *Wilson Daily Times*, May 11, 1949.
"Suicide closes murder mystery." *Cairo Messenger*, March 17, 1950.
"Suppressed story of Dixie terrorism cracked by ANP writer." *Indianapolis Recorder*, March 14, 1942.
Suro, Roberto, and Michael A. Fletcher. "Mississippi massacre, or myth?" *Washington Post*, December 23, 1999.
"Suspect in forgotten Ku Klux Klan killings faces justice after 43 years." *The Times* (London), June 4, 2007.
"Suspect in murder called a Klansman." *New York Times*, February 26, 1966.
"Suspect pleads in 1964 murders." *USA Today*, January 25, 2007.
"Take no action on officer who killed two GI's." *Mt. Vernon Register-News*, May 17, 1951.
"Taken from jail, Negro is killed." *Spokane Daily Chronicle*, June 16, 1943.
Talbott, Chris. "FBI may reopen cold civil rights murder cases." *Tuscaloosa News*, February 24, 2007.
"Talmadge demands killers be arrested." *New York Times*, November 30, 1948.
Teachout, Terry. "Close to home." *New York Times*, May 30, 1999.
"Testimony is completed in Heathsville murder trial." *Richmond News Leader*, December 21, 1955.
"13 accused in Paris slaying to be arraigned Monday." *Commercial-News*, July 14, 1943.
"13 get new date in Palmer case." *Daily Defender*, September 18, 1957.
"This week in black history." Pittsburgh Courier, October 8, 2014.
Thomas, Robert McG. Jr. "Thomas Coleman, 86, dies; Killed rights worker in '65." *New York Times*, June 22, 1997.
Thompson, Krissah. "Civil rights-era cold cases put back in spotlight." *Washington Post*, February 19, 2011.
"Threaten four jailed in teen gang slaying." *Chicago Daily Tribune*, March 17, 1957.
"3 guilty in 1970 Mississippi killing." *Los Angeles Times*, November 14, 1999.
"Three held in lynching." *Times Daily*, January 25, 1934.

"Train hits Negro, body already cold." *Weekly Moultrie Observer*, August 2, 1946.
"Transcripts of two FBI interviews with Frank Morris at Ferriday hospital." *Concordia Sentinel*, August 28, 2008.
Trescott, Jacqueline. "Smithsonian's African American History Museum acquires Emmett Till casket." *Washington Post*, August 27, 2009.
"Troy Combs removed from office of jailer by governor Tuesday." *Hazard Herald,* March 1, 1934.
Tugman, Lindsey. "10 more unsolved Arkansas mysteries." KTHV Channel 11, March 11, 2014.
"12 enter pleas of not guilty in slaying." *Commercial-News,* November 13, 1943.
"Twin counties probe deaths." *Evening Telegram,* February 5, 1951.
"Two accuse sheriff of beating fatality." *Washington Post and Times Herald,* July 7, 1958.
"2 are lynched in Mississippi by white mob." *Chicago Daily Tribune*, July 16, 1935.
"Two eyewitnesses see Louisianan shot and killed in cold blood." *Louisiana Weekly,* September 22, 1945.
"Two face jail in Mallard lynching." *Chicago Defender*, December 18, 1948.
"2 guilty in '69 race riot death get prison." *Los Angeles Times,* December 19, 2002.
"Two handcuffed soldiers slain by police chief." *San Bernardino County Sun,* May 13, 1951.
"$2M settlement reached for '69 race-riot killing." *USA Today*, December 6, 2005.
"2 more join list of Miss. victims." *Philadelphia Courier,* November 7, 1959.
"$2,750 for a death." *New York Times,* August 26, 1959.
"2 whites indicted in Georgia killing." *New York Times,* December 11, 1948.
"U.S. drops case against GI slayer." *Atlanta Daily World,* July 21, 1945.
"Verdict expected today in bumper jack slaying." *Tupelo Daily Journal,* April 4, 1950.
"Victim taken from jail, beaten, marched about with rope around neck." *Louisiana Weekly,* October 14, 1933.
"Victim's friend testifies on slaying at Ft. Meade." *Washington Post and Times-Herald,* November 6, 1963.
"Victim's son, retired detective push for justice in racial killing." WJXT Channel 4, September 29, 2005.
"Visitor shot by trooper." *Southern Courier,* January 28–29, 1967.
"Vote to indict 15 in killing by teen gang." *Chicago Daily Tribune,* March 16, 1957.
Wagster Pettus, Emily. "Reputed Klansman gets life in teen deaths." *Toronto Star,* August 24, 2007.
"Wake man to pay $2,750 to family of Negro victim in playful killing." *News & Observer,* August 25, 1959.
Walker, Laura E. "Race relations in Chattanooga." *Chattanooga Times Free Press,* January 20, 2009.
"Warfel gets 10 years in death of soldier." *Afro-American,* December 7, 1963.
Waters, Enoc P. "Two lynched boys were ace scrap iron collectors in Mississippi town." *Chicago Defender,* March 6, 1943.
"West Point election today." *Delta Democrat-Times,* August 18, 1970.
"White man held in Atlanta slaying." *Corpus Christi Caller-Times,* September 14, 1966.
"White man held in slaying of Negro in Anniston, Ala." *New York Times,* August 30, 1965.
"Wife of Negro minister shot to death." *Milwaukee Sentinel,* January 30, 1967.
Wilcox, Beth. "Man found in Wilcox." *Southern Courier,* May 27–28, 1967.
"Will show self-defense, Warfel's attorney says." *The Sun,* November 14, 1963.
Williams, Arnolta J. "Isaiah Nixon's family enjoying a 'new life.'" *Pittsburgh Courier,* December 25, 1954.
Windham, Ben. "Wilcox County sheriff never needed a gun." Tuscaloosa News, February 12, 2012.
"Windham's murderer captured." *Winona Times,* April 9, 1937.
"Wingard facing assault sentence in stockade case." *Augusta Chronicle,* September 4, 1948.
Winn, Bill. "'Shots in rapid succession' death to Brewer." *Ledger-Enquirer,* March 8, 1988.
Wolff, Henry Jr. "Justice and injustice administered at hanging trees." *Victoria Advocate,* March 9, 2003.
"Worker dead after fight with sheriff." *Pentwater News,* October 13, 1944.
Yee, Min Sun. "Death on the yard: The untold killings at Soledad & San Quentin." *Ramparts,* April 1973, pp. 35–40.
"Young physician killed by blast in N. Carolina." *Indianapolis Recorder,* May 4, 1957.
Younge, Gary. "Justice at last?" *The Guardian* (London), May 6, 2005.
"Youth admits slaying teen with hammer." *Chicago Daily Tribune,* March 14, 1957.
"Youth saved as mob begins to hang him from Bayou Bridge." *Louisiana Weekly,* October 21, 1933.

Official Sources

The Attorney General's First Report to Congress Pursuant to the Emmett Till Unsolved Civil Rights Crime Act of 2007, April 7, 2009.
The Attorney General's First Annual Report to Congress Pursuant to the Emmett Till Unsolved Civil Rights Crime Act of 2007, April 7, 2009.
The Attorney General's Second Annual Report to Congress Pursuant to the Emmett Till Unsolved Civil Rights Crime Act of 2007, May 13, 2010.
The Attorney General's Third Annual Report to Congress Pursuant to the Emmett Till Unsolved Civil Rights Crime Act of 2007, August 2011.
The Attorney General's Fourth Annual Report to Congress Pursuant to the Emmett Till Unsolved Civil Rights Crime Act of 2007, October 2012.
The Attorney General's Fifth Annual Report to Congress Pursuant to the Emmett Till Unsolved Civil Rights Crime Act of 2007, January 2014.

Carrie Lee Jones v. Oscar H. Haynes, Sr. Civil Action No. 2248, U.S. District Court for the Western District of Pennsylvania, 1951.
Caston v. State, Supreme Court of Mississippi, No. 1999-KA-01985-SCT.
Emmett Till Unsolved Civil Rights Crime Act of 2007, 122 Stat. 3934, Public Law 110–344—Oct. 7, 2008.
Federal Bureau of Investigation files. "Emmett Till."
_____. "Isaac Simmons."
_____. "Lillie Belle Allen."
_____. "Louis Allen."
_____. "Mack Charles Parker."
_____. "Mississippi Burning (MIBURN) Case."
_____. "Viola Liuzzo."
Crist, Charlie. *The Christmas 1951 Murders of Harry T. and Harriette V. Moore.* Tallahassee: Florida Attorney General's Office, 2006.
Harrison v. State, 5 So.2d 703, Supreme Court of Florida, en Banc., January 20, 1942.
Iowa Civil Rights Commission Annual Report, 1966, http://publications.iowa.gov/1650.
Ollie Mae Brown and Margaret Brown v. Allen C. Thompson, 430 F.2d 1214 (1970).
People v. Paille 2, 383 Mich. 621 (1970), 178 N.W.2d 465.
Report of the Select Committee on Assassinations of the U.S. House of Representatives. Washington: U.S. Government Printing Office, 1979.
Screws v. United States, 325 U.S. 91 (1945).
Supreme Court of Georgia. *James v. State* 24206, 223 Ga. 677 (1967), 157 S.E.2d 471.
U.S. Commission on Civil Rights. *Justice: Book 5.* Washington: U.S. Government Printing Office, 1961.
White v. State, 135 Tex. Crim. 210 (Tex. Crim. App. 1938).
White v. State, 139 Tex. Crim. 660 (Tex. Crim. App. 1939).
White v. Texas, 309 US 631; 310 U.S. 530, 532 (1940).

Internet Sources

A Doctor's Death Causes Black Professionals to Flee, http://www.civilrights.uga.edu/cities/columbus/doctors.htm.
A Moment Of Insanity, http://deb8islife.blogspot.com/2012/07/a-moment-of-insanity.html
Adams, Hannah. "The Ones Left Behind: The Homicide of Prentiss McCann and NAACP Strategy in Post-War Mobile," http://nuweb9.neu.edu/civilrights/wp-content/uploads/Prentiss-McCann1.pdf.
Allen, Fredric. "The Unsolved Civil Rights Murder of James Brazier," http://jamesbraziermurder1958.blogspot.com.
Anarchy at the Algiers, http://www.detroits-great-rebellion.com/Algiers-Motel.html.
Bass, Jack. The Orangeburg Massacre, http://www.jackbass.com/_u_the_orangeburg_massacre_u_25512.htm.
Beito, David T., and Linda Royster Beito. "The grim and overlooked anniversary of the murder of the Rev. George W. Lee, civil rights activist," http://hnn.us/article/11744.
"Bessie McDowell," http://orangepublicmemory.50webs.com/bessie_mcdowell.htm.
The Birdia Keglar Legacy, http://www.birdiakeglarlegacy.org/1.html.
Blume, Kirsten. "'Not In New Orleans Anymore': A legal history regarding the death of Tom Jones, Jr.," http://nuweb9.neu.edu/civilrights/wp-content/uploads/Tom-Jones-Jr.pdf.
Brasted, Chelsea. "6 civil rights-era murder cases remain unsolved in Louisiana," http://www.lafayettepublicpolicy.com/6_civil_rights_era_murder_cases_remain_unsolved_in_Louisiana.html.
Browning, Lauren. "A chief, a coach, a killer: Two perspectives on Weyman B. Cherry," https://scholarblogs.emory.edu/emorycoldcases/a-chief-a-coach-a-killer-two-perspectives-on-weyman-b-cherry.
Calvert, Tessla. "Clarence Triggs," http://prezi.com/nzm_stbnbkfb/untitled-prezi.
Catherwood, Heather, and Rashida Richardson. "Mattie Green: 'It Cannot Be Walked Away From and Forgotten,'" http://nuweb9.neu.edu/civilrights/wp-content/uploads/Mattie-Green.pdf.
Chicano Moratorium, http://myemail.constantcontact.com/Poster-of-the-Week.html?soid=1011181350183&aid=SvWlkxfRx6k.
The Civil Rights Cold Case Project, http://coldcases.org.
Civil Rights Cold Cases: Who Killed Adlena Hamlett? Birdia Keglar? James Keglar? http://emmett-till.blogspot.com/2010/01/who-killed-adlena-hamlett-birdia-keglar.html.
Cold Case Justice Initiative, http://www.syr.edu/coldcaselaw/index.html.
Civil Rights and Restorative Justice Project, http://www.northeastern.edu/civilrights.
Columbia Race Riots, http://www.tn4me.org/article.cfm/a_id/110/minor_id/26/major_id/11/era_id/8.
"Columbia Race Riot, 1946," Tennessee Encyclopedia of History & Culture, http://tennesseeencyclopedia.net/entry.php?rec=296.
Day 652: Shots Fired—The Marin County Courthouse Incident, http://1000words1000days.com/2013/10/day-652-shots-fired-the-marin-county-courthouse-incident.
E. H. Hurst, http://en.wikipedia.org/wiki/E.H._Hurst.
Ekanem, Janette. "Injustice unveiled: The lynching of Jesse Thornton," http://nuweb9.neu.edu/civilrights/wp-content/uploads/jesse-thornton.pdf.
FBI Seeking Victims [sic] Next of Kin, http://the7thpwr.wordpress.com/tag/jessie-james-shelby.
Federal Bureau of Investigation, "Civil rights era murders," http://www.fbi.gov/news/stories/2010/march/coldcase_030210/civil-rights-era-murders-joint-initiative-yields-results
Fields, Ronald. "Murder on the mountain: The lynching of James Thomas Scales," http://nuweb9.neu.edu/civilrights/wp-content/uploads/Murder_on_the_mountain-Fields-2007.pdf.
Gitin, Maria. "In memory of civil rights martyr David Colston Sr., Camden, AL January 23,

1966," http://thislittlelight1965.wordpress.com/2013/01/27/in-memory-of-civil-rights-martyr-david-colston-sr-camden-al-january-23–1966.

Gordet, Danielle. "Rev. Isaac Simmons (April 1880–March 26, 1944)," nuweb9.neu.edu/civilrights/wp-content/uploads/civilrigh...mons-Paper-for-CRRJ.pdf.

Greenberg, Ben. "A Deep South cold case goes frigid," http://narrative.ly/stories/a-deep-south-cold-case-goes-frigid.

Guzman, Jessie P., and W. Harden Hughes. "Lynching—Crime," http://nationalhumanitiescenter.org/pds/maai3/segregation/text2/lynchingcrime.pdf.

Hamlett, Adlena McKinley. "My great-grandmother Adlena Hamlett," http://lcasalon.wordpress.com.

Harlem riot of 1964, http://en.wikipedia.org/wiki/Harlem_Riot_of_1964.

Harry Tyson Moore, http://en.wikipedia.org/wiki/Harry_T._Moore.

Historical Moments of Police Violence: William Milton—A "Good Man" Killed by the NYPD, http://www.usprisonculture.com/blog/2013/01/24/historical-moments-of-police-violence-william-milton-a-good-man-killed-by-the-nypd.

Ibeabuchi, Chikaelo. "The Lyching Death of Caleb Hill, Jr.," http://nuweb9.neu.edu/civilrights/wp-content/uploads/Hill-Essay-Final-Edited.pdf.

"Isadore Banks (Murder of)." The Encyclopedia of Arkansas History & Culture, http://www.encyclopediaofarkansas.net/encyclopedia/entry-detail.aspx?search=1&entryID=6425.

Jackson State May 1970, http://www.may41970.com/Jackson%20State/jackson_state_may_1970.htm.

"James Reeb," Encyclopedia of Alabama, http://encyclopediaofalabama.org/face/Article.jsp?id=h-2054.

"Johnnie Mae Chappell," http://www.ferris.edu/htmls/news/jimcrow/witnesses/chappell.htm.

"Johnnie Mae Chappell and the forgotten others," http://archive.clarionledger.com/assets/pdf/D06031423.PDF.

Kates, Tasha. "The search for a just prosecution: The story of Willie B. Carlisle," http://nuweb9.neu.edu/civilrights/wp-content/uploads/Willie-Carlisle.pdf.

Kennedy-Smith, Samuel. "Ernest Green and Charles Lang; Shubuta, MS; October 1942," http://nuweb9.neu.edu/civilrights/wp-content/uploads/GreenLang.pdf.

Kempton, Murray, "What have they got to live for?," https://www.soc.umn.edu/~samaha/cases/kempton_what_to_live_for.html.

Klopfer, Susan. "Murders around Mississippi," http://neshobanews.blogspot.com/2005_06_01_archive.html.

"Klunder, Bruce W.," The Encyclopedia of Cleveland History, http://ech.case.edu/ech-cgi/article.pl?id=KBW.

Jones, LaQuinton D. "Mink Slide Riot," http://kennethfrawley.com/Columbia_Race_Riots_Essay.pdf.

Lloyd, Craig. "Thomas Brewer (1894–1956)," New Georgia Encyclopedia, http://www.georgiaencyclopedia.org/articles/history-archaeology/thomas-brewer-1894–1956.

Martyrs Remembered: Bruce Klunder, http://www.splcenter.org/BruceKlunder.

Martyrs Remembered: Herbert Lee, http://www.splcenter.org/HerbertLee.

Mississippi Civil Rights Martyrs, http://www.crmvet.org/mem/msmartyr.htm.

Mississippi Civil Rights Project, http://mscivilrightsproject.org.

Nevins, Rosie. "The murder of Otis Newsome: A legal history," http://nuweb9.neu.edu/civilrights/wp-content/uploads/Otis-Newsome.pdf.

Newman, Michelle Amelia. "'They shot me for nothing': A legal & historical account of William Daniel's murder," http://nuweb9.neu.edu/civilrights/wp-content/uploads/William-Daniel.pdf.

Nguyen, Mary. "Law enforcement involvement in the death of Samuel Mason Bacon," http://nuweb9.neu.edu/civilrights/wp-content/uploads/samuel-mason-bacon.pdf.

1946 Georgia lynching, http://en.wikipedia.org/wiki/1946_Georgia_lynching.

People & Events: Clarence Strider (1904–1970), http://www.pbs.org/wgbh/amex/till/peopleevents/p_strider.html.

Rosen, Georgi A. Vogel. "The murder of Ellis Hutson: A legal legacy," http://nuweb9.neu.edu/civilrights/wp-content/uploads/Ellis-Hutson.pdf.

Samuel Leamon Younge, Jr., http://www.findagrave.com/cgi-bin/fg.cgi?page=gr&GRid=27039291.

Sanderman, Robert. "A legal history of the murder of Malcolm Wright," http://nuweb9.neu.edu/civilrights/wp-content/uploads/malcom-wright.pdf.

Sellers, Cleveland. "Killed: Wayne Yancey," http://www.crmvet.org/mem/sncc50_wayne-yancy.pdf.

Simon, Kaylie. "Lost Life, a miscarriage of justice: The death of John Earl Reese," http://nuweb9.neu.edu/civilrights/wp-content/uploads/Lost_Life_a_Miscarriage_of_Justice_The_Death_of_John_Earl_Reese.pdf.

_____. "Restorative Justice; Securing justice (even) when legal remedies aren't available," http://nuweb9.neu.edu/civilrights/wp-content/uploads/Justice_Restored.pdf.

Slade, Paul. "True lies: The lonesome death of Hattie Carroll," http://www.planetslade.com/hattie-carroll.html.

Southern Poverty Law Center, "The Forgotten," http://www.splcenter.org/civil-rights-memorial/the-forgotten.

_____. "Murder victim's son finds solace at Civil Rights Memorial Center," http://www.splcenter.org/get-informed/news/son-of-soldier-slain-in-racial-killing-finds-solace-at-civil-rights-memorial-cente.

Sovereignty Commission Online, Mississippi Department of Archives and History, http://mdah.state.ms.us/arrec/digital_archives/sovcom.

Stalking the Angel of Death: The Lynching Calendar, http://angelofdeathlynchingcalendar.blogspot.com/feeds/posts/default.

Summerlin, Donnie. "Samuel Younge Jr.," Encyclopedia of Alabama, http://www.encyclopediaofalabama.org/face/Article.jsp?id=h-1669.

Tollison, Courtney. "And then there were 14," http://www.journalwatchdog.com/city/1016-and-then-there-were-14.

Tovar, Nancy. "History timeline," http://chicanomoratorium.org/html/history_timeline.html.

Trescases, Heather. "Edwin Pratt is murdered outside of his Shoreline home on January 26, 1969," http://www.historylink.org/index.cfm?DisplayPage=output.cfm&File_Id=4142.

Unsolved Civil Rights Case: Booker T. Mixon, http://bookertmixoncivilrights.blogspot.com.

U.S. Department of Justice, Cold Case Initiative, http://www.justice.gov/crt/about/crm/cold_case_ini.php.

_____. "Justice Department to Investigate 1955 Emmett Till Murder," http://www.justice.gov/archive/opa/pr/2004/May/04_crt_311.htm.

Warren, John. "'Duck': A legal history of Robert Mallard's murder," http://works.bepress.com/cgi/viewcontent.cgi?article=1000&context=john_warren.

Woodham, Rebecca. "Jonathan Myrick Daniels," http://www.encyclopediaofalabama.org/article/h-1838.

York, Jake Adam, "Ambient Witness," http://www.jakeadamyork.com/2008/10/university-of-new-orleans.html.

Index

Abel, Fred 121
Abney, James 191
Acton, W.M. 123
Adamowski, Benjamin 208
Adams, Clinton 11
Adams, James 209
Adams, Mrs. J.M. 173
Adams, Washington 111–112
Adams, Wyatt 163
Adas, Lawrence 209
Adcock, George 10
Addy, Henry 94
Aiken, Horace 159
Akin, Bernard 57
Alabama 1, 4, 8, 14, 27–28, 32, 67–68, 69–71, 76–78, 80–81, 84, 91–92, 104, 109, 110, 137–139, 143, 162–164, 201–202, 209–210, 212–213, 220, 227, 230–231, 232–233, 240, 246, 252, 254
Alabama Bureau of Investigation 30
Alexander, Diane 28
Alexander, Henry 28
Alexander, Jim 184
Alexander, Lacey 182
Alford, Bernice 132–133
Alford, Jewel 37
Alford, Maud 132–133
Alford, Taylor 132–133
Alfred, David 36
Algiers Motel 235–237
All Star Bowling Lane 94
Allen, Frank 145
Allen, Hank 52
Allen, Hosea 177
Allen, Joe 110–111
Allen, Lillie 247–248
Allen, Louis 44, 51–52
Allen, T.A. 102
Allen, W.L. 212
Allman, Brady 159
Allman, E.L. 155
Altland, Donald 248
Amsterdam News 201
Anderson, Andrew 48
Anderson, Blair 249–250
Anderson, Lula 222
Anderson, Rick 245
Andrews, Frank 64

Anguilla Stockade 160–161
Anniston Star 68
Arbuthnot, Millie 140
Arkansas 15–16, 48, 150, 226
Arkansas Delta Truth and Justice Center 5, 69, 78
Arledge, Jimmy 57
Arline, Geneva 192
Arline, John 192
Armstrong Tire & Rubber Company 89
Arnall, Ellis 10
Arnold, Henry 146
Aryan Brotherhood 241
Ash, J.M. 239
Ashworth, Virgis 239
Askew, Reuben 200
Asman, Lon 197–198
Associated Negro Press 121
Associated Press 94
Atkins, Ed 137
August, Ronald 236–237
Avants, Ernest 85–86
Ayers, Rotha 220

Babcock, Lloyd 162
Baca, Lee 259–260
Bach, Lester 132
Bacon, Paul 169
Bacon, Samuel 168–170
Bacon, Warrington 169
Bagwell, S.L. 194
Bailey, Joyce 77
Bailey, Orville 211–212
Bair, Robert 220
Baker, George 193
Baker, Otha 196
Baker, Philip 107
Baldowski, Clifford 228
Baldwin, Charles 206
Baldwin, J.D. 161
Bandyk, James 209
Bankhead, John 12
Banks, Alice 15
Banks, Claude 113
Banks, Isadore 15–16
Banks, Jim 16
Banks, Willis 113
Barbee, Robert 238
Barbour, Haley 57, 219
Bardin, Tom 196

Barnes, Earl 118–119
Barnes, J.C. 234
Barnes, Roy 11
Barnett, Ethel 40, 215–216
Barnett, Ross 47, 69, 219
Barnette, Horace 57
Barnette, Travis 57
Barrattini, Pearl 219
Bass, Howard 240
Bassett, James, Jr. 223
Batchelor, G.W. 195–196
Bates, Bodie 104–105
Bates, Frank 185–186
Bates, L.C. 15
Battle, Tom 195–196
Battle, Vonzella 196
Battle, William 195–196
Baxley, Bill 4, 28
Beaman, James 190
Beard, T.V., Jr. 149
Beasley, Herbert 122
Beauchamp, Keith 22
Bedford, Henry 100
Begin, Louis 162
Belk, Fred 101
Bell, Albert 140
Bell, Baxter
Bell, Harold 249–250
Bell, Horace 212–213
Bell, Osborne 240
Bell, Willie 140
Bell, Willie E. 160
Bellamy, Norwood 94
Belser, Tom 128
Belvin, Tillman 12, 13
Bennett, Blaney 181
Bennett, Thomas 227
Bentley, Ed 98
Berry, Marion 253
Best, Lorenzo 193
Bicket, William 213–214
Biddle, Francis 122, 132
Bigner, W.A., Jr. 133
Bilbo, Theodore 126
Birdsong, T.B. 86
Birmingham News 155
Birmingham Police Department 172, 175, 195
Bishop, Jim 213
Bissette, Fes 151
Black, Jeff 153

Black Guerrilla Family 241
Black Mafia 256
Black Panther Party 241, 242–243, 245, 248–250
Blackstone Rangers 249
Blackwell, L.E. 242
Bladsacker, Alvin 165–166
Blair, Julius 147
Blair, R.M. 114
Blair, Sol 147
Blanchard, George 200–201
Blanton, David 120
Blanton, Thomas, Jr. 4
Blaylock, Officer 165
Blue, C.M., Jr. 233
Bohannon, James 128–129
Bohannon, Lee 257
Bolden, John 32
Bolden, Preston 15
Bolling, Elmore 164
Bomar, Lynn 136, 147, 148
Bone, Walter 171
Boone, Buford 210
Booth, Carl 138
Borders, C.L. 172
Bouldin, T.T. 204
Bowers, Samuel, Jr. 4, 57
Bowron, Fletcher 175
Boyd, Earcel, Jr. 60–61
Boykin, J.L. 170
Bozarth, Errett 122
Bozarth, Kenneth 122, 123
Bradley, Henry 155
Bragg, Thomas 198
Brake, Robert 197
Branch, Berry, Sr. 153
Brandon News 214
Brasford, Daniel 163
Brazier, Hattie 32
Brazier, James 31–32
Brazier, Odell 31
Breed, Allen 224
Breitbart, Andrew 71
Brewer, Jesse 82, 83
Brewer, Thomas 26
Brewer, Verlina 249, 250
Briley, George 231–232
Briley, Lillian 231–232
Brinson, Frank 179, 180
Britt, Raymond, Jr. 28
Brocato Bus Line 150
Brock, J.C. 101
Brokering, Harry 134
Bromley, Howard 203–204
Bronson, Bo 105
Brookins, A.B. 102
Brooklyn, Earl 12, 13
Brooks, Ellen 28
Brooks, Elliott 148
Brooks, Enoch 128
Brooks, Hilliard 14
Brooks, Roy 165–166
Brooks, Stephen 208
Brooks, Tyrone 11
Broome, Vernon 38
Brown, Ansel 130
Brown, Benjamin 90–91

Brown, Charles 29
Brown, Eddie 51
Brown, Gene 50–51
Brown, H. Rap 253, 254
Brown, Jessie 67
Brown, John 132
Brown, John (patrolman) 94
Brown, Levi 242
Brown, Mack 108–109
Brown, Nicey 142
Brown, Red 156
Brown, Sylvester 231
Brown, Thomas 156
Brown, William 161–162
Brown Berets 249
Brown v. Board of Education of Topeka 218
Brownell, Herbert, Jr. 17
Brownlee, Charles 92
Bruce, Brown, Jr. 82, 83
Brumfield, Carrie 92
Brumfield, Eli 44
Brunswick News 160
Bryan, J.T. 107–108
Bryant, Carolyn 19, 22
Bryant, Danny 177
Bryant, Farris 45
Bryant, John, Jr. 257
Bryant, Mose 197
Bryant, Roy 20–22, 24, 253
Bryant, T.A. 184
Bryars, Clarence 202
Bryson, J.R., Jr. 174
Buck, Harvey 257
Budz, Andrew 209
Buffington, John 257
Buford, K.L. 232
Burchfield, Jasper 74–75
Burnett, John 35
Burney, Ned 183
Burns, Herman 175
Burns, John 175
Burns, Julius 175
Burns, Virginia 175
Burrage, Olen 57, 59
Burts, James 174
Bush, George W. 4, 55
Bush, Jeb 55
Butler, Betty 210
Butler, Richard 222
Byrd, Daniel 132
Byrd, Richard 202–203

Cacurro, Frank 163
Cagle, Charles 47
Cagle, Helen 47
Cagney, Edward 195
Cahalan, William 237
Caldwell, Hamilton 24
Caldwell, Millard 141, 153
California 1, 143–145, 149, 175, 193, 241, 242–244, 250–252, 258–260
Callaway, Austin 118
Callaway, A.W. 137, 143
Camp Ellis 129

Camp Joseph T. Robinson 121–122
Camp Van Dorn 126–127
Campbell, Fred 91–92
Campbell, LeRoy 186
Campbell, Thomas 46–47
Campbell, Walter 145
Cannady, Lola 7–8
Cano, Jose 66
Carlington, John III 189
Carlisle, Willie 190–191
Carmichael, A.A. 109
Carmichael, Stokeley 85, 87, 253
Carpenter, George 183
Carroll, Hattie 216–217
Carroll, Omer 126
Carroll, Petie 98
Carroll County Georgian 76
Carson, Robert 220
Carswell, Tom 183
Carter, Alprentice 242–244
Carter, Angelina 179, 180
Carter, D.V. 176
Carter, Hodding 24
Carter, Hodding II 205
Carter, Hosea 172–173
Carter, Lila 139
Carter, William 179, 180
Carter, Willie 173
Case, Carroll 127
Cash, Lee 99
Caston, Billy Jack 43
Caston, Charles 255
Caston, E.L. 43, 44, 51
Caston, James 255
Caston, Silas 54
Causey, Clarence 241, 250
Causey, Elnora 211
Causey, Jonas 211–212
Cavin, Carl 54
Cawley, Louise 94
Centimano, Joe 256
Chalmers, Lester, Jr. 213
Chambers, Gordon 174
Chambliss, Robert 4
Chambliss, W.F. 7–8
Champion, Hugh 211
Chaney, James 40, 57–59, 216
Chapman, Lucille 34
Chappell, Johnnie 54–55
Chappell, Sheldon 55
Chappell, Willie 55
Charles, Chrispin 185
Chatham, Gerald 21
Chatman, Thomas, Jr. 248
Cheek, L.M. 194
Cherry, Bobby 4
Cherry, Weyman 31, 32
Chessman, Wayne 54–55
Chester, Charles 158
Chicago Defender 37, 136, 138, 169, 170, 202
Chicago Tribune 249
Chiefs (novel) 182
Childs, J.A. 39
Chiles, Joyce 22

Chism, Alma 82, 228
Christenberry, Herbert 133
Christian, Thad 78
Citizens Committee of Greater Little Rock 122
Citizens' Council 3, 17, 21, 38, 77, 207
Civil Rights and Restorative Justice Project 16, 69, 207
Civil Rights Congress 142, 143, 144. 145, 148, 150, 153, 162, 174, 177, 182, 188, 189, 190, 191, 193, 194, 195, 199
Civil Rights Memorial 1, 220
Clare, Richard 193
Clarion-Ledger 34, 56, 57, 113, 133, 205, 208, 235, 237
Clark, James 190–191
Clark, Jim (sheriff) 70, 212
Clark, L.D. 32
Clark, Mark 248–250
Clark, Michael 236
Clark, Reuben 87, 88
Clark, Tom 133, 136, 139, 141, 169
Clay, Cosby 146–147
Clay County Development Corporation 253
Clayton, Frank 190
Clemmons, U.W. 242
Clifton, J. Roderick 180
Clifton, Red 128
Cloninger, Clarence 43
Cloud, John 240, 241
Clutchette, John 251, 252
Cochran, Ruby 120
Cochran, W.S. 120
Cody, Lee 54, 55
Cogdell, C.J. 161
Cohen, Sharon 224
Cohen, Wilbert 142
COINTELPRO 242, 243, 249
Cole, Echol 95
Coleman, Donald 54
Coleman, James 37, 38, 39, 218
Coleman, Luther 197
Coleman, P.C. 197
Coleman, Stanton 168–170
Coleman, Thomas 77
Coley, John 221
Coley, Oscar 30
Colker, John 32
Collier, Robert 238
Collins, Ben 39
Collins, Ernest 106
Collins, George 148
Collins, Joshua 133
Collins, Leroy 199
Collins, Levi 21
Collins, Thelma 133
Colorado 158
Colston, David, Jr. 227
Colston, David, Sr. 226–227
Colvard, Dewey 48
Combs, Troy 97–98
Coming of Age in Mississippi 38, 207

Committee of Six 8
Commonweal magazine 144
Communist Party 18
Concordia Sentinel 60, 65, 74, 90
Cone, Frederick 110
Congress of Industrial Organizations 145
Congress of Racial Equality (CORE) 7, 47, 50, 54, 55, 64, 229, 243
Connally, Charles 206
Conner, Harvey 87–88
Connor, Dudley 218
Cook, Eddie 225
Cook, Elmer 70, 71
Cook, Grady 214
Cook, Oscar 214
Cook, W.G. 116
Cooley, Buck 213
Cooper, Carl 235–237
Cooper, Cynthia 226
Cooper, Hope 121
Cooper, James 196
Cooper, Prentice 136
Copeland, G.W. 167–168
Copling, John, Jr. 229
Corbin, George 213
Corbitt, J.L. 109
Corcoran, Joseph 195
Cornelison, "Tex" 143, 144
Cornish, R.E. 211
Cossar, George 81
Cotton, Cleo 128
Cottonmouth Moccasin Gang 85–89
Countryman, Willie 32, 33
Courts, Gus 17–18, 205
Couser, Raymond 163
Cowart, John 10, 184
Cox, Dale 8
Cox, Joseph 12, 13
Craig, Bill 152–153
Craig, William 239
Cranmore, William 232
Crawford, Isaac 173
Crews, Tom 141
Cribb, John 118–119
Crimm, Harold 255
Crisby, Amos 189
Crist, Charlie 13, 130
Croom, Carl 15
Cross, Arthur 129
Cross, Noah 66
Crowe, Dorman 72
Crowley, Wilbert 209
Culberson, Earthy 41
Culbertson, Frances 40
Culbreath, Lee 226
Culpepper, Robert, Jr. 124
Cunningham, S.T. 234
Cupit, R.A. 75
Curry, Charles 165

Dabbs, G.F. 123
Dahmer, Vernon 81, 84, 85
Dahmon, Vincent 84–85

Dailey, Gwen 82
Daily Clarion-Ledger 113
Daily Worker 18
Dale, Sebe, Sr. 38
Daniel, J. Saxton 129
Daniel, Ruby 155
Daniel, William 154–155
Daniels, Annie 35
Daniels, Jonathan 76–77, 171
Daniels, Lee 218
Daniels, Woodrow 34–35
Darnell, Tom 147
Davies, Elmer 148
Davila, Jose 134
Davis, Edward 211
Davis, Elisha 117
Davis, George 135–136
Davis, Henry 188
Davis, Hugh 168
Davis, James 54–55
Davis, L.C. 37
Davis, Paul 242
Davis, Rayfield 166
Davis, Roderick 236
Davis, Thomas 117
Davis, Willie 128–129
Dawkins, Charles 75
Dawson, Buddy 140
Dawson, Harper 131, 132
Dawson, Mann 132
Dawson, Roger 132
Dawson News 32
Dayton Daily News 229
Deans, Robert 170–171
Deaton, Calvin 222
Deaton, Herbert 86
Debardeleben, Mattie 190
Debow, Luolen 35
Dee, Henry 56–57
DeGraffenreid, Lloyd, Sr. 256
Deitle, Cynthia 5
De La Beckwith, Byron 4
DeLaughter, Frank 60, 64–65, 66
Delta Democrat-Times 24, 205, 217
Delta Ministry "Freedom Corps" 91
DeMascio, Robert 236
Denton, C. Hayes 147
Department of Justice 3, 4–6, 7, 8, 9, 11, 13, 15, 16, 18–19, 22, 23, 25, 26, 27, 28, 29, 30, 31, 32, 33, 34, 35, 36, 37, 38, 39, 40, 41, 42, 43, 44, 45, 46, 47, 48, 49, 50, 51, 52, 53, 54, 55, 56, 57, 59, 61, 62, 63, 64, 66, 67, 68, 69, 71, 73, 74, 76, 77, 78, 80, 81, 83, 84, 85, 86, 87, 88, 89, 90, 91, 92, 93, 95, 96, 97, 118, 129, 130, 136, 141, 232
Derrick, John 194
Dewey, Thomas 146
Diaz, Angel 258
Dickerson, Ben 10
Dickinson, Hattie 248
Dickinson, Jacob 147

Diggs, Charles 20
Dinkins, D.W. 70
Dismukes, Melvin 236–237
Dixon, Robert 201
Dodd, Christopher 4
Dogan, Ellett 81
Donatto, Joseph 200
Donehoo, Paul 109
Dorsey, George 9–11
Dorsey, Mae 9–11
Dougan, Eric 149
Douglas, Ruth 136
Doyle, Chester 110
Doyle, William 45
Drake, S.N. 81
Drane, Hayward 222
Drane, Louisa 222
Drumgo, Fleeta 251, 252
Duchak, Donald 209
Ducksworth, Melva 45
Ducksworth, Roman, Jr. 44–45
Duckworth, Edward 205–206
Duckworth, Wadell 206
Dukes, B.T. 27
Dukes, John 112
Dumas, Joseph 45
Dunigan, Willie 210–211
Dunn, Marvin 130
Dunnaway, William 197
Dunne, George 144–145
Durden, James 46
Dwight, Tommy 213
Dyer, Stonewall 87
Dylan, Bob 22, 217

Eagerton, Carl 118–119
Earle, Willie 156–157
Earp, J.E. 196
Eastland, James 126
Eddins, W.E. 123
Edmundson, Paul 171
Edwards, Charles (deputy) 151
Edwards, Charles (Klansman) 56
Edwards, Cleveland 250–252
Edwards, Joseph 60–61
Edwards, Malinda 28
Edwards, Willie 27–28
Eisenhower, Dwight 212
Elkins, Herschell 213
Ellender, A.J. 114
Elliott, J. Jefferson 12
Elliott, James 122
Elmore, B.F. 44
Elmore, Nesbitt 159
Embry, Frank 28
Emmett Till Justice Campaign 5
Emmett Till Unsolved Civil Rights Crime Act 4–6, 8, 9, 11, 13, 14, 15, 16, 18, 23, 25, 26, 27, 28, 29, 30, 31, 32, 33, 35, 36, 38, 39, 41, 42, 44, 45, 48, 49, 50, 52, 53, 54, 55, 56, 57, 59, 61, 62, 63, 64, 66, 67, 68, 69, 71, 73, 74, 75, 76, 77, 78, 80, 81, 52, 84, 85, 86, 87, 88, 89, 90, 91, 92, 93, 95, 96, 130, 163, 255
English, Maxine 134
Erwin, Andrew 177
Erwin, Tom 159
Estes, J.F. 39
Evans, J.C. 110–111
Evans, Lucius 30
Evans, Pheld see Brown, Gene
Evans, Robert 194
Evanston, James 25
Everett, Ronald see Karenga, Maulana
Evers, Medgar 4, 24, 46, 204, 205, 214, 218, 245

Falkenheimer, J.T. 39
Falvey, Charles 18–19
Farley, Michael 50
Farmer, I.C. 203
Farmer, J.C. 151
Farmer, Saxon 227
Farmer, W.F. 133
Farrior, Rex 98
Farrow, Australia 158, 159
Fayetteville Observer 27
Featherstone, Ralph 252–254, 257
Federal Bureau of Investigation (FBI) 4, 5, 7, 9, 10, 11, 12, 13, 14, 15, 17, 18, 19, 20, 23, 25, 28, 29, 31, 32, 33, 35–36, 37, 38, 40, 41, 42, 43, 44, 45, 46, 47, 48, 49, 50–51, 52, 53, 54, 56, 57, 58, 59, 60, 63, 64, 65, 66, 67, 68, 70, 71, 73, 75, 76, 77, 78, 79, 80, 82, 83, 86, 87, 88, 90, 92, 95, 96, 117, 118, 121, 123, 125, 128, 129, 132, 133, 135, 136, 139, 141, 144, 152, 156, 166, 167, 169, 183, 191, 201, 202, 212, 220, 226, 228, 233, 239, 242–243, 245, 249, 250, 254, 255
Fellowship of the Concerned 209
Ferguson, Alfonzo 145–146
Ferguson, Boyce 86
Ferguson, Charles 145–146
Ferguson, Ellsworth 252
Ferguson, Joseph 146
Ferguson, Richard 145–146
Ferguson, William 140
Ferrell, Charles 181–182
Finch, Tom 108
Fitzharris, Cletus 251, 252
Flanagan, R. Purdy 113
Flay, Gilbert 225
Fleming, John 30, 68, 78
Fleming, William 147, 148
Fletcher, Charles 163
Florida 7–8, 12–13, 54–55, 66, 104, 127–128, 139–130, 153, 176, 186–187, 197, 199–200, 244
Flourney, D.M. 116
Flowers, Lucio 26

Flowers, Richmond 77
Floyd, Jerry 208
Fogleman, Julian 15
Fontana Herald News 144
Food, Tobacco, and Allied Workers of America 145
Foote, Eddie 87
Ford, Geraldine 236
Foreman, Ray 123
Forman, James 80
Forman, Lenox 53
Forrest County Cooperative 218
Fort Benning 119
Fort Bragg 197
Fort Dix 194
Fort Meade 219–220
Fortune, Charlena 233
Foster, Thomas 122–123
Foster, William 188
Fountain, George 171
Fountain, J.A. 183
Fowler, James 68, 84
Franks, S.C. 156
Fraternal Order of Police 250
Free D.C. Movement 253
Freedom, Inc. 256
Freedom of Information Act 242
Frieberg, Arthur 137
Fron, Edward 209
Fugate, Ordley 98
Fuller, Claude 85–86
Fuller, Ed 53
Fulton, Lonnie 118–119

Gaines, Prentiss 140
Galveston Daily News 206
Galvin, Linda 59
Gantt, Benjamin 151, 152
Gantt, Thomas 163
Garrett, Fred 221
Garrett, W.A. 191
Gartin, Carroll 210
Garwood, Edward 122
Gary, Ed 143
Gatlin, John 225
Gatreaux, E.H. 177
Gauss, Barkley 128
Gayle, William 210
Gehrig, James 146
Geiger Field 148–149
Gentry, Leroy 213
Georgia 4, 9–11, 12, 26, 33, 41–42, 71, 76, 87, 105, 107–108, 119, 124–126, 128–129, 139, 149–150, 158, 160–161, 173, 175–176, 177–181, 181, 182, 183–184, 188, 191–192, 197–198, 199, 210, 215
Gerson, Simon 175
Geter, Gordon 54
Gibbs, Phillip 255–256
Gibney, Pat 138
Gibson, John 5
Gibson, Lee 98
Gilbert, Dora 154
Gilbert, Ernest 159–160

Index

Gilbert, John 151
Gilbert, Sam 154
Gillespie, Bob 203
Gillespie, Connis 101
Gilley, Claude 116
Gilligan, Thomas 61–62
Gillis, Dana 49
Gipson, Reese 67
Girarders gang 247, 248
Gist, Kelly 194
Glasper, Herman 181
Glenn, W.T. 116
Glines, Joe 143–144
Glover, Albert 121
Glover, Raleigh 90
Goff, Cynthia 129–130
Goff, Phil 130
Goforth, A.F. 136
Goforth, Henry 136
Goldwasser, Joseph 180
Gonzales, Alberto 5
Gooden, Albert 110
Goodman, Andrew 57–59, 216
Goodwin, Leroy 174
Goodwyn, John 14
Gordon, Jesse 188
Gordon, William 147–148
Gore, Eunice 184
Gore, Lillian 34
Gorski, Edward 209
Graham, James 193
Grant, J.B. 108
Grant, Tommy 36
Graves, Thomas 98
Graves, Walter 211
Gray, Bill 169, 170
Gray, Grafton 81–82
Gray, Mace 106
Gray, R.E. 179–181
Gray, Texas 245
Green, Ernest 123–124
Green, James 255–256
Green, Jethro, Sr. 42
Green, Larry 41
Green, Mary 102
Green, Mattie 41–42, 210
Green, Mr. (alleged killer) 76
Green, Moses 141
Green, Samuel 179
Green, Tom 112
Green-McCray, Gloria 256
Greenberg, Ben 53
Greenlee, Charles 186, 187, 199
Greensboro Record 195
Greenwood, Jasper 59
Grenada County Freedom Movement 234
Gresham, Deloris 205
Griffin, Jack, Jr. 125
Griffin, Jimmie 78–79
Griggs, Son 99
Grimes, Lawton 172
Groat, Gerald 237
Gross, A.M. 97
"Groveland Boys" 186–187, 199–200
Gubow, Lawrence 236

Guihard, Paul 45
Guilbeau, Clayton 200–201
Gumn, Fred 208
Gunn, Canana 154
Gunter, George 141, 169–170
Guthrie, R.E. 126
Guyot, Lawrence 80

Hadad, Chuck 16
Hagood, M.M. 116
Haile, Calvin 159
Hairston, Coleman 195
Hale, Walter 135
Hale County Improvement Association 225
Hall, A.C. 45–46
Hall, Cal, Jr. 71
Hall, Dave 229
Hall, Felix 119
Hall, Robert 171
Hamill, William 163
Hamilton, Beatrice 30
Hamilton, Rogers 30
Hamlett, Adlena 81–83
Hammond, Samuel 93–95
Hampton, Collie 86–87
Hampton, Fred 248–250
Hancock, Robert 33
Hanley, David 188
Hanrahan, Edward 249–250
Hansen, Carl 165
Harbour, Arnold 155–156
Hardy, L.F. 156
Hare, James 70
Harmon, James 165
Harp, Junior 65
Harpole, Earl 197
Harrell, Daniel 226–227
Harrington, Dottie 13
Harrington, Frank 13
Harris, Albert, Jr. 151
Harris, Alphonso 88–89
Harris, Billy 252
Harris, Brenda 249, 250
Harris, Charles 113
Harris, Denice 137
Harris, James 57
Harris, Lewis 105
Harris, L.H. 112
Harris, Madison 137, 143
Harris, Parker 103
Harris, Pete 59
Harris, Romie 222
Harris, Tom 81
Harris, William 172–173
Harrison, Cellos 127–128
Harrison, J. Loy 10
Hatcher, George 154
Hatchett, J.B. 161
Hauser, Henry 132–133
Hawkins, Richard 110
Hay, Abner 121–122
Haynes, Aubrey 78
Haynes, Jerry 78
Haynes, Oscar, Jr. 151–152
Haynes, Oscar, Sr. 151, 152
Haynes, Oscar III 152

Haynes, Oscar IV 152
Haynes, Robert 78
Haynes, W.T. 99
Hazard Herald 98
Hazelwood, George 131
Helfrich, Bob 219
Helm, Jack 227
Helpenstill, Travis 166–168
Henderson, O'Dee 116
Henderson, Russell 160, 161
Hendrix, Bill 12
Henry, Aaron 212, 214
Henry, Ezra 150
Henry, Isaiah 16
Henry, James, Jr. 150
Henry, Raymond, Jr. 12–13
Henry, Tom 130
Henry, Willie 150
Henson, A.L. 143
Henson, George 121
Hentschel, Bradley 53
Herndon, Frank 57
Hester, Barnette 10
Hester, George 10
Hicks, Samuel 148–149
Higgenbotham, Elwood 105
Hightower, Jesse 143
Hightower, Ted 117
Hildebrand, Joe 195
Hill, Arthur 76
Hill, Caleb, Jr. 183–184
Hill, Doc 206
Hill, George 154
Hill, Kenneth 232
Hines, Corinne 202
Hines, Earl 234
Hinton, Ira, Jr. 203–204
Hinton, Meade 203
Hinton, S.C. 115
Hitler, Adolf 123
Hobby, T.C. 218
Hoegemeyer, Frank 106
Hoggle, Namon 70–71
Hoggle, William 70–71
Holden, Joel 133
Holder, Eric 5
Holland, Spessard 128, 130
Holley, Thomas 164
Holliday, Tolbert 97
Holloway, David 224–225
Holloway, Robert 190, 191
Holmes, Cleveland 214
Holmes, Connie 194
Holmes, Inez 214
Holmes, Warren 134
Holt, R.V. 149
Holtam, R.G. 232
Homochitto National Forest 56–57, 85–86, 222
Hood, Timothy 146
Hooker, Leon 214
Hooven, James 165
Hoover, J. Edgar 10, 118, 133, 152, 191, 242
Horrall, Clement 176
Horton, John 51
Houey, Smith 100–101

House Committee on Un-American Activities 75
Houston, James 122
Howard, Golden 10–11
Howard, James 130
Howard, Lula 130
Howard, Robert 11
Howard, T.R.M. 17, 21
Howard, William 143
Howard, Willie 129–130
Howell, Charles 141
Howell, William 180
Hubbard, Connis 219–220
Hudson, Charlean 168
Hudspeth, R.H. 101
Huey, Albert 158–159
Huffman, James 232
Huffman, Rufus 233
Huggins, John 242–244
Huguley, Harrell 190
Huie, William 20
Humphrey, Robert 180
Humphreys, Murray 133
Hunt, James, Jr. 94
Hunter, Ernest 35
Hunter, Frank 155
Hunter, Tip 117
Hurd, Roosevelt 156
Hurst, Eugene 43–44
Hurst, William 239
Hutson, Ellis, Jr. 167–168
Hutson, Ellis, Sr. 166–168

Igleburger, Robert 238
Illinois 122–123, 129, 195, 208–209, 215, 217–219, 248–250
Indiana 28–29, 122, 241
Ingle, Bobby 27
Ingle, Claude 27
International Labor Defense 136
International Paper Company 52, 53, 75
Invaders (militant group) 95
Iowa 228–229
Irvin, Walter 186–187, 199–200
Ivy, Charles 257

Jackson, Chatwick 67
Jackson, David 215
Jackson, Eli 222
Jackson, Exerlena 89
Jackson, George 241, 251, 252
Jackson, Jesse 249
Jackson, Jimmie 67–68, 84
Jackson, Joe 30
Jackson, Luther 39–41
Jackson, Michael 68
Jackson, Nathaniel 146
Jackson, Viola 68
Jackson, Wharlest, Sr. 89–90
Jackson Daily News 21
Jackson State College 90–91, 255–256
Jacobs, Olivia 121
James, Edna 87
James, William 87

James Avenue Church of God in Christ 231
Jefferson, Jesse 174
Jells, Ernest 50
Jenkins, Carol 241–242
Jenkins, Elizabeth
Jenkins, Kenzie 177
Jenkins, Percy 91, 92, 201–202
Jeter, Joseph, Jr. 35–36
Johns, Marshall 42
Johnson, Alexander 97
Johnson, Andrew 195
Johnson, C.L. 190
Johnson, Deborah 250
Johnson, H. 204
Johnson, Harrison 150
Johnson, Hilbert 146
Johnson, Jacob 240
Johnson, James 147–148
Johnson, Jim 176
Johnson, John 172
Johnson, Johnny 176
Johnson, Lyndon 93, 227
Johnson, Nathan, Jr. 68, 84
Johnson, Paul, Sr. 123–124, 126
Johnson, Robert 98
Johnson, Roy 24
Johnson, Versie 162
Johnson, Walter (prosecutor) 204
Johnson, Walter (victim) 153
Johnson, Wes 109
Johnson, Willie 182
Johnston, Erle, Jr. 54
Jones, Alvin 173
Jones, Carrie 152
Jones, Cecil 175
Jones, Curtis 19, 20
Jones, Daniel 51, 52
Jones, Dennis 222
Jones, Edwin 33
Jones, Ervin 139–140
Jones, Eugene 188–189
Jones, Frank 100
Jones, Frank (deputy) 124–125
Jones, James 85–86
Jones, John 151–152
Jones, Joseph, Jr. 39
Jones, Julius *see* Jones, Yoeman
Jones, L.D. 95–96
Jones, L.L. 198
Jones, Lloyd 91
Jones, Madison 123
Jones, Marion 104
Jones, Officer 36, 150
Jones, Robert 100–101
Jones, Sam 193
Jones, Tom, Jr. 140
Jones, Tommy (judge) 68
Jones, Tommy (Klansman) 66
Jones, Wiley 194
Jones, Willie 106, 113
Jones, Yoeman 225
Jordan, Danella 245
Jordan, Leon 256–257
Jordan, Michael 245

Joubert, Jacob 199
Joyner, Bobby 1995

Kane, Buddy 91
Kansas City Star 256
Karenga, Maulana 243–244
Kato, Elmer 54–55
Kavanaugh, Jerome 144
Kazar, Justin 64
Keating, M.C. 112
Kees, Willis 107
Keglar, Birdia 81–83
Keglar, James 228
Keglar, Robert 228
Kelley, Jim 124
Kelley, Tom 248
Kellum, James 184–185
Kelly, John
Kelly, R.B. 70, 71
Kelly, S.C. 174
Kelly, William 45
Kemper County Messenger 156
Kennamer, Charles 191
Kennard, Clyde 217–219
Kennedy, Hayes 182
Kennedy, Herbert 107
Kennedy, Lloyd 147–148
Kennedy, Robert 82
Kennedy, Stetson 139
Kennedy-Smith, Samuel 207
Kennefick, Charles 174
Kenny, Robert 144
Kent State University 255
Kentucky 86–87, 97–98, 188
Kentucky New Era 100
Kernan, Robert 220
Kester, Howard 8, 109
Keyes, R.L. 225
Kiado, Martin 122
Kilcommons, Peter 174
Killen, Edgar 57, 59
Killian, Gaddis 48
Killian, George 48
Kimball, Elmer 23–24, 204
Kimball, Sammy 24
King, Alfred 246–247
King, Alveda 246
King, Camright
King, Martin, Jr. 5, 209, 212, 213, 227, 233. 246
King, Martin, Sr. 246
King, Naomi 247
King, Richard *see* King, William
King, Tima 117
King, William 205
King, Willie 233
King v. Chapman et al. 9, 26
Kinser, Bill 98
Kirby, N/A 110
Kirby, Shelley 78
Kirk, Tommy 245
Klavalier Klub 139
Klopfer, Susan 82, 205, 208, 217, 222, 224, 225, 228
Klunder, Bruce 55–56
KMEX television 258
Knight, Bunion 211–212

Knight, Claxton 227, 229
Knouse, Rick 248
Knox, Alfred 52
Knox, Gordon 161
Knuckles, W.C. 97
Kollmann, Geraldine 106
Kozlowski, Raymond 209
Kramer, Joseph 209
Kroft, Steve 52
Ku Klux Klan 1, 3, 8, 9, 10, 12–13, 26, 27–28, 40, 42, 45, 47–48, 49, 50, 51, 52, 56–59, 60–61, 64, 65, 66, 68, 69, 70, 72, 75, 77, 80, 81, 82, 84, 85–86, 88, 89–90, 128, 139, 147, 151, 175, 178–179, 181, 192, 197, 199, 207, 210, 211, 212, 221, 222, 225, 226, 227, 229, 232, 241, 246
Kwanzaa 243

Lacey, Robert 231
Lafargue, Malcolm 151
Laffoon, Ruby 98
Lamar, Bedsole 137
Lamarr, Robert 155
Lambert, J. Frank 190
Lancaster, C.D. 100
Lanclos, David 201
Landry, E. 185
Laney, Gene 240
Lang, Charles 123–124
Langdon, John 238–239
Lanier, Joseph 94
Lanier, W.L. 180
Lathers, George 134
Lattimer, Tobe 33
Laurel Leader-Call 225
Lauridson, James 28
Lawing, Roy 188
Lee, Aaron 235
Lee, Beverly 162
Lee, Cager 67
Lee, George 17–18, 205
Lee, Herbert 43–44, 51
Lee, Howard 31, 33
Lee, J. Floren 37
Lee, J.F. 37
Lee, John *see* Lee, William
Lee, Vaughn 131–132
Lee, William 68–69
Levine, Sam 161
Lewis, Clayton 40
Lewis, Jannie 255
Lewis, John 4
Lewis, Robert 65
Lewis, William 188
Ligon, Allen 189
Lillard, Richard 35
Limpus, Charles, Sr. 197
Lindsay, Virgil 239
Lingo, Albert 68, 77
Lippitt, Norman 236
Lipscomb, James 111
Littlebrant, Marland 134
Little, Bill 206
Little, Ruby 25

Littles, Elree 167
Liuzzo, Viola 71, 77
Livingston, Sonny, Jr. 28
Lockhart, Rich 257
Loggins, Henry 21
Lollar, Michael 96
Long, Huey 103
Long, Kenny 146–147
Long, Meron 146–147
Looby, Z. Alexander 136, 148
Look magazine 4, 20
Los Angeles County Sheriff's Department 258–259
Los Angeles Police Department 175, 243
Los Angeles Sentinel 144
Los Angeles Times 258, 259
Lott, Pat 234
Louisiana 16, 37, 42, 53, 60–61, 64–65, 66, 71–73, 74, 92, 99, 100, 103, 114, 122, 133, 148, 151–152, 167, 208, 229, 241
Love, George 31
Love, J.A. 203
Love, Joe 98–99
Lovett, Willie 217
Lowery, Arthur 166, 168
Lowndes County Freedom Organization 254
Lucas, Robert 136
Luckey, George 205–206
Luckey, Herman 206
Luckie, Charles 164
Lunsford, H.L. 192
lynching 3, 7–8, 9–11, 12, 36–38, 46, 57–59, 97–101, 102, 103–111, 112, 114–118, 119, 120–121, 122, 123–124, 128, 129, 134–136, 151–152, 153, 156–157, 158, 175, 180, 181, 183–184, 208, 224

Mack, Percy, Jr. 51
Madden, Ike 172
Maddix, R.A. 252
Maddry, Sam, Jr. 151
Maddry, Sam, Sr. 151
Madison County Herald 116
Mafia 53
Mahone, Maybelle 27
Malachy, Norman 36
Malcom, Dorothy 9–11
Malcom, Roger 9–11
Mallard, Amy 179
Mallard, John 181
Mallard, Robert 177–181
Mann, Joseph 198–199
Mann, O.B. 205
Manning, Glenn 206
Manor, Marlon 25
Mants, Bob 30
Marbury, Luke 220
Marshall, Barnes 257
Marshall, Thurgood 117, 121, 130, 132, 138, 141, 148, 150
Martin, Dorothy 123
Martin, Harlon 168

Martin, J. Robert 157
Martzell, William 127
Maryland 44, 47, 188, 216–217, 219–220, 252–254
Mason, Mark 100–101
Mason, R.W. 134
Mathis, Prentiss 52
Matthews, Charlie 12
Matthews, Delbert 65
Matthews, Linwood 188
Matthews, Marvin 163
Matthews, Sutton 149–150
Matthews, Van 196
Matthews, Zachary 31
Maxwell, Sylvester 46–47
Mayo, Johnnie 127
McAdams, O.B. 113
McArthur, Donald 213
McCain, McCauley 101
McCall, Willis 13, 186, 187, 199–200
McCamy, A.L. 107–108
McCann, Prentiss 138–139
McCann, Rena 139
McCarron, Walter 209
McCarthy, Ray 221
McCaskey, David 92
McClendon, Ed 123
McCord, Jim 136
McCrimon, R.M. 176
McCullers, S.B. 130
McCurdy, George 30
McDaniel, Edward 66
McDaniel, John 8
McDaniels, Robert 109–110
McDonald, David 140–141
McDonald, Randolph 31
McDonald, Willie 112
McDowell, Bessie 27
McDuffie, Della 201–202
McDuffie, William 201–202
McDuffy, W.E. 179
McElroy, Taylor 185
McElveen, Ernest 228
McEnery, Daniel 187
McFadden, Sam 141
McFayden, Dudley 138
McGarrh, Lee 23–24
McGee, Joe 101
McGee, R.D. 103
McGettingan, Manus 163
McGough, T.H. 15
McGowan, Wilder 115
McGraw, Mike 256–257
McKeithen, John 73
McKinney, Gwendolyn 135
McKnight, Leo 52
McLauren, Judge 206
McLean, Charles 170
McLeod, Andrew 99
McLeod, Blanchard 70
McLin, Clarence, Jr. 238
McMillan, M.S. 34
McNair, Lesley 127
McNair, Robert (governor) 94
McNair, Robert (victim) 79–80
McNeal, Lloyd 123

McPharland, Ernest 42
McQueen, Connie 242
McQueen, Shirley 241
McTatie, Leon 149
McWhorter, Diane 221
McWilliams, Matt 155–156
McWilliams, Nettie 155
Mears Newz 134
Meeks, Donald 238–239
Melton, Beulah 24, 204–205s
Melton, Clinton 23–25
Melvin, John 195–196
Memphis Press-Scimitar 108
Meneweather, Thomas 252
Meredith, James 46, 84, 85, 217
Mergerson, Willie 166
Messersmith, Arthur 248
Messersmith, Robert 248
Metcalf, Red 54
Metcalfe, George 89–90
Metts, Colie 94
Mexican American Legal Defense and Educational Fund 260
Michael, David 238
Michigan 20, 96, 117, 134, 162, 215, 225, 235–237
Middleton, Delano 93–95
Middleton, Virgil 253
Milam, John 20–22, 23, 24
Miles, E.W. 181
Milledgeville State Hospital 42, 192
Miller, Alvin 250–251
Miller, Horace 166
Miller, Hosie 71
Miller, James 63
Miller, Leighton 212
Miller, Opie 252
Miller, Orloff 69, 70
Miller, Pearl 122
Mills, John 252
Mills, Marvin 14
Milton, Jack 174
Milton, William 174–175
Minakotis, Basil 194
Minninger, James 169–170
Minor, Flossie 59
Mississippi 4, 17–22, 30, 31, 34–35, 36–40, 43–45, 46–47, 51–54, 56–59, 60, 63–64, 65, 68–69, 72, 74–76, 78–80, 81–83, 84–86, 88, 89–91, 97, 100–101, 102, 103–104, 111–112, 123–124, 126–127, 131–132, 139, 140–141, 149, 168–170, 174, 177, 184–185, 202–203, 205, 207, 208, 214–216, 217–219, 222–224, 225–226, 228, 229, 239–240, 245, 252–253, 254–256, 257
Missouri 120–121, 187–188, 244, 256–257
Mitcham, Doyle 190–191
Mitchell, Bennie, Jr. 106
Mitchell, Jerry 56, 57, 208. 219
Mitchell, John 200–201

Mitchell, Lester 229–230
Mitchell, Lizzie 239
Mitchell, Vance 161
Mixon, Booker 39
Mize, Wiley 131
Mobile Register 138
Mohr, Ferdinand 160
Montenegro, Eugene 149
Montgomery, Anna 42
Montgomery, Neimiah 63
Montgomery, Sam 172
Montgomery Advertiser 210
Montgomery Improvement Association 212
Moody, Anne 38–39, 207
Moody, W. Osborne 36
Moore, Bert 103–104
Moore, Charles 56–57, 80
Moore, D. 208
Moore, Edward 94
Moore, Harriette 12–13, 187
Moore, Harry 12–13, 130, 187
Moore, James 184–185
Moore, Jamie 233, 234
Moore, J.T. 104
Moore, L.S. 70
Moore, Oneal 71–73
Moore, O.P. 106
Moore, Thomas 56
Moore, William 47–48
Moore, W.O. 217
Morace, E.D. 66
Morgan, A.D. 86
Morgan, David 91, 92
Morgan, E.M. 194
Morgan, Juliette 97, 209–210
Morris, Fee 136
Morris, Frank 60, 64–66
Morris, Guy 122
Morris, Luther 118–119
Morrisroe, Richard 76–77
Morton, A.J. 147
Morton, Dooley 103–104
Moseley, Berry 107
Motley, James 87–88
Murder on the Suwannee River (film) 130
Murphy, Frank 115
Muske, A.H. 121
Myles, Elijah 160

Nash, John 180
Nash, Levie 215
Nash, Otis 215–216
Nashville Globe 136
Natchez Democrat 168
National Association for the Advancement of Colored People (NAACP) 7, 8, 12, 15, 17, 20–21, 24, 25, 26, 38, 39, 42, 43, 46, 50, 51, 52, 54, 67, 71, 81, 84, 89, 91, 109, 114, 115, 116, 117, 119, 121, 122, 123, 127, 130, 132, 133, 136, 138, 140, 141, 144, 148, 150, 151, 152, 154, 161, 162, 167, 168, 169, 176, 179, 187, 198, 199,
200, 201, 204, 205, 212, 214, 218, 232, 242, 245, 248
National Chicano Moratorium Committee 258
National Funeral Home 140
National Negro Congress 158
National States Rights Party 50, 72
National Urban League 244
National Young Lords 249
Neal, Claude 7–8
Neff, Gregory 248
Neil, William 135–136
Nelson, Johnnie 23
Nelson, Joyce 23
Nelson, Stanley 60, 61
Nelson, Thomas 116
New Jersey 165, 194
New Journal and Guide 199
New York 8, 61–62, 145–146, 163, 171, 174–175, 181–182, 187, 189, 192, 194, 201, 215, 254
New York Times 46, 104, 160
New Yorker magazine 157
Newberry Street Boys 248
Newman, David 245
Newman, Michelle 155
News & Observer 195
Newsome, Otis 170–171
Newton, Calphus 154
Newton, Demetrius 155
Newton, Dennis 254
Nguyen, Mary 169
Nixon, Edgar 162
Nixon, Isaiah 175–176
Nixon, Richard 93
Nixon, Sallie 176
Noble, Marion 172
Nobles, G.R. 206
Nolen, W.L.
Nonsectarian Anti-Nazi League 139
Norquist, Griffin 25
Norris, Mary 158–159
North Carolina 26–27, 28–29, 43, 104, 151, 158, 170–171, 194, 195–196, 197, 213
Northeastern University 16, 69, 91, 206, 207, 214
Norvell, Aubrey 85
Nowobielski, Frank 209
Noyes, Mary *see* Norris, Mary

Obama, Barack 5
O'Brien, Lloyd 132
Office of Independent Review 260
Ogden, Bill 60
Oglesby, T.L. 86
Ohio 55–56, 119, 168, 229–230, 238, 244, 255
Olsen, Clark 69–70
O'Mara, Gerald 208
O'Neal, William 249–2
O'Neill, John 174
O'Quinn, Ida 38

Index

O'Quinn, Samuel 38–39,
Orange, James 67
Orangeburg Massacre 93–95
Oregon 55
Original Knights of the Ku Klux Klan 227
Orlando Morning Sentinel 162
Orlando Sentinel 181
Orlando Sentinel-Star 197
Orsby, Herbert 63–64
Overbey, Arch 159
Owens, William 26–27
Owsley, Cliff 192

Padgett, Norma 187
Padgett, Willie 186
Page, Grafton 100
Paille, Robert 236–237
Palmer, Alvin 208–209
Palmertree, R.W. 52–53
Palumbo, Louis 194
Parchman Penitentiary 218, 219
Parker, Jack 49
Parker, Leroy 188
Parker, Mack 36–38
Parker, Thomas 224
Parker, Tony 225
Parmley, Hagan 167
Parrish, J.D. 232
Parrish, William 232
Passmore, Louis 197–198
Pate, Earl 113
Patterson, A.T. 185
Patterson, Clark 35
Patterson, John 212
Patterson, W.B. 80–81
Patton's Chapel Negro Church 99
Pavlik, Lawrence 209
Payne, Jesse 153
Payne, Larry 95–96
Payne, William 254
Pearson, H.L. 208
Pennsylvania 163, 247–248
Pentwater News 134
People magazine 242
People's Law Office 250
Perkins, Joe 175
Perrigan, Hess 120
Perry, James 187–188
Perry, Joseph 250
Perry, Will 10
Person, Rosa 213–214
Person, William 213–214
Persons, James 122–123
Peters, H.L. 11
Peters, J.L. 133
Peters, Ray 159
Peterson, James 208
Peterson, T.E. 240
Peterson, Virgil 127
Pettiford, John 219
Phifer, Anne 182
Phifer, Charles 182
Philadelphia Tribune 127
Phillips, Herbert 141
Phipps, Hiram 225

Pickett, Clarence 30
Pickett, Fred 54
Pierce, Malcolm 183–184
Piercefield, William 74
Pigdons, Charles 234
Pilcher, Lee 239
Pillow, William 147
Pinckney, J.L. 143
Pinella, Victor 177
Pittman, Nathaniel 196
Pittman, William 158
Pitts, Albert 42
Pitts, Clayton 240–241
Pitts, David 42
Pitts, Henry 239
Pitts, McLean 239
Pittsburgh Courier 169, 176
Poissot, O.C. 65–66, 90
Pollard, Aubrey 235–237
Pollock, H.G. 110
Pool, Rainey 254–255
Pope, Lonnie 149
Porter, Floyd 210, 211
Porter, Melvin 138
Porter, Sonny 195
Porter, William 253
Porterie, Gaston 200, 2001
Posey, Billy 57
Poteat, Manley 125
Poteat, Walter 125
Potok, Mark 5
Powders, Ernest 110
Powell, Jack 104–105
Powell, James 61–62
Powers, Lillie 225–226
Poynter, Ernest 122
Prather, William 41
Pratt, Bettye 244
Pratt, Edwin 244–245
President's Commission on Campus Unrest 255
Pressly, St. Claire 142
Prettyman, Fred 195
Price, Cecil 57–58
Price, Charles (judge) 28
Price, Charles (lyncher) 122
Price, Mrs. Elmer 185
Price, Otis 114
Price, Paul 234
Price, Roland 163
Prince, George 81
Prince, Ralph 23
Pritchard, Robert 75
Pritchett, Kermit, Jr. 213
Privette, A.A. 170
Progressive Voters League 12
Pugh, Ernest 233
Purl, T.H. 137
Purnell, Guy 239
Purvis, Dennis 183–184

Queen, John 74–75

Raby, J.G. 196
Rainey, Lawrence 40–41, 57–58, 215–216
Randle, Henry 202–203

Rankin County News 223
Rasberry, Charles 232
Rasberry, Donald 69
Ratcliff, Walter 214
Ray, Nathaniel 193
Ray, Nolan 165
Red Guard Party 249
Reeb, James 69–71
Reed, Allen 206
Reed, John 54
Reed, Joseph 175
Reed, Willie 110
Reeder, L.L. 233
Reese, John 22–23
Reeves, Mrs. Emory 159
Reeves, James, Jr. 238–239
Reeves, Jim 226–227
Regional Counsel of Negro Leadership 18
Rehling, Carl 213
Reyer, Columbus 37
Rhodes, Doris 117
Rhodes, James 229
Rice, Glenn 256–257
Rice, Michael 188
Rich, Jasper 184–185
Rich, J.W. 54–55
Richardson, Bill 40
Richmond, Dan 245
Richmond, Earnest 239–240
Richmond, Kenneth 241–242
Rider, Narville 132
Rider, Noble 131–132
Ridgen, David 56
Rigdon, Mrs. M.A. 207
Riles, Holis 188
Riley, Archibald 239
Robbins, Jerry 219
Roberts, Alton 57
Roberts, Joe 158
Roberts, Johnny 218
Robertson, Charles 248
Robins Air Force Base 198
Robinson, Amelia 229
Robinson, Fred 42–43
Robinson, Johnny 48–49
Robinson, J.T. 90
Robinson, Noverta 154
Robinson, Plater 52
Roebuck, M.C. 167
Rogers, Creed 71–73
Rogers, Joe 116
Rogers, J.P. 120
Rogers, William 40
Rogge, John 118
Rolen, Billy 213
Romeika, Joseph 145–146
Romney, George 235
Roney, Henry 245
Roosevelt, Franklin 119
Roper, Samuel 9
Ross, L.A. 214
Ross, Perry 23
Rowe, Gary 70–71
Rudolph, Tom 155
Rushin, John 107
Russell, Allen 94

Russell, C.W. 20
Russell, Milton 205
Russer, Joyce 208
Rybka, Ronald 209

Sahue, E. 185
St. Petersburg Times 199
St. Tammany Farmer 177
Salazar, Rubén 258–260
Sales, Ruby 77
Salky, Irvin 96
Sallis, Eddie 228–229
San Quentin Prison 241, 252
Sanchez, Gilardo 258
Sanchez, Guillermo 258
Sanders, James 99–100
Sanford, Willie 28
Sapp, Robert 119
Satchell, Ronald 249
Sauls, Henry 45
Scales, Charlie 223–224
Scales, James 134–136
Scarborough, James 66
Schaad, Henry 248
Schemanski, Robert 236
Schrade, Alan 32
Schultz, Herman 37
Schwartz, Joseph (activist) 222
Schwartz, Joseph (killer) 208–209
Schwerner, Michael 40, 57–59
Scott, A.M. 130
Scott, H.E. 135–136
Scott, Marshall 66
Scott, Morris 193
Scott, Notie 135–136
Scott, Rexwell 97–98
Screws, Mack 124–126, 129
Seale, Homer 229
Seale, James 56–57
Seattle Post-Intelligencer 245
Seattle Weekly 245
Segrest, Marvin
Sellers, Cleveland, Jr. 94
Senak, David 236–237
Shafer, Raymond 248
Shapiro, Joseph 74
Sharpe, Jerry 57
Sharpe, Thomas 180
Shaw, Almas 172
Shaw, Lint 107
Shealy, David 94
Shelby, Jesse 26
Shelby, Ollie 67
Shell, Lester 32
Shell, Mickey 230
Shelton, Anthony 230–231
Shelton, Isaac 17–18
Shelton, Mack 230
Shepard, J.E. 150
Shepherd, James 186
Shepherd, Samuel 186–187, 199–200
Sherrod, Shirley 71
Shields, T. Wilmer 193
Shoffiett, Paul 191

Sholtz, David 8
Shores, Arthur 221
Short, Barry 144
Short, Carol 144
Short, Helen 144
Short, O'Day 143–144
Shuttlesworth, Fred 221, 233
Sikes, Barney 180
Sikes, Herschel 180
Silmon, Joe 190–191
Silmon, Roy 191
Silver Dollar Bar 258–259
Silver Dollar Group 60–61, 66, 90
Silver Moon Café 70, 71
Simmons, Eldridge 132
Simmons, Isaac 131–132
Simpson, F.W. 189
Simpson, Floyd 48
Simpson, Joe 23
Simpson, Richard 82, 83
Simpson, Robert 198
Sims, Donald 227
Sims, Larry 50
Singletary, V.L. 31
Singleton, George, Jr. 28–29
Singleton, Sarah 29
Sixteenth Street Baptist Church 48–50
60 Minutes 52
The Slaughter (novel) 127
Slick, Ezra 248
Small, James 232–233
Small, Perry 224–225
Smirely, Anthony, Jr. 127
Smith, Andrew 217
Smith, Arthur 38, 192
Smith, Bob 185
Smith, Carnie 18
Smith, Charles 163
Smith, Daisy 32
Smith, Edward 32
Smith, F.A. 231
Smith, Frank 226–227
Smith, George
Smith, Hazel 203
Smith, Henry (suspect) 235
Smith, Henry (victim) 93–95
Smith, Herbert 8
Smith, Lamar 18–19
Smith, Mack 18–19
Smith, Mamie 192
Smith, Noah 18–19
Smith, Otis 158, 159
Smith, Sallie 8
Smith, Toby 159
Smith County Reporter 206
Smith v. Allwright 176
Snead, Roy 78
Snell, Lee 115–116
Snipes, Maceo 9
Snowden, Jimmie 57
Social Action Committee of 257
Soledad Prison 241, 250–252
South Carolina 29, 42–43, 73, 93–95, 118–119, 139, 141, 142,

152–153, 156–157, 163, 174, 188, 248
Southern Christian Leadership Conference (SCLC) 5, 69, 226
Southern Conference Educational Fund 209
Southern Negro Youth Congress 155, 169
Southern Poverty Law Center (SPLC) 1, 5, 6, 11, 14, 63, 69, 88, 217, 220, 224, 225, 246
Southern Tenant Farmers' Union 102
Southern Women for the Prevention of Lynching 115
Spears, Brad 101
Spell, Jesse 94
Spence, Porter 190
Spencer, Arthur 66
Spencer, Henry 32
Spicola, Joseph 177
Spidle, J.R. 99
Spivey, Edward 12
Spivey, James 180
Spradley, Pad 167
Stacey, Reuben 104
Standard Burial Association 140
Stanley, Seth 257
Stapleton, Louis 214–215
Starr, Amos 162–163
Starr, Dave 197
Stasiuk, Eugene 182
States' Rights Democratic Party 176
Steckler, David 254
Steele, Charles, Jr. 5
Steiner, George 243
Steiner, Larry 243
Stephen E. Howe Elementary School 56
Stephens, Lewey
Stephens, R.A. 110
Stephenson, Gladys 147
Stephenson, James 147, 148
Steptoe, E.W. 43
Stevenson, Coke
Stevenson, Luther 79–80
Steward, Bernard 238–239
Stewart, Allen 137
Stewart, Eddie 86
Stewart, J.D. 41, 42
Stewart, Napoleon 147
Stillman, Rabbit 131
Stimson, Henry 119
Stokes, Joe 128
Stokes, W.M. 193
Strickland, J.W. 122
Strickland, U.C. 170–171
Strider, H. Clarence 20–21, 24
Stripling, Hal, Jr. 167
Student Nonviolent Coordinating Committee (SNCC) 43, 80, 85, 94, 217, 223–224, 243, 248, 252–254, 257
Sturgeon, Grace 120
Sullivan, Herbert 54

Index

Summerour, Phinazee 137, 142–143
Sutherland, J. 143
Sutton, Rayfield 104
Swango, Curtis 34
Swearingen, M. Wesley 250
Sweeney, Taka 247
Sykes, Alvin 5

Talmadge, Eugene 9–10, 175, 178, 179, 199
Talmadge, Herman 175, 178–180
Talton, John 197
Taplin family 39, 207
Taylor, Herman 214
Taylor, Isaiah 63
Taylor, Johnny 240
Taylor, Samuel 189
Taylor, Sidney 94
Taylor, W.H. 32
Teche Greyhound Lines 140
Temple, Fred 235–237
Tennessee 29, 32, 35, 47, 56, 85, 95–96, 99, 102, 106, 110, 116–117, 122, 134–136, 145, 147–148, 155, 211, 223
Tennessee Coal and Iron Railroad Company 116
Texas 4, 15, 20, 22–23, 66, 96, 99, 106, 120, 121, 122, 133, 134, 146–147, 153, 165, 166–168, 181, 204, 258
Thagard, T. Werth 77
Thigpen, A.J. 114
Thomas, Ann 96
Thomas, Bobby 234
Thomas, Edgar 143
Thomas, Ernest 186–187
Thomas, Eugene 71
Thomas, Freddie, Jr. 75–76
Thomas, George 155
Thomas, Isaac 98–99
Thomas, J.D. 193
Thomas, John, Jr. 257
Thomas, Joseph 237–238
Thomas, Nellie 118
Thomas, Theodore 236
Thompson, Carl 60
Thompson, Hattie 40
Thompson, H.T. 223
Thompson, Jolly 25
Thompson, O.C. 233
Thompson, Scott 245
Thompson, Walter 206
Thornton, Jesse 117–118
Thrash, Cecil 162
364th Infantry Regiment 126–127
Thurmond, Strom 156
Till, Emmett 4, 19–22
Till, Louis 20, 21
Tisdale, Bruce 118–119
Tolliver, James 165
Tolliver, Tom 233
Torgersen, Thore 66
Townes, Roosevelt 109–110

Towns, Thurmond 192
Townsend, Berry 106
Townsend, W.B. 208
Travers, Nick 131–132
Treloar, James 34–35
Trial by Fire (play) 145
Trierweiler, John 122–123
Trigg, Selma 67
Triggs, Clarence 229
Triggs, Emma 229
Triggs, Saleam *see* Trigg, Selma
Truelock, Louis 249
Trujillo, Rafael 154
Trujillo Seitas, Jose 154
Truman, Harry 10, 146, 175
Trybula, Thomas 209
Tuck, Stephen
Tucker, Herman 57
Tupelo Daily Journal 185
Turner, Bobbie 192
Turner, David 173
Turner, Hattie 192
Turner, Hollis 210
Turner, Jake 213
Turner, James 191–192
Turner, Jimmie 192
Turner, J.T. 192
Turner, L.O. 34
Turner, Officer 36
Turner, Percy 75
Turner, Porter 139
Tuscaloosa News 202, 210, 224
Tuskegee Institute Advancement League 80
Tweedy, Hubert 122
Tyrone, R.J. 103

Underwood, Curt 36
Underwood, J.J. 147
unidentified victims 101, 103, 105, 182, 193, 210, 221, 222, 223
United Nations 142, 143, 144, 145, 148, 150, 153, 162, 174, 177, 182, 189, 190, 191, 193, 194, 195, 199
U.S. Bureau of Internal Revenue 190
U.S. Civil Rights Commission 69
U.S. Department of Agriculture 71
University of California, Los Angeles 243
University of Mississippi 45, 217, 219
University of Southern Mississippi 217–218
Ureste, Ladislado 15
US (organization) 243

Vail, Ed 226
Vail, James 226
Van Landingham, Zack 39, 218
Vanderford, J.W. 155
Vandiver, Ernest, Jr. 41
Varner, Hulet 87

Varner, J.C. 201
Vaughn, H.S. 34
Vaughn, W.J. 110
Ventril, Charles 161–162
Verner, James 11–12
Verner, Tom 11–12
Vickers, Tommy 200
Vicksburg Evening Post 59
Vilsack, Tom 71
Vinson, Bos 105
Vinson, Willie (Florida) 181
Vinson, Willie (Texas) 122
Virginia 3, 13, 159–160, 189, 194, 198–199, 203–204, 220
Vittur, Cliff 139
Vonbatten, Francis 162
Voting Rights Act of 1965 3, 68

Waddell, George 182
Walker, Clifton 52–54, 222
Walker, Deputy 86
Walker, Jacob 191
Walker, James, Jr. 152–153, 171
Walker, J.P. 37–38
Walker, Matt 140
Walker, Robert 95
Walker, William 126–127
Wall, L.D. 206
Wallace, Albert 233
Wallace, Martha 75
Wallace, R.C. 192
Walling, William 206
Walter, Jimmy 36
Walter, June 36–37
Wampler, J.W. 205
Warbington, Ronald 87
Ward, Anderson 101–102
Ward, Charlie 218
Ward, Eugene 172
Ward, Govan 104
Ward, Lynn 258
Ward, Sam M. 98
Ware, James 50
Ware, Virgil 49, 50
Warfel, William 219
Warren, Fuller 12, 197, 199
Wash, Howard 124
Washington 244–245
Washington, Cynthia 253
Washington, D.C. 7, 34, 88, 119, 193, 228, 232, 233, 253
Washington Post 31, 33
Waters, Lester 42
Watkins, George 98
Watson, Dee 181
Watson, J. Tom 153
Watson, Joe 254
Watts, Curtie 224
Watts, James 90
Watts, John 98
Watts riot 243
Waymers, James 73
Weatherspoon, Archie 52
Weeks, M.A. 189
Welch, William 193
Welch, Willie 197
Wellborn, Gordon 23

Wells, Edward 27
Wells, Hub 225
Wells, J.M. 112
West, George 189
West, Rebecca 157
West, William 198
Westmoreland, Lynn 5
Westray, George 187
Wexler, Laura 11
Wheeler, David 234
Wheeler, Elton 160
Wheeler, J.A. 195
Wheeler, L.H. 242
Whitaker, Richard 126
White, A.E. 188
White, Ben 84, 85–86
White, Bob 120
White, Charles 158
White, F.A. 149
White, Fred 79
White, Hugh 20
White, J.C. 150
White, John 56
White, Lucille 78
White, Ronald 209
White, T.W. 172–173
White, Turner 167
White, Walter 8, 114, 117
White Knights of the Ku Klux Klan 82
Whitfield, R.W. 111
Whitfield State Hospital 212, 215
Whittaker, John 63
Whittle, Kennon 160
Whittle, M.G. 173
Whittley, Jesse 120
Wilder, John 73
Wiley, Robert 219
Wilkerson, Jesse 155–156
Wilkerson, L.L. 155–156
Wilkerson, Richard 99

Williams, A.C. 119
Williams, Annie 117
Williams, Billy 60, 90
Williams, Charles 95
Williams, Charlie C. 27
Williams, Ed 208
Williams, Elbert 116–117
Williams, H.O. 233
Williams, James 170, 171
Williams, Jim 196
Williams, Marcelina 16
Williams, N.G. 194
Williams, Pat 214
Williams, Roger 213–214
Williams, Ruby 140
Williams, Samuel 189
Williams, Virgil 173
Williams, W.C. 114
Williams, Wilbur 202
Williamson, Ed (policeman) 10
Williamson, Edward (killer) 9
Williamson, Rodell 91–92
Williford, W.E. 195
Willingham, James 125
Willis, C.H. 38–39
Willis, Gordon, Jr. 240
Willis, Holley 119
Willis, Richard 40, 57
Willison, Herbert 169
Wilpitz, Howard 121
Wilson, Billy 253
Wilson, Eddie 91
Wilson, Harvey 193
Wilson, Jerome 101
Wilson, John 24
Wilson, Luther 101
Wilson, Moise 101
Wilson, Tom 258
Wilson Daily Times 170
Windham, George 109
Windham, Joe 155
Wingard, Horace 173

Winter, Harrison 220
Winter Garden Elementary School 197
Wisconsin 146
Woddall, R.C. 174
Wolff, Paul 144
Womack, Melvin 197
Wood, Delos 101
Wood, M.G. 134
Wood, M.L. 231
Wood, Phillip 232
Wood, William 190–191
Wooden, Archie 92–93
Woods, C.W. 230–231
Woods, Douglas 220
Woods, Stuart 182
Woodson, George 24
Worthy, H.G. 160
Wright, Cleo 120–121
Wright, E.E. 109
Wright, Henry 185
Wright, Malcolm 174, 184–185
Wright, Mary 185
Wright, Mose 20
Wright, Roy 87
Wright, Virgil 104
Wright, Virginia 185

Yancey, Wayne 223–224
Yarbrough, L.L. 63
Yates, James 186
Yeager, William 165
York, Gregg 250
York, Jake 235, 237
York, James 28
Young, Ab 102
Young, Buckie 108
Younge, Samuel, Jr. 80–81

Zantzinger, William 216–217
Zureki, Alan 209

www.ingramcontent.com/pod-product-compliance
Ingram Content Group UK Ltd.
Pitfield, Milton Keynes, MK11 3LW, UK
UKHW050703160426
5217IPUK00038B/2027